Also by Alexander Frater

Chasing the Monsoon:
A Modern Pilgrimage Through India

Beyond the Blue Horizon

TALES FROM
THE TORRID ZONE

TALES FROM THE TORRID ZONE

Travels in the Deep Tropics

ALEXANDER FRATER

Alfred A. Knopf New York 2007

THIS IS A BORZOI BOOK
PUBLISHED BY ALFRED A. KNOPF

Copyright © 2004 by Alexander Frater

All rights reserved. Published in the United States by
Alfred A. Knopf, a division of Random House, Inc., New York.
Originally published in Great Britain by Picador,
an imprint of Pan Macmillan Ltd., London, in 2004.

www.aaknopf.com

Knopf, Borzoi Books, and the colophon are
registered trademarks of Random House, Inc.

Library of Congress Cataloging-in-Publication Data

Frater, Alexander, [date].
Tales from the torrid zone : travels in the deep tropics / Alexander Frater.—
1st American ed.
p.   cm.
Includes bibliographical references.
ISBN: 978-0-679-40871-0 (alk. paper)
1. Frater, Alexander, 1937—Travel—Tropics. 2. Voyages and travels.
3. Tropics—Description and travel. I. Title.

G910.F73 2007   910.913—dc22   2006049552

Maps by Reginald Piggott

Manufactured in the United States of America

First United States Edition

For Tania and John

Tropic (trop·ik). *n.* Late ME. *tropik;* LL. *tropicus;* Gr. *tropikos,* meaning "belonging to a turn," and *tropos,* "turning," relating to the sun's "turning" at the solstice.

Tropically (trop-ika˘li), *adv.* 1852. Hot, sultry or torrid. With tropical heat, luxuriance or violence.

Contents

Prologue 3

A Place Called Pandemonium 16

The Sagacity of Dr Manson 31

Can You Grow Prozac? 55

Vive Les Tropiques! 70

Great White Bird 88

Grandfather's Presbytery 106

The Place with the Drive-in Volcano 133

The Garbage Dump at Millionaire's Point 157

The Voyage of the Portuguese Grocer 163

Notes from the Lost Continent 176

The Tree of Life 190

The Miraculous Reflection 203

Big River Blues 216

In the Doldrums 239

How to Be Boss: Politics in a Hot Climate 259

The Fragrant Isle 280

The Elusive Turret Bell 306

Confessions of a Beachcomber 313

The Hum Note 349

Acknowledgements 381

Bibliography 383

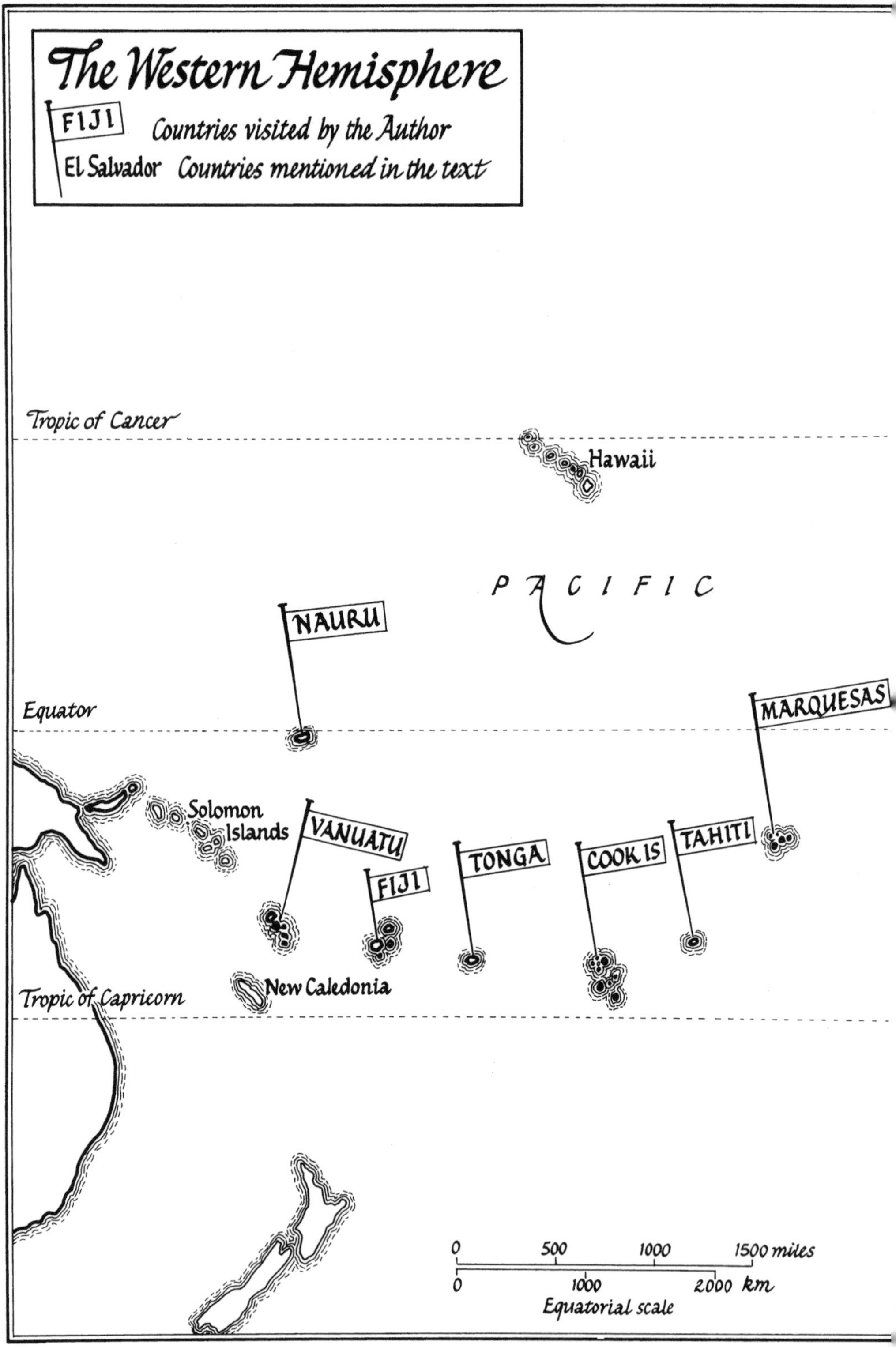

The Western Hemisphere
FIJI
Countries visited by the Author
El Salvador
Countries mentioned in the text
Tropic of Cancer
Hawaii
PACIFIC
NAURU
Equator
MARQUESAS
Solomon Islands
VANUATU
FIJI
TONGA
COOK IS
TAHITI
New Caledonia
Tropic of Capricorn
0
500
1000
1500 miles
0
1000
2000 km
Equatorial scale

ATLANTIC

OCEAN

OCEAN

CUBA

Bahamas

BR. VIRGIN IS

ANGUILA

Haiti

Puerto
Rico

El Salvador

JAMAICA

Barbados

GUYANA

SURINAME

GALAPAGOS

Panama

Ecuador

Peru

Chile

Paraguay

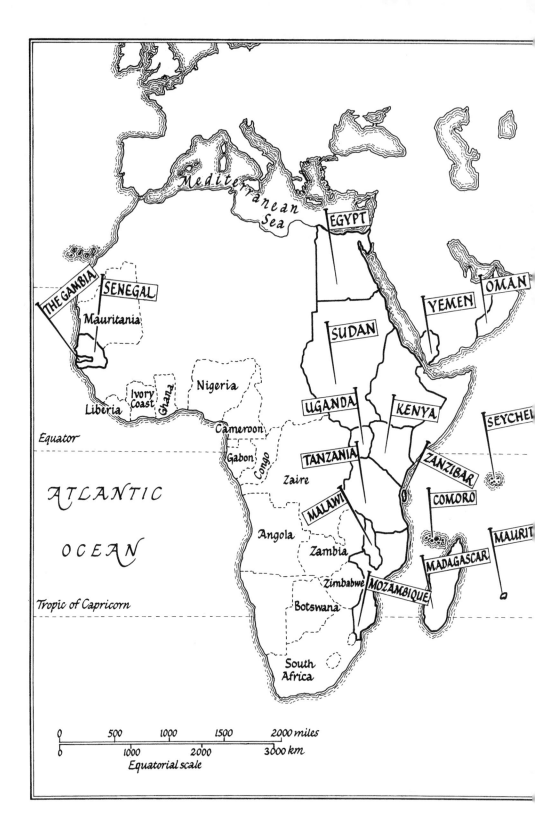

THE GAMBIA

SENEGAL

Mauritania

Mediterranean
Sea

EGYPT

YEMEN

OMAN

SUDAN

Nigeria

Ivory
Coast

Ghana

Liberia

Cameroon

UGANDA

KENYA

SEYCHEL

Equator

Gabon

Congo

Zaire

TANZANIA

ZANZIBAR

COMORO

MALAWI

ATLANTIC

Angola

Zambia

OCEAN

MADAGASCAR

MAURIT

Zimbabwe

MOZAMBIQUE

Tropic of Capricorn

Botswana

South
Africa

0   500   1000   1500   2000 miles

0   1000   2000   3000 km

Equatorial scale

CHINA

MYANMAR

LAOS

INDIA

Bangladesh

Taiwan *Tropic of Cancer*

Hong Kong

THAILAND

Cambodia

VIETNAM

PHILIPPINES

CEYLON

Maldives

MALAYSIA

Borneo

INDONESIA

PACIFIC

OCEAN

Papua
New Guinea

INDIAN

OCEAN

AUSTRALIA

The Eastern Hemisphere

EGYPT *Countries visited by the Author*
Nigeria *Countries mentioned in the text*

Prologue

For years Frank Clarke, a traveller in bells, had brought a certain plangency to the islands of Oceania. He worked for a London foundry whose Edwardian managers still referred to our part of the world as the Torrid Zone. Out here, Frank liked to say, due to the moist equatorial air and reverberant properties of water, his Clerkenwell bells gained an acoustic bounce and echo found nowhere else. He called it "tropical sonance."

Frank turned up one morning aboard a small steamer bound for Tonga. It made an emergency stop at Port Vila and my father, summoned to the ship, returned with Frank slumped comatose in his launch. After administering an intramuscular quinine shot—7½ grains—he saw him through the cycles of malaria: first the teeth-chattering rigor when they piled on blankets and force-fed him hot fluids, next the acute vomiting and mind-expanding headaches as the clinical thermometer stuck at one hundred and five, finally the "heavy sweat" after which they changed his sodden sheets, gave him Atabrine by mouth and waited for it to happen all over again. He recovered, but, too weak to travel, left the hospital and came up the hill to recuperate in our house. My father had told us about the Englishman who'd cracked jokes at death's door. My mother, intrigued, had taken him books.

Small, skinny and white-bearded with a shock of uncombed ash-white hair, he had rheumy blue eyes—which held your own in a very steady way—and a surprising voice: deep, patrician and carrying echoes of the old British ruling class. He told us little about himself. Once he received a letter addressed to "Frank Clarke MA (Oxon)" yet, when asked what he'd studied, he simply said, "Oh, something relating to my work." An Oxford degree in *bells*? That seemed about the size of it. Frank would not be drawn.

Our island, Iririki, lay just a stone's throw from Port Vila, and each

3

day he sent Moses, our gardener, off in his canoe to the Burns Philp store for a bottle of Bundaberg rum. This, he claimed, contained all the nourishment he needed. Though my mother badgered him—"For God's sake, Frank, you need building up"—he barely touched his food, just moved it distractedly around the plate as he talked. Yet he could make her laugh. The unexpected re-emergence of that sound, like a dry stream bed suddenly in spate again, was a sharp reminder of its rarity. And I noted Frank's pleasure when it happened. She was a pretty, brown-eyed woman whose face shone with intelligence, he a wry, gossipy, alcoholic bachelor old enough to be her father. Yet I saw the way his gaze followed her around, and the effort that went into keeping her amused. The entertaining stories never stopped.

Uneasy with children, he simply addressed them as adults and spoke to them about adult matters. For example, sitting under the banyan tree one morning with an unopened P. G. Wodehouse on his lap, he said to me, "Do you think your mother is happy?"

I'd never given the subject a moment's thought. She had frequent "moods" but these were always attributed to neuralgia; then she took APC tablets and went to lie down—often for days on end. It was the most disturbing question I'd ever been asked and Frank, doubtless noting my bewilderment, volunteered an indirect answer.

"I think the tropics are getting her down."

I stared. *The tropics?*

"Yes. These are the tropics, Sandy, it's a region of the world. You *live* in the tropics. But they don't suit everyone."

He told me a little about our region and its unique relationship with the sun; it was, apparently, the only section of the planet over which it passed directly. Everyone else saw it obliquely, angled and aslant; indeed, during midwinter in the frigid zones it apparently tumbled so far off the perpendicular they never saw it at all. But here, every single day of the year, it rose metronomically at about six in the morning and set twelve hours later, with only the briefest of dawns and dusks.

Frank seemed to imply her headaches were somehow solar-induced or -related yet, when I put this to my mother, she said brightly, "He's talking nonsense as usual. I love it here. You know that." But, years later, I realized he was right.

My mother feared the tropics. The victims of its diseases, often incurable, sometimes disfiguring, were to be seen every day down at the hospital. My sister and I were constantly monitored for a whole sweat of fevers, while our personal hygiene regime included the routine checking of stools for blood; blood probably meant dysentery, which in those days could kill a child in hours. She hated a climate which threatened to make her prematurely old and sallow, and which slowed up her mental processes. "We're all at least a beat behind," she would sigh, lamenting too our chaotic behaviour and disorganized personalities. The tropics made you garrulous; everyone, she claimed, talked at once—whereas in more temperate, reflective latitudes conversations tended to be linear; speakers there took turns.

The tropics also jammed the keys of her piano. At first she extemporized to cover the missing notes then, as more failed and Chopin started sounding like jungle music, she stopped altogether.

And she found the mind-clouding, energy-sapping heat that begins building at noon (and takes a four-hour chunk out of the day) the enemy of initiative. The interesting thought you had at breakfast, atrophied by heavy afternoon sleep, was a poor, wizened thing by dusk. Science, literature, engineering, architecture, the arts, abstract ideas—not much came out of the tropics.

What came out was life—seeding, breeding, buzzing, barking, fluttering, squawking, germinating, *growing*. Sex, of course, figured worryingly in this. Tropical sexuality meant children matured early—girls in particular budding like hothouse flowers (little heads full of carnal thoughts even as their little busts bloomed).

She was a BA (Hons) education graduate who built two excellent schools and taught in both. Then I believed her languors were due to nothing more than exhaustion. Now I believe she worked to blot things out. Work was her revenge on the tropics.

Yet my father adored the region, loved its warmth and the exuberance of its people, its forcing-pit fertility, its astounding colours and amazing skies. He had spent much of his childhood, and most of his working life, in places like this, and always feared that in a cold country his heart would stop. The matter of the latitudes in which they lived would remain a bone of contention between them until, in late middle age, she finally won the argument and moved him to cool, temperate New Zealand.

She could never have budged Frank. Like an old gorilla, he was only truly at home in warm, wet countries and, though entitled to home leave every ten years, always left the ship before it left the tropics—in Panama City, it was said, to see a mysterious widow. He often talked to my mother about his travels, told her how he'd smoked opium in various Indo-Chinese *fumeries,* got drunk with Hemingway in Cuba, visited the caboclos of Brazil—who prayed to St Andrew to steer the winds as they burned the forests—and even sold bells in Burma. (To *Buddhists!*) I recalled him speaking of African tribes with names that created sharp little mind pictures; today when I read about the Tivs and Yorubas of Nigeria, the Congo Balokis and the Bembas of Zimbabwe, I think of Frank.

The tropics occupy one-third of the earth's land surface and are inhabited by 1.7 billion people—one-third of the global population; they contain eighty-eight nations wholly and a further twenty partially, many of which lie within the Third, or Developing, World. Over eight thousand species of fish, or a third of the sea's total, inhabit the coral reefs, while (to conclude that trinomial equation) two-thirds of the original forests are already destroyed beyond recovery.

Chronically poor soil and topographical irregularities—such as surreally steep slopes and an excess of sterile laterite—mean tropical agriculture often struggles to sustain dense populations. It comes down, naturally, to land quality: under Zimbabwe's old *chitimene* system 200 acres were required to sustain a family of five, while in Sumatra just 15 acres suffices. The Cameroons' Ndikis manage with a 0.6 acre kitchen garden, a quarter-acre patch of savannah, and two pocket-handkerchief-sized forest clearings for dry-season green vegetables and wet-season sweet potatoes. Meanwhile, throughout the region, the needs of an undernourished, expanding population leads to the extinction of seventeen thousand species of flora and fauna annually by tree-felling—a staggering two species *each hour.* Life in all its forms has always been hard.

But not for Frank. "Every community needs a church, and every church needs a bell. Tropical congregations may be poor but they're passionate; that's where you'll find the old revivalists with that old-time fire in their bellies. They always get the money."

*

As a young man he had spent a year in Tahiti, managing a beachside restaurant near Papeete. Among his regular customers was a middle-aged, taciturn French artist who had gained some local notoriety for his strong sexual appetites and bizarre use of colour—blue trees, orange dogs, green nudes and so on. When he had money he paid for his meals, when he didn't they went on the slate. Then came a drought period so prolonged the artist finally settled his bill by painting an erotic masterpiece on a mirror in the gents' toilet. (Frank, while primly declining to describe the picture, hinted he himself had been in it, peering through the leaves of a strangler vine.) Soon afterwards police closed the place down and Frank left Tahiti; my mother reckoned it had been a bordello with bistro facilities attached.

He took the mirror with him, and several years later it hung in his Pago Pago villa. What happened next depended on how much rum he'd swallowed, but one version—the best—concerned a Swedish opera star who came to supper and sang for him, her sonically resonating upper register shattering every glass object in the room. (But not even Callas could have broken a slab of heavy-duty speculum like that.) It's more likely to have fallen off the wall—at any rate, it finished up in fragments which the servants swept up and threw out with the rubbish.

My mother told me the story shortly before she died. "Poor Frank. A pornographic Gauguin! That would certainly be worth a bob or two today."

*

A whizzo who took all the journals, he saw himself not just as a bell scientist but also as a scientific generalist. And he had a schoolmasterly streak which, she said, responded to my sudden interest in our region. "I certainly remember him sitting you down and talking." I too have vague recollections of that, and assume he started with the equator and the two circles of the celestial sphere, Cancer and Capricorn, which run parallel on either side. Set 23° and 28° north and south of it, the solstitial points—or extremes of the ecliptic—contain a hot, rainy girdle 3,200 miles wide.

These are the tropics.

The sun, "moving" from one extremity to the other, acts as both engine and fuel cell. Its migratory cycle brings it to Cancer, its northern terminus, on 22 June. Here it creates the summer solstice yet, even as the Northern Hemisphere floods with light and warmth, those exalting in midsummer's day below never see it *directly overhead*. At high noon the shade made by their beach umbrellas registers a slight tilt from the perpendicular. The sun still lies somewhere off to the south—directly over the Tropic of Cancer, in fact, and only those living on that ecliptic may then (cloud cover permitting) glimpse it right above their rooftops.

On the map Cancer is depicted as a continuous dotted line. Picked up in, say, the Caribbean, it swings just north of Havana and south of Anguilla, transits the Bahamas at George Town on Great Exuma and Sims on Long Island, before heading across the Atlantic to the Middle East: Aswan and Muscat are Cancerian cities. Crossing the Indian subcontinent it passes Ahmadabad, shaves Calcutta and Dhaka, clips Hong Kong then, passing above Kaui in Hawaii, enters North America at Todos Santos, Baja California. Anyone south of the line can claim to be a *tropicano,* or citizen of the world's warm, wet belt.

Cancer might be seen as a firewall protecting our temperate regions from the thermal energy boiling around inside the Torrid Zone. On 22 June the sun "bounces" off it and "heads" back south. Travelling at a sedate 17½ m.p.h. it crosses the equator on 22 September and arrives over the Tropic of Capricorn precisely three months later: 22 December is summer solstice for the Southern Hemisphere—and winter for the Northern.

Capricorn's line bisects Australia. It traverses the Gibson Desert (and Lake Disappointment), passes north of Alice Springs and arrives at the Pacific at Rockhampton, Queensland. It enters South America at the Chilean town of Antofagasta, touches Concepción in Paraguay and Maringa in Brazil, exits again at São Paulo. Heading across the South Atlantic to Africa, it makes its landfall at Namibia's Walvis Bay, cuts through the Kalahari Desert and the Kruger National Park, leaves via Malova on the Mozambique coast then heads back across the Indian Ocean.

I was born in the Tropic of Capricorn just twelve days after the sun "turned" over Lake Disappointment. This makes me a Capricornian twice over—the second manifestation being zodiacal. Anyone raised under the sign of the goat will know we are plodders who, devoid of inspiration or big ideas, rarely set the world alight. Yet we persevere and, in our dogged, rather curmudgeonly way, tend to get there in the end.

What happens when the sun passes directly overhead? Frank, I don't doubt, marched me outdoors to witness the fact that, for a few strange moments, we leave not the faintest umbral trace of ourselves. People standing on their shadows cast no shade; the sun causes their heads to be swallowed by their feet, so they wear their shadows like shoes. Each of us, creating our own personal solar eclipse, turns into a tiny moon.

*

Then there was Frank's bell lore. Reading the subject up half a century later, it too stirred memories.

The hundred-and-eighty-ton Great Bell of Moscow, known as the Tsar Kolokol and cast in a pit between 1733 and 1735, was the biggest in history. After its dismayed founders realized they couldn't lift it off the ground—it had also been cracked by fire—they turned it into a chapel; people confessed and got married in the bell, and attended Old Church Slavonic services preached by patriarchs whose voices, acoustically boosted, rang around an instrument that, had it been hung, might even have been heard in Finland. Russian Orthodoxy believed you spoke to God through your bells; thus the bigger the bell the more prayers it could carry.

Buddhists relished the instant after it stopped ringing. The tingling, fading hum—air still vibrating after all sound had ceased—was charged with spiritual significance. (The barrel-shaped Asian bells, non-swinging and inert, hung motionless; cast without clappers, they were struck—either by wooden mallets or swaying horizontal beams—like gongs.)

Bells may have been around for four thousand years, but their acoustical structure has only recently been understood.

It revolves around variously pitched frequencies known as partials; lower partials are harmonious, higher partials discordant. This converging chromatic principle applies also to fog bells, gong bells, clinkum bells, jingle bells, shriving bells, school bells, sleigh bells, saucing bells—and church bells. And oddly, though they were Frank's living, churches brought out the worst in him.

My mother told another story.

Outside Port Vila a big one had just been completed, its steeple mute but already rigged with lignum vitae corbels. One day he learned that a rep from a big Marseilles foundry had arrived and, even now, was talking to its elders. "His name," she said, "was Christoff, and Frank certainly knew about him. He *bristled*." M. Christoff had been a celebrated *carilloneur* who, wearing heavy gloves, played his chime-stand keyboard like an organist, coaxing music (popular classics, marches, even jazz) from his bells—row upon row, *tons* of bells, hidden away in the rafters. After arthritis struck he brought that same flamboyance to his marketing.

Frank, by now pretty well recovered, also went to call on the elders. He told them that, in Windsor Castle's archives, lay a deposition from a Surrey milkmaid who, in 1580 in a hay meadow, heard the voice of God. Among the truths revealed to her were that French bells were 50 per cent cheap, low-grade tin guaranteed to rust. God stressed that when it came to quality, workmanship, reliability and honest-to-goodness value for money, British bells had no equal.

Frank won the order by acclaim and, ignoring threats from Christoff's lawyer, remained unrepentant. My mother said, "And, do you know, he wasn't even a Christian? For him churches were just places to be supplied with fixtures and fittings."

"So what was he?"

She smiled broadly. "Frank was a Druid!"

*

The tropical year, 365 days, 5 hours, 48 minutes and 45 seconds of mean solar time—the time between successive vernal equinoxes—is the one used in the Gregorian calendar.

*

At sunset on the evening of my sixth birthday the sky erupted in an emerald flash. I waited, incredulously, for the end-of-the-world bang that must surely follow. But the mysterious viridescence vanished, as suddenly as it had come, leaving behind the same molten-copper sky I had noted a split second earlier. My father, when I breathlessly reported back, told me I had seen the Zodiacal Light. Caused by refracting dust particles in the plane of the ecliptic—a region called the Zodiac—it's perhaps witnessed only once or twice in a lifetime. It was the moment, probably, that I caught the virus. We tropophiliacs are not bleeders or chokers, do not have fits and spasms. There is a fever, recurring after long periods of dormancy, but it's all in the head and won't kill you. Known as *le coup de bambou,* it's a mild form of tropical madness for which, luckily, there is no cure.

I never saw Frank again, but assume he finished up becalmed and befuddled in his own shadowy green acres, heart registering one beat for the tide coming in, the next for the tide going out. And even before I heard the story of the mirror I'd somehow associated him with Paul Gauguin; the fact they were acquainted came as no great surprise. The question was: had the tropics made them like that—or would such personalities have behaved in much the same way, say, in Greenland or Patagonia?

*

Today, among our number, I have met inadequates and no-hopers, sex tourists, runaways and petty crooks. But there are also yachties, surfers and sun-freaks, and First World retirees on underperforming pensions hoping to live well in the low-cost, debt-ridden tropical Third World (where fruit grows wild by the roadside). All in all, we're a pretty mixed bunch—and Gauguin is our man. Not only did he lead the life we craved, he left behind sublime evidence of what it could be like. How solemn and beautiful he made it! What grace he bestowed on the tropics!

Once, in Papeete, I boarded a tiny propeller-driven Twin Otter and flew north-east for seven hours. It refuelled at various atolls on route—the Tahitian pilot using binoculars to make his landfalls, we half-dozen passengers jumping out to hand-pump the gas from drums—then, late in the afternoon, finally descended towards a lofty island, angular and densely wooded. I noted pines on Hiva Oa's crown and, at its foot, the palm-fringed black volcanic beaches which, famously, he had painted a luscious pink.

Exasperated by Tahiti's petty provincialism, Gauguin sailed off to this obscure outpost in the Marquesas. There, aged fifty-two, he scandalized the French by seducing, then marrying, a thirteen-year-old Polynesian schoolgirl named Marie-Rose. He built his child bride a villa—the "House of Pleasure"—and bought her the first pony and trap the island had seen. (The authorities promptly fined him for driving without lights.) Creating his final pictures, he also began drinking himself to death. Ben Varney's store, across the road, supplied him with absinthe and *six-hundred-litre* hogsheads of claret (he kept his absinthe down a well to chill it).

Today the house, along with Varney's store, has reverted to the forest. But the well remains, as does the Magasin Pierre Shan, a two-storey trading emporium where he and Marie-Rose did their household shopping—and which, during my visit, received a shipment of Gauguin T-shirts: suddenly, right across the island, people were walking around in his masterpieces.

Otherwise only his grave provided tangible evidence of his presence. Fashioned from slabs of heavy rust-coloured rock, it had a gnarled frangipani tree growing from its head (and putting forth so many flowers it may have taken root in his skull).

I stayed in the house of Gabriel Heitaa, a retired ship's cook, and his graceful wife, Feliciene. One afternoon they threw a birthday party for their four-year-old daughter. Grave young mothers brought their children on horseback then lounged in the tangled garden where, as if stepping into one of his paintings, I met the current owner of Gauguin's sewing machine ("A Singer, still goin' fine") and a friend of Gauguin's youngest daughter. She, I learned, had recently died from elephantiasis, leaving his great-grandson—allegedly "good at drawing"—working as a fisherman over at Paumau, or Shadow of the Flower. Looking around, I reflected the old artist should have slipped away on an ebb tide of contentment yet, according to Feliciene's tattooed great-uncle, he had finished his days in torment.

The French, sick of his complaints about the shabby way they treated the Marquesans, charged him with treason and summoned him for trial in Tahiti. Soon afterwards the money ran out. "Then Marie-Rose leave him," the great-uncle said, "also his health not good, he get plenty pain, was *hypocondriaque,* always want to see doctor." It did him little good.

Early on the morning of 8 May 1903, a neighbour, Tioka, called in to find him sprawled motionless across his bed. Weeping, he did what Marquesans always do to ensure life is extinct: bit his head. A few days afterwards a letter arrived from Paris with news that two of his beautiful, sombre Hiva Oa pictures had been sold to a collector for a handsome 3,300 francs.

It was returned with *"Decédé"* scrawled across the envelope.

Before returning to Tahiti I revisited his grave. Several visitors—grief-stricken Scandinavian women, as far as I could judge—had tied messages to the branches of the frangipani tree. All were slightly crazed, the work of victims like me. Crouching by his head I looked, so to speak, along his line of sight. Mount Temetiu soared four thousand feet overhead. Frigate birds rode the thermals as thunder rumbled up in the cloud forest (marked *nuage* and left blank on the map). Beyond the cemetery children played, someone strummed a ukulele. Then I heard a distant, melodious church bell and, for the first time in fifty years, the phrase came back—tropical sonance!

*

My father died just as he predicted. One wintry morning in New Zealand, recently turned sixty-five and climbing the steps of a post office to mail a letter to my small daughter in London, it happened: a massive coronary. (I keep imagining, apart from the violent shock of pain, some awful inner turmoil, like a huge rockslide.)

Eventually, against his better judgement, I had decided to become a writer and, persuaded I couldn't really succeed in the tropics—"Name one writer who has," said my mother—turned down a job on the *Fiji Times & Herald* and headed for Europe.

In Venice, one leaden day in early spring, the sky suddenly filled with whirling volcanic ash. I wondered where the eruption had occurred, and if any tidal waves had been triggered, then, realizing I was seeing my first snow, rushed out to catch the flakes and eat them. For a day I loved the way it transformed the city, changed its contours and neutralized its colours, but then it all turned to slush and we were breathing freezing air from the Alps. In Venice I had a relapse, a bad attack of *le coup de bambou,* and, reaching London, didn't need histology checks to tell me the bug had struck again. The only treatment was tropical proximity and, down the years, to keep it at bay, I managed to persuade a succession of editors to send me off on tropical assignments.

*

Of the seventy or so warm, wet countries I've visited thus far, a particular moment in Guyana comes to mind. Late one afternoon I found myself aboard the *Jesus Shall Reign* water bus as it sped up the mighty Essequibo River. A setting sun lit the forest canopy and picked out macaws, troupials and flurries of white egrets. I chatted to a dark-haired, pretty woman, Dominique Bones, who owned a small hotel on one of the riverine islands and had family links with the forest. She recounted the story of her great-grandmother, known as Missi, who spent her teenage years logging a species of tree found only along the Essequibo and Demerara.

Greenheart, famously durable, listed second in the table of hardwoods rated A1 at Lloyd's, possesses modules of rupture stronger than oak or mountain hemlock; the lock gates of the Manchester Ship Canal are made from it, as are the butts of the finest billiard cues. Missi, having built a greenheart mill on the site of an old leper colony, married a Georgetown rake named Willems and bore him four children. (Known to Georgetown's whores as the Pharaoh—he daily showered gold coins on them from his carriage—Willems went on to father eighty-one more.)

The water bus trailed a rooster-tail wake. Jack Black, a grizzled old pork knocker, or prospector, passed around a rum bottle and told me that Eldorado lay up in the interior. "I actually headin' foh a stream drainin' from dat locality." Then, unpacking his kit, he showed me some of the items a pork knocker carries: cutlass and *criminal* (patois for a Brazilian spade), diamond sieve, gold scales and scoop.

Dominique said her brother, just twenty-four, had also gone after gold. "He got lucky, he actually found a mine! I'd just returned from school in England and he wanted to show me. But as I jumped out of his boat the propeller pin sheared and he was swept away over rapids. It took nine days to find his body, it was my mother who made them go on looking." She shuddered. "These damn *rivers.*"

"Aaah, Mizz Bones," sighed Jack. Then, brightening, he pointed ashore to a timber concession where the previous day an emerald boa constrictor had been found looped, like a giant liana, around a bombax tree.

The antique *Lady Northcote*—a smoking pile of scrap beneath a steamer-shaped carapace of rust—bustled downstream, leaving a heavy wash; idly, as she passed, I noted the sun slip below the water. And then I saw it again: the green flash.

Incredulous, up on my feet, I told my friends about the Zodiacal Light. And when, right on cue, *a church bell tolled* from some shadowy village, my whoop of laughter startled them even more. It was there in the heart of the deep tropics—feeling at home and content—that I first thought about doing this book.

A Place Called Pandemonium

Some years ago I returned to my birthplace and found it had become a luxury holiday resort. Described in the brochures as "Iririki, Island of Elegance" and lying snugly in Port Vila's blue harbour, its forty-four acres were crowned with flowering trees and contoured like a tall polychromic hat; you could walk the shadowy path around its brim in twenty minutes. It was a comfortable spot; when the mainland sweltered, Iririki usually got sea breezes and cooling showers. Once it had contained just two houses: our mission bungalow and—set in parklike grounds with a flagpole flying a bedspread-sized Union Jack—the palatial residence of the British Resident Commissioner. Now seventy-two air-conditioned accommodation units were strung across its northern end.

By the resident's jetty a signpost read "Old Hospital Ruins." Directed back half a century, I saw myself as the guests drifting over on parasails might see me: an ageing, perspiring, overweight man hurrying towards a jungly acre that looked like an abandoned archaeological site. Somewhere in there, among the creeper-strewn hillocks and slabs of mossy concrete, my father had delivered me with forceps; now I expected, if not a thunderclap, at least an acknowledgement, some audible sign.

That, however, only came at the check-in desk when a porter cried, "Welcome to the Champagne Resort!" and handed me a complimentary fruit punch. Drinking it, I realized the vaulted reception area, built from local hardwoods, stood on the site of our vegetable garden. Then, having spelled my name for the clerk, I told her about my links with the island. She went "Uh-huh," and asked for my credit card. Handing me a key she said, "Enjoy your stay, Mr Fraser." My unit overlooked a tiny, fan-shaped beach where I had learned to swim; two topless women lay sunning themselves on the spot where I once kept my canoe. Later, eating a Big Riki burger at the poolside restaurant, I was relieved to find the restaurant's location held no associations at all.

My son turned up and said, "How do you feel? Have the squatters moved in?"

I felt pretty good, actually—indeed, oddly gratified that so many people seemed to be getting pleasure from the place. "What do you think?"

"It was probably nicer before."

But John detested resorts of any description. He had arrived a couple of weeks earlier, a Royal London Hospital medical student out here to do his elective at his grandfather's old hospital—today named Vila Base and re-established over on the mainland. Looking tired and preoccupied, he said a nine-year-old girl from Tanna had been admitted that morning with cerebral malaria. "Her parents tried a custom doctor, that didn't work, so they brought her in: Western medicine, last resort, it happens all the time. A few hours earlier and we might have saved her."

I watched my son pondering one of the diseases which my father, for much of his life, had fought so obsessively. That oddly jolting moment was interrupted by the arrival of Dr Makau Kalsakau, escorted to our table like a visiting head of state. Three waiters tussled to pull out his chair, a portly Australian manager hovered anxiously. Dr Makau, trained by my father and perhaps our oldest family friend, had promised us an Iririki island tour. A handsome, black-skinned pensioner with amused eyes and a wispy Assyrian beard, he held John's hand and said, "You look like your grandaddy, there is a definite similarity. He was my teacher. And now you are working in our hospital! About this there is, uh, a kind of . . . what is the word?"

I had disappointed him by not going to medical school, but words were my business and now I was oddly eager for his approval. "Symmetry."

"Hmm, yes." (Symmetry would do.) "So what do you make of our new Iririki?"

"Not bad. But I'm still a bit confused."

"Let us climb the hill. John, you should see what is up there. The tourists never go, they don't know. And for you, Sandy, it will be more familiar."

Dense undergrowth walled off our garden. But we found a way in, a dozen paces spanning fifty years and leading to a half-acre so still and shadowy I felt I had broken into my own childhood.

The place was running wild but evidence of our tenancy remained. The flowering trees my mother planted grew with a jungle exuberance, the grass was knee-high and the banyan that loomed so massively over our front veranda had acquired half a century's extra girth and a further forty feet of elevation.

Our house, said Makau, had been demolished after we'd gone, whirled out to sea by the great 1948 hurricane. But the garden endured, and I knew its tangled boisterousness would have delighted my mother.

Beneath the banyan Makau paused. "Here Mummy built her school." John raised an eyebrow at this nursery nomenclature, but among the old-timers hereabouts it was routine; to Makau I would be perennially juvenescent, an ageing toddler with a worrying weakness for cigars. I was touched to see the spot where the *smol skul* had stood. When the British and French refused to countenance any form of state education my mother took matters into her own hands. It proved so successful that later, a few yards away, she also built a teachers' training college.

Our garden thus became a centre of academic excellence. The school produced—to the unease of both metropolitan governments—two streams of keen, bright kids. One entered the teachers' training shack, the other headed down to the hospital where my father taught them to be doctors. That was how Makau, one of the first garden graduates, had learned his medicine. "All this bougainvillaea Mummy planted. She planted these frangipanis. You planted that orange tree. These hibiscus Daddy planted."

I noted the absoluteness of the silence. Several dozen holidaymakers were making merry below, but the density of the bush excluded their voices. We clambered down forty broken steps to the razed Paton Memorial Hospital. This wilderness was Makau's old alma mater. Sweeping aside a spinnaker-sized spider's web he nodded towards a small depression carpeted with prickly sensitive plant. "Labour ward, you were born there." We stumbled on through heavy scrub. By a young sandalwood tree he said, "Hospital front steps. At seven sharp every morning Daddy came down from the house wearing a tie and held a service for patients and staff. After that he did his rounds." That startled me. The idea of a tie in this climate was one thing, officiating at morning prayers quite another. He had been a Presbyterian *misinari dokta*, Glasgow-born, ordained after finishing his MB BS, but I never thought of him formally facing a congregation, couldn't equate that with the quiet, rather shy and private man I remembered. We toured the sites of the general wards, the path lab, the theatre and, set by the beach like an elegant little Edwardian boathouse, the shell of the mortuary. The evening sun made the wooded hills above Port Vila a landscape worked in silks. An outrigger canoe slid past, propelled by a woman in a crimson dress.

"Gud naet!" she called.

As we strolled along a coastal path the resort guests were abandoning the beach for Happy Hour. They glanced curiously at Makau; normally the only native Vanuatuans, or ni-Vanuatu, hereabouts were employees. We progressed through the lobby to the pool bar and the staff rushed to secure a table for us. Makau walked in as though he owned the place—which, in a sense, he did—and called for orange juices all round. His home island, Ifira, lay less than a quarter of a mile away, its eight hundred people long regarded as Vanuatu's elite; a progressive, industrious, enterprising crowd, they flocked to my mother's schools and, today, play a major role in the country's affairs. Iririki belongs to Ifira, and it was a typically shrewd Ifira move to lease it to an Australian development company. Makau said, "In seventy-five years we get the island back—plus a top-quality international resort. They build it. We keep it."

The guests, mostly well-heeled Australians in designer evening wear, began drifting in for cocktails, and as a band played island music I thought of my parents living quietly up on the hill, making do on their mission stipend, poor as church mice.

But there had been compensations and we were witnessing one now—a sunset so stunning that around the pool bar all *tok tok* ceased. The horizon was invaded by an unearthly lavender light which came spilling across the sky then fell into the harbour at our feet, empurpling the air and water, painting our faces with amaranth. Makau told John about Vila Base, built by the American navy in 1941 on the old Belleview Plantation. "It had one thousand beds and thirty-six doctors, all top people. Every day C47s flew up to Guadalcanal to bring the casualties. At Bauer Field forty ambulances would be waiting, hospital ships called all the time. I remember the *Solace,* painted white with a big red cross on the funnel. She used to sail at night, all lit up like a cruise boat. There were Jap subs everywhere, but . . ." He shrugged. "The old Paton Memorial nameplate is now at Vila Base. In reception."

John nodded. "Yes, I know." But he didn't know that Makau had been its first post-independence superintendent. My father's best student had succeeded him at the infinitely superior hospital he had long badgered the condominium government to build.

It was getting late. Makau rose. *"Lookim yu!"* he said.

See you later.

*

Vanuatu's eighty islands, routinely rattled by earthquakes, lie twelve hundred miles east of Australia. Named the New Hebrides by Captain Cook, they became a nineteenth-century Anglo-French condominium—a territorial trade-off in which two metropolitan powers with a thousand years of mutual enmity agreed to share power. It never worked; the Brits complained endlessly about the duplicity of the French, the French bemoaned the constant, furtive manoeuvrings of the Brits.

Their determination to yield nothing led to the duplication of everything: two flags, two anthems, two political doctrines, two currencies, two languages, two sets of postage stamps, two police forces, two legal systems, two jails (the French served better food), two hospitals (my father's practised better medicine) and allegedly, for an utterly surreal few days, two rules of the road: Brits on the left, French on the right. Locals never spoke of Condominium. They called it Pandemonium.

In 1980, faced with growing UN disquiet, they finally agreed on a joint course of action—to allow the new Ripablik Blong Vanuatu to hoist its gaudy, jungle-hued flag. Yet, six centuries after Agincourt, the native population, schizophrenically split between Anglophones and Francophones, began re-enacting the Hundred Years' War. An early Anglophone government sacked not one, but two, French Ambassadors, while the first act of the Francophone administration succeeding it was the mass sacking of Anglophone civil servants.

*

In one of the seismic family splits not uncommon here, Makau's older brother Dr John—also trained by my father—threw in his lot with the French. Both were clever and ambitious; while Makau, before independence, ran the British hospital, John ran the French. Makau received an OBE and a gold lighter from the Queen at the British Residency, John a Légion d'honneur (plus a kiss on the cheeks) from De Gaulle at the French Mission. They remained close, but there was an edge to their relationship. And when the new Anglophone government shut down John's hospital and declared that Makau's would henceforth be Vanuatu's major infirmary (and he its medical supremo) it grew distinctly sharper.

During a previous visit, a month before independence, I dined with them both—Dr John, a stringy, inquisitive, excitable old man, wore horn-rimmed glasses and did brilliant De Gaulle impressions. Now, little more than a decade later, I found the Francophones had again forced the Anglophones into opposition. Makau deflected questions about his brother; he was OK but inaccessible and, somehow, no longer in the family loop.

*

At dawn I was woken by the *ringim*. Makau spoke without preamble. "You will eat with us tonight. John and you should be at Iririki wharf by seven o'clock."

He replaced the phone. I sighed and went back to sleep.

At breakfast a waiter told me that Vanuatu's Anglophone President was under house arrest.

I looked up from my grapefruit. "What's he done?"

"He refused to support laws Korman wants."

Maxime Carlot Korman was the new Francophone Prime Minister. "So what happens now?"

"There will be trouble."

I called a friend in Port Vila who said he had recently seen the

President, Fred Timakata, strolling past the post office. The PM, he added, was just back from Paris, where he mislaid his passport and plane ticket home; he was not in the best of moods. Reports of a rift between President and Prime Minister continued all day. Much *bigfala trabol* was anticipated.

Nothing happened.

*

Kal Kalsakau and his wife, Maria, a clever, vivacious Fijian, were waiting at the wharf where the *aotbod*-driven Iririki shuttle punt docked. Kal, one of my childhood playmates, had become prosperously overweight and owner of the only BMW in the country. Makau, his father, sat brooding, a silent presence in the back. They took us to Le Rendezvous, then Port Vila's *nambawan* (number one) restaurant. Set on a hill overlooking the harbour and "written up in *Vogue*," it was a very classy place.

We shared it with a dozen Australians—the women tanned and bejewelled—and a bunch of high-spirited American yachties who had just completed a *dipsi* (ocean) crossing from Guam. Makau, Kal and Maria asked the waiter for orange juices, John for a cold Tusker, or local premium beer. So did I. Makau pursed his lips and I knew exactly what he was thinking.

Drinkers.

We both ordered fish soup and coconut crab. But when the soup came, nobody moved. An air of expectancy hung over the table. Then Makau spoke crisply.

"Say grace!"

That killed all adjacent conversations stone dead and, in an electric silence, I muttered the dimly remembered words. "Amen!" he proclaimed, and took up his spoon. Yet it turned into an excellent evening, one which would have delighted my parents. The Kalsakau family had, to all intents and purposes, adopted them on their arrival in 1935. Makau's wife, Thelma (who had died two years earlier), became a surrogate mother to me and my sister. Now he seemed to be keeping a patriarchal eye on me and my son.

The Kalsakaus had left us way behind. Dr Makau OBE had dined with the Queen ("a nice young woman") on Iririki while Kal, in

1980, became Vanuatu's first Finance Minister. Now Chairman of Air Vanuatu, he found that running an airline owning just one aeroplane— an ageing Boeing 727—allowed him time to conduct a remarkable social experiment on Ifira island. "We're involved in shipping, retailing, roadworks, hotels—Iririki—and quarries. As a result everyone over fifty gets a pension. Scholarships are available to any kid wanting an overseas education, cheap housing loans are available for their parents. Our people will never go without."

My attempts to talk politics were neatly deflected by Makau. "You ask about the President," he said reflectively. "Well, I will tell you something. Daddy baptized him. Fred Timakata. Yes, I think he did."

The waiter came to take our pudding orders. *"Yufala wantem sam aeskrim? Sam gato? No? Jes kofe? Faef kofe? Tangyu tumas!"*

My son, who had grown very quiet, gave me a look which said: *What am I doing here?*

*

Efate island, on which Port Vila stands, can easily be driven around in a day. During my childhood there had been no road; that was built by US Seabees in 1942. But the man from whom John and I rented our clapped-out *haeakar* warned that heavy cyclonic activity had resulted in certain sections being reclaimed by the beach; others, he said, would shortly revert to primary rainforest.

Yet the views it kept offering were stupendous—old shadow-puddled French plantations, soaring bush-clad volcanic peaks, every escapist cliché in the book. James Michener set *Tales of the South Pacific* in the wartime New Hebrides and, wherever you looked, you saw locations for the movie—bright seas, misty offshore islands, miles of sparkling sand.

"If you listen hard enough you might hear Ethel Merman singing 'Bali Ha'i,' " I remarked.

"Who's Ethel Merman?" said John.

Sighing, I told him all this had been part of his grandfather's practice. He made his house calls in a thirty-foot launch powered by a Kelvin marine engine—which he tended like a baby, doing all the maintenance and *fisksimap* himself. But he steered clear of Havannah Harbour in 1942 when, as the US fleet mustered for the Battle of the Coral Sea, it was stacked shore to shore with men-o'-war. Now, by the beach, a stall assembled from driftwood displayed spent tracer shells and World War Two Coke bottles with "San Francisco Calif" inscribed on their bases. You left your coins in an honesty box.

A bearded axeman told us he had been felling a tree for a new canoe. The cartridges and Coke bottles? He shrugged. Heaped in the bush, they were harvested by kids for pocket money. Driving home through rolling green hills we wondered about the men who, half a century earlier, had drunk from the souvenir bottles we'd bought, and what became of them.

*

Alec, my father, spent his childhood on the island of Paama, one hundred miles to the north and the apostolic domain of *his* father, Maurice, a Scots-born Presbyterian missionary who lived there for thirty-nine years. After studying medicine in Australia, Alec joined the same mission; they kept in touch by launch—a twenty-four-hour trip across big ocean swells. I had last visited in 1980 and wanted to return. But John couldn't get time off, and the twice-weekly *smol plen* that went part of the way was fully booked. At Port Vila's police station we called on Lewey Sahe, a likeable, shrewd Paamese who, when the government in one of its more ebullient moods threw his boss into jail, did a stint as acting deputy commissioner. Were any copra boats going north? Not for ten days, he said, but, meanwhile, we must come to dinner. "Paama people will be there. And there is something you can do for us."

That was my first intimation they were planning to make an evangelical video.

Six men turned up, among them two pastors and a young cop carrying a Sony camcorder. We sipped lemonade and chatted about my grandfather. Recalling a companionable, entertaining old man who read *Punch* and knew all Harry Lauder's comic songs by heart, I listened incredulously as they described the figure now incorporated into their mythology: part wise proconsul, part Nonconformist warrior facing the devil armed only with a Bible.

Gentle Mrs Sahe, unperturbed, produced a staggering array of dishes cooked in European and island style. The Maurice talk became more general. On Malekula a ferry had been named for him, on Santo a football team. A football team! (They'd even won a cup.) His two descendants exchanged wondering glances. But the big news was that on Paama his main church had been flattened by a hurricane. "So now we are building another," said Lewey, "but work goes slowly. Whenever we get money we add a bit more."

"It will be very big," said Joe, a pastor.

Then Lewey told a curious story. Bad things were happening on Paama—indeed, with sinister regularity, all over Vanuatu. "Men enter houses and steal. They also commit sexual offences."

"Why don't you lock them up?" John asked.

Lewey hesitated, and I sensed we had moved into an area not covered by the operational manuals. "Because we don't know who they are. They break in at night. When they rape the women, the women experience it as a nightmare and do not wake; only in the morning do they understand what happened. Then they find things are missing: radios, tinned goods, jewellery." He leaned forward. "But no finger-prints. Windows are not broken and the locks are untouched. Our CID experts don't know how they get in."

"But they're real people?" I asked.

"Oh, sure, they even have conventions."

"Conventions!"

He nodded. "And they can act like this because many of us have stopped going to church. We are losing God's love."

These were murky waters. A baffled policeman urgently needed advice but, undeniably, it was from Maurice he wanted it.

Then he asked if I would film a message for Paama. "What, now?" I said, and he nodded. Joe adjusted his camcorder and called for silence. I knew what Lewey had in mind—words of succour for islanders destabilized by their weird crime wave. My message should comfort the victims and strike iron into the souls of the perpetrators; he needed references to Christian values, family life, church attendance and, crucially, to Maurice. I said all that then, running out of inven-tion, stopped. "Well, goodnight, everyone."

"Great!" Lewey was polite. "You really put it over."

But of course I hadn't even got close, and, tucking into a pudding of bananas cooked in coconut cream, wondered what Maurice had really been up to all those years. The bond between him and the Paamese, strong as ever, remained exclusive and private to both. Lewey said, "There is one more thing. The new church will need a bell. We would like your family to give it to us."

Sudden memories of Frank, trailing rum fumes and Capstan Navy Cut cigarette smoke, made me smile—but, actually, I liked the idea. A well-cast bell was a flawless artefact, pure and transcendent as the note it struck. It was also supposed to be timeless; so what had become of the one custom-made for Paama by the Glasgow Foundry Boys' Bible Class in 1903?

Joe said, "It was broken by the hurricane."

Lewey said, "The church will not be ready for a while. You can send it in five years. There is a bell-maker in London?"

"The Whitechapel Bell Foundry," said John, "is almost next door to my hospital."

"OK," I said. "But I won't send it. I'll bring it."

*

Air Vanuatu's 727 stood on the apron as the Bauer Field departures hall filled with passengers for Sydney. I noted some familiar faces, Iririki people ending their package holidays.

"How old's that plane?" John said.

"Don't ask."

"Where are you sitting?"

"Up the back. I got a ticket from a bucket shop in Earls Court. The girl had never heard of Vanuatu, she said, 'It's a *place*?'"

Makau and Kal emerged from the crowd, each holding a translucent pink shell. "For your missus," said Makau. "You give her our good wishes." He beamed. "So, John, how are things at Vila Base?"

John said, "Oh, you know, too many sick people, not enough time for wind-surfing." Now he addressed Air Van's chairman. "Kal, Dad's travelling steerage."

"Uh-huh," said Kal.

"Not many people checking into business, though."

I waited for my old chum to get the point and summon his station manager. Instead, he delivered a brief monologue on the vagaries of business-class traffic—slow at the moment, certainly, but destined to grow with an economy already stirring. In a few months his executive cabin would be packed.

"But it's not packed today," said John.

"No." Kal glanced at his watch. "Want a lift? I'm going past the hospital."

It was a straight choice between a ruined airport minibus and the chairman's air-conditioned BMW. John grinned wryly as we said goodbye. He had got the upgrade.

The instant we were airborne Kal's female cabin attendants, all unsmiling, comfortably built Anglophile Presbyterians, wheeled out their drinks trolleys. My neighbour, a grocer from Manley, asked for whisky. As he took a tumbler filled to the brim with neat Bells the Australian captain came on the PA to say our hydraulics were malfunctioning. Though his tone remained unconcerned one worrying fact emerged: the problem was serious enough to send us straight back to Port Vila. "First we'll dump some gas. Then we'll try and get the undercarriage and flaps down manually."

I immediately ordered a large whisky too. *"Try?"* muttered the grocer. "What's that mean, for Chrissake?" The stewardess frowned. "Sir, do not take the Lord's name in vain." He seemed to assume she was in Holy Orders and meekly said, "Sorry, Sister." As the 727 continued discharging aviation fuel into the blue Pacific people broke open their duty-frees. The atmosphere grew party-like. Voices rose and the laughter grew louder. Everyone smoked.

The pilot now sounded very stressed. "Folks, the wheels are down but the flaps aren't—not fully. So it's going to be a very fast landing. Please remove all spectacles and false teeth, and adopt the crouch position." Hurtling into Vila, carrying a planeload of drunks with their heads between their knees, his touchdown was as violent as a car crash; overhead lockers burst open, oxygen masks sprang from the roof, then wild applause rang out. Speaking a little breathlessly he said, "Welcome back to Bauer Field! You folks enjoy that? The repairs shouldn't take too long. We'll be off to Sydney in an hour or so."

*

The repairs took four days.

I reclaimed my quarters on Iririki and left a message at the hospital. Moments later Makau phoned. "I heard about the plane. Are you OK?"

"Sure."

"I have found a book. Written by Daddy. I will send it around."

He'd written a *book*?

"Yes. And you take care of it. I am just lending it to you."

An hour later, from reception, I collected "Lecture Notes for Medical Students by A. S. Frater, Vila, New Hebrides"—114 worn, yellowing pages typed (probably by my mother) and bound in blue cartridge paper. Sobering up fast, I leafed slowly through.

He began by listing things that had once lived ("thatch for roof") and never lived ("a shilling") and the characteristics of things living now: these included *growth* ("plant a stone and it will never grow"), *movement* ("a stone moves when you throw it, but by itself cannot move at all") and *reproduction*. "The banana makes suckers which form new trees. But usually living things have children by making seeds. When two seeds are joined they make a new body, and this grows up like the parent."

I hadn't, actually, grown up like him at all, and hoped John hadn't grown up like me; I wanted him to be more like my father—which, indeed, seemed to be the case.

Then he listed fifty-four "Parts of the Body" ("Learn these names") and sixteen bones. "You have seen cargo lifted into a steamer by means of the steamer's derricks. The bones of the arm are like derricks, and they enable us carry heavy things." The muscles, strung from those ossicular derricks, are "the ropes and winches that do the work," the heart was an "engine which has four rooms," the kidneys passed two and a half pints of urine daily. (Red or dark urine indicated blackwater fever, milky urine certain forms of filariasis.)

He introduced "Parasitology" by evoking the giant banyan and the way parasitic visitors fed off the host. "Medicine" described fifty-two tropical conditions, "Surgery" was mostly burns and fractures—the latter rare "because there are not many accidents with motor cars as in white man's countries." He urged students to visit the forest if splints were required; good ones could be fashioned from bamboo.

There was a knock. A weary-looking woman asked if I had any

laundry. She told me she came from Ifira and knew Makau. When I mentioned our family connection her face suddenly lit up: my father had delivered her mother. *"Gud naet, dokta!"* she called.

"Hygiene" was mostly practical. "Do not sleep with your head under a blanket." Kids with head lice needed scalp massages of kerosene and coconut oil. Too many clothes stopped sunlight from benefiting bones and teeth—"People should not be ashamed of their bodies." Nor should they defecate in the bush. A closet, set over water, was the ideal solution. Diseased dogs should be killed, floors regularly scattered with clean coral. "When a house begins to break, it should be pulled down and a new one built."

"Pharmacology" contained dispensing notes and dozens of prescriptions for liniments, lotions, ointments, paints and powders. (For yaws you stirred 15 gr. of Potassium Iodide and 15 m. of Ext. Glycyrrhizae Liq. into ½ fl. oz. of water.)

Sitting in my five-star suite just a stone's throw from where he had written this I recalled, in the hospital, a room containing desks and a blackboard. There, between eleven and twelve each morning, he lectured. I usually went down to collect him for lunch and, dawdling on the veranda, would listen to him speaking his fluent island pidgin with its interestingly exotic traces of a Glasgow accent.

That memory had a curious tropical weight. It came complete with midday heat, stillness, sea glitter, greenery, the whiff of damp earth and, closer to hand, ether and disinfectant (hospital smells, for me, still conjure up the noon hour on that Iririki veranda). I knew he had been teaching barefoot doctors when Chairman Mao was still on his Long March but now, a decade after his death, reminders of him kept cropping up almost daily.

*

His Little Blue Book, and the quality of the people he turned out, led to his next job. Appointed a professor in Fiji by British Colonial Office headhunters, he accepted the long hours and beggarly salary (he was always hopeless about money) because Fiji, crucially, lay in the tropics. So, on New Year's Eve 1946, a Qantas flying boat took us from Rose Bay, Sydney to Suva, its hot, sprawly, harbourside capital. There, at the

Central Medical School, he gave students from all around the Southern Pacific a four-year, no-frills course in surgery, obstetrics, tropical medicine and public health. Public service featured in the syllabus too, and graduates returning home as assistant medical practitioners were expected to take an active part in community affairs. (At least three, in due course, became Prime Ministers.)

The Sagacity of Dr Manson

One night six years ago I returned to Fiji and, stepping off the plane, relished the moment of transformation. The tropical air was silky and oven-roasted, the stars bright as headlights and arranged in such novel configurations you needed time to adjust your mental compass. The interior of Viti Levu, the main island, is an old volcanic egg box of impassable mountains and plunging ravines that keeps the highway hugging the coast. I caught a minibus from Nadi, the international airport, around to Suva, and spent the long drive happily re-acclimatizing. At Sigatoka a dense little shower drummed on the roof, split an adjacent rainbow like a wishbone then, crossing a jungly area irradiated by sunbeams, became vaporized steam. The old aura of romance remained. "I still love you Sanjay Bali" read a message on a roadside cliff face. Three storeys high, the cliff possessed a slick buttery glaze indicating the author had risked her—or, perhaps, his—neck to publish that despairing proclamation; and I recalled having my heart broken here by hazel-eyed Miranda Sims, aged nine.

Suva seemed unchanged. It had kept its Edwardian architecture and, years after independence, its imperial nomenclature. Strolling down Victoria Parade towards Albert Park I was stopped by an American who wanted directions to Disraeli Road—which, after half a lifetime, I was able to supply (head up to Gladstone and bear right)—then moved on, a stranger in a familiar town, looking for someone to talk to. I was hailed by a handsome, smiling woman who spoke in an educated way. I took her for a teacher and, delighted by her friendliness and spontaneity, even summoned up a few words in Fijian. She waited patiently for me to finish then said, "You want a blow job?" Dismayed, I began handing over money and learned she was an unemployed midwife, now destitute. The money was supposed to buy time for a chat—about the state of Fiji's economy, among other things—but an elderly Taiwanese tourist caught her eye and she waved me away.

On Saturday afternoons at Albert Park—set beside Suva's triumphalist Government Buildings—my father and I had watched the Central Medical School team play dazzling barefoot rugby.

Now three Indian kids were knocking a football about. "What country?" they cried.

I told them. One said: "You know Cambridge? My brother is there."

"Really?" I said, interested. "Which college?"

He frowned. "No college. Curry place."

The Grand Pacific Hotel, once the finest between Sydney and Honolulu, faced the park too. A Palladian structure erected by a shipping company to vaguely maritime specifications, it had a Cunardian dining room, decklike balconies and foaming saltwater baths. (After arriving on the flying boat we spent several pampered weeks at the GPH, our bill paid by the British government.) Once part of any sophisticated traveller's compendium, it now stood boarded-up and abandoned. A seller of shark's-tooth swords said it was owned by an island community who hadn't the money to pay for its restoration. "So what will happen?" I asked.

He shrugged. "It will tumble."

Sliding into a state of despondent nostalgia I took a taxi up to the airy, designed-for-the-tropics house (starlight being specified as a source of illumination) my parents built at Tamavua. A quiet wander down the drive became a wild sprint back up, pursued by a bellowing Rottweiler, while a stout Indian woman stood grinning in the garden. Somewhere around the Domain area we passed a handsome bungalow with deep verandas. The driver said it belonged to a senior officer in the police and then I remembered.

Old Clinton, oblivious to his celebrated name and illustrious medical pedigree, had once lived there.

*

Hippocrates, in *Airs, Water and Places,* written in the fifth century BC, was the first to recognize diseases of travel as a specific category. Yet diseases brought home by visitors to the tropics remained a mystery until the "germ theory" evolved in the latter part of the nineteenth century. Louis Pasteur proved diseases were caused not by spontaneous generation but by bacteria. His pupil, Pierre-Paul Emile Roux, discovered viruses. And Patrick Manson realized that agents—such as mosquitoes—could transmit them. A new science was born (which my father included in the letters after his name: DTM, or Diploma of Tropical Medicine).

One of his colleagues in Fiji was a big, balding, extrovert Englishman named Clinton Manson-Bahr. We boys liked the way he created excitement and controversy wherever he went, organizing manhunts, tug-of-wars or rugby and soccer games in which, sometimes, he would suddenly merge the codes so you could score tries with a round ball or flatten a goalkeeper with a flying tackle; he teased our sisters, flirted with our mothers and joked with our fathers, and always left behind eddies of laughter and a marked improvement in the social climate. He was the consultant physician at Suva's War Memorial Hospital and a good family friend. (When I headed for Italy to try to become a writer Clinton, out of the blue, turned up one day and hustled me off to lunch. Over two or three bottles of strong Umbrian wine he offered shrewd advice, passed on the gossip from home and, as always, told some excellent jokes.)

I knew he had a famous grandfather who, at the age of fourteen, had shot a neighbour's cat and surgically removed a tapeworm from its intestines; Clinton always argued this act of hooliganism hinted at future greatness. Perhaps it did. Sir Patrick Manson, having qualified as a doctor at Aberdeen, went on to found the School of Tropical Medicine in London, while his work in lymphatic filariasis, according to one authority, had "a more profound effect on the human race than any other discovery which can be attributed to an identifiable individual."

The Wellcome Trust have a photograph, taken in Ceylon in 1912, of chubby, confident four-year-old Clinton—the booming voice, I sensed, already troubling the servants—seated on the knee of his legendary ancestor. The beaming, handsome old patriarch, luxuriantly bewhiskered, radiates geniality. Universally known as "the father of tropical medicine"—though he tended to wince when called that—he's remembered too for his personal modesty and professional generosity: co-workers always got extensive credit. He was dogged and lucky but also, no question, a ranking genius up there with Pasteur.

In 1898 Sir Patrick wrote a slim textbook. As new illnesses continued to be identified—often by him—the volume grew and, when the fifth edition came out shortly before his death in 1922, it was already regarded as a classic. Today it has become an institution, and the massive twenty-first edition of *Manson's Tropical Diseases,* published in 2003, is 1,847 pages long.

His realization that mosquitoes can transmit germs led to the discovery of vector-borne sicknesses and, eventually, the cracking of the codes governing malaria, plague, typhus, yellow fever and countless other parasitic and viral infections.

Lymphatic filariasis, a condition still affecting over ninety million people in Africa, Asia and equatorial South America, is caused by worms that inflame the lymphatic system and trigger conditions such as elephantiasis. This, when it attacks the scrotum, can produce testicles of such size some men are obliged to move them around in wheelbarrows. The largest on record, removed by a surgeon in Senegal, weighed two hundredweight.

The microfilariae of a filarial worm had first been noted in the blood of a dog. When Timothy Lewis, a young Calcutta-based Aberdeen graduate, spotted them in human blood, Manson, working in China as medical officer to the Amoy Customs Service, grew interested. He found microfilariae in the blood of Hinlo, his gardener (who has his own place in medical history), and at some point during 1877 asked him to sleep in a "mosquito house" where, nightly, he was bitten by dozens of pre-caught local species.

Manson, examining the sated insects under his microscope, saw the haematozoon drawn from Hinlo undergoing dramatic changes; *inside the mosquito* they became tiny worms with their own alimentary canals. The mosquito, acting as a "nurse," developed and nourished the robust, disease-bearing creature which it then injected into its victim. *It was the carrier*—Manson had made his quantum leap. (And though an Amoy street vendor who draped a cloth over his testicles and used them as a counter sued him for cutting off his unique selling points, he continued operating on elephantiasis cases.)

The arrival of the drug diethylcarbamazine, and the startling decision of the Beijing government to mix it with domestic salt, virtually eliminated lymphatic filariasis from China. Yet elsewhere it persists and, in the 1980s, the World Health Organisation issued a poster showing a slender Asian girl with grotesquely misshapen lower limbs. "Should tender feet meant for dancing become deformed?" said the caption. "We must destroy mosquitoes that deform beautiful damsels."

*

One humid morning, shortly after the end of the Cultural Revolution, I watched a man having his leg amputated at a hospital in Canton. A nurse sat by an open door plucking a chicken, open windows overlooked a yard where roosters crowed. Two sweating young surgeons took turns with a blunt saw while an acupunctural anaesthetist used needles to ease the man's agony. They didn't work; when his howls grew unbearable a hypodermic syringe (we Western observers were not meant to see this) was produced and he grew quiet. As the nurse carted away the severed leg—in a carton labelled "Golden Moon Lychees"—I told my companion, a veteran Hong–Kong-based British journalist, about Manson's Amoy vendor; that operating theatre, I suggested, must have been very like this one. He said, "At least the poor bugger probably got chloroform." To this day, of course, infirmaries just as dreadful are to be found in many corners of the neglected, fiscally desolated tropics. There local ingenuity often provides substitutes for drugs and equipment; in Senegal, for example, an ancient form of music has been used, with notable effect, to help make sick people better.

*

At certain Senegalese hospitals, when all orthodox treatments have failed, a physician may turn his patient over to a team of specialist drummers. "Each of us," said Mark Sunkett, "is supposed to have a unique set of personal rhythms, a kind of sonic DNA. If the drums can reproduce it, then a dying person's planets all suddenly line up and he recovers. They call it Ndeup."

I met Dr Sunkett in the coastal village of Bargny where the Seck family—a Muslim mother and ten daughters—took in paying guests. In the evenings (as Mme Seck wrote prayers with her fountain pen— exquisite little works of calligraphy—on the palm of her hand) we chatted under a neem tree filled with squalling cats. There I learned about the remedial powers of Ndeup, and the families who could trace their drumming lineage back two hundred years. "Any male child, whether he become a gas-pump attendant or a high-court judge, first and foremost remains a drummer." On the faculty of Arizona's State University School of Music (also principal timpanist with the Phoenix Symphony Orchestra), Mark knew the signature of every drummer in the Bargny region. So when we heard, for example, an eruption of ground-level thunder coming from down near the beach, he would say, "That's the Feayes, a father and ten sons, rehearsing a *sabar,* danced by the women and *very* sexy."

Nobody around here, though, could do Ndeup.

"Oh, the local guys are all strictly social drummers. You'll find the Ndeup specialists further along the coast."

"But how could they know about a sick person's rhythms?"

"Friends or relatives would tell them, maybe tap them out with a pencil. The way you come to recognize your tune isn't fully understood, you usually find it early in life, perhaps you even fall down on first hearing it. But the treatment works so well it's even recognized by the Senegal government—and now it's catching on in the US; I know of Americans who've had drummers flown over and felt a whole lot better for it."

Curious about how such drums were made I went, one day, to meet the Sow brothers of Rufisque. The older brother, whiskery and red-eyed, said they carved their instruments from *dimba,* a hardwood heavy as mahogany; other specialists then applied the skins—goat at one end, baby crocodile on the other. And, yes, they had Ndeup men among their customers.

"And can they cure sick people? Really sick people? With cancer? Heart disease? Maybe even AIDS?"

"Of course." He raised a cautious finger. *"But only if the right song is played."*

Patrick Manson, the pragmatic Victorian, would certainly have dismissed all this as mere jungle medicine. Yet had he seen drummers cause a comatose patient to suddenly stir and twitch, it might have started him thinking. A response so puzzling needed the kind of imaginative leap that, famously, he made when in 1889 he turned his attention to malaria.

*

Today it kills two million annually and, in India alone, is reckoned to cost two billion working days; the lassitude of tropical peoples doesn't stem entirely from their climate. The most dangerous of its four strains— the malignant, tertian *Plasmodium falciparum*—can lodge parasites in the brain which cause coma and death.

The anopheles larvae require the same conditions for life as rice seedlings; both like heat and water. Some prefer their water sunlit and running, others dim and still. (Mosquitoes in Brazil's Sierra do Mar lay their eggs in the rain-filled leaf-cups of epiphytic Bromeliaceae fever trees. As each tree may carry three thousand of these tiny ponds, a small forest could inflict more damage than a civil war.) In Sri Lanka and Cambodia malaria has, without fuss, wiped out civilizations.

Identified over four thousand years ago, it has probably been around for a million, first emerging from the tropical forests of Asia and Africa. Apes and monkeys get it; so do birds. Indeed, three Calcutta larks with avian malaria, dissected in 1889 (at Manson's suggestion), provided a crucial breakthrough.

Hippocrates, "the first malariologist," identified the telltale splenic enlargement and advised his patients not to drink from stagnant marshes. Italians attributed it to bad air, "mal aria." (Horace Walpole probably anglicized the word when, writing home in 1740, he complained of "a horrid thing called the mal'aria, that comes to Rome every summer and kills one.") The belief that infection was due to poisonous miasmas persisted until 1880 when a French army surgeon, Charles Laveran, examining the blood of a soldier diagnosed with malaria at Constantine, Algeria, detected agitated movement among his red cells— living parasites which, he surmised, might have caused the disease.

Manson, home from China, started a London practice and had himself appointed physician to the Seamen's Hospital Society. There, pondering the blood of sick Indian sailors, he saw the weird, exflagellating parasites for himself and knew instinctively that mosquitoes had a role—yet he discounted their bite; malaria, he believed, came from drinking larvae-infested water in which an insect had laid its eggs. Then, in 1890, a young British doctor on furlough from the Indian Medical Service sought an interview.

Ronald Ross, intense and prickly, with a movie star's looks, had grown so bored in India he had taken to writing romantic novels and reducing "space, matter and motion" to a series of wonky mathematical formulae. A sudden, obsessive interest in malaria (allegedly triggered by his marriage) brought him to Manson. Yet Manson, to Ross's astonishment, talked not about miasmas, but mosquitoes—and his belief that though mosquitoes infected man, man first infected mosquitoes; they weren't born with the fever but somehow picked it up and passed it on. Using his new-found fame and influence, Manson (who now dined at 10 Downing Street) persuaded the India Office to allow Ross, on his return, to do three years' research on full pay.

Ross sent Manson a hundred and ten letters and sketches. Following Manson's advice he fed his mosquitoes with infected human blood then dissected them to look for parasites. Initially he used "grey" and "brindled" insects which yielded nothing. Then, stumbling upon brown ones with "dapple wings," he unwittingly found the anopheles. Yet just as they showed promising signs, he moved house and mislaid the lot. New dapple-wings were hastily collected then, unexpectedly, he ran out of sick people.

Manson told him to try birds. Ross acquired three malarial larks, fed their blood to his mosquitoes and watched the parasites appear, then saw them shift from the stomach walls to the salivary glands, *ready to be injected into a new host.* In July 1898 he sent an elated telegram to Manson who, though ill, immediately left his bed and took a train to Edinburgh to break the news to a meeting of the British Medical Association. Ross returned home to a post at the new Liverpool School of Tropical Medicine, located in a great trading port with a constant supply of tropical patients.

In 1902 Ross received a Nobel Prize and suddenly everyone was talking about mosquitoes—though most revealed a fathomless well of ignorance. The British Museum commissioned a taxonomic study which ran to five volumes and described 1,050 species. Today the number has risen to 3,300, of which 410 belong to the anopheles tribe; of those 70 can, and do, transmit malaria.

*

Buying bottled water in the market at Pakse, beside the Mekong in Laos, I came upon a pretty, tangle-haired woman sitting crooning, half-naked upon a sack of rice. My interpreter, Xa Thepvongsa, said she spent her days wandering bare-breasted through this buttoned-up, highly conservative provincial capital *singing* the story of her life. "She lost a child and is quite mad. Since that day she never speak, only sing."

Checking out of my hotel, haunted by her story, I mentioned it to the clerk; overworked and kindly he said, "Poor woman, I know her; the dead baby, yes, but afterwards, I think, she had malaria." He tapped his sweaty forehead with his leaking Hanoi-made biro. "Up here."

Staring at the livid mark it left behind—it would take days to scrub off—I caught his drift. "Cerebral malaria?"

"In the *brain*. You are paying dollars?"

"Yes."

"Excellent!"

I wasn't unhappy about leaving the Champasak Palace. A lizard-infested, mock-Ming fantasy fortress, it had been built by a developer who accommodated his guests in dim, airless little rooms sporting notices demanding that all weapons and ammunition should be deposited at the front desk.

I said to the clerk, "So what's been handed in today?"

"Just one flamethrower," he grinned. It was our joke.

In town I stopped the car to pick up a Dutch blonde. Corine Eeltink had been my neighbour on the Chinese-built seventeen-seater doing the flight down from Vientiane. (Chewing gum had been stuck into its rattling, loose-fitting windows by passengers fearing explosive decompression.) When I mentioned I was headed for the Bolaven plateau she said, "Hey, me too!" and told me its weavers were famous; she had bags crammed with fabrics acquired during several weeks wandering around Indo-China. Would there be room in the car for her? I nodded. She said, "Bring medicines. In those villages many children are sick. Malaria is bad up there."

Xa was awed by her size. Over six feet and skinny, with Nordic colouring and a face displaying strong aquiline planes, she had trained as a nurse in Amsterdam and now, at thirty-three, practised as a masseuse in Manhattan. Charging a hundred bucks an hour, working seven days a week, she visited her clients by trail bike; regulars included superjocks on Wall Street and Fifth Avenue, models and movie stars. Yet her overriding ambition was to buy a big house in Calcutta and start an orphanage.

At Khieng Khong, a motley village, she loped towards the shacks where the weavers lived, pausing to play with the kids and distribute pencils. Xa and I slipped off to see the killing house in which Nge animists, under a harvest moon, engaged in the ritual slaughter of water buffalo. (Drunken men danced around tethered beasts and stabbed at their hearts; the depth and musculature of a buffalo's heart meant at least fifty knife-blows were needed.) Summoned back by raised voices we found Corine confronting a woman who held a bolt of cloth in one arm and a whey-faced baby in the other. "Malaria!" cried Corine. "He will be dead in three days. Where is the father?"

The father, a small, spindly built youth, said the shaman had advised him to kill a cow; the baby's fate now rested with the forest spirits. *"Spirits?"* yelled Corine. *"He needs mefloquine!"* As she pulled tablets from her tote bag a second woman approached, suckling an infant and smoking a green cheroot. Corine glared at the child. "This one has pneumonia!"

Grim-faced, handing out pills, crying "Boil your water!" she hectored cheroot-puffing mothers whose kids had worms, goitres, dengue fever, fungal infections, dysentery and, above all, malaria. Villagers too old or frail to join the scrum got their mefloquine from me, along with multivitamins, hydrocortisone cream for rashes, Nurofen for aching joints and, for those plainly on the point of death, Boots rejuvenating ginseng tablets.

"Next village," said Corine.

"Yes, ma'am," said Xa.

"And go faster. You are a very slow driver, Mr Xa."

He sighed. "You don't want nice ethnic fabrics?"

"No." In the car she fell asleep then suddenly woke and said, "It was the Nazis who developed the first anti-malarial chemicals." That was news to me. I knew quinine was extracted from the bark of the cinchona tree, identified in Peru in 1630, and that in the East Indies the Dutch created plantations of such size they controlled the world's supply. When Japanese invaders cut the link the Allies, knowing their armies would soon be fighting on malarial battlefields, urgently needed a synthetic substitute.

She said the Germans, shortly before the outbreak of war, had produced a promising four-amino quinoline compound named Sontochin. America "acquired" several tablets for analysis ("Don't ask how!") and from these developed chloroquine—while British scientists, working independently, developed Paludrine; within twenty years, however, mosquitoes everywhere had developed a resistance to both. "So now quinine is making a comeback." The Laos insects, it seemed, were already displaying some mefloquine resistance.

Corine disrupted three more villages then, as darkness fell, hit a rural pharmacy stocking Thai-made Western medicines. She turned that shop over, had its bewildered small-boned proprietor and his wide-eyed daughter produce all their antimalarials and antibiotics, made Xa write out lists of all the sick children we had visited, plus the drugs and dosages each required, paid the pharmacist a treasury of bank-notes and had him promise to deliver them first thing in the morning.

We found rooms at Tad Lo, beside a waterfall. During dinner Xa complained of exhaustion. Corine jumped up and, with her big, strong hands, went to work on his shoulders. She left him sighing with pleasure, attended to me ("Sit up straight, Alex!") then finally massaged the cook. I left this remarkable woman noisily drinking a whole tureen of watercress soup and went to my room. Moonlight bouncing off the river filled it with such radiance you could read a fortune cookie. I felt a bit feverish and wondered if I was coming down with malaria myself, though I now realize it was probably the early symptoms of *mal de jaune*—a condition said to be common among those who yearn nostalgically for Indo-China.

*

Dutch physicians in the East Indies, puzzling over a strange, intractable new malady, named it *Indische Sprouw*. Manson, after treating five patients in Amoy, dubbed it tropical sprue and wrote a celebrated paper which put the disease on the map—yet it was his son-in-law (Clinton's father) who went on to do extensive research. Originally calling himself plain P. H. Bahr, he followed the great man into tropical medicine, married his daughter and, through a hyphenated nominal link, also acquired his name. Then, helped on his way by sprue, he made a considerable one for himself, embellishing it with a knighthood and ending his days as Sir Philip Manson-Bahr.

In 1912, invited over by a sprue-plagued Tea Planters' Association, young Bahr spent fourteen months in Ceylon and concluded it was caused by an infection named *Monilia albicans*. That was contradicted by a Dr Rogers, who said the problem was streptococcal, while a Dr Nichols spoke of a deficiency disease and a Dr Fairley blamed "ill-nourished bone marrow." Nobody, it seemed, had a clue what to do about tropical sprue.

Deadly if untreated, it causes the body to stop absorbing food. Any solids taken by mouth go straight through the system and emerge as frothy white stools ("Like a mixture of chalk and beer," observed William Twining, a nineteenth-century Calcutta physician), unusually heavy in faecal fat and smelling particularly foul; post-mortem examination usually reveals intestinal putrefaction. Aside from chronic diarrhoea the symptoms include an ulcerated tongue, sallow complexion, debility, torpor, emaciation and a fretful temper. "It sinks their Spirits very much," wrote William Hillary, an eighteenth-century Barbados physician, who prescribed bed rest and opium.

Popularly supposed to be confined to Europeans living in the tropics—the one certain cure was to ship them home quick—it struck at Allied troops during World War Two's Burma campaign. Since the thousands who caught it along the Irrawaddy included Africans and Indians, the whites-only myth, at least, was laid to rest. A century earlier, a British professor of military medicine had published a full account—he called it diarrhoea alba—so the army medics knew what to do. Yet, even while successfully containing the outbreak, they had no idea why it happened.

In 1953 Philip Manson-Bahr called it "one of the outstanding conundrums of tropical medicine" and, though research has since moved on, certain aspects of the disease continue to baffle scientists. They know antibiotics usually work (tetracyclines being favoured) but, really, it remains an enigma still.

*

It was Clinton who, noting I was at a loose end during a university vacation in Suva, suggested I visit a leper colony. From him I heard about Joseph de Veuster, or Father Damien, who, caring for eight hundred lepers on the Hawaiian island of Molokai, contracted the disease himself. (In 1936 they exhumed his body for a solemn pontifical mass in Honolulu before bringing it home to Antwerp.) And he spoke too of Gerhard Hansen, the Dane who discovered the leprosy bacillus and, to prove it was transmissible, injected it into the cornea—the *eye!*—of a hapless non-leprous woman in his Bergen hospital. This, an example of the ambition-driven side of medical research, got him struck off for life.

Molokai had been the inspiration for Makogai, a small Fijian island now given over entirely to lepers; yet, aboard the Medical Department ketch, I wondered what I'd let myself in for. In 1774 Captain Cook, visiting Tonga, "happen'd to peep into a house where one or more of these people were, one Man only appeared at the Door . . . but the intolerable Stench which came from his Putrified face was alone sufficient to keep me from entering, his Nose was quite gone and his face ruin'd being wholly covered with ulcers, or rather covered with one ulcer so that the very sight of him was shocking."

After a wild night at sea we sailed in to find Tonga's lepers had all finished up here—and, that very day, were celebrating a visit by their monarch. I heard singing and speeches, saw Tongans dressed to the nines in palm-leaf mats. Makogai's breezy Irish MO showed me around a settlement of tidy bungalows, introduced me—"Sure, you can shake hands"—to residents with unmarked faces. Where was Cook's shocking putrefaction now? "Gone for good. We diagnose early and hit them with sulphonamides. So how's old Clinton? Still bossing everyone about?"

Queen Salote, an imposing six-footer, made her name when heavy rain fell on Queen Elizabeth's coronation parade. Sharing an open carriage with a shivering Jawaharlal Nehru ("Her lunch," Noël Coward remarked), she famously refused to hoist its retractable roof and, soaked to the skin, wowed the English crowds with her cheery indifference to their awful climate.

Her dinner, that night on Makogai, was grilled fish eaten in the Irish MO's house, with me seated opposite. "The knife and fork, young man," she said, "should be returned to the plate when you are chewing. Also, it is impolite to lean your elbows on the table"—*in front of me,* she meant. Carrying on like the last of the Edwardian royals, she gave off a faint fragrance of coconut oil, and had a resonating, up-from-the-boots contralto voice. Yet I detected a certain mischievousness and, sure enough, she broke off formal exchanges with the doctor and his wife to question me closely about a stunningly beautiful Suva girl who had won Fiji's Miss Hibiscus crown. Had I met her? Actually, I'd been trying to meet her for weeks and Salote, noting my discomfort, boasted, "She is part Tongan, you know." (She was also part Fijian, part Chinese and part German—one of those spectacular racial diversifications that can only happen in the tropics.)

We heard that Elizabeth and Salote, being island monarchs, shared an islander's sea-girt view of the world. She was talking about the dangers of introspection when a wrinkled old lady-in-waiting, forgotten on the floor behind, jumped up: "Her Majesty will retire now." Next morning, before embarkation, I had to hand over the shoes worn on Makogai for burning on the beach: a precautionary public-health measure.

*

While tropical sprue was supposed to attack only Europeans, Europeans were thought to be immune from African trypanosomiasis, or sleeping sickness. But in 1901 Everett Dutton, a young parasitologist from the Liverpool School and one of Manson's brightest protégés, spotted trypanosomes in the blood of Captain Kelly, master of a government steamer on the River Gambia—the first recorded infection of a white. (Steamers still shuttle between decrepit, crime-stricken Banjul and Basse Sante Su two days inland to load peanuts—the large brukus and small chopper species—for export; the old, sunk-long-ago *Lady Wright*, perhaps Kelly's own command, became a philatelic oddity: the only vessel on earth to issue its own postage stamps.)

Lucky Manson, naturally, got to record the second infection: Mrs. S., a missionary's wife from the Congo, came to see him in London complaining of fever; he identified the same "wriggly worm" trypanosomes and knew that within a year her entire nervous system would be under siege. Shortly before she lapsed into a coma, he was able to tell her the cause of her impending death. Just six months earlier the Second Sleeping Sickness Commission, meeting in Entebbe, Uganda, had finally identified the trypanosomiasis vector. Mrs S. had been bitten by a tsetse fly.

*

The dozen or so people seated around the Kampala dinner table included a couple of cabinet ministers, the Deputy British High Commissioner and various other scions of Ugandan society. The talk was of Amin and Obote.

My companions spoke of them in a way that was anecdotal, dispassionate, almost disinterested. A tall, strikingly handsome woman well known for her work with AIDS victims said, "Obote was the worst. He was a master butcher, a truly dedicated killer. At the end of a long day he liked to wind down by watching people being thrown off the roof of the Nile Hotel. It is multi-storey. It was his favourite Happy Hour activity."

"How many died?" I asked.

The Hon. Dr Rogunda, a burly, bearded physician turned Minister for Transport, called across the table to the Hon. Sam Sebagereka, Minister for Tourism, Wildlife and Antiquities (present with his wife, Vicki), "Brother! How many, would you say, perished at the hands of Obote last time?"

Mr Sebagereka said the number would never be known.

"Half a million?" I persisted.

They shook their heads. It had become just another awful historical abstraction.

We sat drinking Chardonnay and nibbling smoked tilapia fish while garden scents wafted through the house and, in the trees, roosting marabou storks rattled their bills. The tall woman said Churchill's "Pearl of Africa" had become a dual-purpose killing ground, the era of the bullet now followed by the apocalyptic virus. "Our first cases were diagnosed in 1983, all contracted at a small port on Lake Victoria. Today, in that area, whole communities have been wiped out, the gardens have gone back to the bush and you can walk for several miles without seeing anyone. Any houses are probably inhabited by orphans. On my last visit I came upon a seven-year-old girl looking after her baby brother, both quite alone. She said to me, 'Mother, is it the end of the world?' "

I told them my son had spent a summer vacation working at Kampala's Mengo Hospital, overwhelmed with AIDS victims. Dr Rogunda said, "The Mengo has a place in medical history, you know. It was Uganda's first hospital—built in 1897 by Sir Albert Cook, the first British doctor to settle here. And at the Mengo he wrote the first description of Burkitt's lymphoma."

"That is a terrible affliction," said Sam Sebagereka.

He nodded. "Cancer of the face in small children. For a long time it was thought we sub-Saharan Africans did not get cancer. Cook proved we could. Then Dr Burkitt came in 1946 and showed how widespread it was."

At the Mengo, around the turn of the century, Albert Cook examined a child with a facial growth half the size of his head. In Tanzania and Mozambique I had seen youngsters with those same tennis-ball tumours, some attacking all four quadrants of the jaw, displacing muscle and bone while rearranging the features into a distorted Picasso-esque parody of a face. (Their parents dared not let them look in a mirror for fear they might die of fright.) The under-sevens were most at risk, and while I simply wondered about a God who condoned such violation of the innocents, a doctor coming upon it for the first time would also have felt intense curiosity. What *happened* to that kid? When Dennis Burkitt, a young Ulsterman from Enniskillen, arrived in Uganda he knew instinctively the condition wasn't uniquely Ugandan; like the gorillas roaming the Ruwenzoris—Ptolemy's Mountains of the Moon— these sarcomas would not observe national borders. A Colonial Medical Service surgeon, he wanted to know how many children were afflicted and where they lived. So, funded by a £250 grant from the British Medical Research Council, he and two colleagues set off in a clapped-out Ford station wagon on a ten-thousand-mile journey that took them to twelve countries.

As an off-the-wall travel narrative their trip is remarkable enough. Chaotic post-war, pre-independence Africa threw absolutely everything at them: tribal conflicts, bad borders, impassable roads, impossible weather and, always, a few local surprises. (When, half a century later, I drove down a highway they had followed, a garrulous, disturbingly thin teenage girl—was she HIV positive?—sold me three *matooke* bananas and warned that, just a few miles ahead, a cyclist had recently been taken by a lion.)

As an odyssey of discovery, though, it's simply amazing. Burkitt's quest yielded something any travel writer would die for: a new map of tropical Africa. His African cancer chart delineated the latitude, longitude *and* elevation of high-risk areas—with malaria playing an unexpected sniper's role, bushwhacking victims from the sidelines. As he set about establishing causes and treatments, the international medical community became fascinated by these giant jellyfish tumours that kept on killing small African children. In 1966 several dozen top overseas specialists attended the first Burkitt's Lymphoma Conference in Kampala. With Dennis in the chair they set up the Uganda Cancer Institute, and today direct their considerable resources and expertise towards research. Burkitt, lean, aquiline, bespectacled and amused, looking a bit like Samuel Beckett, died in 1993, a genuine hero.

*

Dr Rogunda said to me, "So! What is your boy up to now?"

"Well, he's finished his degree. And he's thinking of doing research at Imperial College in London."

He grew interested. "Research into what?"

"AIDS."

He sighed deeply and drank some wine. "Will it ever go away?"

The auguries were not good. In the *New Vision,* a Kampala daily, I found a health column which dealt with little else. A typical letter said, "Dear Dr Amref, I am 26 years old and a virgin. I am threatened that if you become above 25 years without having sex, you become impenetrable. Is this true?" The doctor wrote: "The rumour that you mention is common, but has no truth in it. In Uganda today such misinformation contributes to the spread of AIDS."

One morning I called on a Kampala GP, a crisply spoken Englishman in his fifties who tried to put things into perspective. "Some of the figures being bandied about are preposterous. You must remember it is rare in children under fifteen and adults over fifty. So that leaves fifty per cent of the population at risk and, of that number, I would estimate that probably thirty per cent are HIV positive." I calculated that came in somewhere under three million, and asked, "How do you tell your patients?"

"There is no easy way. But I then urge them to forget their positivity. I tell them that, as with every personal catastrophe, they will enter a three-month period of mourning and then they will forget it. They will get on with their lives. And that, inevitably, is what they do."

Yet John had reported that some at the Mengo, on hearing the news, swallowed the tiny cadmium batteries in their digital wrist-watches. Death followed within hours.

*

One day near Kabale, in western Uganda, a driver named Abu took me in search of a forest where a tribe of sure-footed lions slept like possums high in its trees. But the road was flooded so we took a red-clay high-way ("first-class murram") that wound through millet fields to a small pool containing thirty or forty motionless figures, naked to the waist and seated on ledges of black volcanic magma. Their dark forms, glimpsed through wisps of drifting steam, represented patience, sadness and resignation. I knew they were dying. It was a heart-rending tableau.

A beaming young man appeared, doing a drum-majorette's twirl with his furled umbrella. "Good morning, my friend! How are you? Welcome to the hot spring Merembo-Kitigata!" He wore a soiled cotton jacket with four buttons which, briskly, he proceeded to do up in the wrong order. "It is good for rheumatism and skin conditions, but these people are sick with everything. They are from a hospital up on the hill. It has no medicines. They hope the waters will help them."

He pointed to a buxom, handsome girl who smiled shyly. "She will live six months maximum." (Her sudden sharp look seemed to say, "Don't write me off yet!") "That fellow has cancer, that one poison blood."

"Do any have AIDS?"

"Of course! Many!"

An old man with a furrowed face courteously showed me the fissure from which steaming water trickled. As a skeletal woman dipped her calabash into the pool and gave me some to drink, I reflected that Amin and Obote had pursued policies that required the doctors, with scarcely an aspirin between them, to make their sickest patients sit in a warm pond tasting faintly of aloes: so, post factum, the killing went merrily on. The guide urged me to roll up my pants and climb in. He frowned at my refusal—*how do I get this fellow to enjoy himself?*—and spoke of the springs as a future stop for tourists. "They can swim, take picture, it will be nice."

Back at the Land-Rover he wanted money. "I am official here," he said, holding his umbrella in a two-fisted quarterstaff grip. Distracted by the sudden onset of darkness—my watch, powered by a cadmium suicide battery, indicated nine minutes before noon—I handed over some devalued Ugandan shillings (100/- wouldn't even buy him an egg). Giant cumuliform clouds, approaching from Rwanda and Burundi and flickering with lapis-lazuli light, collided directly overhead. Their crack-of-doom impact made us flinch, and as grape-sized drops began splatting on the windscreen I looked back and saw those doomed people still sitting there, impervious to the storm. Our wipers, set at monsoon pitch, merely redirected the torrent and, moving off, a thought began to gnaw worryingly: I really shouldn't have drunk that water.

Next morning we picked up an agitated man needing a lift to the maternity ward at a nearby clinic. Was his wife in labour? Abu smiled faintly. "I think she is not his wife." We drew up beside a rambling, low-slung structure with busted guttering that had not coped with yesterday's rain; a moatlike puddle now encircled it. As our passenger raced up the steps I said, "Abu, can you give me a moment? There's somebody I want to see."

It was cool inside, and quiet. I asked a plump woman in a spotless white coat if I could talk to a doctor; wordlessly she pointed to an empty whitewashed cell with a barred window. There, above the examination couch—its grubby sheet bearing the imprint of a very tall man—a bookshelf contained the Koran, a Liverpool football annual with a mop-haired Kevin Keegan on the cover, and a worm-eaten, pre-war edition of *Manson's Tropical Diseases*. I took it down. The fragile pages contained underlined passages and some cryptic annotations, for example, "Cane-cutter's cramp, thrashing & crying out, give isotonic saline." The many stains included a few ochre smears of blood.

This edition had been edited by Philip. Certainly worth keeping in the family, I reflected, wondering why Clinton hadn't followed in his dad's footsteps: good money, nice London house, privileged membership of Britain's medical establishment. But, I guessed, he saw the bacteria of the tropics as an ornithologist might regard the birds of Amazonia: vibrant and numerous, with amazing new species constantly popping up.

Finally the doctor walked in. He looked about eighteen, hollow-eyed and exhausted, like a boy soldier just back from the front. Yet he smiled as he watched me restore Manson to its shelf. "Our bible," he said, "but, of course, it is out of date."

"Nothing about HIV." That section would be their Book of Revelation.

He nodded.

"Actually, it's what I wanted to see you about."

I noted his confessor's suppressed sigh: yet another tourist owning up to sex with infected Kampala hookers. So my worry about drinking the water at Marembo-Kitigata actually made him laugh. "*AIDS? No. But you've got antibiotics?*" Now the boy soldier used a military analogy. "This country's a medical minefield."

For some days I became a walking compendium of tropical symptoms—faint discoloration of the elbow indicating yaws, a reluctance to get out of bed sleeping sickness, flavescent urine a sure sign of yellow fever. (There were others.) But nothing happened. Or has actually happened since.

*

In Taiwan, in 1879, a British physician named Ringer carried out an autopsy—a rare event since post-mortem mutilation of Chinese corpses was forbidden by law. This particular cadaver, a Portuguese, yielded up a curious pealike parasite which, since the dead man had once been Patrick Manson's patient, Ringer posted to him pickled in spirits of wine. Manson knew a similar organism had been found in a dead tiger at Amsterdam Zoo, but never before in a human; he identified it, correctly, as an Oriental lung fluke. Soon afterwards a thirty-five-year-old mandarin named Tso-Tong had a violent coughing fit in Manson's Amoy surgery. When he spat on the carpet Manson noted the spit's odd reddish colour, and once the man had left, put some under a microscope and found it contained eggs. Sensing a connection with Ringer's parasite he left a solution of Tso-Tong's sputum to ferment on his mantelpiece.

Weeks later, after his wife complained about the smell, he saw the eggs had grown into creatures he reckoned to be embryonic lung flukes that had originated in snails. *Snails?* How did he know? In truth he didn't; snails had been an inspired guess yet, later, he would be proved right on both counts—and find himself the first person in history studying the lung fluke's life cycle. An organism lurking in bad water and uncooked food, it becomes a worm in the gut, reaches the lungs after penetrating the intestinal wall, in a few cases continues upwards to lay its eggs in the dark little cerebellic burrows of the brain.

Manson, contemplating another big breakthrough, denied luck had anything to do with it. "A man may search for a shilling," he said, "and find a sovereign. *The important thing is to search.*"

Of the forty diseases that flourish between the ecliptics Manson studied no fewer than a quarter—and created a more profound understanding of them all. Giant statues should be raised to him throughout the region.

*

I wonder now how Clinton coped with all that ancestral baggage and the weight of expectations: legendary grandfather, knighted father, Nobel superstars like Ronald "Malaria" Ross coming to dinner, family fireside chats periodically straying away from cricket and school to developments in dumdum fever, beriberi and porocephalosis (an affliction caused by parasites which infest the lungs and windpipes of snakes). Clinton, having read medicine and headed for the tropics, arrived in Fiji as reports began filtering through of a weird new disease in the Papua New Guinea highlands.

Kuru, meaning "trembling" in the local dialect, was a fatal degenerative condition caught from eating the brains of loved ones killed in battle. Though the brains had been boiled in cooking pots the virus proved impervious to heat. Victims at first grew feverish. Shivering and twitching, they adopted a swaying, shambling gait, became incontinent, developed acute joint pains and strabismus—a severe squint that made the world muddled and unfocused—then towards the end, unable even to sit unsupported, suffered violent mood swings. Daniel Gajdusek, an American virologist, realized it bore a pathological resemblance to scrapie, a sickness of sheep. When he injected chimpanzees with a broth distilled from the brains of victims they developed kuru too. It was the cannibals' version of Creutzfeldt–Jakob—and it won him a Nobel Prize.

Clinton must have known about kuru—my father certainly did. Old Manson would have been off to New Guinea like a shot, but his grandson remained contentedly in Suva. Comfortable with his ancestors but not overwhelmed by them, he was kind, funny, noisy and sociable, a man forever hitching up his trousers with one hand while, with the other, lifting a finger for attention. Born into a different family he might have become a popular Tory politician, or ringmaster of a very interesting little circus.

*

In 2001 a World Health Organisation report claimed that, though tropical diseases form half the world's illnesses, only 3 per cent of the funds available for medical research are devoted to them. While health expenditure in the USA, Canada, Japan and Western Europe averages $400 per person per year, in the poorest countries of the tropics it averages less than $5. Professor Barry R. Bloom, chairman of the WHO committee on research and training in tropical diseases, claims that while the First World "is on the cutting edge of malaria and a dozen other killer diseases, the lack of profitability has caused them to withhold funding for research, with dire consequences for the inhabitants of the tropical zones."

*

Every eighteen months or so my childhood sends me off to hospital to have a memento of those days surgically excised from my face. It's a lesion or skin cancer, sun-induced and possessing the most baneful name imaginable: a rodent ulcer. Germinating like seeds, these things need fifty years to bloom, and each time one appears I hear my mother's well-intentioned voice ordering me out into a garden drenched with solar radiation. It may be a bizarre way of exploring one's past, but doctors insist the half-century incubation period is accurate. So I always try to work out where I was, and what I was doing, when the sun activated that particular cell.

It tends to be an old man's affliction. A rodent ulcer looks like a rat bite and, ironically, some of the other rodent regulars at Queen Mary's Hospital, Roehampton, are old Desert Rats, Eighth Army veterans who got their overdoses at Tobruk and Alamein. Over the years I've got to know a few. Arthur, who was in tanks, even carries an anthology of poems written by various sun-blasted Rats dug in among their sand-bagged dunes and wadis.

The procedure is carried out under local anaesthetic so the worst bit comes first. "Ouch!" warn the surgeons a second before they start sticking needles in your face. The cutting only takes a few minutes and you feel nothing—though some may jerk your head around while inserting stitches. Occasionally there are indications of problems. "Oh, shit!" once muttered a bossy female registrar; "Oh, Gawd!" once mur-mured a youth who had recently qualified at Oxford. You simply go with the tug of the thread, and at home in the mirror, note that the damage seems no worse than usual. There may be heavy bruising under the eyes, and blood on the pillow for a few days afterwards.

If you're lucky you'll be done by a consultant. We regulars all have our favourites—many, in the manner of senior Royal College person-nel, garrulous and a bit starry; they do the neatest jobs and tell the best stories. I've had some laughs on that table—the scalpel always with-drawn a split second before the punchline is delivered. Then, a plaster over the wound, you drink a cup of strong NHS tea, nibble a biscuit and leave with a wave. The ward sister calls, "Bye bye, Mr Frater, see you next time."

In Germany I have noted nostalgia in the eyes of certain folk who think I am sporting *duellieren* sabre scars. On the plus side, the NHS provides me with an ongoing facelift: we old rodent ulcermen tend to look a lot younger than we actually are.

*

The fifty-year time-lapse indicated that a particular ulcer, blooming by the lip, was probably activated on the Fijian island of Toberua during a family holiday. Now, having finished my work in Fiji, I decided to spend my last night there. Like Iririki, it had become a luxury offshore resort and seemed as good a place as any to get my laundry done.

I sat and listened to a fitful southerly trade leafing through palm fronds, heard the occasional whump of a falling coconut and knew again the pleasing sense of being parked in one of the world's lay-bys. Those of us born in the tropics have lassitude bred into our very bones and now, yielding to it, I felt the old waypoints—sunrise and sunset, the rhythm of the tides—quietly reimpose themselves. Then the afternoon grew dim. Rain purring on my palm-thatch roof invoked such contentment I drifted off to sleep.

On islands you can be woken by silence. I woke in good time for an evening drink with Michael Dennis, Toberua's lively minded manager who, learning I was a journalist, said, "We made headlines a few years back, you know. One morning I found an empty yacht sitting on my reef. There was a British passport in the name of Ian McNair, but no sign of him; I told the police we had another *Marie Celeste* on our hands. Eventually some Indian fishermen brought him in; a windshift had put him on a reef—not this one—and after he'd gone for help in his dinghy the tide moved his boat over here. He stayed for six months, my shipwrecked sailor, while he carried out repairs."

I vaguely remembered the story. "What was he like?"

"Tall, red-haired, quite introspective, always talked in a self-deprecating English kind of way; he was a very amusing chap, actually. He'd been wandering around the tropics in that boat for thirty years—don't laugh, but I think he was looking for paradise." Dennis shrugged. "Toberua got high marks, but not the full score. He found it, apparently, in South Africa. He even sold his boat and settled down—only to be run over and killed by a car."

But much of South Africa lay south of the tropics; he'd strayed off-limits, run out of luck. Luck, or the lack of it, came to mind again next morning when five scrawny frigate birds appeared and, but for a slight axial spin, hung motionless overhead. "Aren't they bad omens?" I asked the boatman who would take me to the mainland. He laughed. "No, they are just omens for storm."

It arrived as we set off, the launch breaching the swell in blinding rain. In just thirty-six hours, going via Los Angeles, I would be back in the wintry Northern Hemisphere, where the sun appeared only briefly, and low on the horizon. I longed to see my family, but also felt the tug of sadness that always came when leaving the torrid regions. A dolphin rose nearby then slapped back hard, drenching us with spray. As it kept pace I could hear the whistling sounds of its breathing and see its bright, round eye upon me. And all the way home I seemed to fly cocooned in its benevolence.

Can You Grow Prozac?

Only two tropical outdoor leisure activities have seized the world's imagination. Since both use natural forces (oceanic energy in the first instance, gravity in the second) to generate momentum, they're not the kinds of exercise normally expected to raise a sweat or make you fit. But they can make you frightened—and, in extreme cases, they can even kill. We *tropicanos* like a touch of spice with our sport.

Surfing originated around the islands of Oceania. There is evidence that, when big seas were running four thousand years ago, people were out walking the noose, doing their Stone Age versions of loopers and quasimodos. In 1778 Captain Cook witnessed Tahitian families riding the waves, while in Hawaii the board-makers offered up prayers and sacrifices before taking chisels to their slabs of *koa* or *wiliwili* wood. Mark Twain, visiting Hawaii in 1860, became a devotee (though he kept falling off) but local missionaries abhorred it. They called it "the devil's pastime."

Bungee jumping was invented on the Vanuatuan island of Pentecost. The world first learned about it on 6 February 1974, when John Mark, a local youth, sprang off a ninety-foot-high tower and broke his neck at the feet of Elizabeth II, England's *Kwin*. He was a land diver, exponent of a tradition in which men, with vines tied around their ankles to break the fall, launched themselves from spindly timber platforms high as four-storey buildings. Yet that Royal Command leap remained a source of controversy. John Mark's father, complaining that he was obliged to use green, immature vines (cut pre-season, they snapped at the critical moment), had spent years trying to claim damages from the British government. Also, some say he died because he carried a charm intended to make him irresistible to women.

Women are taboo to a land diver; during his period of preparation he may not go near them, must void his mind of all sexual thoughts. So John Mark—evidently thinking of little else—was asking for trouble. Indeed, all these years later *Jif* Willy still called him an idiot. The tragedy, he claimed, led directly to the creation of a big overseas industry *based on a stolen idea.*

Some beady-eyed foreign entrepreneur, following the media coverage, realized an obscure fuzzy-wuzzy ceremony intended to ensure a good yam harvest possessed, with a few health-and-safety amendments, strong commercial possibilities. (You'd need to use heavy-duty industrial elastic in place of vines, perhaps include personal videos in the price of a jump.) There was bitterness about that, certainly, when I turned up on Pentecost. Yet I detected an odd sense of excitement too; *samting* else seemed to be going on.

In Vila friends had told me that folk here spent their days asleep on the beach. "They've let all the old plantations go back to the bush," they said. That set me thinking about the Leles of Zaïre's Kasai valley who, understanding the debilitating effects of hard labour in the tropics, had awarded themselves more public holidays than anyone else on earth. Every third day was a day of rest—along with Sundays *and* the day following the departure of any visiting personage. Thus a week during the busy September planting season went like this:

Sunday: Day off.

Monday: Work.

Tuesday: Day off in honour of a VIP who had left on Monday.

Wednesday: Day off. After lunch an important agricultural scientist turned up to inspect the fields. He persuaded several women to accompany him with baskets of groundnuts but, since this was a rest day, no groundnuts were sown.

Thursday: Work cancelled due to rain.

Friday: Day off in honour of the agricultural scientist who had left on Thursday.

Saturday: Day off.

On Pentecost, though, people seemed to take holidays simply when they felt like it. Bagging a ride from the *efil* (airfield) on the public truck I saw some lazing, others lurching out of the forest bent double under heavy sacks. And the plantations, sure enough, lay abandoned; it was Charolais cattle grazing among the palms—lofty Fiji talls, trunks dusted with the saffron mould denoting age—that kept the bush at bay.

Now I was back in the hot, silent, slow-beating heart of the Torrid Zone. Mountainous and bursting with greenery, Pentecost was so fertile you could imagine a pencil stuck in the ground turning overnight into a leafy twig. The truck passed hot springs where women wreathed in steam sat cooking eggs, and followed a coast veined by rivers; every half-mile it slid down a bank and splashed through swirling mountain torrents.

In the back *Jif* Willy Orion Bebe held court. My landlord for the next few days, he organized the *nangol,* or land-diving festival. And, making all ground arrangements, he tried to ensure that the tourists— from *Ostrelia, Niusilan, Inglan, Amerika, Franis, Jemani, Spen*—stayed at the Nangol Bungalows (which he owned).

In his late forties, burly and clean-shaven with large, oddly luminous eyes, a charismatic smile and wild hair compressed willy-nilly beneath a baseball cap, he exuded a force field of energy—now insulated by a Back to Basics T-shirt, shorts and, on his big brown callused feet, flip-flops worn razor thin.

He joked that I'd arrived six months too late for the *nangol.* When I told him I was here to research a book he questioned me closely about the financial side of the "book business"—the role of agents, in particular, appearing to interest him. "They get ten per cent?" More, I said, if—for example—movie rights were sold. His jaw dropped. But selling was what he did! He sold vegetables to Australia! Then, abruptly losing interest in me, he gave his full attention to a small blue yacht that had just sailed in and dropped anchor. Leaping from the truck he ran down the beach, shouting. An overweight, heavily bearded American rowed himself ashore and Willy wasted no words. "There are pirates in this bay."

The man gaped. *"Pirates?"*

"They come in canoes at night, when police all sleep, take money and clothes. Stick up."

"Jesus!"

"In Bay Homo, next one along, you will be safe. You can't miss it, it has a bulldozer on the beach."

The man lingered, suddenly wanting to talk. He told me life at sea had made his wife very, very stressed; any pirates turning up ran a serious risk of being shot. "By her. She's got a pistol and an AK47, she can hit a dime at a hundred paces and, right now, she's in a real shitty mood."

Back on the truck I asked Willy, "Is Bay Homo your bay?"

He nodded. "My place is there."

"Anyone else staying just now?"

"Nobody been for some time."

The truck dropped us by a crescent-shaped gulf. Huge trees lined a beach of polished pebbles which clinked and rattled under a heavy surf. The landmark bulldozer, standing well out to sea, had waves breaking over it. A dark, cavernous cookhouse and three thatched bamboo shacks—each furnished with rough-hewn, home-made bamboo beds— made up the Nangol Bungalows.

At the end of a forest path stood a wooden privy which seemed to have taken root; tendrils curled from a beam, small crimson flowers hung over the entrance—along with a humming, undulating curtain of sewage-dependent insects that glittered in the late sun like sequins. A fork led to the river where I would wash. I enquired about drinking water. Willy told me a bucket would be filled at the Salop village tap.

"Is it good water?"

"Very good."

"And I can get hot water also?"

"Hot water for coffee? Or you like tea?"

"Coffee."

"Me too." He patted my shoulder. "Listen, Alex, maybe I come to London and be your agent. Stay in your house."

"But I already have an agent. He wouldn't like that."

"Well, we talk some more." He whistled tunelessly for a moment. "Is the Governor of the Bank of England your friend?"

"No."

He seemed surprised. "But you come from there."

I caught his drift; if you lived in England you banked with the Governor; he supervised your account, gave fiscal advice and met you on social occasions. I said England had many banks quite independent of the Governor's, and he nodded slowly. "They speak about him on Radio Vanuatu. I think he could help my business."

"Maybe." Then, feeling that by failing to befriend the Governor I had somehow let Willy down, I went to my shack.

*

In the cookhouse his slim, silent, preoccupied wife—never introduced— sat peeling yams by lamplight. The blue yacht motored round the headland and moored offshore. An elderly one-legged man hobbled out of the night, laid down his crutch and, speaking in a deep, sonorous voice, introduced himself: Fred, a retired accountant with pen-friends in *Itiopia* and *Ijip*. "I hear you and Willy bin talking business. That is good. He will make money for you. You know about his kava deal? With those people in *Jemani?* One million *vatu* [£4,800] per ton! *Ten tons per month!*"

I realized the men carting those sacks from the forest had been bringing in the gnarled, mud-encrusted roots of the *Piper methysticum* plant. Why should these be of interest to Germans? From them you extracted a drink known as *aelan bia* (island beer) with a sappy, earthy, oddly medicinal taste; containing soporific alkaloids and numbing the mouth like Novocain, it caused drowsiness and a sense of lazy contentment. James Cook called it "the intoxicating pepper" yet, alcohol-free and officially certified as non-addictive, it occupied the same Customs & Excise category as tea. But when fifty people were hospitalized after a New Year's rave concert in LA, police blamed a hallucinatory substance alleged to be kava-based.

I'd heard that kava derivatives were prescribed for blood pressure, post-menstrual stress, kidney disorders, even cancer. And I knew that with its antibiotics and analgesics, its appetite suppressants, diuretics, decongestants and God knows what else, it had been the mainstay of bush medicine for a thousand years; custom doctors spent half a lifetime learning its chemistry. But ten tons a *month?*

"What are the Germans planning to do with it?"

Willy said, "Make medicine to stop them getting old. If they drink kava they live long time. Like my grandfather."

"How old's your grandfather?"

"Two hundred."

I stared. "That is absolutely impossible."

"Maybe more."

I did some calculations. "If he was just a little older he could have seen Captain Cook."

"I think he has mentioned him."

But when I asked for a meeting he grew evasive. His other grandfather, meanwhile, had died aged a hundred and thirty. He drank kava also but, in other ways, hadn't looked after himself—no exercise, smoked *tumas,* stayed out late. Then a pretty teenage girl walked by carrying a package wrapped in blood-soaked newspaper. "That is Nelly, bringing your meat. My other daughter is Daisy."

"Aren't we all eating together?"

"No." Out in the darkness the yacht rode quietly, a light at its masthead as the wife fixed supper and loaded her guns. Glumly Willy said, "I must make improvements here." He wanted Nangol Bungalows to have electricity, en suite bathrooms, a handicrafts shop and, on a plinth, the wreckage of an American C47 which had crashed into Bay Omo during World War Two.

It was, he said, still there and, some day, would form the centre-piece of his property. "Many tourists will come." I wasn't so sure; it seemed a pretty spooky notion. "No bones," he promised, "but we found a clock—it *was still going.*" I pointed out the clock must have been under water for thirty years. "Sure. US technology! But now I need dollars for this place. You know, maybe these bungee millionaires can help."

"Our government," said Fred, "has tried at the highest level—the PM himself told the overseas bungee companies they should give something back to Pentecost."

Nelly brought me a plate of rancid, half-raw beef and slabs of gluey yam. I ate the yam but left the meat untouched; Willy, too preoccupied to notice and ignoring the women's eloquent frowns (such waste!), said, "Alex, could you write a letter?"

"You want me to ask them for money?"

"Yes."

"And they'll send it out of the kindness of their hearts?" I shook my head. "Not a chance, you'll have to offer something in return."

"OK. So we will invite them to dive in the *nangol*—in the *kastom* way, with vines around their ankles. It is against the law for foreigners, but next season we will let them."

It wasn't, actually, such a bad idea. The bolder chairmen and CEOs, caught on camera, could even star in their own corporate videos and brochures. Specify it was a once-in-a-lifetime opportunity, and they might even shell out sizeable sums.

"All right," I said. "I'll see what I can do."

*

In Bay Homo an opalescent dawn light seemed to lend the water extra buoyancy. Floating on my back, I watched the smoke from distant breakfast fires signalling the locations of villages deep in Pentecost's shaggy green hills.

Willy, bearing ship's biscuits and Nescafé Niugini Blend instant, appeared with his daughters. As they lit the stove he said, "Daisy has brought peanut butter for you."

Daisy, good-looking but rebellious, banged the peanut butter down then stalked off to sulk by the sea, leaving bright-eyed Nelly to prepare the coffee. She had a special smile for me. Had her father intimated he might start a new life in England? Was she planning to come too? Willy, though, spoke only about a new bungalow to be named the Queen Elizabeth 2 Memorial Resort. I said, "You can't call it 'memorial' unless she's dead."

"Then it will be Bay Homo Royal Resort; the yacht *Britannia* anchored here when she come for the diving." He spooned peanut butter into his mouth. "Have you started the letter?"

"First I'll need some background. You must tell me what it is like to jump."

"Me?" He looked incredulous. "Far too dangerous! For that you must talk to Clement."

Clement, who operated the public truck, had jumped eight times. Handsome and softly spoken, he had three infants of his own and seemed to acquire more all the time; indeed, he often drove around with a sleeping child on his lap. Mothers handed their wailing babies to Clement and instantly, as if bewitched, they grew quiet. I found him, in Salop village, tenderly changing the nappy of someone's tiny daughter and asked if the land-diving scared him. He chuckled. "Always!"

The fear started, he said, when you went into the forest to cut your vines, grew worse as you stood on your platform (you had a choice of levels) while the dive *masta* bound the vines around your ankles, peaked as you addressed the crowd; it was a tradition that before leaping you could say anything you liked and, since it might be your last word, no one dared interrupt. Then you crossed your arms and toppled forward. Proceedings went on until late, the last men landing by torchlight.

*

One morning we set off for Bunlap, a custom village where the men were shifting kava. Clement's truck climbed so high our ears popped. I sat in the back with a woman breastfeeding four-month-old Ivanhoe, who wore an Everton strip and a bib with a duck on it. At the summit we came upon some Bunlap men, staggering along under laden sacks, stark naked but for brief twists of leaf that enclosed their penises like sweet wrappers. When Willy leaped off to harangue them they lit cigarettes and squatted on the verge, balls jiggling as they coughed. He told them their kava would shortly be sent to Vila then loaded onto a jet *plen* for *Jemani*. They shook their heads wonderingly. *Jemani!* Where was that?

The road ended in a secluded valley. I looked around for Bunlap but Willy said, "*Smol* walk," and moved off into the cloud forest. As we attacked our first gradient it began to rain; the track, sleek and slippery, sent us climbing past treetops—big banyans with parrots in their canopies. I grabbed at knotted roots while Willy, slapping along in his flip-flops, slashed at the undergrowth with a bush knife. After an hour, scaling a limestone bluff glazed with moss, I saw that Bunlap was set on a mountain peak blocked by a giant stile. Constructed from logs lashed with vines, it had perhaps been put there for a defensive ambush.

Willy, scrambling over effortlessly, made some fluting bird calls; a naked youth with a spear appeared, and walked us up the final small escarpment to the village. "I am Sam," he said.

In the compound Willy hurried to embrace a sinewy old man. "This my father."

I stared. "Your father!"

"*Kastom* father. I adopt him. He is Bunlap's Big *Jif.*"

"*Gudmoning,*" said the Big *Jif,* extending a gnarled hand.

Willy explained that this Big *Jif* was not, in fact, Bunlap's biggest; there was also a paramount seigneur who had abandoned his people (and wives) to live with a fat woman in Port Vila.

"She *very* fat. And *ugly*," growled the Big *Jif.*

This was a famous land-diving place, with five towers raised and all the men jumping in season.

"Does your head actually hit the ground?"

The Big *Jif,* smiling, said it had to hit *hard enough for your hair to fertilize the yams.* But he had no hair at all.

Willy, here on kava business, began handing over wads of banknotes. Out on the horizon a copra ship crawled across a dull sea. Bunlap, smelling of wet earth and wood smoke, was a recyclable village built entirely from forest products. Plaited, woven, trimmed and tied—without a single nail or screw—it went spilling down the hillside as if sprung from a single seed.

A tiny white floatplane, whizzing out of nowhere, splashed down on the bay a thousand feet below. It taxied in, a man jumped out, heaved it onto the beach and ran for the trees. Moments later he reappeared buttoning his trousers, heaved it back and flew off again. Watching, I recalled two equatorial journeys made a few years earlier in a veteran flying boat: crossing the Torrid Zone through heavy moist air, thermals, erratic winds, twelve-mile-high cloud formations and storms of quite extraordinary ferocity, I'd finally understood the primacy of air over earth; every element that sustained the tropics came from the sky. And it was happening now. Ten miles away a sudden, violent little rain squall suddenly materialized and went chasing after the copra ship.

A pretty woman appeared and stared hard at me, her breasts bearing intricate hieroglyphic symbols tattooed in blue ink. She wore an ankle-length skirt woven from wild hibiscus fibres and looked about thirty, though—since working wives hereabouts have a shorter life expectancy than their lazy husbands—may have been a lot younger. I wanted to know what the symbols meant, but when I asked she frowned and turned away.

Sam, leaning on his spear, keen to practise his English, drew my attention to a limping teenage boy with staring eyes and a nervous jittering manner. "Crazy feller! Devil got 'im." Bunlap's village idiot, badly malnourished, displayed severe bruising on the face and arms; aware that pastoral psychotherapy hereabouts often took the form of beatings, I asked if he had ever seen a doctor. What *dokta*? Sick people saw the sorcerer; *kastom* remedies did the trick. No *dokta* here, no dispensary, no drugs, no dresser, no health visitor or district *nas.*

And no *skul* either. As some whooping, bare-arsed kids chased by after a piglet I learned that schools didn't fit with *kastom* thinking. Children learned about traditions, kava, the forest and land. What use was reading and writing to anyone?

He said he had once tried my world for himself, on Santo even owned a motorbike—and claimed he didn't like it one bit. (A tiny spasm around the eyes indicated he was lying.) So how did he spend his time? Naked teenagers presumably weren't interested in clothes, but did they listen to music on the radio? And what did they think about *hambag* (sex) before marriage? He shrugged. "*Kastom* tell us what to do."

"Has anyone ever run away from Bunlap?"

"Never!"

Yet the Big *Jif*'s eldest son had joined a *dipsi* fishing fleet and fled to South Africa. The *Jif* himself sadly told me this in the meeting house, a shadowy, mud-floored shack off-limits to women. Here he explained the mysteries of grade-taking, the means by which a male climbs high enough up the social ladder to ensure a warm welcome in the next world. It's done by largesse, the giving of pigs and hosting of feasts; the more you give the higher you rise, the higher you rise the poorer you grow—a state of grace being finally achieved when you have nothing left at all.

Suffering personal ruin for the public good is what a great man strives for, and upon these bankrupts much power devolves. Pondering a society administered by the people who threw the best parties, I saw the demarcated areas where the members of each grade sat: the Birang, Bossis and Bumangarie, the Arakon, Leebus and Naime, the Melgorokorue and Mol; the Mel, containing cold ashes and an empty iron cooking pot, could be entered only by the Big *Jif* himself.

We said goodbye to this decent man, and on the way down met a breathless middle-aged French agronomist on the way up—who, it turned out, knew what the Germans were actually doing. Mopping his face he explained that the kava species contained twenty elements called kavalactones—five important to chemists; Vanuatu kava incorporated all five in the one plant, and Pentecost yielded Vanuatu's purest crop. From it the Germans hoped to produce a powerful non-addictive anti-depressant enjoying worldwide sales. "It could be even bigger than Prozac. You guys may have struck oil," he told Willy.

"*Prozac?*" said Willy. He grew thoughtful and, for the next hour, never spoke a word.

Riding home on the truck we stopped to harvest armloads of wild island cabbage growing by the roadside. He promised I could have some for dinner, cooked in coconut milk; his silent wife, placing the leaves in a pot, soon filled the cookhouse with sublime smells yet, when Nelly put the dish before me, I saw she had stirred it into yesterday's rancid leftover beef.

Willy said, "Cabbage no good?"

"The cabbage is fine, Willy."

"You don't like it! Well, you can have a tin of fish instead."

*

Once the inhabitants of the tropics picked much of what they ate—in Ghana, a hundred and fourteen kinds of edible fruit, forty-six types of leguminous seeds and forty-seven variations of spinach. In the Ivory Coast's Mossi district sauces prepared from crushed peanuts, pounded sesame, tomatoes, okra, red pepper and hibiscus seeds added flavour to spinach variants that included the leaves of the silk cotton, butter and baobab trees. A Mossi adult male, annually, ate a thousand pounds of leaves boiled either in oil or water.

*

Prozac became the subject of muttered conversations between Willy, Fred and several other men who now appeared each evening. Questions put to me were mostly to do with potential profits. They wanted a figure, I could only say it would certainly exceed Vanuatu's entire national budget.

Not knowing if the letter to the bungee tycoons was still needed, I wrote it anyway. It concluded with a flourish: "Our ancient test of a man's courage has brought us few rewards. Yet an investment in Nangol Bungalows will help put something back—while offering a unique opportunity to jump in the legendary Pentecost way. Photographers will record your historic leap for that company brochure or Christmas card (guaranteed to impress staff and clients alike) while a new European miracle relaxant, distilled from our own kava, should be available for those last-minute nerves. We promise a happy, stress-free dive!"

He read it, folded it and slipped it wordlessly in his pocket.

"OK?" I asked.

"I think maybe we get the money from *Jemani*."

While that certainly made sense, I couldn't help wondering if a professional judgement had been made, and that the letter had been assessed and rejected. Also, from that moment on, he never again spoke of coming to London; I was left with the uneasy feeling that Willy had sacked me.

*

Yet he continued to behave with good-humoured courtesy, and at the *efil* introduced me to a dozen listless market women who drowsed over their coconuts and live string-shackled crabs. "These girls come to see the plane, this place no good for retailing." I told him about some airports—giant shopping malls with runways attached—which seemed to do little else.

His eyes narrowed. "And they make profits?"

"You bet."

"Selling souvenirs?"

"Among other things. For example, here you could have land divers on key rings."

"Or palm-leaf penis wrappers, Pentecost National Costume," he chuckled, catching on fast.

As one of the girls, a butcher's wife, suggested takeaway cow's tongues fresh from the slaughterhouse, a Twin Otter landed and parked by the market. The pilot, in his forties, had close-trimmed greying hair and a prominent nose; a certain rangy, raw-boned aspect made me think he might be a New Zealander. He wandered over, hands in pockets. "Don't see many white faces here. You a missionary?"

Willy laughed.

The Kiwi had a trick of listening intently, half smiling and nodding encouragement. When I'd explained myself, he said, "You better sit with me. I can point out things. We'll push off when you're ready."

I said goodbye with both relief and regret. Willy, fixing me with one of his limelight smiles, asked if I knew anyone at the Harvard Business School; there had been *samting* on the radio. I told him I knew not a soul and went scrambling up the steps.

On the cramped little flight deck the pilot extended a large hand. "Norm Sanson. Haven't we met before?" I said I didn't think so. He told me his forty-year-old plane came from Panama and had once belonged to General Noriega. Its age and provenance seemed to please him and, twin engines yammering, he got it airborne within seconds. As the *efil* slipped away I had the oddest feeling that Willy, already, had forgotten all about me.

*

Three thousand feet above Pentecost, Norm pointed to a ragged tear in the forest. It was a hurriedly made clay road—with no logical beginning or end—built by Malaysian loggers. "They lift the timber, take the profits and leave a wasteland behind. The government won't do anything, so I got some portable sawmills and found some local men who know which trees should be left alone; the timber still goes abroad but control stays here. So does the money." A small eddy rocked the plane. "Now I've handed the mills over to them. And they're going great guns."

"Bit of a missionary yourself, then."

He grinned. "Aw, to be honest, the responsibility was running me ragged."

Over north Pentecost he prepared to land at Sara, set on a hilltop. It looked a real bush pilot's stop, with grassy undulations and conflicting gradients, yet, chatting still, he settled the Otter as lightly as a bee. The only boarders here were two sunburnt young Australians off a yacht who, the previous evening, had drunk kava. "I threw up," she said.

"I was hallucinating," he said. "I saw herds of *blue horses*, all stampeding. Then I passed out."

She shuddered. "It's shocking stuff."

Airborne again, Norm talked about gravel. All Vanuatu's roads, he said, needed to be resurfaced and sealed. Lacking any local aggregate, the authorities planned to import overpriced stuff from New

Caledonia. "For years I've been flying over an island, uninhabited, about two miles long. Something about it tickled my interest so one Sunday I borrowed a mate's floatplane and took a look." The Otter lurched as he fished in a pocket and produced four tiny black stones which, very carefully, he tipped into my palm.

"That's pure, twenty-two-carat aggregate," he said. "There's millions of tons, just waiting to be scooped up."

I returned them. "It's an aggregate island."

"Top to bottom, mate."

"So what did you do?"

"I made an offer to buy," he said.

Norm proved to be a companionable man doing a job that meant hours of solitude. Mention of a floatplane reminded me of the one I'd seen a few days back, and when I mentioned it, his eyes shone. He'd become a pilot due to a boyhood passion for slow, leaky aircraft operating from water, spent years flying them around New Zealand and the South Seas. Their relegation, in aeronautical terms, to machines from the horse-and-buggy era had made him master of a largely redundant trade—yet he remained bewitched. "One moment you're racing the canoes, next you're up there with the frigate birds!"

I told him that once, making a documentary for the BBC, I travelled from Egypt to Mozambique in such a contraption, an antique Catalina with retractable wingtip floats. Now I vaguely recalled being told the plane—which I grew to hate—had been sold to some enthusiasts in Auckland. Had he ever come across it?

He gave me a strange look. "Yes. I have. I'm one of your enthusiasts, actually. I'm a part-owner."

"I'll be damned."

"And I've got that video back in Vila. *The Last African Flying Boat,* right? Still watch it from time to time." He grinned. "You do the chat. Knew I knew you!"

We popped into Longana and Redcliff on Ambae, made a brief halt at Santo then headed on home to Vila. Norm spoke of his partner in the aggregate venture, a Frenchman who had recently bought a big property out on Mele Bay. Then we overheard Vila air-traffic control giving clearance to a helicopter carrying a photographer and requesting a north-north-east track that, evidently, would take him right over the aggregate island. "Problem is," Norm said, "we still haven't got our quarry permit. So far only nine people know where the island is—and three are in the government. What if one of them wants it for himself, or knows someone who'll pay big bucks for its location?"

He called up Vila ATC and, casually, asked about the photographer. A crisp English voice said, "He's a freelance out from LA, interested in volcanoes."

"Good-oh." Moments later Norm pointed to a fragment of bruise-coloured land. *"Over there!"*

To him it may have given off an adamantine glitter, but I saw only an atoll inhabited, probably, by creatures from some *kastom* bestiary: anthracite-eating lizards, blindworms subsisting on charcoal. Yet it could make someone—Norm and his *Franisman* partner, a rogue government minister or itinerant Taiwanese carpetbagger—fabulously rich.

We arrived over the old US anchorage at Havannah Harbour to find it irradiated by late-afternoon light, then crossed jungly ravines pooled with shadow. Dropping into Vila he made a small diversion over an estate extending from the coast to the foothills. "Guy's place! See the beach? Ideal for unloading barges!" He made a brushstroke landing. "Got anything planned for tonight?"

"Nothing much," I said.

"I'm having a few beers with him. Want to come? Meet the family? He's got a lovely wife."

"Sure. And I now make ten, Norm."

"You make ten what?"

"Ten people who know where your island is."

He chuckled. "I better put dogs on it."

*

The Salop village phone was permanently out of order, Willy didn't reply to my letters and no one in Vila seemed to know what was happening on Pentecost. Then, a year later, a German friend who worked in pharmaceuticals said he'd heard some gossip about kava. But he laughed when I mentioned the Prozac replacement. According to him it was being used in a range of homoeopathic household jellies—fruit-flavoured, emollient and mildly narcotic.

Vive Les Tropiques!

A Catalina flying boat is the perfect tropical aeroplane. Impervious to weather and climate, air-conditioned by its own obsolescence—draughts from countless structural leaks keep its occupants comfortably cool—it can, in amphibious mode, operate from just about anywhere. Like the region itself it's low-tech; it uses oil available at village stores, its spark plugs may be changed by any competent village mechanic, while its engines (developed before Orville Wright even drew his pension) are as simple as a tractor's.

There was a certain appropriateness about Norm and the New Zealand connection. During my years in Fiji the New Zealand Air Force operated Catalinas from a base outside Suva. My parents had friends there, and while visiting I'd sometimes be allowed down to the slipway and hangar where tolerant young mechanics fielded my questions. The Catalina—or PBY—made its maiden flight at San Diego, California, in 1935. It was a thing of beauty, all right, its contours created by sculptors, its soaring wing indicating an albatross-like ability to stay up indefinitely. Back then the PBY was a technological miracle, it was Fiji's stealth bomber.

I learned that 3,271 were built for service in virtually every theatre of the war. (The Russians assembled 150 under licence beside the Sea of Azov.) Their endurance became the stuff of legend. In 1943 Catalinas operated the non-stop double-sunrise run from Ceylon to Perth, cruising at eighty knots for thirty hours; to maintain the centre of gravity its passengers were obliged to squat motionless—at a point just aft of the cockpit—for the first six.

And I learned some Catalina lore. In 1941 a Soviet sailor, who had never before even set foot in a plane, stole one from under the noses of the Germans at Sevastopol and flew it all the way to Cyprus. Catalinas hunting Japanese shipping got shot down so often their crews allegedly radioed, "Enemy sighted, inform next of kin." In 1948 a Cathay Pacific Catalina going from Hong Kong to Macau became the first aircraft in history to be hijacked. A gangster named Chio Tok, after its cargo of gold bullion, pulled a gun on the pilot, blew his brains out by mistake and sent "Miss Macau" plunging straight to the bed of the Pearl River.

Around the South Pacific the Kiwi boats did all kinds of jobs—mercy flights, air-sea rescue and supply missions. Freight that wouldn't fit inside went outside; they flew with ladders and timber lashed to their hulls. Catalinas could go anywhere and do just about anything.

One day the mechanics had a word with Lofty, a pilot about to take his machine up for an engine test. Lofty shrugged and placed me in the charge of Popeye, a supercilious young flight engineer who, as I followed him aboard, said he would shortly be going home to read law at Auckland University. "I'll be able to print my own money, it's what lawyers do. What about you?"

I said I wanted to be a writer.

"That's pathetic," he said.

Then, whistling tunelessly, he began venting his bilges, hand-cranking his Twin Wasp radials, activating the strainer drain cocks and clearing the sumps, directing carburettor heat, setting the cowl gills, vigorously maintaining fuel pressure with a hand pump, finally throwing his starter switches. During the clamorous take-off run he read a comic, pausing only to smack the floats-operating lever into the "up" position and squint through his tiny windows.

The flight, quite brief, ended in a bridal train of spray. Then Popeye, unexpectedly, said, "Now *this,* kiddo, is what I call writing," and handed me a souvenir sky-blue booklet entitled *Catalina Pilot's and Flight Engineer's Notes Promulgated by Order of the Air Council, Reproduced by Permission of the United States Government.* Within a week I had memorized every word.

*

One afternoon in Cairo, forty years later, I began a journey that would traverse the tropics, take me from north of Cancer to half a degree south of Capricorn. Standing among a buzzing, expectant crowd I watched the old machine splash buoyantly down on the Nile. *The control column may be eased back to reduce water coming over the cabin and engines.* She surged to a halt while flankers of foam made the felucca men yell with alarm. *Give warning signal on horn. Station rigger and assistant in bows, put a man on each drogue and one in the front turret with a boathook.*

Coughing and barking, aged a sprightly forty-four, she came ploughing towards us, the first flying boat to land in downtown Cairo since the days of King Farouk. *Place the grommet over the bollard. Remove the mooring bridle from its stowage and shackle the free end to the mooring pendant. Mouse the shackle, cast off the short slip, make fast to the buoy.* Now she lay ready to take her passengers off to the far end of Africa. Sun caught her dimpled skin, as battered by age and hard usage as the hull of a coaster. My edgy companions thought she looked like an ark under an ironing board, but I knew she would be as much at home in the sky as a monsoon wind; any reservations I had regarding her reliability—our route crossed a very active war zone—melted away.

Aboard she seemed familiar yet weirdly different, like coming upon an old friend who had changed sex: the waist deck flanked by Plexiglas gun blisters, once a clutter of flame floats and sea markers, had been turned into a glass-walled lounge with upholstered seating, a library and a bar. And beneath the engineer's tower (I thought of Popeye, now aged fifty-five or so, and either in jail or a millionaire QC) lay a sophisticated little galley, its wine cupboard occupying the spot where parachutes had once been stowed.

Around seventy Catalinas remained in use, some employed for fighting forest fires, others converted into airborne yachts (Farouk ordered one with polar-bear-fur-lined cabins). Ours, an amphibian, had flown in from Vancouver then, at Cairo Airport, spent the night under the eye of Pierre Jaunet, a tousled, donnish Frenchman who smoked a churchwarden pipe and planned to operate cruises down Africa's old Imperial Airways route. Today he would set off on his proving flight, taking a few friends and associates—including the BBC's David Wallace, and myself; Wallace, a quietly spoken, fiercely focused man who looked like an ageing rock star, planned to charter it for a film about Imperial's route; I would write and present it; this was to be our recce.

Pierre, who owned a safari company, knew a lot about Africa but nothing about flying boats. Jim Ladegard, the American pilot, knew plenty about flying boats but absolutely nothing about Africa. And Oliver Evans, our twenty-five-year-old Canadian co-pilot, had flown floatplanes in Botswana so knew a bit about both—yet, worryingly, was not certified to fly Catalinas.

Our first take-off attempt, down a river turned windless and glassy, lasted a mile, the boat rising on its step—the flared base of the hull— in a paroxysm of noise. Nothing happened. Jim turned and tried again, this time struggled to an altitude of three feet and stayed there a full minute, cursing quietly, with his floats up. *In conditions of flat calm the floats may be retracted while still on the step at 60 knots or over.* We lumbered aloft as a bridge, clogged with traffic, hove into sight.

Residents of high-rise riverside apartments waved as we climbed by. The Pyramids cast long shadows; dusk darkened the world below but up here it remained full of light and buoyancy. I sat in the waist where blister gunners once threw back their crystal turtleshells to engage the enemy, a tiny covered quarterdeck now offering the best views in aviation.

Squeezing into a niche behind the cockpit, yelling over the racket, I introduced myself to Jim, a stocky, fortyish, bespectacled chain-smoker. Resting his hands on the Bakelite wheel (lacking its bomb-release button) and flicking ash out the window, he wearily neared the end of his first full day in Africa. Beside him Oliver, tall, tow-headed and boyish, frowned over a chart. The airspeed indicator registered eighty-five knots.

We arrived over Luxor in darkness; this would be a dry landing. But the squeal of tyres was followed by a thunderous bang. Swarms of ignescent firefly sparks swirled gaily by as the nose, clanging like an angelus bell, struck the tarmac twice more. "Fucking wheel's stuck!" Jim yelled, getting airborne again. *In the event of failure the nose wheel may be lowered manually by a hand crank.* The socket, though, lay under a hundredweight of luggage, now frantically being heaved aside. Instruments did not record the nose wheel's status; it could only be tested by another landing and, this time, applause filled the plane.

The baggage handlers had been summoned to prayers by their muezzin. Jim, excused unloading duties, plucked a pebble from the nose-wheel stanchion. Someone said we owed our lives to the speed of his response. He shrugged. "Put that down to naked fear."

When Oliver yanked out the bilge plugs Nile water gushed across the tarmac. Firefighters in a braying appliance mistook it for spilt fuel and girdled the Catalina with foam. An airport official drove up and, by insisting we pay cash for their anti-conflagration measures plus two landings, restored the normal tempo of Egyptian life. Pierre sighed and drew dollars from his wallet.

At the Mina Palace Hotel I met a rich, retired Alexandrian doctor who claimed he had seduced Narriman, the last Queen of Egypt, in the back of his Lagonda. "Out by the Pyramids," he recalled. While a student at Cambridge he had flown back and forth in Imperial's boats; Wallace signed him up for the shoot as I asked the pilots what they planned for the evening. "Going Indian," said Oliver, meaning some very serious drinking. In the lobby I was approached by a young woman with the plumpness that comes from a surfeit of sugared almonds. She proposed sex in my room—payment in US currency only—and looked astounded when I said no. Then, wheeling sharply towards the bar, I went Indian too.

*

We entered the tropics above Lake Nasser, our shadow crossing the demarcated Cancer line then skating over Sudan's thorny desert. Down there grew parasol-crowned acacias from which they extracted gum arabic, spiny trees that produced frankincense and myrrh, giant succulents (called spurges) and cacti possessing an architectural dimension: pillared, domed and bottle-green, they looked like structures made from Roman glass. Here we learned that Khartoum's air-traffic controllers were on strike. "They haven't been paid," said Pierre, busy planing wood in the galley, still making fixtures and fittings for his old tin clipper.

Later he pointed: "Fourth Cataract!" Pondering a wilderness of white water and black granite, I idly thought: *not* a good place for a birdstrike. Yet around here, on our filming flight several months later, the Catalina would run into a flock of sacred ibises. (And be forced down; at Moroe, in the Baiyuda desert, we found gobbets of flesh hanging from the engines, a section of fuselage seemingly peppered by apple-sized hailstones. Jim, producing his tools, had us airborne within the hour.)

Over the Sixth Cataract a faint radio voice said, "OK, you can come now." It may have been the Minister of Tourism himself; an old crony of Pierre's, he awaited us at the airport with a crew from Sudanese TV. In the late afternoon sun both Niles, Blue and White, gave off a coppery shine, while Khartoum went sprawling along their confluence like a speculative idea for a city sketched in chalk. Pierre, locking away the liquor, said, "We have entered an Islamic state. Here we drink limoon. And remember—there has been rioting due to food shortages."

At a decaying riverside hotel I watched the waiter hand my glass to a portly figure in a morning suit. He unlocked a brass-fronted safe, withdrew a one-pound bag of Tate & Lyle sugar, spooned in a measure, then replaced the bag and locked the safe behind him. Was this the manager? The waiter said, "The manager is in prison, sir." Dinner, subdued without alcohol, grew more so when Bill Cragg joined us. An English pilot working locally, he expressed surprise at the idea of taking a forty-four-year-old flying boat across a very bad civil war. "You'll have to stay at twelve thousand feet," he warned. "The SPLA rebels are shooting at everyone, even the Red Cross. But they're using SAM 7s, only effective up to eight and a half thousand feet. If you lose an engine get down among the treetops. The missile has a gyroscope that needs forty seconds to wind up; you'll be past the operator before he's had a chance to work out your speed and bearing."

Height may be maintained at low altitudes provided the propeller of the dead engine is feathered.

Jim sat with his head in his hands. "Sunday we're heading down to Lake Turkana in Kenya," he said. "What's that like?"

"Tiger country!" beamed Cragg. "The radio beacons don't work and the maps feature many areas described as 'Relief Data Incomplete.' Basically you'll need a good eye, a compass and a watch—old-fashioned, seat-of-the-pants dead reckoning."

"Jesus." Wearily Jim rose to his feet and went to bed.

The morning-suited man signalled the closure of the dining room by walking through it waving a Union Jack. As we adjourned to the terrace the lights went out. "Owawa," remarked Cragg. "Local mnemonic: Oh, Well, Africa's Won Again." Engaging, crisply spoken, retaining his old rugby physique, he seemed amused when we asked him to be in our film. Born in Amritsar of an Indian mother and an English father, he owned a Lincolnshire estate once comprising 2,700 acres. "My dad went in for fast women and slow horses, a huge tax demand when he died is what brought me here. But I've still got 'Lord of Spanby' in my passport—useful for getting into the VIP lounge at Amsterdam airport."

We said we wished to film at Juba, a Nilotic town once a key stop on the Imperial route and now at the heart of the war zone. He shrugged. "You'll need to come in high then spiral down. Could a Catalina manage that?"

Intentional spinning and aerobatics are not permitted.

A shadow figure approached, spoke a few words to Cragg then moved on. "He was a professor at the university," said Cragg. "Last month he retired after twenty-eight years and now they're refusing to pay his pension. They say there's no money."

"And is that true?"

He shrugged. "Sudan is the world's eighth largest importer of Mercedeses; they retail here for £125,000 each. And you should see how some of the ministers live."

"Why doesn't he sue?" asked Wallace.

"Because the judges are on strike. They're not getting paid either."

The Sudan, Africa's largest country, possesses many physiographic characteristics of the tropics—desert, savannah and grassland, the Sudd's equatorial swamps and rainforests—and some social ones too. A small ironclad gunboat that Kitchener brought upstream in pieces and assembled for use against the Mahdi was, when I visited, thronged with descendants of the Mahdi's warriors; it now belonged to the Khartoum Yacht Club. Two gum-arabic dealers told me they couldn't tap their trees due to the war. A youngish academic responsible for pronouncing the arrival of Ramadan complained that shaving cream was unobtainable. Shell's local manager, a wry, sad-faced Dutchman, said oil was unobtainable too. But I had overheard Jim claiming we needed a hundred gallons. He murmured, "You do. And I have barely enough aviation fuel to get you to Kenya." He gave a weary smile. "Welcome to our fair city."

One evening we attended a party thrown by the Khartoum Guild of Brewers. Held in a walled garden strung with lights, its most remarkable feature was a long table swaybacked beneath countless bottles of imported wines and spirits. Our ebullient English host poured me a tumbler of malt whisky. "The key to survival," he said, "is a good bootlegger; I've got one who even delivers to my door. But since we can't always depend on a regular supply we've had to master the black art of home brewing, and are thus known around town as the KGB. Many expats are members; we hold competitions and award silver trophies. Cin-cin!"

"What about the authorities?" I asked, astonished.

"As long as we're discreet they turn a blind eye. Our big problem is exploding bottles. Fermentation is done behind corrugated-iron barricades so there's no risk to the public, but nervous soldiers sometimes mistake them for bombs." He sipped his gin. "We had a beauty last week. At a certain stage you're supposed to add Epsom Salts as a clarifying agent, but some idiot used Eno's by mistake. That's like putting a match to gunpowder, they probably heard the bang in Cairo."

One of the KGB's founders, an elderly Polish crop-sprayer, entertained me with stories of bracken-clearance work in the Lake District. Then, growing serious, he talked about our run to Kenya. "Stay away from dams. The soldiers guarding them get five thousand Sudanese pounds for shooting down an aeroplane. To men who are supposed to live on one date a day that is a great incentive."

My stomach gave a nervous lurch.

"To feed themselves they ambush the aid convoys. But if they can get a plane—oh boy!" He popped out, returned with a Michelin road map, then, frowning over his half-moon specs, borrowed my pen and circled the areas he deemed unsafe: dams, airstrips, army camps and a few villages, all set along the Nile. "Take it," he said. "It's better than the charts. Good luck!" Then he shook my hand and slipped away.

I gave Oliver the map at breakfast. He, pale and distracted, barely glanced at it. Yet his mood improved when, prospecting for oil at the airport, he happened upon an oil-rich Canadian mission aviator happy to assist a fellow-countryman. We climbed to thirteen thousand feet over lush, Nile-watered cotton country; told to watch out for the blossom of incoming rocketry, I fell asleep.

The eight hours passed slowly. Jim, bleakly contemplating Africa, displayed fatigue, uncertainty and exasperation in equal measure. He smoked continuously and, watching his butts go out of the window, I joked, "Aren't you worried about starting a forest fire?" Back home in

Washington State he fought forest fires for a living, his Catalina water
bomber fitted with a retractable scoop that filled a tank during the
course of a low pass across the nearest lake. So he treated my question
with the contempt it deserved; forest fires may make firefighters rich,
but firefighters don't make forest fires; they abhor them. This prickly,
difficult man wasn't saying much today so, turning to Oliver, I asked
where we were. He, sucking oxygen from a bottle, a pile of discarded
charts (including the Michelin map) around his feet, spoke distractedly.
"The beacons are all dead—all I know for sure is we're still over SPLA
territory."

He kept checking his compass and watch as Jim, banking through
afternoon cumulus to find the smoothest passage, kept making devia-
tions. Then, six hours out of Khartoum, those of us seated aft witnessed
the genesis of another problem. The starboard engine was venting oil.
Droplets splattered on the Plexiglas blister and stained the rudder the
colour of teak.

Wallace wondered what we should do if both engines conked out.
"Do we stay by the plane or run for the trees?"

"Does it matter? I mean, what would the SPLA do with a pile of
junk like this? Turn it into spoons?"

He said, "It's the lions that worry me," and I looked at him with
renewed interest.

With two hours to run we saw distant glimmers of water, passed
west of the Kenamuke and Lotagipi Swamps, then the Machar
Marshes. A friendly Lufthansa cargo pilot, heading north with carna-
tions from Nairobi, helped Oliver establish his position. As we crossed
southern Ethiopia and the Gamo Gofa, Pierre raised someone at Lake
Turkana—call sign "Tusker"—on his HF radio.

"Expect us at 5 p.m., local time!" he shouted. We entered Kenya
near Ch'ew Bahirtea and overflew the isolated waterside lodge where
we would be quartered for the night. A low-level equinoctial wind
enlaced the lake but, up here, the aircraft drifted through heavy
rubescent light. Jim, choosing a spot several miles on, came down like
a breaching whale; waves burst over the cabin and plunged us into
bottle-green dimness. Then he began to motor, taxiing on the step at
forty-five knots, bucketing through a burgeoning swell and gathering
darkness. Later, anchor secured, I sat star-gazing on a wing; the wind

had dropped, and as small watery sounds played around the hull, a forcefield of silence came out of Africa.

Our landfall, made from rubber dinghies, was supervised by grave El Molo tribesmen in silver bangles and crimson robes. Pierre warned of crocodiles and added, as four men in suits loomed towards us: "These are officials from Nairobi; this is an international flight; I had to pay for them to come."

On the lodge's lamplit balcony we had our baggage examined by Customs, our yellow fever certificates by Health and our passports stamped by a stout Sikh from Immigration. The fourth man said, "I am Civil Aviation. At eight in the morning you will proceed back aboard aircraft and do one take-off and one landing, full-laden. Then I am assessing each of you disembarking with baggage." He had sunken, yellowish eyes and taut features.

Jim stared at him. "No way," he said.

"This is order I am giving!"

Jim's face had grown brick red, Pierre spoke placatingly. He knew Kenya and its bureaucrats, badly needed their support if his venture was to succeed. Thoughtfully we went to our rooms.

The lodge had its own airstrip and a dozen other guests, rich Nairobi folk up for the weekend; in the bar they kept staring at Jim, the Yankee barnstormer who had brought our exotic old aeroplane all the way from the New World. I bought him a beer. Homesick and unhappy, he was threatening resignation. Then his Kenyan fans closed in, laughed at his cornball jokes, shouted him drinks, showed respect. He cheered up—only to suffer a further mood swing when, midway through dinner, the Catalina began to sink.

Pierre brought the news, bounding into the dining area wild-eyed and hollering. Jim and Oliver shot out the door, and Wallace murmured, *"Owawa";* if it went under our film went with it. But it was nothing, a small bilge-pump problem; all seemed well.

Next day he and I planned to hitch a lift down the Great Rift Valley, in a Cessna flown by an ex–white hunter, to Kisumu, then make our way south to Maputo in Mozambique. Over a farewell drink Pierre said he had his eye on a new engine. "Well, not new, exactly, but fully reconditioned by the Papua New Guinea Air Force."

Waiting at the airstrip, we saw another Cessna make a jinking little sideslip then a very classy touchdown. The white-haired pilot, wearing a baseball cap at a jaunty angle, scrambled out and hauled a bag after her. Anne Spurry, a seventy-four-year-old French medic working for the Kenyan Flying Doctor Service, had arrived for her clinic with the El Molo. "What's wrong with them?" I asked.

"Depression—life on the lake is hard—plus almost every tropical complaint you can think of." Cheerily she agreed to take part in our film. "Last week I flew a woman to hospital with an axe in her head. She was unconscious on departure, but suddenly woke up during a very bad storm. Then she tried to get out. Flying in Africa, you must cope with the unexpected." Muted thunder sounded out on the lake and a moment later the Nairobi-bound Catalina swept over, spilling water like a rain cloud. "Ah, beautiful," murmured Dr Spurry.

In two months Wallace and I would re-board with a film crew and do the whole thing again, setting off from Alexandria on a journey that would take us across *two* civil wars to the Ilha de Moçambique—the most extraordinary tropical island on earth.

This, though, seems an appropriate moment to report the death of Bill Cragg. During our shoot he spent the better part of a day with us, charming and spectacularly good on camera, amiably tolerating the wasted time and endless retakes. Then, shortly after transmission, he was gunned down over Juba while flying in medical supplies. *Juba!* "You must come over the airfield very high then spiral down for your land-ing." What went wrong? I kept thinking of his wife and kids back in Lincolnshire, of a decent man who took a high-risk job just to settle an outstanding tax bill. Bill Cragg gave his life for his father's death duties.

*

Now I had a date with one of the Catalina's current owners. Norm, waiting at the Iririki landing, still seemed tickled by the coincidence. The Auckland consortium used it for sightseeing and joyrides; he, though, had invested simply for the dubious pleasure of being at its controls.

He had a weakness for old machinery; we boarded a Toyota 4x4 which, during his logging venture, had been repeatedly rammed in the rear by giant hardwoods breaking loose from the trailer. "Never lets me down," he said, starting an engine that clattered like a tumble-dryer full of cutlery. He told me Guy Benard, his partner in the gravel venture, adored the tropics. "*He'll* have some stories. Used to be a sailor—and a dead ringer for Steve McQueen; Guy got mobbed all over the world."

We bought beer at a supermarket reeking of rotting meat ("Freezer bust," said the check-out girl) then set off along blacktop which soon turned into particulated coral, deeply rutted; our dust created a localized fog belt. "There are a hundred miles of this," Norm said, "all needing tarmac." Out on the darkening horizon huge flat-bottomed clouds, rippling with electricity, burned like fireships.

Near Mele a big unlit house faced a breezeblock church, and a paddock containing two chestnut mares and a wild pig. Norm said, "This used to be a French mission; he's going to put a thirty-foot bar in that church." Our arrival startled the mares. But, as they galloped off, the pig galloped too; spindly legs working like pistons, it somehow kept pace. When the mares stopped, so did the pig; staggering, flanks heaving, it never took its eyes off them.

"The bar's made of *pure copper.*"

"Norm, what is that pig doing?"

"It's being a horse. Came out of the bush one day and fell in love with the mares. It adores them, follows every move they make."

He pointed to the church. "Guy's turned that into his kitchen— the bar's still in the hold of his ship: a five-hundred-ton *gravel* carrier he sailed out from France six months ago. Before we even met. Isn't that weird?"

A trim, well-preserved man in his fifties hurried towards us waving a handful of greenery and crying, "Edible leaves!" Guy had greying hair, steady blue eyes and a crushing handshake and looked, presumably, pretty much as Steve McQueen would have looked today. "Try one!" Serrated and pinkly veined, it had a bitter medicinal taste. "I will put them in the salad." We followed him into his church—boxy and barnlike, an equatorial structure designed to let the air circulate freely. Though built cheaply from local materials, it seemed to retain lingering traces of incense.

Otherwise it had been efficiently deconsecrated: the nave now cluttered with corrugated iron, the vestry with old furniture, the chancel containing a scrubbed pine table and a gas stove; the copper bar, I learned, would fit snugly into the transept. As Guy took fish from the fridge I learned their quarry permit was now being chased by a famously adversarial Vila lawyer. "He will also be a partner," said Guy, who spoke fast cosmopolitan English, spikily accented. "I love gravel more than gold and I want to make a gravel commune; I want my partners to build their houses here."

Norm, opening beer bottles, went "Hmm" in a way that made me wonder if, putting the idea to his wife, he had learned only that he must never, *ever* mention it again. Guy salted the fish and sliced wild cucumbers. "But I am not a communist. My commune wouldn't be for the masses. They must stay out."

"While you all sit here counting your money," I said.

"Precisely." He gulped some beer, placed a bucket of scraps on the spot where, perhaps, a rood screen once stood, then went to a window. *"Mr Pig!"* he yelled.

It came skidding up the nave. The men watched fondly as, sway-backed and slobbering, it plunged a hairy pink snout into the food. Norm said, "He only leaves the horses for his dinner. And they always wait patiently, I reckon they're in love with him, too. Sweet, huh?"

I suggested that, some day, Mr Pig could be turned into a very smart suitcase.

That got flinty stares; pigskin-luggage jokes had no place here, and in the midst of this awkward silence a beautiful woman arrived and cried, "Ugh, my God, that animal!" In what seemed like a single graceful movement she kissed her husband, ruffled Norm's hair, gave my hand a summary shake and grabbed a beer. Norm did the introductions: meet Alex, born locally, now resident in London, once worked on a film about his Catalina's journey down Africa. "I'll bring the video over, Lore. It's got things that might rekindle a few memories."

Lore had a trim figure and features so fine you could discern the play of muscle and sinew beneath. "You come from here but you live in *London?*"

"That's right."

"And you are happy?"

"Sure."

"After many years in Africa," she said, "Guy and I moved to France.

But it was like a house without a garden. We thought of returning—but Africa has gone crazy. So we came to Port Vila."

Guy, opening the oven door, sang, "For the coconut trees!"

She smiled. "For surf on the reef. For starry nights."

He popped in the fish. "For heat that warms your bones. For fantastic colours. And the light! Well, the light is amazing."

"The early mornings I love," said Lore. "Pure magic."

"Even bad weather. The wind smells good, the rain is warm." He raised his beer. *"Vive les tropiques!"* She cried, *"Haut les tropiques!"* Norm grinned, a party atmosphere was developing. But how many tropical subsistence farmers, I wondered, ever spared a thought for tropical aesthetics? Settlers able to afford top-dollar accommodation (with domestics who daily checked the pool for anopheles larvae), fully climate-proofed Range Rovers and the latest refrigeration gizmos might be arriving by the jetload. Yet to any indigene they must seem alien as Eskimos.

She rested her chin on her hand. "I come from an island like this one. Réunion. In the Indian Ocean? It is spoiled now: too many French tourists. But we longed to live in a tropical environment and, one day, we read about Vanuatu in a book. We thought: sounds good, let's go. But you went the other way."

I listed the usual stuff about family and friends, familiar terrain, the analeptic buzz that comes from being around a great city: that she accepted. Then, as a secondary reason, I mentioned—because it was how I made my living—quality Sunday newspapers. "Britain has the world's best," I added, instantly realizing how silly that sounded. She looked incredulous.

"On Sunday you have nothing better to do? We are out with our children and friends. Sunday is for sailing, swimming in the ocean, for relaxing and talking. It is a day for nourishment . . ."

"Nourishment, certainly," muttered Guy, stacking spaghetti in boiling water.

"Yes, but I also mean we speak of ideas, books and movies, the state of the world—and we gossip . . ." She had, of course, just described the objectives of good Sunday journalism. "And you are content to sit reading the latest lies your politicians are telling?" She shook her head. "Alex, remember where you came from, it's not too late."

I laughed. "You're saying I should move back?"

"Why not?"

"And what would I do?"

Guy said, "Buy a glass-bottomed boat and take tourists to the reef. All the coral types are there—shrub, brain, mushroom, staghorn. They will pay anything, specially the Russians."

"Or write a novel," said Norm, who plainly found the conversation absurd. "With plenty of sex and gravel." As he turned to Guy and began discussing barge procurement, I suddenly remembered something I hadn't thought about for years—a solemn promise made to my wife then, most comprehensively, broken.

*

I had courted her with visions of life in the British Colonial Service. Most colonies lay within the tropics and we dreamed of a posting east of the sun and—as my father used to say—west of the moon. I coveted the job of district officer. These versatile men, in their pith helmets and snake-proof leggings, shouldered many roles: social counsellor, health adviser, road builder, agronomist, tax gatherer, riot controller, bomb-disposal expert, magistrate and white hunter. Never a dull moment, I swore, inventing idylls which, I now realized, belonged in a glossy brochure. But then Britain began nervously shedding its colonies and, around the time of our marriage, shed the Colonial Office itself; quietly subsumed into the Foreign Office, it was allowed to wither and die on the Whitehall vine—taking my job with it.

For almost two centuries the profession of district officer had attracted muscular, rather dim boys from England's minor public schools. Like me, they aspired eventually to the rank of governor, a proconsular post which entitled the holder to live rent-free in a palace and wear a hat decorated with pink flamingo feathers. He commanded an enormous personal staff, threw parties, consumed much good food and liquor in the service of the crown and, by and large, did remarkably little work. Then the whole edifice—supporting huge numbers of people—simply vanished. It was as if Parliament, overnight, had abolished the armed forces.

I told Lore, who nodded. "What does your wife think?"

The matter, actually, had gone clean out of our heads; now, though,

it was restored to mine with pitiless clarity. Instead of becoming
Sanders of the River I stumbled on an alternative career by accident;
my career, in effect, chose me.

"Journalism, eh?" Her tone implied this was something only dysfunctional people did.

In or out of the Colonial Service, I'd always wanted to write, and a
few casual pieces sent to a humorous London magazine had led, unexpectedly, to an offer of a staff job. For a hundred and forty years *Punch*
had kept the Empire laughing, and when the Empire went out of
business, business at *Punch* went inexorably downhill. My time there
coincided with its most spectacular years of decline—not entirely due
to laboured wit or dreary editorial content, but also to big changes at
home. Britain, seeking a new role for itself, needed radical new jokes.

That era produced the satire boom. So, seated at A. A. Milne's old
roll-top desk in Bouverie Street by the Thames, I turned out quirky stories about current events, our imperial past and a childhood spent
among the Outposts of Empire. Whenever I felt remorse at bringing
my own children up in an overcrowded European city I would mentally list what they might catch out there, anything from beriberi to
cerebral malaria. Then there was education. Once they reached ten or
eleven you were supposed to send them abroad to school; we would
have resisted—yet I knew what happened to the stay-at-homes. The
tropics claimed them: at fifteen the girls got pregnant, the boys got
arrested; public-disorder charges were badges of honour, their rites of
passage.

"It's different now," said Lore. "Our kids will go away to university.
And then they'll come back."

"Will they? You'll seem so far away. Overseas."

"OK, but we have always been overseas people."

Once that had been a word resonating with glamour and opportunity. To my forebears it meant the world beyond the privet hedge, freedom from a class-ridden society governed by a haughty old widow with
chilblains. Overseas could turn escape into a smart career move.

My grandfather believed the Empire flourished because it allowed
so many Brits to flee the country.

Lore said, "But, look, if you had joined your Colonial Service you
would be coming up for retirement. Quite soon, I think."

That, unbelievably, was true.

"I know such people, so many years working abroad for France—but what have they got to show for it?"

I imagined my wife and I, sallowed by sun and fevers, filling a Home Counties cottage with artefacts—stuffed birds, monkey-skull ashtrays, elephant's-foot umbrella stands, pygmy funerary figures containing human bones and shrivelled human hearts—guaranteed to upset our children.

Guy passed me another beer. "So by closing down their Empire," he said, "the Brits may have done you a favour."

But the tropics? Well, that was another matter.

From the fridge Lore produced pots of yogurt. "Here I have a yogurt machine. But in Africa we made it just with sunshine."

Her daughters walked in, one a languorous blond teenager, the other dark-eyed and intense. They ate a little supper—the younger, a choc-ice on a stick—then retired to watch videos.

Guy, serving up wonderful fish, said he had been born in Algeria and enlisted in the Paras at seventeen. "Then, along with half the French army, I joined the rebellion against De Gaulle. He had offered the Algerians independence; one half, who didn't think it was a good idea, fought the other half; I still have a French bullet in my leg. We even prepared to invade France, but the evening before I was supposed to parachute over Paris—a city armed to the teeth—peace was agreed. For the rebels there was no amnesty. I fled to Madagascar and started fishing, when the amnesty came I bought a trawler and went after cod in the North Sea; those were the days when they just jumped into your net. Later, to see the world, I joined the merchant marine."

Lore fetched a photo of a young Steve McQueen look-alike standing on a ship's bridge. He said, "That was in Yokohama; even there people wanted my autograph! Down at the wharf I have a complete fish factory crated up on my ship."

"Which Norm says is actually a gravel carrier."

"Yes. I also had a good gravel business. What has happened here is just a happy coincidence."

Norm produced a pair of bowls heaped with birdseed-sized stones. "These ones are New Caledonian, those are from our island. Judge for yourself." The stones looked absolutely identical.

"Judge what?"

"The quality." He scooped some up and tipped them back, spilling lithoidal treasure from his hands.

Lore caught my eye and winked. "This film Norm mentioned. It was a travel thing, uh? Where did you go?"

"From Alexandria to the Ilha de Mozambique."

She stared at me. "You went to the Ilha?"

"Yes."

"In the war?"

"Yes."

Guy produced four glasses and a jug filled with pale, cloudy liquid. "Tropical home brew. I make it from rum, grapefruit, vanilla and green peppers. It's tart and quite strong. Try some."

It was sensational.

He sat down. "So tell us," he said.

Great White Bird

One evening over Africa I saw a silver MiG leap from a puddle of crimson cloud, hang there for two beats then plunge back. It reminded me of a trout jumping from a claret barrel yet carried rocketry that could have vaporized the Catalina; its black pilot, exuberantly cutting loose after a long day, failed to note we had trespassed into his war. Lumbering along at eighty knots I surveyed the beautiful wooded battleground below, knew the trees hid trigger-happy troops but didn't know which side they were on, or how either side regarded us.

A Canadian mission pilot had warned that both would shoot and, aboard, we took bets on the lot more likely to do so. In a grim and protracted conflict, Mozambique's Marxist regime fought a free-enterprise guerrilla consortium—which left us, working for the BBC, ideologically stranded somewhere between the two. In the air we talked politics while the soldiers below, watching our weird old aeroplane through the calibrated sights of their missile launchers, probably decided not to fire for housekeeping reasons; a single SAM 7 cost more than the heap of scrap droning overhead.

As we dropped towards Pemba the sun looked like a blazing oil well, semi-opaque behind its own smoke. We left the plane in the charge of nervous kids toting AK-47s and went to a small, dank hotel so unaccustomed to guests the public crowded in to look. They saw ten weary, dispirited Europeans who all wished they were somewhere else. Pierre had just learned his London insurers had withdrawn cover while Jim, in the grip of a black-dog depression, gulped beer and announced the imminent arrival of a tropical storm; for him the trip had become a nightmare.

Three weeks earlier, departing from Alexandria's harbour, we retraced the route we had followed two months before, overflown Sudan's civil war, crossed the equator between two Kenyan lakes,

Turkana and Naivasha, moved on towards Zanzibar and Dar es Salaam, saw tropical savannahs with elephants making rippling wakes in the long grass, and heavenly blue jacarandas flowering everywhere. Apart from the bird strike over the Fourth Cataract the flight had been uneventful. We met some interesting people, got some good interviews and shot plenty of film. Falling into bed that night I discovered dead scorpions and mouse droppings among my soiled sheets, but was too tired to care.

Heading on after breakfast we spotted tank tracks on Mozambique's empty beaches, and when our port engine began leaking oil, turned inland to Nampula where Jim, grim-faced, tinkered with a bypass valve. Airport officials shook their heads when they learned we were making for the Ilha de Mozambique; the small unlit strip opposite the island, they warned, became part of Renamo's rebel domain after dark. We met the storm funnelling up from South Africa. It bounced the old boat around, making its wings flex and creak—their trailing edges fashioned not from metal, but reinforced oilskin. The faulty Pratt & Whitney radial continued spewing Shell Multi-Grade as, late in the afternoon, Jim and Oliver confirmed they had completely lost their bearings.

With twenty minutes of daylight remaining we flew out of the weather and across the coast; ahead lay the sinewy, two-mile-long Ilha. Past travellers may have regarded this as the most remarkable tropical island on earth, but even their accounts hadn't prepared us for what began unfolding below. Hidden away among the mudbanks and mangroves of the Mozambique Channel lay an exquisite little European city: the abandoned capital of Portuguese Mozambique. As Jim made a low pass to check the sea state I identified the sixteenth-century granite fortress of St Sebastian, ringed by cannon and ranged before other lovely period structures: the Chapel of Our Lady of Baluarte, the convent of St Domingo and the airy pink church and palace of St Paul—erected by Jesuits then claimed by the Governor-General for his chapel and residence. Elegant public buildings looked over spacious paved squares; I glimpsed statues, bandstands, parks and boulevards.

After the emptiness of Africa it seemed miraculous, a glittering mirage likely to dematerialize at any moment. Nigel Meakin, our cameraman, muttered, "Jesus!" and sprang to work, while the rest just stared—Oliver so entranced he forgot to lower the retractable floats. A flying boat alighting floatless on water self-destructs in a series of splashy, diminishing cartwheels, and warning yells filled the plane. As we surged to a halt I reflected on the historical symmetry of having an accident here. In 1937 one of Imperial's legendary Empire machines had crashed at this same spot, killing its flight clerk and radio officer.

Then we noted the people. Dense crowds massed on the beaches and pressed into the sea, and when Jim cut his engines their cheers echoed across the water like voices from the Anfield terraces. An old motor-driven whaler came bouncing through the swell. It carried the harbourmaster, his pretty lady assistant in a blue sailor suit and a burly able seaman wearing a lime-green smock embroidered with white anchors. Half a dozen local dignitaries accompanied them: thin, solemn, threadbare old men who surveyed us gravely. One caught my eye and smiled. *"Bom dia,"* he said.

In the gathering darkness they put us ashore at a baroque pier with much of its decking gone, murmuring apologies as we followed them across the few rotting planks still in place. Outside the pink palace of St Paul a crackling tamarind-wood fire lit the square. Men warmed their drums in the flames; ululating women with clay-daubed faces began to dance. Soon everyone joined in, three thousand or so spirited Africans bringing this moribund, forgotten fragment of Europe exhilaratingly back to life. What a party! Gleefully grabbed and passed around, I stomped and shuffled with agile grannies, an earnest little girl desperate to practise her English ("Good morning, sir! Do you like toast?"), mothers with babies on their backs, the harbourmaster's sailor-suited lady assistant, even the harbourmaster himself. Drums boomed, voices whooped and harmonized, shadows leaped, the reek of palm oil, wood smoke and sweat made the evening intoxicating; none of us, ever, had witnessed anything remotely like this.

What made it so moving for me was that those welcoming us were hungry, impoverished refugees now squatting in the marble palaces and fine houses abandoned by the Portuguese. What made it so moving for the film crew was that the light had gone, and as the amazing spectacle unfolded they couldn't shoot a single frame; Wallace sat with his head in his hands while Meakin, an ace documentary cameraman famed for his civility under pressure, paced agitatedly—then shrugged and began dancing too.

That night at the semi-derelict Pousada, our interpreter, Juan, rummaged through the busted freezer and unearthed, from beneath a pile of stinking fish, several cans of South African milk stout. A slim, bright young civil servant from Maputo, he said government forces had probably captured it from Renamo who, in turn, would have had it shipped from the Cape by submarine. I stared at him. "They're sending milk stout to the guerrillas in submarines?"

"Well, that is the way they send the guns. The submarine is called the *Emily Hobhouse*. Fishermen see it in these waters quite often."

He said South Africa supplied Renamo to keep the Marxist regime destabilized. The war had dragged on for years and brought Mozambique to its knees. "That is where Pretoria wants us. And that is where we stay until their evil regime is brought down." (Nelson Mandela would be released two years later.) He tasted the stout. "God! Pure poison! But we have nothing else to offer you."

Ours, he said, was not the only alien flying machine to visit the Ilha. Recently a UFO had made several calls. "It is about fifty metres across, green and very pretty, like a big firework. It hovers over the island for a minute or two, quite silent, then goes in a flash of green flame."

"Have you seen it?"

"No. I only arrived last night, but they're all talking about it." He smiled grimly. "It is not delusional paranoia, not some stress thing brought on by hunger and fear. It's *real*."

"How many refugees are here?" I asked.

"Ten thousand, perhaps. A thousand have come in the past two weeks alone."

"Where do they get food?"

He shrugged. "Where they can. At low tide they find shellfish. Or seaweed. Sometimes there is rice. There are plants they can cook. And rats. They can eat grass."

"Is there food over on the mainland?"

"Sometimes. But if they cross the causeway they must be back on the island by sundown. After dark the whole area over there is in the hands of Renamo. From here you can even see the village that is their base; last week it was bombed by government MiGs. This afternoon MiGs were around the village again. Did you pass any in your flying boat?"

"We saw one yesterday, but it was far away."

Now, alarmingly, I was being revisited by my own stress thing: a worm crawling across the right eye's conjunctiva and making a shadow like a partial eclipse. (I first heard about Calabar swellings from my father and, years later, diagnosed my own in Zanzibar; there, at the One Coconut Hospital, a jolly but ignorant Polish doctor laughed and told me to get new glasses.) Anxiety-related and lasting barely an hour, it affects me only in the tropics.

We dined off green, half-cooked crayfish, the remains—with fragments of meat still in their claws—carefully gathered by the cook; later I glimpsed him distributing them to shadowy figures clustered around the kitchen door.

The lights went out. We lit a palm-oil lamp but it flickered and died too; Pierre said blowing the mains was a classic prelude to a guerrilla attack. We wondered what we should do if Renamo troops came over the causeway. Juan thought this unlikely. "Here they would be bottled up. Our forces would follow and corner them. They know that."

Pierre, concerned for his Catalina moored out in the moonlight, asked, "What kind of arms do the rebels have?"

"The best Pretoria can supply," said Juan. "Bazookas, mortars, high-velocity automatic weapons. It is all good stuff."

"Is the Catalina within range of them just now?"

"Yes," said Juan. "And so are we."

A year earlier Renamo had blown the pipeline bringing water from the mainland; at the Pousada you got half a bucket daily and showered with a tin cup. My room had been unoccupied for so long the rats, wholly unafraid, seemed tame, even playful; the cockroaches, though, were predators with stinging bites. At midnight, drifting off to sleep, I heard shouts and the sound of people running. Had Renamo invaded after all? Then silence returned, leaving only the bony click of coconut fronds and the reassuring swish of the tide rising in the Mozambique Channel.

*

Work began here half a century after Vasco da Gama first visited in 1498. The old *descubridor,* seeking India, had sailed south to find a monsoon wind that would carry him there, and coming upon the island and the fertile, possibly mineral-bearing mainland beyond, wrote home suggesting that Portugal stake its claim with a fine new city. His idea received royal support; *cedulas* signed by the King authorized the dispatching of craftsmen to create a miniaturized replica of Lisbon itself—a capital for the King's faraway African dominions. It remained the seat of government until 1898, then flourished as a commercial centre and vacation destination for expats from the interior (our ruined Pousada was once thought to be the last word in luxury seaside chic). In 1975 Frelimo independence fighters threatened to overwhelm the island, and within three days, the Portuguese had packed and gone. They left their stunning little metropolis with all its fixtures and fittings intact and, to my mind, resonant eddies of shock which seemed to linger still.

*

Two polished five-barrelled Maxim guns bearing plaques saying "Nordenfelt Co. Ltd. London 1889" flanked the fortress of St Sebastian's vaulted gatehouse; rusting cannon embossed with the Portuguese crown lay strewn around its battlements. Many pointed uselessly at Mossuril, the rebel village half a mile across the water (now a picture of pastoral calm—smoke from breakfast fires, children's voices) where Renamo officers planned their eventual conquest of the island, perhaps also the destruction of our Catalina; swinging at anchor (as Jim, shirtless in the sun, worked on his port engine), it looked awfully vulnerable.

Within their city the Portuguese built a fort, and within the fort a township for their militia. Churches, chapels and bell towers occupied a paved three-acre courtyard. In the barbican we found shadowy, low-ceilinged living quarters, around the inner bailey's perimeter a warren of halls, galleries, audience chambers, waiting rooms, grand staircases and ornate balconies from which, once, governors-general had reviewed their armies. Troops had been garrisoned here until 1975 but now an air of dank, cobwebbed desolation hung over the place. Dennis stared at a wall scored with strange charcoal graffiti.

"Voodoo art, next time we'll hire a witch doctor." A can-do Yankee optimist with a lumbering, ursine physique, boyish looks and an immense capacity for enthusiasm, Dennis Kane owned the only company in America then dedicated exclusively to the making of television documentaries. He had put up the money—*lots* of money—for this one, and though ostensibly we were all employed by the BBC, right now we actually worked for ABC/Kane Productions. In an old "doco" specialist like him the Ilha tapped reserves of enthusiasm even he didn't know he had. He wanted to return and shoot a special. Screw the war; he could sell it round the world. "How you fixed for next month?"

"Next month's OK. But why don't we stay a while longer and do it now? We're here, we've got a crew . . ."

He stood staring as a line of boy soldiers shuffled raggedly by, malnourished children in baggy, oversized adult uniforms that emphasized their skin-and-bone shapes. Under the command of a shrill teenage NCO they began drilling, using whittled acacia wands for rifles.

"Holy shit," he muttered, "they're aged what, twelve, thirteen?" He shook himself. "Why not shoot now? Because our film stock's running low and because of those sons-of-bitches over there." He pointed to Mossuril.

"They'll still be around next month."

"Look, Alex, just one big push from the government . . ."

"Maybe," I said, "these kids *are* the government."

Wherever the crew went thousands followed, and now we tracked the noise to a reeking, feculent beach buzzing with blowflies. Ron Brown, a sandy-haired sound man whose wit thrived on adversity (Ron's best jokes always eclipsing the worst occasions), had crossed into a realm beyond humour. Bleakly he warned, "We're on take *ten*," and pointed to some fishermen in a wooden boat. Bobbing several yards offshore they held out a few mullet to Pierre, who stood thigh-deep, brandishing money. The beaming men, untroubled by the retakes and ignoring Wallace's shouted directions, kept tossing their heads and employing sweeping, operatic gestures. They were hamming it up like pantomime dames, playing not just to our camera but also to their cheering supporters. Pierre looked helplessly at Wallace who, flushed and sweating, spotted me. "Alex! Get in there with him."

"Sorry?"

"Get in the water with Pierre! Buy some fish!"

He meant *pretend* to buy some fish; we would not be eating those. This, my first foray into television, had already shown the distinction between drama and the glossy travel documentary to be a fine one. Here in equatorial Africa I stood clad head to toe in gear bought at Blazer's in London by one of Wallace's BBC lady assistants ("the camera likes blue shirts") and sported a haircut from a London stylist who worked under the same lady's close ("leave it thicker over the ears") personal supervision.

I found myself acting out a series of vignettes fastidiously, almost lovingly choreographed, in which I played the Catalina's lone passenger— someone traversing tropical Africa with its two pilots and eccentric French owner. Though I fully understood the pressures on Wallace I also understood I was not an entertainer, couldn't manage the spontaneous, off-the-cuff stuff that, for example, Michael Palin does so brilliantly. I was accustomed to performing with pen and notebook; what we were doing here was a stunt requiring acting skills I didn't have. Pierre could play his own scene.

"No," I said, and set off to see the town.

The dimensions of the Café Restaurante Ancora D'Ouro indicated it must once have accommodated several hundred candlelit diners and a palm-court orchestra. Now, though, the premises contained only four chairs and a pair of wrecked mattresses. A toothless old man lying on one sprang to his feet and tried to sell me a broken flute. At the padlocked Supermercado Populare de Mozambique in the Rua dos Arcos I glimpsed bare wooden shelves in a shadowy interior, pondered a window display left oddly intact: one tin of Nugget Equimal Icbal, one bottle of Sopal fruit cordial, a tin of Andorinha olive oil, two plastic buckets, a plastic baby bath, three glasses and a wooden bowl. The dusty objects seemed to imply that trading had been suspended only temporarily but, more likely, were testimony to the haste of the evacuation.

Gunmen had shot at the padlock on the Cinema Nina, an airy 1930s building on a beachside boulevard, leaving it bent and buckled. (Yet it still held.) A breeze soughed through a stand of casuarina trees shading a mosaic marble pavement intricately patterned in pink and white.

In the vestibule of the old French consulate I found refugees living under the staircase. When I went to climb the stairs a young woman suckling a boy of two indicated they were unsafe. Much of the vestibule had been reclaimed by the forest. A vigorous *Figueira brava* had burst through the wainscoting and grown up the wall, wildflowers sprouted from the grassy floor. I saw other fine old mercantile houses being slowly crushed and swallowed by the burgeoning *Figueira,* each leaving fragments of a house visible within the structure of the tree. But even these fragments, provided they still possessed a roof, sheltered families.

In the apse of the Misericordia Church a man beckoned urgently. He led me to a chapel containing the corpse of an elderly black male, face catastrophically imploded around a prominent hooked nose. Wrapped in a shroud and lying in an open coffin, his mummified remains gave off a musty smell, like unaired linen. Three kneeling stools covered in worn red velvet flanked the coffin. My companion dropped onto one and indicated I should do the same. I declined.

"I speak English," he said. "Pray with me."

"I cannot do that."

"It will bring you luck."

"Who is this man? How long has he been dead?"

"He very important saint. He give protection from Renamo terrorists. If you pray he give you protection too."

When, unprotected, I left the church, he followed holding a stolen plastic lily. Short and balding with odd, deep-set eyes he told me he had once been a tour guide, and as if to prove it, waved his lily at the facade. "Gable elevation contain Arabic and Indian influence but overall effeck is Portuguese Baroque. You please give me cigarette."

He placed the lighted end inside his mouth and asked if I wanted a girl. "Very young, sir, very juicy." Unperturbed by my response he strolled on, showed me the spot where, years earlier, diggers from a sewage crew had uncovered Roman buckles and falcon bells. "Portuguese colonialists install underground pipes for foul waste, but they all fill with sand." He smiled faintly. "So now followers of 'scientific socialism' must shit on the beach. You know, when all this war is finish, we will get out."

"Where will you go?"

"Portugal!" he cried.

*

I found myself recalling Suriname, a tractless wilderness of rainforests and caramel-coloured rivers set high on the eastern shoulder of tropical South America. It too possessed a ruined capital, Paramaribo, and its citizens also behaved like a people in transit—which most, I discovered, would seriously like to be.

Jerry A-Kum, a likeable young Creole who showed me around, said, "Our official language is Dutch, which we call Wooftie-Blooftie. But among ourselves we speak Sranan Tongo. That's Suriname Tongue, which the Dutch call Taki-Taki."

Destitute Paramaribo is home to half the nation. Built largely from pitch pine and tin, badly in need of paint, it was permeated by miasmal petrol fumes and a semi-submerged air of desperation.

At its heart, coddled in mahogany trees, lay a deserted Dutch fort and a few crumbling seventeenth-century Dutch mercantile houses— the gorgeous empty centre of yet another European tropical dream. This one, though, had not been wrecked by foreign-backed guerrilla raids. Instead, it was simply dying in its sleep. Part of the country's heritage it may have been, but there was no money to save it. Paramaribo was broke.

At the Torarica Hotel a notice warned: "Due to present economic downturn crime and prostitution have been on a steady increase."

Out strolling in the evenings I adopted the rotating-head gait I had seen British soldiers use in Ulster, sometimes even walking backwards. (This evoked soft laughter from thieves keeping pace in the shadows.) The whores, all wearing the same stale bazaar perfume, literally fell on you—stepped up close and toppled over so you instinctively grabbed them. Then they'd offer, in Wooftie-Blooftie, to let go without fuss for a dollar.

Jerry A-Kum talked a lot about emigration. "I would rather be living in Holland. More than two hundred thousand Surinam people are there."

"But that's half your population!"

"You bet. Next time, Alex, we will meet in Amsterdam!"

*

At the Pousada the District Governor joined us for a lunch of corned beef and canned peas. A tall, personable man in a well-cut safari suit, he made a disjointed little speech which Juan translated.

"Thank you for coming to our Ilha. Four hundred years ago the inspiration for our builders were the houses of the Algarve. Yet the early twentieth century is also represented here—we have a neoclassical police station and a functionalist primary school. Every time it rains, however, another house falls down. Once we were famous for our pretty doors, but most have been burnt for firewood. And our pretty birds have all finished up in the cooking pot!" Nobody laughed, he hurried on then, a moment later, stopped and looked at us expectantly.

Juan murmured, "Now His Excellency would like you to interview him for BBC current affairs. But he will not speak about the security situation, he will speak only about old buildings."

Wallace nodded. "Sure; OK, Alex, do an interview?" To Nigel he said, "I think maybe a strawberry filter for this."

"Right," said Nigel.

"Everyone ready? Action!"

I put my first question. This time the Governor, a political appointee, spoke in a grave, measured way, his demeanour statesmanlike. Even while describing the evolution of seventeenth-century window design he sounded like a man putting down markers for future advancement. After five minutes Wallace cried, "Cut! Very good! You happy, Nigel? Was that all right?"

"Fabulous!" said Nigel.

As the beaming Governor shook our hands I asked, "What will happen here when the war is over? Will everyone go back to their villages?" He said, "There are many landmines, the villages are dangerous. Here we have a city. In the Third World a city always has possibilities. The Ilha will get moving, they will stay."

"Don't they want to go to Portugal?"

Grinning, he kicked an imaginary football. "Sure! But I think only the next Eusebios will get there." Then he hurried away, leaving me with a gritty residue of guilt. A strawberry filter meant there had been no film in the camera.

Dennis told the crew to go and grab every view they could. They didn't need me, so I walked to the Palace of St Paul's State Apartments where a courteous, quietly spoken retired headmaster wearing spectacles with a lens missing asked me to remove my shoes. I placed them beside a green sedan chair which, he told me, once belonged to the Kings of Portugal. "It was carried by slaves."

"Can the people come in here?" I asked.

"No. They must stay away. But they do not mind. There is nothing they can eat."

The European powers knew that a grand palace had the same effect as an efficient army, kept a subject people awed and pliable. Following beacons of crystal and gilt I wandered past tapestries, carpets and furniture crafted for great occasions, visited huge, dim rooms resonating with wealth and privilege. In the banqueting hall I found an inlaid ebony table set with silver candelabra. The Governor's private chambers boasted two vast canopied beds intricately painted with Indian birds and reached by sets of teak steps. Even the room of the wet-nurse had chandeliers, the ebony cradle beside her bed clinker-built by shipwrights in the form of a galleon's hull.

I found chambers where the Governor and his family had stayed cool in the hot season and rooms where they gathered for warmth during the rains. In a study hung with stained silk brocades the caretaker sat reading in a wing-backed Regency armchair. He said, "Please admire the garden." I looked out over vigorous primary forest halted by a crumbling brick wall; it needed an effort of will to recall what lay beyond. He closed his book. "So you came in the aeroplane. What is flying like? Can you describe it?"

Surprised, I started telling him about our tropical journey: kaleidoscopic colours, a sky full of light, the stars seemingly closer, the organization of clouds. But this was not what he wanted.

"I mean defying *gravity*! Does it make you breathless? Are you giddy? Can you see straight?"

"You can see for miles. If you go high enough you can even see the curvature of the earth."

"You can leave all your troubles behind."

"Exactly."

"Ah!" His wistful smile exposed a mouthful of ruined teeth. "I am alone here, nobody comes. I practise my English by reading books from the library. Today I am reading a Portuguese one that says Adam and Eve were black, and the Garden of Eden was in southern Africa— I think maybe on the Ilha!" I'd been taught the Garden had bloomed by the Euphrates, a degree or two north of Cancer. Yet it could have been a metaphor for the tropics, with the apple symbolizing a much sweeter fruit, such as the mango. In time, presumably, those who reclaimed the Garden cut it down for firewood—perhaps even went to war over it.

Thunder rumbled and rain began to fall. Outside the palace church, with its fabulous gold altarpiece and carved seventeenth-century pulpit, an old woman called to me and indicated hunger by rubbing her stomach. Three boy soldiers strolled by, carrying Russian-made grenade launchers carelessly as skateboards. I came upon Dennis, bouncing along, and wheeled him straight into the State Apartments, brought him out wide-eyed and feverish. I said we must film them. "We got no goddam lights!" he cried.

Back at the Pousada his agitation made the exhausted crew despondent. "We might as well strike matches," said Nigel. At dinner I started describing the dead saint in the Misericordia then, realizing I was compounding the gloom, fell silent; he'd need lights too. We would be departing the Ilha with only part of its story told, and privately knew we would never return. Any last hopes flickered when the electricity failed, were finally dashed when Juan—who had been summoned to see the military commandant—returned grim-faced. "Tomorrow Renamo will attack your flying boat. You must leave at once."

"We can't take off in the dark," said Pierre.

"You go at first light. And I am coming with you. This place is not healthy for me."

We mustered before dawn for a breakfast of bread and weak unsugared tea. A tall, wild-looking man, face daubed with clay, stepped through an open window, wordlessly snatched at cups and swallowed the dregs, grabbed crusts and stuffed them in his mouth. Then he ran out, jumped the wall and vanished.

Nigel filmed our notional departure as Jim and Oliver took off for the mainland strip—held by friendly forces during the hours of daylight. We made our actual departure covertly, across the rattling timber causeway in a minibus with an escort of troops, found the Catalina parked by a tiny terminal clad with pretty blue tiles miraculously undamaged by those alternating day-shift, night-shift armies. Airborne, we made a low pass over the Ilha de Mozambique and saw many people waving; a heavy emotional silence transcended the racket of the engines.

*

Looking back, I thought of other desolated cities lying within the tropics. Sri Lanka's Anuradhapura, founded four hundred years BC, was a monumental capital (its nine-storey bronze-roofed Brazen Palace accommodated a thousand monks) set among canals and giant man-made tanks. In southern Laos I visited a metropolis fashioned from sandstone and laterite six hundred years earlier, and beside a giant pond dug for boat races chatted to a family who had fled to California when the hardline, pro-Hanoi Marxists took over in 1975. But in Fresno, the man told me, his Bulgarian doctorate in nuclear physics had been received with derision. "So now I fix Toyotas." He wanted his grand-children to see what their ancestors had accomplished when Fresno's Native Americans *still lived in the Stone Age.* "I guess," he mused, "we were cleverer back then." The same might be said of other tropical peo-ples. In pre-Columbian America the Mayans invented a hieroglyphic script, made precise astronomical observations, drew up a calendar and perfected a vigesimal numerical system notable for its development of zero—on which the binary computer is based.

*

Over on the African mainland the Zambezi was in spate. It carried liquescent topsoil and looked like oxblood broth; a mile from its gaping mouth it went foaming over a couple of wrecked freighters, lying on their sides. Down on the delta, refuelling at Quelimane, I talked to a wiry Zimbabwean pilot loading his DC3 with Red Cross supplies. "What's happening here," he said, "is a children's war. If a SAM 7's got my name on it I'll die knowing it was probably fired by a kid who should have been at school."

The authorities at Beira airport made us spend the night aboard the Catalina. Heavy rain sweeping in from the Indian Ocean caused it to leak continuously.

Dennis, sitting with a wet blanket over his head, talked about the American version of our film. It was scheduled to be networked on ABC Television, so a major star would be needed to narrate the script.

"You can read some too, Alex, but since the US public don't know you from a hill of beans we're gonna need a personality like . . . Sean Connery." (In the event, Connery said no; Roy "Jaws" Scheider said yes—and did a fine job.)

We dozed, at one in the morning were wakened by the howl of powerful turboprops. A big executive twin taxied to a halt nearby and I spotted glow-worm-green instrument lighting in a computerized cockpit, black leather seats in a pastel-toned cabin. Dennis peered groggily through the blister. "Where's he headed?" Ron hailed the pilot ("I say!") as he commenced an external inspection with a torch and golf umbrella.

"Joburg." *Cheuberk.* The pilot was South African.

"Joburg!" Dennis gulped. In Joburg they had rat-free five-star hotels with king-sized beds and twenty-four-hour room service. He yelled, "You got space for one?"

The pilot laughed. "Bad as that, eh?" This, he said, was a company machine but if his boss agreed, there shouldn't be a problem. "It's just him and two others. They're coming through now, we're ready to go."

Dennis seized his bag. "See you dudes around!" he cried and raced, whooping, through the deluge.

Soon after dawn we left for Harare and the end of our odyssey but, somewhere over the forests of Manica Land, Jim lost his bearings again; a kindly flying farmer far away in Zimbabwe heard his distress calls and put him back on track. On the ground a telegram awaited us. At Nairobi, Nigel had shipped the first batch of exposed film back to the processors in London, ever since waited anxiously for news. The message said simply, "Every frame a Rembrandt."

*

There was an unexpected postscript to our journey.

One mild March evening a year later the Catalina brought us, as it were, to dinner at the Grosvenor House, Park Lane. There we joined a thousand exquisitely dressed people for *mousse d'avocat en crêpe,* fillet of sole, baby guinea fowl in a lime sauce, *parfait* Drambuie and as much Mouton Cadet—presented, according to the programme, by Baron Philippe de Rothschild (UK)—as we could hold. More to the point, the programme also listed tonight's nominees. They included Julia

Roberts, Michelle Pfeiffer, Sean Connery, Tom Cruise, Robert de Niro, Al Pacino and, at the very back of the Grosvenor's Great Room—second last, after Best Film Not in the English Language—the occupants of Table 111.

At 8 p.m. sharp, after a trumpet fanfare and before a prime-time Sunday night audience of around fifteen million, the British Academy of Film and Television Arts awards ceremony got under way. As it proceeded I noted, idly, that a roving cameraman arrived at the winners' tables thirty seconds before they were announced, filmed their ecstatic reaction and long trek up to the platform. "Got something ready to say?" I asked Wallace. He shrugged. "Won't be necessary." I wondered if he meant that. Quiet and ferociously dedicated, he gave little away; we had worked together for months yet I still barely knew him.

Of the four films nominated for the Flaherty Award for Best Single Documentary the smart money was on a powerful Channel 4 piece about disadvantaged children in Romania.

The Bafta awards ceremony seems, retrospectively, an odd venue in which to conclude I had no long-term future in television. (Television soon came to the same conclusion about me.) As the evening wore on, sluicing down the baron's vino and looking fondly upon my friends— we'd had some laughs on that trip—I recalled the moment on the Ilha's beach when I finally understood it's mostly done with mirrors: a lesson reinforced only months afterwards while making a documentary on the Indian monsoon.

When it failed to materialize we drove north, following its projected path with a big red Indian fire engine in tow. By imaginative use of their hoses the firemen simulated monsoon rain so heavy and splashy that the real thing, when it finally showed up, seemed like passing drizzle. (They could even make rainbows.) The inventive, affable, gum-booted firemen, unacknowledged in the credits, had turned our piece into a majestic tribute to the Indian rains, and I felt uneasy about people assuming that what they'd seen was how it had been.

I felt uneasy too about the way a TV crew can overwhelm a place and change its nature. Even in the most obscure backwaters crowds gather because they know the camera is a window through which, intoxicatingly, they may be glimpsed by the world. And I was unhappy about its inability to handle the tiny, revelational incident that sends you scrabbling for your notebook, the way it couldn't—unless you had first scripted and rehearsed them—do the chance encounters, the glimpses and insights, all those little balancing acts going on in the mind: anxiety, boredom, elation, the way you can feel lucky one day and lousy the next.

It was getting on for eleven when the roving cameraman appeared. I waited for him to stop at the Romanian table but he didn't. He stopped at ours. Up on the platform someone ripped open an envelope and cried: "David Wallace, *The Last African Flying Boat!*" The camera's eye glowed and Wallace, suddenly live on national TV (and ignoring the pandemonium at 111), began walking. In the spotlights he cut an unexpectedly glamorous figure and, of course, made the coolest speech of the evening.

*

"Well, you certainly had an adventure," said Lore, but I guessed it wasn't the Africa she remembered, and that she would not care for the video. Under a tropical moon she and Guy walked us over to their house and an upstairs floor crammed with books; in a white sitting room the daughters, in their nightdresses, slept before a flickering video screen. Guy scooped them up as Lore murmured, "Here we have something special," and, from a cupboard, plucked a wonderful set of signed Dalí lithographs. Norm, yawning, said it had been a long day; tomorrow he was doing the early run down to Tanna. Saying goodbye to the hospitable Benards, I suddenly saw their tropical dream as a sequel to *Tales of the South Pacific*—the handsome French planter, played in the movie by Rossano Brazzi, now resembling Steve McQueen and pursuing a career in aggregate.

Norm, driving back to town, asked about Jim.

"As far as I know he's still fighting forest fires in Washington State. And I heard somewhere he'd been with Steven Spielberg, flying Catalinas for a movie. I believe Oliver joined an airline in the States. He's on 737s, something like that."

Norm grunted. "Fate worse than death."

Back on Iririki I had a nightcap and listened to the barman raving about a new evangelist due to preach in Port Vila on Sunday. Would I be present? I told him I had other plans.

"Church plans?"

"No."

He gave me the look Melanesians reserve for backsliders, apostates and other hopeless cases and, mildly irritated, I said I was actually an infrequent church-goer; recently, indeed, I had become interested in Buddhism.

"Buddhism!" He gulped. "The son of *misinaris!*" His demeanour indicated that, in certain quarters, that would really put the *puskat* among the *pijins.*

Grandfather's Presbytery

The heavily forested summit of a dormant marine volcano, or sea-mount, Paama measures six miles by three and, from a distance, has a curiously polychromatic appearance; it shines with many colours. Maurice, my apostolic grandfather, claimed its beauty had "burst upon the eye of Captain Cook, the great navigator" during HMS *Resolution*'s transit of the group in 1774. Maybe so. Yet Cook's decision to remain aboard may have been due to the thousand or more yelling men menacing him from the shore; led by psychotic cannibals, the Paamese had a shocking reputation for cruelty. Maurice, dismissing this bloodlust as mere "hostility to Europeans," chose not to describe how it intensified when the first white traders and planters showed up; local braves went after them with pitiless single-mindedness.

So when he wrote, "In October 1900, Mrs Frater and I landed on the beach of Paama," he chose not to dwell on their terror (though he did admit to "a few misgivings"). Unworldly, newly wed young Scots who'd never been abroad before, they turned up dressed in their Sunday best—only to cower as missiles clanged off their schooner and wild howls drifted over the water. Finally the chief of Liro village, Hilly Along, said they could stay for a week. The schooner crew, having rowed them ashore across a clicking parquet of floating arrows, threw their furniture into the sea and hoisted sail. (Carried in by the tide, the warped drawers and jammed cupboard doors became a feature of the household.)

They stayed for thirty-nine years, and on Paama alone built twenty-one churches. For the hundred and fifty ash-grey people who lived among the blast clouds, lava flows and spatter cones of Lopevi—a beautiful, volatile marine volcano rearing from the sea nearby—they built three more; regularly he preached in all. The cannibals had been transformed into ardent psalm-singing Presbyterians.

In his book *Isles of Illusion* Robert Fletcher, an English planter, described the view from his Epi plantation. "In the distance (about seven sea miles) are two islands, Pauma [*sic*] and Loperi [*sic*]. Pauma is high and bush-clad. At this distance it is an ever-changing impression of wonderful tints . . . Loperi is an active volcano, almost perfectly conical in shape, some 4,000 feet high. The tracks of the lava reflect and refract light in the most astounding way. Every now and then it gives a weirdish growl and crash and a great bubble of smoke forms and bursts, and one can see the shining snake of lava traced out down to the blue."

That was my grandfather's presbytery.

*

In 1922 he wrote his own book. Published by James Clarke & Co. Ltd of Fleet Street, *Midst Volcanic Fires* enjoyed respectable sales and some decent reviews. My parents' only copy came to the attention of giant winged insects—equatorial versions of the book louse—present on Iririki in large numbers. Some just craved ink and paper, others (as if favouring rump, rib or sirloin) went for specific bits of books: the spine's sweet glue and crunchy muslin, biscuity strawboard covers, a comfit of gold leaf licked from the titles. Having reduced it to a pile of powdery dust they removed it almost entirely from my memory.

In London, thirty years later, a magazine editor sent me to interview Sir David Attenborough. I found a brisk, likeable man untroubled by celebrity (television had made his one of the most famous faces in England) who led me into a study where an entire wall was lined with books on the South Pacific. It was the most formidable Oceanian collection I had ever seen and, bemused, I mentioned my ancestral connection. He looked at me curiously. "You're not related to Maurice Frater, are you? Well, well." Then he plucked down a mint-condition copy of *Midst Volcanic Fires*. Holding it again brought back a rush of memories. I asked him to sell it to me. He said, "I really can't, it's very hard to come by."

A week later, out of the blue, he sent a handwritten note and a catalogue from a Cambridge antiquarian bookseller featuring a copy slightly foxed but otherwise in excellent shape; given its rarity, Sir David thought the price a fair one. Buoyed up by this act of kindness I rang the bookseller and, within days, it arrived. I looked through its thick, musty, rough-cut pages and noted bits of turgid Edwardian pulpit prose. Oh *Gawd*. I didn't actually want to read this; I just wanted to own it, so it went on the shelves and there it stayed, unopened, an exotic family trophy.

Years later, visiting a Brisbane flea market, I came upon another copy—hinges cracked, cover stained, spine chipped—going for ten Australian dollars. Handing my money to the gimlet-eyed woman running the stall I boasted rashly, "My grandfather wrote that." She glanced at the banknote but not at the book. "Jeez, my useless husband, this one's actually a hundred bucks!" I walked away; she called me back (who else was going to buy it?) and a deal was struck. It left her smiling.

Next morning I would travel up to Thursday Island, twenty miles beyond Cape York, Australia's northernmost tip and, now suddenly curious, felt an obscure Pacific outpost would be a good place to finally get stuck into Maurice's memoirs.

Thursday is the administrative capital of the hundred Torres Straits islands—which include Tuesday, Wednesday, Friday, Coconut, Booby and Yam—and a famous hideaway for social degenerates. (A Melbourne friend claimed Lord Lucan had been sighted there.) I went to check out its pearling history; while it wasn't in the same league as Broome on the mainland, where in 1917 they brought up the legendary drop-shaped "Star of the West," Thursday Island, or TI, had been a busy centre.

Yet all I found was a cemetery containing the remains of five hundred and sixty Japanese divers, and the tomb of a Kyoto princess who'd owned a fleet of luggers. TI had been effectively fished out. Nobody had seen Lucan, and the degenerates had all moved on to a smaller, unpoliced island where the marijuana grew like prairie wheat. That evening, at the bar of the Federal Hotel, I bought a Foster's stubby and settled down in a corner with Maurice's book.

Certain chapter headings—"Storming the Heathen Citadels," "An Evangelistic Campaign" and "The Winning of Paama"—suggested the Church of Scotland had once been a covert branch of the British War Office. With growing unease I began learning about a side of him that had remained hidden: fundamentalist Maurice, launching his attack on the devil's domain. On Paama "every beam of sunlight, every vision of tropical splendour, seemed to intensify the degradation of a people living in darkness." He bemoaned their "cruel and treacherous nature," claimed "anarchy and the attendant evils of heathenism" were still rampant. "Licentiousness was without limit or restraint of shame . . . under the accumulated influences of the vices which prevailed," the Melanesians "had fallen to the lowest depths of degradation."

Phew!

In the Federal's bar a crowd of drunken islanders, also Melanesian, stood menacing each other. A huge woman grasped a billiard cue in a two-handed axeman's grip, and, as if splitting a log, brought it down on the bald head of an old, wrinkled man. He went "Ungh!" and slumped to his knees. Both sexes began trading blows, the females punching harder and meaner and lower. Soon the males began limping back to the table where the women, impassive, joined them; quietly they resumed their game.

I read on. Maurice had been one of God's warriors, all right, with fulsome references to the Generalissimo peppering every page. Yet, ploughing through all that patronizing, old-time religion I sensed his dawning realization that the locals were, in fact, decent people. "Savage and revolting as was their external appearance," he growled, "they gave us a hearty reception"—acknowledgement of human qualities as village after village welcomed him, offered food and shelter. (At Fangbang, visited with a friend named Weir, a kindly man proffered a pudding made from fern leaves. "Queer tack," remarked Weir, putting it aside. Not so queer, Weir, I thought; here on TI I had already been urged to try *dinagwan,* a bitter concoction of vinegar and pig's blood.)

Since the Paamese coexisted with "evil spirits who peep and mutter at them from trees and mountain caves," Maurice preached remorselessly—unaware his Jesus was gaining a very cool *kastom* resonance. Born of a woman who had never had intercourse, he could walk on water, conjure up feasts from a fish and a loaf of bread, heal the sick with a wave of the hand then, pronounced dead, miraculously return to life and go hurtling off into space; all that was very strong magic. But where exactly had he gone? And where was he now? People who after dark had little to look at but the night sky required stellar waypoints; Maurice, according to my father, would gesture past Zeta Ursae Majoris—a binary star bejewelling the Big Dipper's handle—to a region somewhere up in the Fifth Magnitude; that was where heaven lay. Afterwards, by candlelight, he wrote up the day's events.

Thus, when a witch doctor continued casting malign spells after death, the victims opened his grave, tossed in dynamite and blew his bones to bits. Villagers went "surf-riding"—an activity he had not witnessed before: "Mounting the roller with the surf-board in a slanting direction they reach the crest and . . . career ashore in a maelstrom of foam." A "bevy of little girls" who glimpsed him as they gathered breadfruit in a forest ran for their lives crying, "Woe is me, mother! The white man has caught me!" The glee with which he recorded these encounters indicated more than just a benevolent interest. Something more profound seemed to be taking place. But that could wait. I dined on belly *pwaka,* or chewy fried pork, and went to bed.

*

Next morning, strolling, I came upon the Quetta All Souls Memorial Church. A luminous window depicted a tall-funnelled Victorian liner, awash and sinking, which the verger—speaking Torres Strait Creole, or Broken English—identified as the 3,200 ton steamship *Quetta.* London-bound in 1890, she struck an uncharted rock off TI one wind-still evening and vanished with the loss of a hundred and thirty-three souls. Among the survivors was a baby English girl scooped from the sea by one of the rescue team, a Torres Strait pilot named E. L. Brown. Adopted by her saviour, Cissy Quetta Brown lived out a long and contented life on Thursday.

I knew the pilots, a famous seafaring fraternity, once awaited their southbound rides on TI. "Still do," said the verger.

"They're in the phone book?"

"T for Torres."

*

Every ten years Maurice and Janie got home leave. He spent a good part talking in draughty Scottish halls where, with his good looks, splendid voice and charismatic way with an audience, he made a modest name for himself. People queued. His autograph was requested. Even the press came. Mostly, he just told stories—a favourite being about the night seven new volcanoes erupted on Ambrym. From Paama, a few miles away, Maurice witnessed "a display of fireworks such as is given to few mortals to behold." (One appeared in the grounds of the mission hospital run by his friend Dr Bowie; as Bowie ran for his life "fragments of his house and hospital" roared skywards in a column of compressed steam that rose twenty thousand feet in less than a minute.) Maurice summoned Mr Roxburgh and Herr Grube, local traders who owned cargo launches, then, boarding his own flimsy whaler, led Paama's mercy mission off through choppy seas.

Approaching Ambrym's exploding coast, blizzards of hot ash and cinders engulfed them. Moving through a slurry of dead fish and steaming pumice, they saw fiery rock bombs and fragments of Pele's hair (spun glass) while lava flows tossed trees in the air—visible in the light of the molten magma surging along beneath. Lava entering the sea made it boil. Choking on sulphurous smoke while steering for a beach crammed with refugees, they had to ride scalding tidal waves— a mile offshore an eighth volcano was rising.

Yet, running shuttles all through that extraordinary night, half-deafened by seismic bangs and using Ambrym's "unearthly brilliance" to guide them, he, Roxburgh and Grube brought seven hundred people to safety. One of them, Robert Fletcher—who wrote that fine description of Paama—now found himself "comfortably installed in the house of a very decent missionary." (That surprised me; they should, by rights, have been at each other's throats.)

*

Robert James Addison Gerard Fletcher left Oxford with a good degree and a boxing Blue. Shortly afterwards, in 1910, inspired by R. L. Stevenson's Vailima letters and determined to pursue his own tropical dreams, he set off for the New Hebrides. There, marooned for seven years in a succession of dead-end jobs, he showed his employees much casual violence, scandalously had sex with his house girl, fathered a son he adored (then abandoned) and drank like a fish—the whisky also used to wash down daily cocaine "lozenges." Regular dispatches home to Bohun Lynch, an old university chum, unflinchingly chronicled the progress of his breakdown.

In 1923 Lynch published his letters under the title *Isles of Illusion*. They were never intended for public scrutiny—indeed there are hints that Lynch, who had literary aspirations but no talent, spitefully sprang the anthology on his gifted friend. Fletcher, insisting his name be kept out of it, chose a nom de plume almost comical in its anonymity: Asterisk ("conjectural, obscure, etc." says the *Shorter Oxford*). Yet the book went on to become an Edwardian bestseller.

Fluent in French, Fletcher first found work as an interpreter at the Joint Court. "The witnesses," he grumbled, "are mostly French traders. Can you imagine the babel? On Friday the Court sat from 9 a.m. to 6 p.m. in stifling heat, and at the end of the day I was nearly dead."

The prevailing view, according to the Vila lawyer Edward Jacomb, was that since the natives occupied "one of the lowest rungs in the ladder of the human race" they should be treated like wayward children. Fletcher, untroubled by such niceties, called them niggers and kanakas, complained about their smell, personal habits and hygiene, and treated them with a bizarre mix of brutality and compassion. Once, having beaten a labourer senseless—"my left," bragged the old Blue, "landed right on his squat nose and split it"—he assumed first "the swine was dead." Then, realizing the man was still breathing, he fetched his medical kit and, "by expending much time, drugs and energy I got him round."

Fletcher sneered at his fellow planters for their uncultured ways (a faded set of Beardsley's *Salomé* prints hung in every miserable plantation bungalow he inhabited) and upset their wives by sleeping with Topsy, his good-natured house girl. She gave him two children—the second stillborn after he fought for seventy-two hours to save mother and child. (Having revived Topsy he found himself sitting, exhausted, on her dead baby.) Meanwhile his son knew "with a dog's instinct that I am going to leave him, for he hangs around my neck with 'Darling Daddy, darling Daddy' until I have to cry like the neurotic I am fast becoming. Topsy, too, seems to smell desertion in the air . . . two or three times I have caught her weeping quietly and have been refused explanation. I do feel an utterly damnable cad."

He left the boy (who would now be in his eighties) and Topsy ("my slut") to fend for themselves; there is no record of what became of either. Back home Fletcher returned to teaching. His students recalled a short, corpulent, powerfully built figure with aquiline features set off by a monocle on a black ribbon. Perhaps England softened him a little for, in her autobiography *About Time,* his niece, the novelist Penelope Mortimer, referred to her Uncle Bertie with affection. This troubled, gifted man—who wrote wonderfully well about a corner of the tropics he came to detest—died at Deal, Kent, in 1965, aged eighty-seven.

*

I phoned the Torres Strait Pilots and received an invitation to dinner. Walking through a smoky, ochreous sunset I arrived at a colonial-style house set in a deep garden, was greeted by Wally, a lean, middle-aged man with direct blue eyes. He made it clear the place ran on Christian-name terms. "How you doing, Alex? Glad you could make it. Certainly won't hurt us to see a new face in the mess. It's steak and kidney pie tonight."

We entered a room gleaming with silver trophies, nautical pictures and a gilded honours board. Bottles of excellent Aussie claret stood, uncorked, on a massive sideboard. Four cheery master mariners made me welcome, said decent food helped compensate for the tedium of hanging around. "Waiting for a ship south you can be stuck for days."

As stewards in starched white jackets served swordfish entrées Wally told me the Torres Strait service, founded in 1884, was the longest single-handed pilotage on earth. "Our licensed area covers 1,260 nautical miles, from the Queensland–New South Wales border to Booby Island, a hop and a skip from here. Most of it runs inside the Reef."

"And most of it's in the tropics?"

"All but the last few miles. We wear whites to work."

Greg, due to pick up a Greek at 1 a.m., said recently he'd had a Welshman out of Cardiff—a rarity, due to Britain's sad maritime decline. "Mind you," said Laurie, "we still get the *QE2.* She did the fastest-ever recorded run from Brisbane to Booby. Averaged twenty-six knots. Bloody hair-raising, actually."

"And Lew took the *Ark Royal* down to Sydney," said Charles—who once, bringing a massive nuclear-powered American carrier up to Booby, found the officer of the watch to be a stunningly pretty woman. He sighed. "Smart as paint, and so damn *nice.*"

"You can go from that to some scruffy Korean in one hit," said Wally. "It's a lottery."

I asked about the pearling days. Charles said, "You seen the

Japanese cemetery? The divers worked in suits and helmets, with an air tube up to a pump on the lugger's deck. But in these waters storms can spring up in the blink of an eye."

Laurie said, "A skipper, if he saw one coming, would cut the air tube and go for his life. Leave the poor bastard down there."

"My God," I said.

"In time they'd return and bring up the body. Sign of respect, of course, but also because those suits were worth good money."

These hospitable men told me about life on TI—where the cops ran a sly grog disco, and rough rugby was played; a recent knockout fixture killed one player and put twenty-three more in hospital. "They're combative people. They like a fight."

"And that's just the women," said Charles.

Wally said, "It's a good spot if you can handle the climate. The tropics don't suit everyone. I took the wife to Bali last year—she got rashes, prickly heat, a touch of fever, the lot. Hates the region generally, reckons we're all sitting here just rotting away."

His friends grinned. Laurie swallowed several fluid ounces of brandy. "Cheers!"

I said I had once bought a Balinese picture (of farmers planting rice in a coconut grove) which, had it stayed on Bali, would have disintegrated within twenty years. The island's corruptive humidity, according to the artist, ensured that he, and the dozen apprentices who did much of his routine work (they had painted, leaf by leaf, the blizzards of palm fronds in my landscape), were always employed; everything they made eventually had to be replaced.

"So where's your picture now?" asked Wally.

"At home. And, thirty years on, still in mint condition."

*

Mission work, early in the twentieth century, reflected the manly ideals of Dr David Livingstone ("Fear God, and work hard"), who died while saying his prayers beside a malarial African swamp. In Scotland it became fashionable to support such causes. Working-class Maurice, a carter's son from Cumbernauld, found himself hobnobbing with some very grand families, saw his first crystal chandelier in an Edinburgh banker's house once visited by Burns. His fans gave generously—not just money for Bibles, but money to teach benighted, far-away tribes about British values. Literacy would lead to an understanding of free-market economics, taxes, democracy, self-denial and the Protestant work ethic. (Most savages, Maurice gloomily reported, were indolent by nature; he kept talking about the dignity of labour while battling against "the contempt which the heathen attach to it.")

He had written *Midst Volcanic Fires* to celebrate the ideals Livingstone once preached and, finishing it, I realized that behind all the rhetoric lurked a fine travel book. He had a sharp eye for detail and wrote crisp, grammatically perfect, fastidiously punctuated prose. Yet I wondered what they had made of it on Paama. Indeed, I wondered if anyone there even remembered him.

*

I made my first return trip to Vanuatu in 1980, when Britain and France announced the islands would finally be granted independence. In Port Vila, after a day spent talking to morose British officials, I happened upon some Paama men in a bar and mentioned the family connection. Later I got a call. Was I free this weekend? If so, on Saturday morning I should catch the little Air Melanesia plane up to Lamen Bay, on Epi. I did, and found a decrepit old launch, its decking slippery with fish scales, waiting at the end of the grass strip. Its young, unsmiling three-man crew started the engine and set off, very fast, for Paama.

We motored past Lopevi, rearing from the sea and active today, swirling smoke indicating that its own weather system was producing winds around the summit. Paama hove into view: "set in opal-tinted waters," Maurice wrote, "and clothed with the luxuriant vegetation of the Tropics, it presented a beautiful spectacle with the primeval bush stretching from the water's edge to the summit of the mountains." Yet, during his time, earthquakes had sent "the cliffs falling into the sea." Then you couldn't see the island for dust but now, on a fine morning with unrestricted visibility, it glittered.

"Where are we heading exactly?" I asked.

"Liro," said the youth at the wheel.

Liro was the village where Maurice and Janie built their mission; that, however, had been eighty years ago. We passed a headland and turned into a wide green bay where dense crowds had massed; hundreds of voices carried strongly across the water. "What's going on?" I demanded.

"They singing a hymn," said the youth.

"A *hymn*?"

He grinned and cut the motor. "They waiting for you. Now you must jump in the sea."

I jumped, and, standing waist-deep, watched an arthritic old woman labour towards me. She carried a pink sunshade and a bunch of flowers and, breathlessly, commanded me to stay still. For a full half-hour she shaded my head (but never spoke another word) as, on the beach, a white-suited pastor prayed and preached. Finally beckoned ashore, I faced a shouting, jostling mob determined to shake hands with a direct descendant of a local legend. Escorted to the church I saw, behind the pulpit, a smallish picture of Jesus hung beside a giant gilt-framed photograph of Maurice—smiling broadly, with a cocky, vice-regal gleam in his eye.

At the mission guest house the Elders led in two skeletal crones, whiskery and half-blind. They hugged me, sobbing uncontrollably. "His laundry girls," said the smiling Elders. "Now they have seen his grandson. They can die happy!"

I felt swept along by events utterly beyond my control. "Have you read his book?" I asked uneasily.

"What book?" They held my hands and urged me to take Sunday service next morning. I agreed to preach but not to pray, made my sermon a plea for political unity—heard by a congregation four hundred strong. During the pig-roast that followed, a brisk little earthquake shook the mangoes out of the trees, and I began pondering a question that, on and off, has troubled me ever since: what cryptic hold had my dead grandfather over all these folks?

*

That church, built by Maurice, was the one flattened by a hurricane a couple of years after my visit. Back in London, after Lewey Sahe had relayed news of a new church over dinner in 1992, I phoned the Whitechapel Bell Foundry and learned they had many models suitable for a South Seas island. Would a tenor bell fit the bill, I wondered, or would the Liro folk want a big bass bell with an ear-splitting bong? I couldn't raise Lewey, but spoke to other friends in Vila. None knew what was happening in Paama. "Don't worry, Lewey will send word," they said. But he never did.

*

In 1999, down south again to gather material for this book, I made an early stop at Paama. Almost two decades after my last visit it had finally acquired its own *efil*—a sharply sloping paddock set between the sea and primary forest—on which my Twin Otter made a grass-strip version of a carrier landing. This time I found no crowds, just the elfin figure of Louis Obes, the jockey-sized paramount chief, now bald and self-consciously missing his front teeth.

A retired ship's master, Louis had taken rickety steamers around hazardous reef-strewn waters as calmly as he helped steer Paama through its post-independence political storms. My arm draped around his thin shoulders, we headed for Paama's only motor vehicle. "So how's the new church coming on?"

"It was finished two months ago."

"Finished!" I stared at him.

He chuckled. "We had big celebrations. They cost two million *vatu*! You should have been here."

But nobody had invited me. "Have you got a bell, Louis?"

"A *bell*?" He coloured slightly. "Oh!" He gave an uneasy yip of laughter and, as we went pitching down boulder-strewn gradients in the truck, refused to meet my eye. "Where's Lewey Sahe?" I asked.

"In Santo, Luganville police station."

"Did you know he asked me for a bell?"

"Uh, maybe. Yes, I tink so."

They'd forgotten all about it.

Liro, the largest of Paama's twenty-one villages, lies in a grassy amphitheatre set between high jungly hills and a black sand bay. Outside the *nakamal*, or meeting house, people waited by a fly-swarmed table heaped with sweet biscuits and sliced pawpaw—the table itself surrounded by croton twigs haphazardly stuck in the ground. After a hymn—*"Hapi dei! Hapi dei! Jisas i mekem mi mi fri"*—I was formally welcomed by Andrew Manoa, Liro's custom *jif*. Yet his words seemed oddly threatening. Moving around the twigs, pointing and declaiming, he said I could go from here to there, could walk in this direction or that, indicated landmarks that delineated access; all others, by inference, and possibly under pain of death, remained exclusion zones. I must stay in my territory.

Kastom, it seemed, had been revived on Paama. Maurice fought to stamp it out, yet I was receiving a custom welcome from a custom leader who (I later discovered) was also an elder of the church, and leader of its male-voice choir. *Samting* very odd was going on. Custom people could argue that the sun moved around the earth and water flowed uphill—yet I sensed other, hidden currents here.

A silence fell. Then, during my own stumbling speech, I spotted a young white couple in the crowd, and over the pawpaw and biscuits met Anton and Erin Zuiker, Peace Corps volunteers from Ohio. Anton, with clever, aristocratic features and a gold earring, had edited a successful Cleveland magazine; now he worked as a teacher while Erin, dark-haired and pretty, managed Liro's clinic. He said, "For the new church celebrations they re-enacted your grandparents' arrival. I was Maurice and Erin was Janie, we were on the beach wearing old costumes. Did you know they were led here by a white bird?"

I did not. But did they share my bewilderment at the stubborn way Paama clung to their memory?

He shrugged. "It can get a bit heavy."

Louis walked me up to a single-storey building with white-timbered walls and a red corrugated-iron roof. It looked like a large villa—the pool, patio and barbecue area doubtless located round the back—and, idly wondering who might own such a place, I saw a crudely painted sign: "Rev Maurice Frater Memorial Church 1900–1939."

Louis said, "What you tink?"

I thought Maurice might have questioned a set of dates implying his life had begun when he arrived on Paama, and ended the year he sailed away.

"It's great! He'd be very proud."

"Elders are waiting inside."

Outside, though, on the grass, stood a giant bucket-shaped industrial container. Made from pig iron, it had been designed to run on elevated rails and tip its contents into a trough of industrial sludge.

Louis grew uneasy. "It's from a New Caledonia manganese factory. It is a manganese tub."

Then it dawned on me. "Louis, it's your *bell*!"

He sighed. "But nobody can *move* it. So we are using this." He pointed to an oxygen cylinder strung from a tree. "We hit it with a spanner."

I picked up a rock and, whacking the manganese tub to test it for pitch and resonance, got a thud like a slammed car door.

Louis gave me an anxious glance. "Is the English bell still available?"

Suddenly fed up with their careless ways, I said nothing.

Shrewdly, he took it for yes. Indoors, several lounging elders straightened as he broke the news. A new photograph hung behind the pulpit: Maurice and Janie posing together, wearing strained smiles. It was stiflingly hot, and I thought of my friend Ian Marshall, tropical architect turned maritime painter, who once built a small coral church in Kilifi, near Mombasa. His wizardry—he wryly called it "being climate-responsive"—produced a structure with a double-ventilated roof and, located at the front and rear, contrasting pressure zones; one faced windward, the other leeward. Both caught the prevailing monsoon breeze and, like synchronized weather fronts, ensured that a constant current of cool air funnelled through. (Then he'd crowned it with a four-bell peal from the Whitechapel Foundry.)

Louis asked me to say something. I said their church had neither turret nor tower, no place to actually hang a bell. What should we do?

Donald Mail, a storekeeper with a forceful personality and a prizefighter's build, took charge. As a whispered conference got under way I leafed through a hymn book, its lyrics in Paamese and titles in English, and many, like the declamatory "Paama for Christ," bearing Maurice's name. (The British national anthem, "Ahi mutati Queen," had also been credited to him.)

Janie's "Work, For the Night Is Coming" triggered memories of a bony, dour, taciturn woman driven by duty to the point of exhaustion; though several years younger than her husband she looked like his mother. Had this, I wondered, been a marriage made in heaven? She was stiff, awkward and shy, he restless and endlessly engaging; with his easy charm, vivid blue eyes and—even in middle age—crisp, shiny black curls (he claimed descent from a band of Border gypsies), Maurice effortlessly bent people to him; she remained stranded, always in his shadow.

Her father had been a minister in a deprived, working-class area of Glasgow, his—Joseph—a town carrier who carted goods between Cumbernauld and Glasgow in his four-horse dray. Maurice, tipped by friends as a future Moderator of the Church of Scotland, was supposed to lead both families into the sunny uplands of middle-class gentility. But, dazzled by Livingstone and R. L. Stevenson, and subversively urged on by *her* grandfather (Alexander Russell, a Clydeside ship-worker and frustrated explorer), he whisked Janie off to the deep tropics. In place of a brownstone manse he built her a pandanus-palm shack, instead of admitting deferential, cap-in-hand folk wanting a wee moment with the reverend, she confronted savages—naked but for dwarf haystacks over their genitals—demanding guns and whisky.

Donald Mail roused me by noisily clearing his throat. He said a dedicated bell shack would be erected. I said OK, and asked why the pulpit seemed so familiar.

"It's the original one," he said, "made in Scotland from oak. Maurice ship arrowroot and cotton there, they ship top-quality furniture back. *Nambawan* businessman!"

That was true. An advocate of free enterprise, he persuaded the Paamese (despite their "reputation for stinginess") to plant cotton for export and give 10 per cent to the church. Though an early collection yielded only "£7 14s. 9d., made up of 585 coins"—*he counted the coins!*—after "the entrance of Christ into their hearts unloosed their purse strings" there was "joy and thanksgiving when the handsome total of £125 10s. 9d. was announced."

"I have a question," I said and paused, wondering just how to put this. "Maurice left sixty years ago. That's a very long time. Why have you called this church after him?"

Donald Mail spoke at once. "He brought the Gospel to this citadel of heathenism. We were sons of the devil."

"Worshipping hideous idols," said Louis. "Making vile practices."

A white-whiskered old man whispered, *"Eating our enemies."*

*

Janie, and many other mission wives transported to the tropics, drew strength from the deeds of Mary Slessor, the daughter of an Aberdeen shoemaker. When her father's alcoholism left the family destitute she took a job, aged eleven, in a local factory; seventeen years later, in 1865, we find her working in Calabar, south-eastern Nigeria, busy putting an end to such rituals as the strangling of twins and trial by poison. Then, introducing measures to tackle the women's thirst for gin, she soon had the roaming bands of female drunks singing temperance hymns instead. "In our immediate neighbourhood," she reported, "it is an extremely rare thing to see a woman intoxicated, even on feast days and funerals." Also, she argued furiously with the parents of her mission girls who, as soon as they learned to read, were deemed ready for marriage and whisked back to their villages for "seclusion and fattening."

Ma, as she was known, struggled with Calabar's isolation, its squalor, its weather ("the climate and its forces," she sighed, "are leagued against us"), its sorcerers, spirits and goblins, and forests so menacing it was "dangerous for children to go without an armed escort." A confrontational Aberdonian, when surrounded by angry mobs she simply glared them down. Yet she grumbled at having to do all this, as a female, on her own. "Is it fair to expect results under such circumstances?"

Quite fair, said the men back at head office. So, enlisting various newspaper editors to her cause, she mounted a personal recruitment campaign aimed at the "warm-hearted" women of Britain. I imagine Janie's pulse quickening as she came upon, "Don't grow up a nervous old maid! Gird yourself for the battle, and keep your heart young . . . I'm witness to the perfect joy and satisfaction of a single life."

Mission work was done by males. Around the evangelical fraternity some giant egos competed for the kind of celebrity Mary had won. No question, though, she had been lucky; the press were seduced by her sex and, in Calabar, God gave her challenges to die for. How could any Paamese outrage ever match the gruesome newsworthiness of twin-strangling? *It rankled.*

*

The hundred-year-old mission bungalow, with its million-dollar views, still stood, somehow glued together by its rotting timbers. Painters had left the walls a streaky, silvery blue and the doors deep burgundy—almost matching the rich ochre of the rusted iron roof. I found the place locked; this was now the office of the Liro Council, and its staff had gone home. A veranda (where in the evenings Maurice told jokes and declaimed poetry) now displayed notices relating to sewing circles, shipping movements, earthquake emergencies, play groups and sexually transmitted diseases.

The mission guest house, a wooden structure on stilts, was located nearby. I sat on the steps, watching the sun sink into a cloud-bound horizon and listening to Louis listing the missionaries who came afterwards: Ham Bell, Mr Childs, John Poon (John *Poon?*), Mr Good and so on, giving their dates and years in office as if they had been Prime Ministers or legendary football coaches. An unshaven man in a Mickey Mouse T-shirt wandered up and took my hand. "That was a good sermon you preached."

I stared at him. "Sorry?"

"When you spoke in the church."

"It was almost twenty years ago!"

"Well, you certainly made me think." To Louis he said, "I am looking for the pastor."

Louis said the pastor was in the forest. The man walked away. As the sun slid into the sea and a cool breeze started out of a fiery sky, Louis stood. "Some funny tings happening here." He shyly ducked his head. "I will come tomorrow."

Whatever problems these people were facing, I reflected, they still looked to my dead grandfather to pull them through. And, since he did not seem to be responding, I had an uneasy feeling they expected me to do something in his place.

*

In Havana, Cuba, darkness steals over a theatrical jumble of decaying real estate—pre-baroque, baroque, neoclassical, Moorish—and hides the ravages wrought by years of neglect and economic incompetence. Then when the lights come on (and the stars come out) the city seems to grow weightless and float. Once I dined in a gorgeous nineteenth-century Italianate townhouse with a curving facade and sculpted gable elevations. A tout had brought me to this "home restaurant," newly enfranchised by the regime and seating twelve. His mother cooked *aljibe,* a dish of chicken, rice, black-bean stew and fried bananas, which I ate beneath photographs of his dead father's idols. Yuri Gagarin and Betty Grable I knew, but who was the third? "Capablanca, chess master." Yet the masonry bore apocalyptic cracks, many of the carved adornments had dropped off; I saw more plaster than paint. He told me, "Maybe next year it won't be here. Houses fall all the time."

So a muffled whump in the next street meant another baroque villa had imploded; walking back to my hotel, listening out for the structural death rattles likely to precede each, I found myself obsessed with thoughts of decay—not unusual in the tropics, with so many reminders (the stench of uncollected garbage, the hasty way its dead were buried, the cloying putrescence often emanating from its sick).

Paama, too, had a Cuban element: vegetation decomposing in the forest, fish rotting on the beach, human effluent carried by the breeze. And here I had intimations of my own decay when, without warning, something began happening to my hands. Gradually the outer fingers on both seemed to turn raptorial, curling inwards and locking against the palms. I would sit in the mission guest house, staring at them, fighting back panic. What did this signify?*

Man's ultimate role, I told myself, is to supply the trace elements which nourish higher plants and lower animals. Each of us ends up fertilizing something, yet in the tropics it's all so wildly accelerated the whole region seems to be feeding constantly on itself.

*

---

* Back in London my doctor said, "Oh, that's Dupuytren's contracture. It's a flexion deformity; Mrs Thatcher had it when she was PM. I must say you've got quite an interesting droop there."

Named for the French army surgeon who first treated it, the cause remained unknown—though he warned it might be alcohol-related. "Better get your liver tested."

Summoned back to be told, with little attempt to hide his surprise, that my liver was in good shape, I asked what people were most at risk.

"Well, allegedly, the descendants of Vikings. But I've also heard coachmen mentioned. Horse-handlers."

"My great-grandfather handled horses."

"Well, I suppose you might have inherited it; frankly, it's all a bit of a mystery. Surgery's the only answer, but there's no particular rush: you'll live."

An elder told me Maurice possessed a mirror in which he could see every inch of the island, look into every house and peep behind every tree. I guessed he had once told them the legend of Prester John, who used such a mirror to survey his kingdom (and slept on a bed of cold sapphire to subdue his lust). Now, by attributing this magic to my grandfather, they were quietly bringing him into the *kastom* tradition.

In recent years there had been twenty fatalities caused by shark attacks. *Kastom* said each victim died as punishment for a sin or crime, the shark was merely the executioner. That was its job.

The best-known rain-maker lived over on Ambrym. Able to conjure up deluges at will, he was friendly and approachable and, if the lines weren't down, could be contacted by phone.

*

Lopevi, the graceful, classically proportioned oceanic volcano on which Maurice erected his trinity of churches, reared from the sea just three miles away. Though elegant as Mount Fuji, it had a nasty disposition, steamed constantly, bubbled and spat like a leaky kettle and in 1970 erupted so violently its population was evacuated to Epi and warned never to return. Maurice had written, "To appease its wrath, the sacred men sent up periodically to the lip of the crater, 5,000 feet above sea-level, numbers of young fellows with loads of cocoanuts to throw in as a peace-offering." He had respect for the resilient islanders who inhabited its few acres of coastal moraine—and enjoyed telling his Scottish lecture audiences about preaching in a smoking wasteland of ash and sulphur. One fine morning I said to Louis, "Could we go over?"

He found a fisherman prepared to take us. "It is a very small boat. He says it will cost twelve thousand *vatu*."

That was one hundred dollars. For half a dozen sea miles.

"Fair price?"

"Very fair," said Louis. "He is also an elder of the church, very devout man."

Then I understood what Louis was implying; a sizeable chunk of my fare would go into the collection plate. At Donald Mail's store I ran into Anton. Had he and Erin ever been to Lopevi? He shook his head. "Want to come? In about an hour?"

"Erin had dengue fever a while back. She's not feeling so great today. And Lopevi's been pretty restless these past few weeks. Noisy, smoking like crazy." He paid for his loaf and grinned. "But hey, why not? Sure, I'll come. Love to."

The boat turned out to be little more than a dinghy welded from sheets of steel. The elder, lean and prematurely balding, had brought a couple of friends along. Carrying six souls plus a spare outboard his boat rode low in the water—and took more over the bows while riding some big oceanic swells. Anton, snug in his Peace Corps life jacket, looked unconcerned as Louis announced, "We are now, actually, in mid-Pacific." Lopevi, over a mile high with a feather of superheated steam flapping from its perfect cone, cast an ecliptic shadow that soon wiped out the eastern sky. I saw vertiginous flanks stained with black basalt and biscuit-coloured rhyolite and, fringing its shore like moss, the forest that once harboured the villages. An owl made a low, leisurely pass, flying fish whirred by like thrown knives. "Catch one!" yelled Louis.

The beach—hot charcoal sand, ochre rocks, scuttling green lizards—was remarkable for its silence; not a breath of wind, no sound from the volcano, not the smallest swish of surf. Then, from somewhere, we heard voices and surreal bursts of laughter. *A party?* We headed inland. Trekking through tangled jungle we picked up wood smoke and snatches of talk so animated I began to feel a gatecrasher's unease. Louis called out, a man answered; he smiled. "I know these people." The clearing contained two huts and, seated around the embers of a fire, five middle-aged couples who seemed to have turned breakfast into happy hour.

They welcomed us with cries of pleasure, shook our hands and cracked jokes. Louis, beaming, said they were an exiled Lopevi family who had returned for a week to tend their gardens. "Meet Esau. He is head man." Esau, displaying lots of twinkly charm backed by a faintly authoritarian manner, said, "My father was baptized by Maurice Frater." I stifled a groan but everyone smiled, ripples of merriment eddied around the clearing.

Anton remarked on a clothes line hung with bunches of pink-stalked greenery. A handsome, grey-haired woman in a blue cotton dress identified it: wild cabbage. We must stay for lunch and try some, they would catch a fish, cook yams, grate coconuts . . . No, no, we said. The men grabbed bush knives and led us off through a forest which, as if plugged into the volcano, boasted its own interior lighting system. Within the emerald dimness bright birds shot around like rockets, tropical flowers gleamed and shone. "It's the Garden of Eden," I said to Louis, who muttered, "Yea, verily." Someone shinned up a tree and returned with an island apple the size of a cabbage, honey-sweet on the tongue. Esau said, "We have an abundance of fruit and vegetables, also many nuts."

Later, scooping ash from shards of cement, we found the foundations of two churches, and in an isolated garden paused while a man cupped a hand to his ear and pretended to hear his melons creaking as they swelled. Back in the clearing the women had grilled a fish and squeezed fresh lime juice. We drank the juice from tin mugs and ate the fish with our fingers. I asked if they weren't afraid of staying on Vanuatu's most volatile volcano. Esau said, "Only the women are afraid." The handsome woman in the blue dress laughed. "The women are only afraid when it goes BANG! And, Esau, so are you!"

As they stood waving us off the Elder confided in me. "That family owns the volcano. *Esau tells it when to erupt.*"

I stared at him. "How does he do that?"

"What do you mean?"

"How do you tell a volcano to erupt?"

He gave me a patient look. "You talk to it."

*

The last volcano I visited had been privately owned, in the Philippines. Attorney Dante Carandang, a beefy, good-natured lawyer who wore a baseball cap bearing the legend "Guns and Ammo," was accompanied by his friend Elsa Payumo, an ex-beauty queen (Miss Caltex) now turned politician. The Taal volcano, in the centre of a large lake, lay seventy miles from Manila. Aboard Dante's Toyota-powered *banca,* or double-hulled canoe, I learned the lake was itself a volcanic crater; the Taal's crater contained another lesser lake suspended a hundred feet above the first like a small secondary prism. "It hasn't erupted for eighty years, it's actually the most unique volcano in the country," said Dante, who talked mostly about cock-fighting. "Chicks from Texas are the best but, take it from an old cocker like me, they need plenty of luxury food and vitamins, such as B12 for stress."

At the foot of Dante's volcano we encountered a Hong Kong film crew shooting a kung fu movie, at the top a target bearing the life-sized outline of a man. Dante handed me a Colt .45 and bade me shoot. It made an appalling noise and he, routinely hitting the target's heart and head, grew exasperated by my inability to hit nothing but its elbows. "Are you trying to kill this guy or just stop him doing press-ups?" he cried. Elsa, no mean shot herself, said tropical volcanoes erupted more violently than those in temperate regions. "As the earth spins around you get centrifugal force. It throws all that molten rock and stuff into the middle. The pressure under us now is looking for a weak point. And we're on it!"

*

At the mission guest house one showered under a pulley-operated bucket filled from a barrel of well water. Holes punched in the bucket's base meant you needed a dozen hoists for a basic scrub, six more to wash your hair. Early one morning, woken by a thunderstorm, I dispensed with these procedures and (having checked there was no one about) carried out my ablutions on the back steps in the sheeting rain. Later, finding mice had been at my bread, I went to Donald Mail's dim, airless little grocery for more. Avoiding my eye he muttered, "Once we went naked also. But Maurice teach us that is wrong."

Oh, *Christ*. "I'm certain no one saw me."

"Many did! Women too." Today his shop smelled of kerosene, treacle and yellow laundry soap.

I changed the subject. "Can't you do something about the weather?"

He handed me a hard white loaf. "Maybe."

"How?"

"There is a place up there," He jerked a thumb towards the hills. "One hour walk. You just lie on the ground and tell it—*stop!*"

"And it does?"

"The rain? Sure."

I gave him his money. "Lie which way? Looking at the sky?"

"No, other way, face on ground."

As I left he cried, "Jesus loves you, Alex!"

So that was all right. Or was Jesus now *kastom* too?

*

In the forest I came upon three sweating, axe-wielding youths clearing trees for a new garden. Wouldn't burning them be easier? But they knew better. Fire used to clear tropical bush destroyed timber, wood pulp and leaf manure; for every acre burned nine hundred pounds of nitrogen went up in smoke—leaving nothing but potash to be leached away by the first showers. (Pierre Gourou, in *The Tropical World,* stated that a mere 2½ acres of rainforest at Yangambi in the Belgian Congo was found to contain 30 tons of litter and dead wood, 39 tons of leaves, 55 tons of twigs, 364 tons of branches, creepers and stems of small trees, 210 tons of trunks of average diameter and 266 tons of large boles; that totalled 964 tons of useful organic matter.) A treasure house awaited those who preferred the blade to the flame.

Maurice, by nature a settler himself, believed people should stay at home. How could an eye be kept on nomadic hunter-gatherers who remained beyond the mission ambit? Settlements were the answer, communities of agrarian families bound to house and garden. The tropics, he knew, abounded with fateful stories of those who strayed. Many Portuguese migrants in Brazil, for example, gave up their farms to go scavenging for logwood, *cravo* bark, maté leaves, ipecacuanha root, oil-yielding *babassú* nuts, *mangabeira* gum, the poisonous *timbó, tonka* beans, fan-palm wax and other jungle products European importers clamoured for. Townships were abandoned, sugar plantations allowed to rot.

Often, when they returned to their old lives, inertia set in. Families resuming rubber-collecting along the Rio Negro at the turn of the century couldn't be bothered to grow food. Thirty years later these riverine people, still lounging in their hammocks, continued to eat shipped-in junk—worthless beans and dried fish (while live, juicy, protein-rich fish jumped all around)—and produce degenerate, malformed children. Maurice raised his own pigs, chickens, fruit and vegetables, wielded his own spade, led by example. Work for progress! Dig for the Lord!

(But he missed a trick when it came to Liro's big harvest of juicy Swatow oranges. In French Guinea wily Jesuits noted the abundance grown by the villagers of Juta Fallon—who subsisted on oranges during times of famine—and by 1939 had turned that obscure, febrile little country into the world's top exporter of aromatic essential oil extracted from the cast-off skins. For a time, in the early thirties, he dreamed of exporting Panama hats. Popularized by Teddy Roosevelt and Renoir, the originals were made not in Panama but in rural Ecuador. There magicians, weaving reed filaments *under water,* created hats so supple they could be pulled through wedding rings. The Paamese, however, were never likely to master such artistry, so his idea, born of the prices they fetched in Glasgow, came to nothing.)

*

As I sat, one evening, on the guest house steps drinking rum from a teacup, the man in the Mickey Mouse T-shirt wandered up. I offered him some, but he just wanted to talk and, after a moment's reflection, told me Christianity on Paama was in decline. "People are losing interest." He took a deep breath. "We need a new idea, a new God everyone is happy with."

I stared at him. "What kind of God?"

He shrugged.

Then, out of the blue, I remembered the Thursday Island Solution.

There I had called on Jaki Gothard, the energetic young editor of the *Torres News* (circulation 1,650), who said, "You should meet Tony Hall-Matthews. He's Bishop of Carpentaria and he's invented a whole new theology for the tropics. Imagine!"

I became interested. "Do you think he'd see me?"

"Yeah, sure, he's one of my columnists."

She made a call, learned he was now away on Wednesday Island but, by Friday, would be back on Thursday; this was Tuesday. She shrugged and made an appointment. "Tony flies his own Cessna; that guy puts in more hours than a Qantas captain."

So on Friday I reported to his elegant wooden residence. Mrs Hall-Matthews said her husband was running late. She gave me tea and I admired a tapestry depicting a tiny aeroplane crossing brightly stitched seas and islands. "That was done by local women. Tony carries everything in the Cessna—parishioners, hymn books, communion wine, even coffins. I have a two-way radio in the kitchen and he talks to me on that. A typical message might be that he's just left Yam for Coconut and should be home for dinner."

Bishop Hall-Matthews—Tony Carpentaria—came hurrying through his garden. Stocky, keen-eyed, darkly bearded and faintly piratical, he had the kind of energy that gave no quarter to the climate. It was hard to equate this forceful priest with the Anglican spooks who, tacitly conniving with the Australian government in its genocidal policy towards the islanders a century earlier, had defined their role as "soothing the pillow of a dying race."

When he spoke I detected excitement in his voice. "One of the things we're doing is developing a Torres Strait theology. It's an attempt to merge tribal beliefs with Christian ones. The Bomai Malu cult has a hero, a godlike figure called Malu who has turned up on Murray Island as an octopus. There is an understanding that when Malu died, he died for us all. So could Jesus, they are asking, be Malu incarnated?"

"And could he?"

He smiled. "Why not?"

*

My friend gave a soft whistle of astonishment.

"Jesus is an *octopus?*"

"Yes." I wanted to know if the octopus featured in the *kastom* theogony of deities and he shrugged; maybe as a minor godling. But, he wondered, how did the crucifixion fit into this? What kind of cross could accommodate a Christ with eight arms? He did not see Malu ever uniting Paama and, frankly, neither did I.

*

I had business in Vila and, on my last evening, the church folk threw a party. By the light of hurricane lanterns we feasted on *laplap,* pork, fish and rice prepared by women required to remain in the shadows until the men had filled their plates. Afterwards Liro's ancient generator—a huge bellowing diesel normally only switched on to power the photo-copier—erupted into life. Everyone filed out to sit beneath a huge orange moon and watch the headmaster's collection of rock videos. All at once I was weary of Paama. A woman passed me some mosquito repellent. "It smell of lilies," she said. It also carried faint, disturbing overtones of something else, and a word suddenly came to mind: *cadaverine,* the volatile amine that accompanies putrefaction.

*

The truck supposed to take me to the airfield never showed up. Louis said, "We must find a boat." Sheltering from a shower we heard the sound of an approaching *aotbod* and waved down a fisherman. He dropped us at the head of a forest path. It led to a bay bordered by a boulder field, satin-smooth and slick with rain, which had to be crossed. I took my neck brace from my bag, went to strap it on then, realizing it would impede mobility, put it back. Louis stared, wide-eyed. I told him I had a whiplash injury (an old souvenir from the Karakoram Highway) while telling myself the plane was due in twelve minutes and there wouldn't be another for three days. There was no alternative route.

The boulders seemed to keep tipping, one unsecured boulder pitching me onto the next while small seismic clicks and rumbles underfoot indicated the whole edifice might soon slide into the sea. Lurching along, hearing the voice of the neurologist back in London's National Hospital— *"One heavy fall could paralyse you for life"*—I knew this was heavy-fall terrain of the most consummate kind. Soon sweat was impairing my vision, fear my sense of balance. Louis saw me start to stagger and wobble. "Put your hand on my shoulder." We seemed to progress like this for miles but, probably after a mere two hundred yards, this calm, sure-footed man led me off the field and onto another forest path.

In a clearing we came upon an ancient, skeletal woman washing clothes in a bucket. She had deeply sunken cheeks and eyes milky with cataracts, and when he spoke to her, suddenly scuttled over and seized my hand. Louis said, "Her husband passed away ten years ago."

I expressed regret.

"Maurice married them."

She began to cry. I heard the plane.

"You are a link with her past."

I went to remove my hand but she wouldn't let go.

"You are bringing back memories."

I tried again and the grip became vicelike. She sobbed quietly, yet when finally I gave a sharp, exasperated tug, her old tendons tightened like whipcord; briefly I considered clouting her with my bag.

At Paama the planes spent only minutes on the ground; for the pilots it was a bank-raid stop, in and out. "Plane's coming, Louis," I muttered. He secured my release with a few quiet words then, running hard, we arrived at the ocean end of the field to find the Twin Otter parked at the farther, forest end. Vanair's agent, chucking in the cargo, grunted, "Flight closed." Louis gasped, "This is grandson of Maurice Frater!" and the man said, "Flight open—but give me ticket quick." Several elders wandered across the grass. How had they got here? "In the truck." *In the truck?* "Yes. We have come to say goodbye and to confirm that you will bring us a bell." I said, "I've been in touch with the bell people." We were airborne even before I fastened my seat belt. Lopevi was smoking like a coal-fired steamer today, Paama seemed irradiated with light and colour. As they fell away I felt a surge of relief—finally freed from the spell of my immortal grandfather.

*

Claude Lévi-Strauss once encountered three Jesuit Fathers who had established a mission station near the remote Mato Grosso village of Utiarity. They comprised "a Dutchman who prayed to God, a Brazilian who was preparing to civilize the Indians and a Hungarian—a former nobleman and an expert hunter—whose function it was to keep the missionaries supplied with game." But the Hungarian, who had evidently entered the priesthood to atone for a tempestuous youth, grew surly and unreliable, perhaps suffering an attack of *coup de bambou*. After the Dutchman had cast out his devils, he put him on bread and water for a fortnight—though there wasn't a crumb to be had for miles around.

Maurice, however, always worked solo. Yet, the men he came most to admire in his latter years had been two grandees from the English upper classes—who bonded so closely he came to see one as the flint, the other the fire.

The Place with the Drive-in Volcano

On 11 August 1849 the *Undine,* a twenty-two-ton schooner, arrived in New Hebridean waters under the command of a scholarly Old Etonian named George Augustus Selwyn. Son of a top London constitutional lawyer, and a friend of Gladstone's, he had a remarkable talent for seamanship; always pushing himself and his boat to the limit, wiry, sunburnt Selwyn specialized in voyages of high risk and extreme audacity. Yet they were merely his way of getting where he needed to go—and going the way he liked best. (Years later his son John recalled "the dingy cabin of his little schooner, creaking and groaning in a gale of wind, and a figure in wet and shiny oilskins coming down from the long watch on deck to see how my mother and I were faring below.")

Selwyn was an authentic Victorian hero. Bold, clever, an accomplished artist and outstanding linguist—new languages were simply downloaded into his brain—he had exceptional good looks and a personality that could charm the birds off the trees. His was a life measured in superlatives.

After Cambridge he joined the Anglican Church and, aged only thirty-one, was appointed Bishop of New Zealand—a job offering excellent sailing opportunities. These improved even further when, idly studying his letters patent one day, he realized the Lambeth Palace cartographers had accidentally quintupled the size of his diocese. The area assigned to him was supposed to include all the territory between 50° and 34° south; they, however, had extended it from 50° south to 34° *north*—ranging right up into Melanesia and the tropics. Instead of pointing out the error he gleefully prepared the *Undine* for sea.

For Europeans this was a volatile region. The natives, seeing their sandalwood stolen and their able-bodied males kidnapped for overseas sugar plantations, reckoned the only sure way of dealing with a white man was to kill him. Whenever Selwyn anchored off a new village his companions remained aboard while he swam ashore with presents tucked in his hat. Once there his warmth and transparency did the trick—while his attempts to start learning their language on the spot meant, often enough, that potentially murderous confrontations ended in laughter. (Any close shaves he put down to his own clumsiness.)

Over a four-year period he visited fifty islands. But, instead of establishing Anglican missions, he shipped, with the approval of their families, forty bright kids back to Auckland for a year at St John's Anglican College. There, along with English, Bible studies, general studies and the liberal arts, they were taught—reflecting his own fascination with Melanesia—about their own cultures and traditions: of these, only cannibalism and headhunting were deemed wrong. Back in the islands an Old School network evolved. His worldly teenage leaders helped their communities with the dizzying pace of change; one, having observed how things were done abroad, built himself a two-storeyed house, then advised those neighbours wanting similarly spacious accommodation.

So many clamoured to join the scheme Selwyn needed help and, on furlough in England, persuaded twenty-seven-year-old John Coleridge Patteson to be his chaplain. Coming from a similar background—Eton and Oxford, a linguist (specializing in Arabic), son of a judge, related to the poet on his mother's side—Patteson complemented him perfectly. Impressed by the spirited cannibals' sons in his Auckland classes, he treated them "as if they were Eton boys."

One day, cruising through the New Hebrides aboard *Undine,* they moored off tiny Mota island where the people, owning neither clothes, adornments nor weapons, gave them such a boisterous welcome Patteson adopted it as his spiritual home. And when, at an Auckland ceremony in 1861, he was consecrated the first Bishop of Melanesia by Selwyn, he chose Motan as the liturgical language of his mission—and, for his cathedral, a great cloistered banyan in the main village. (Mota lay a hundred miles north of Paama and Maurice, I know, had made a pilgrimage to see it.)

Selwyn, summoned home to be Bishop of Lichfield, died in 1878. An army of eminent Victorians—Gladstone included—attended the funeral; several years later a splendid new Cambridge college *paid for by public subscription* was founded in his name. By happy coincidence that was where John, my son, studied for an MA, and Part One of his medical degree. He was a Selwyn man.

                                        *

Patteson, spare and angular, with aquiline features and a shaggy beard—an Arabist who looked like a desert prophet—became known around the New Hebrides for his jokes; he loved company, found any excuse to throw a party; wherever he travelled supplies of port and brandy were always to hand. After moving his headquarters to Norfolk Island—its semi-tropical climate suited the students better—he began his work on Melanesian linguistics, and produced *seventeen written languages* (millions of disparate sounds pouring through his head, all scrupulously notated). Then in September 1871, midway through setting down ten more, he went to see what could be done about the Santa Cruz islands.

There white blackbirders often won local trust by claiming they brought messages from the bishop—some, wearing crude crosses made from sticks, even claimed to be Patteson himself. On Nukapu five men had recently been abducted, and as Patteson's ship waited outside the reef for a wind to carry her in, the islanders held a meeting; finally a course of action—vehemently opposed by the women—was agreed.

When Patteson landed he was escorted to the meeting house and invited to sit; grim-faced, he listened to their slaving tales. As he was getting to his feet a man standing behind shattered his skull with a heavy lignum vitae mallet: a huge shout from all present was clearly heard on the ship. The executioner delivered a second blow to the head and a third to his chest; the killing, as planned, had been quick and merciful. After the women stripped off his clothes—though they left his boots on—two more wounds were inflicted. They laid a palm frond, knotted five times, on the body, wrapped it in a chief's finely woven mat and placed it in a canoe. By now the mission ship's master, Captain Bongard, had ordered a boat to be lowered and was sitting in it brandishing his revolver. Two brave women launched a second canoe and took Patteson in tow. Nearing Bongard they cast him adrift—as a second huge shout erupted from the islanders.

The Two Great Shouts of Nukapu were, it seems, directed at Queen Victoria (who got the news via a clipper round the Horn); Selwyn himself helped decipher them. Five wounds, five knots, five stolen men; the message was clear enough: we have killed one of your best people in protest at what some of your worst have done. Patteson, the newspapers told a mourning nation, died with "a sweet calm smile" and, when Norfolk Island's church was dedicated to him in 1880, it boasted commemorative stained-glass windows designed by Sir Edward Burne-Jones. His pectoral cross was taken to Cambridge and now lies in the chapel—on the altar—of Selwyn College. (There is a memorial at Merton College, Oxford, where he had been a Fellow.) Selwyn's son, John, was appointed the second Bishop of Melanesia.

*

Early one morning, in Vila airport's shabby little domestic terminal, the two bishops came up in conversation with a youngish, yawning, overweight American who dumped himself next to me with a force that shook the linked plastic seating; a white woman at the end spilt her coffee and glared. Oblivious to the warning signs he produced a pack of Camels, lit one and gave a single explosive cough. "No ashtrays," he observed. "No smoking!" snapped the woman. He ignored her. "You waiting for Tanna?"

"Yes," I said.

"These shitty little planes. I'm mildly nephelophobic—that's fear of clouds? When they bounce around in cloud, I *sweat*."

A gold eyebrow stud implanted in a long, unshaven face lent him a vaguely menacing appearance, yet he had the kind of intimate manner that sucked you, willy-nilly, into his confidence. Within moments I was learning that he'd dropped out of a media studies course in LA to become a freelance personal bodyguard—no movie stars, just dependable, well-paid corporate work. Pretty soon he began feeling there must be more to life than nannying self-indulgent millionaires, and late one night in a Toronto hotel found his vocation. "My client was next door with a rent boy; I had to wait up and pay the guy." His room contained a bookshelf and, idly killing time, he came upon *Structural Anthropology* by Claude Lévi-Strauss. Hooked after a few pages, he stole it, and a week later determined to go back to college. Now a graduate student, he was gathering material for a doctorate on the significance of volcanoes in Vanuatu's ethnic religions.

It was a quarter of an hour before he got around to asking about me. Mention of Maurice made him frown. "Claude met some missionaries in his time. Only a handful weren't doing actual harm. Tell the truth, a lot of the baddies came from the States, ignorant Midwest farm boys who thought a few years cracking down hard on the natives would get them to heaven. Good ones? Well, there used to be a couple out this way, British Anglicans . . ."

"Selwyn and Patteson."

"Correct! Up in Santo last week some people were talking, they're still remembered. So are a few Presbyterians—but not always for the right reasons. I guess guys like your grandfather never really understood the key to their spirit world. It was called mana. You heard about this?"

"Yes, I have."

He paid no attention. "It represents potency or power—the vital spark—and it's located partly in the liver but mostly in the head. Cannibals liked to eat brains because they were mana-rich. Mana was intellect; it was intelligence and imagination, genius even. That's how headhunting started, collecting the skulls of great men was like building up a fine library." A pretty, elegantly dressed black woman arrived at the check-in desk with a piglet asleep in a basket. "And *things* had mana—animals, insects, trees, plants, sticks and stones—even your island, that had special mana. It was also a force; mana made the grass grow and the tides turn."

"It's certainly a big idea," I said. "But . . ."

"Gets bigger." He looked around for an ashtray, then ground the butt under his heel. "*Possession.* Take sandalwood. Chopping it down was no big deal. If you gave the chief enough guns he'd let you take a whole damn forest, no problem. Trouble came when you started shipping it away. Hey, you're stealing our mana!"

The piglet awoke and began making noises like a fire alarm. We watched the woman produce a gold-wrapped Ferrero Rocher chocolate, peel it and pop it in the piglet's mouth.

"But they had no supreme being," I said. "No lord of the mana."

He shrugged. "The tawny-breasted hawk was sacred because it flew highest and got close to . . . who knows? They had songs and dances dedicated to important spirits—and to sex; sex had a *big* religious pull. Blowing the conch was also religious. Feasts were religious, drinking kava was like taking *communion*. These were devout people, but also very sociable; they loved to party."

The flight was called. He said, "Know how to spot a Presbyterian village?"

"Tell me."

"Nothing interesting going on during the day, silent as the grave at night." We stood. "Missionaries! They're just busybodies who been imposing their ideas on the rest of us since *pagan* times. And I don't just mean the Christians."

His name was Ed.

*

Buddha's followers were imbued with his own missionary zeal. One, Asoka, an Indian king who wore monk's robes, sent his son to Sri Lanka which, today, remains a stronghold of Buddhism in its purest form (and, in Kandy's Temple of the Tooth, behind a bullet-proof screen installed by the Japanese government, displays its most precious relic: an inch-long incisor plucked from the Gautama's funeral pyre). In AD 538 a Chinese delegation brought Buddhism to Japan. The Shogun ordered a family to test their Wall-Gazing Zen principles and see what happened; a major outbreak of plague followed, yet the family remained devout. Zen became the sect favoured by Japan's medieval military class, then flowered into the unity of religion and beauty—artfully placed rocks, intricately raked sand—we know today.

Islam was one of the most zealous missionary religions the world had ever seen. Muhammad, initially opposed to compulsion, changed his tune in 662 and offered infidels three choices: become Muslims, pay tribute or die. Soon afterwards his evangelizing armies burst out of Arabia and routed the superior forces of Syria, Persia, Egypt, Nubia, North Africa and Spain. They did not, however, venture south to the tropics.

Columbus and Da Gama opened up that surprising world to the Christians, with missionaries arriving on every ship. In 1493 Pope Alexander VI, alarmed by the apostolic rivalry between Lisbon and Madrid, divided the globe—Spain to the west, Portugal to the east—

yet the Portuguese, going west, still colonized Brazil while the Spaniards, sailing east, annexed the Philippines. The distinction between priest and adventurer grew so muddied Madrid felt impelled to create a new post, Protector of the Indians. It went to Bartolomé Las Casas, a Dominican who, convinced his Indians hadn't the strength for forced labour, came up with the idea of shipping slaves over from West Africa.

Count Nikolaus von Zinzendorf, a wealthy Moravian with estates in Saxony, organized the first Protestant invasion of the tropics, and in 1728 began sending volunteers to the East Indies and several South American slave communities, including Suriname. He inspired John Wesley and the saintly Baptist cobbler William Carey (who, clerking in a Calcutta indigo factory, translated the Bible into Sanskrit, and as a teacher at Fort William College made it illegal for widows to be immolated with their husbands in the burning ghats). Both helped found the Society for the Propogation of the Gospel in Foreign Parts.

In the deserts of French North Africa the mysterious White Fathers, wearing Arab robes and operating like a liturgical arm of the Foreign Legion, carried their canonicals and communion gear in saddlebags and evangelized the Bedouin on camelback. Mobility down south was dramatically improved in 1885 by the introduction of J. K. Starley's new Rover bicycle; the first "modern" machine, with same-size wheels and rear chain-drive, it was ideally suited to the eighteen-inch-wide paths which crisscrossed much of the continent.

A group of American students decided to fight idolatry abroad while hiding under a haystack during a thunderstorm. Their "Haystack Prayer Meeting" gave rise to the American Board of Commissioners for Foreign Missions and, early in the nineteenth century, their first equatorial postings. (These included Samuel J. Mills, who created Liberia, an African home for freed blacks, and Hiram Bingham, who claimed Hawaii—and its sugar crop—for Christ.)

Many of today's recruits, responding to slogans such as "Two-thirds of the global population are still waiting for their first phone call," attend colleges offering degree courses in Mission Studies. Candidates who complete a doctoral thesis—on, say, "Church-planting in Islamic countries"—are awarded a D.Miss. and, in many cases, a job in the tropics. Though most organizations are genuine, a few turn out to be shamelessly exploitative, others mere oddball outfits. (In Papua New Guinea the British writer Edward Marriott came upon "Have Christ Will Travel" and "Habitat for Humanity Incorporated.")

Now the Bible has been translated into 1,118 languages, while mission schools, hospitals and orphanages circle the world. God knows how many expatriate evangelists work in the tropics—there are said to be over ten thousand Americans alone—but they do a range of jobs that would have astonished Maurice. Current personnel include retail specialists, financial analysts, recruitment and development executives and media, advertising and PR consultants. Christianity has grown into a global multinational more powerful than any concerned with oil or mining.

*

In the early hours of Friday 5 August 1774, James Cook pointed HMS *Resolution* towards "a great fire" flaring on the horizon. At daybreak he found himself off a bulky two-hundred-square-mile island displaying a pair of three-thousand-foot-high mountains, extensive savannah, virgin forest and "a Volcano which threw up vast quantities of fire and smoak and made a rumbling noise which was heard at a good distance." Tanna's bewildered natives, contemplating their first white men (one a seventeen-year-old able seaman named George Vancouver), thronged the beach.

It was the kind of confrontation which, for more than three centuries, had traumatized communities throughout the tropics. Explorers flocked ashore to plant flags, dispense baubles, rape women, check for spices, minerals and timber and note sites for future missions; they left behind incredulous populations able to talk of little else. (The question of whether or not their visitors were gods was settled by Puerto Rico's pragmatic Indians who, having captured a party of fair-skinned intruders, drowned them all—then left the bodies immersed to see whether they would rot.) On Tanna, however, folk were more cautious and conciliatory.

This was partly due to Cook's famous good manners, and a steely determination to complete his great Second Voyage without incident. The biggest problem, to date, had occurred back in Deptford where, preparing *Resolution* for a series of exploratory sweeps through the

Torrid Zone (including copper-sheathing her hull), shipwrights added the extra cabins ordered by Joseph Banks for his entourage—among them Johann Zoffany, a fashionable painter of domestic tableaux, and a couple of horn players. The First Voyage had established ambitious, well-connected Banks as Britain's premier naturalist and botanist. He was determined to profit also from the Second yet Cook, tacking down the Thames to Sheerness, found *Resolution* top-heavy, and told his carpenters to remove the new accommodation. Banks stormed ashore where, according to Midshipman Elliott, "he swore and stamped upon the Warfe, like a Mad Man." In his place Cook appointed a German father and son: Johann Forster, though often prickly, proved to be a fine scientist while the boy, George, a precocious teenager, showed flashes of genuine brilliance.

It was Johann Forster who, on Wednesday 10 August, took the launch ashore and asked Paowang, an old chief, for the island's name. He did so with a downward gesture, so Paowang, thinking he wanted the word for "earth," said *muk-tana.* Forster, catching only the latter part, reported back and Cook inscribed it so on his chart. Thus Tanna was christened in an atmosphere of confusion and muddle which, aside from a seventy-year break until the first traders and missionaries arrived, has continued ever since.

*

These days tour groups fly down to see Yasur, billed as the world's only drive-in volcano. I went hoping to meet up with an old bushman who, twenty years earlier, I helped make briefly famous. Then, with photographer Colin Jones, I visited his forest hamlet and found him worshipping a Greek-born god who lived at Buckingham Palace. Jones's picture of grave, naked *Jif* Niva holding a signed portrait of his deity, flanked by the six buxom, bare-breasted teenage virgins chosen to share his marriage bed, appeared on the cover of the *Observer* magazine and caused a minor sensation. (Later it became a Vanuatu postage stamp.)

Wistfully he told us how his people longed for Prince Philip to join them. Jungle had been cleared so his plane might land, a house prepared; his brides awaited. I pointed out that Philip already had a wife. Niva knew about her. He said if she also chose to come they would give her the duties—yam cultivation or firewood collecting—appropriate to a woman of her age. Yet she must observe the rules; stumbling, for example, upon men drinking kava she would be thrashed like any other female. And, mischievously, he added that at feasts, when she joined the dancing grannies who shuffled and stomped all night, she might wear her crown.

Eyes heavy from kava, he showed us the schoolhouse where, today, kava was the main subject on the syllabus. A grass-skirted teacher taught a dozen naked boys about its cultivation, preparation, remedial qualities, mythology and central role in their lives. Someone had scrawled "Hav yu loose yor horse?" on a blackboard and I asked the teacher, himself stoned, if they studied English. Yawning, unfocused, he said no: that question was part of a circumcision lesson; initiation was the other thing they learned about here. Watching the kids mooning around I wondered if this was a reaction to the mission schools where their ancestors wrote—in copperplate—essays on Cromwell, Drake, Nelson and Henry VIII and the Dissolution of the Monasteries.

*

One day at the *Observer* a colleague named Desmond Balmer strolled down from the News Desk. Aside from pleasantries exchanged at the coffee machine we were barely acquainted; now, though, he told me his grandfather had also been a missionary in the New Hebrides—on Tanna. Dr Campbell Nicholson, he added, knew Maurice; indeed, according to his diaries, Maurice baptized his daughter. He added, "The daughter who's now my aunt."

I stared. "My grandad christened your *aunt*?"

"He did." We smiled and went, "Well, well." A few years younger than me, he was a likeable Ulsterman with a low golf handicap and much easy Irish charm. In time our careers would eventually collide then run on twin tracks.

When the post of Travel Editor became vacant we both applied. He got it; and to the loser went the job of Chief Travel Correspondent. For ten years Desmond and I, the Mission Twins, had manned the Travel Desk and now, back on his grandfather's old stamping ground, I made a mental note to send a postcard.

*

The first missionary to set foot in the tropics was Doubting Thomas, the sceptical apostle. Yet, like many who eventually followed he was, essentially, a practical man; the Incredulity of Thomas consisted merely of questioning the risen Christ's miraculous recovery (touching the wounds) and astounding intentions. Early in the first century he travelled to south India and, after converting the Malabar Syrians to Christianity, was killed by a spear thrust and buried at Mylapore, near Madras. In 1552 the Portuguese found his empty tomb there; eleven hundred years earlier the remains had been moved to Edessa. Since, allegedly, he built a palace for an Indian king, artists sometimes depicted him holding a T-square. St Thomas is the patron saint of architects.

*

At Tanna's White Grass Bungalows they served grilled parrotfish for dinner. The only other guest, a bald, thickset old European wearing a tie, blue blazer and glasses opaque as milk-bottle bases, barely glanced up when I entered. Stabbing at his food with a fork, muttering as he grubbed for bones with stubby fingers, he acknowledged only the youth who cooked and served our meal. Finally, pushing his plate aside, he lit a big cigar and beamed over. "*So!* What protection do you use?"

"I'm sorry?"

He produced a spray can. "I have Aerogard Personal Insect Repellent, Tropical Strength. Even vospz are keeping away. You will take a beer?" Sending the youth off for Tusker Premiums, he told me he also was in pursuit of a grandfather—or, rather, a descendant he left behind. His family, I learned, once owned a Dresden factory making curving staircases: using premium timber and advanced mathematics they built everything from one-bend oak flights for suburban villas to great forked mahogany *escaliers* (exquisitely inlaid with rainforest exotica) that spiralled up into the cupolas and frescoed ceilings of palaces and town halls.

As a young man *Opa* Otto—"Same name as me"—set off for the tropics in a chestnut yawl with a couple of friends. Curiosity about sandalwood brought him to Sulphur Bay. He wasn't buying, merely wanted to see it growing in its natural state. Here he met Mary, a pretty local girl—and a visit that was supposed to last a week stretched into a scandal-ridden two months. When the Presbyterians' mission "police" abducted Mary and threatened the Germans with violence, they weighed anchor and sailed away.

Back home Otto, saying nothing about his island romance, got married. Yet he had kept a *wanderjahr* journal which, decades later, was found by his widow. It contained many fine drawings of the girl—often posing nude, looking "like a Gauguin woman"—and recorded his remorse at the news she was pregnant. Though the widow immediately burned it, word of its contents had passed down to Otto, a retired Munich language teacher. He finished his beer. "So maybe in Tanna I have a great uncle or aunty."

"You've asked around?"

"Yes. But when I speak about it people think I am crazy." He smiled. "But if such a relative exists he, or she, will be different."

"Oh?"

"We are Jews."

I laughed and warned him Tanna had become such a maelstrom of faiths his part-German Jewish relative might now be worshipping a Greek-born Brit with a Scottish dukedom. Before heading for bed I asked the youth, Tony, if he knew *Jif* Niva. He did, and in the morning would arrange for a 4WD vehicle to take me to his village. "You want something to read?" The proffered book, marked "For Guests Only," was called *The Travelling Skier—20 Five Star Vacations*. But I had books of my own, and back in my hut settled down with the story of John G. Paton, the Scot who, in 1858, brought the Good News to Tanna.

With it also came whipping posts and public floggings for anyone defying his edicts—including those who couldn't, or wouldn't, sing his hymns in *four-part harmony*. A vain, well-fed, full-bearded man bursting with energy and ambition (he wore out, and buried, two wives), publicity-hungry Paton finally got what he'd always craved: international recognition. His self-regarding memoirs, cleverly mixing heroic endeavour with schoolboy-style ripping yarns, resulted in such massive sales they even did a spin-off edition for children: *The Story of John G. Paton, Told for Young Folks; or, Thirty Years Among South Seas Cannibals*, became required reading for every red-blooded kid in Britain. Sighed a *Daily Telegraph* review: "There are enough hairbreadth escapes and deeds of cool—if unostentatious—courage in these pages to stock half-a-dozen ordinary books." He became, briefly, the world's most famous missionary.

The Tannese detested him.

Island mythology says they finally chucked him out but, in fact, he ran. When measles—introduced by sandalwooders—eradicated *one-third* of the population, survivors of this European infants' ailment vented their anger on the evangelists. After a couple were killed on neighbouring Erromango, Paton left hastily for Australia where, in a series of ranting interviews (while striking bellicose poses for the cameras), he demanded action. The British government loaned him HMS *Curaçoa*. Though commanded by an embarrassed Commodore Sir William Wiseman, it was Paton who ordered the guns turned on his "beloved darkies." After several Stone Age villages had been flattened a man in a canoe appeared waving a piece of paper. The same people who once told Paton that his God "goes against our customs, and condemns the things we delight in" now forlornly promised that "in future we will be good and learn to obey the word of Jehovah." Yet, pointedly, the message was addressed not to Paton, but to Queen Victoria. Prudently moving to Aniwa island, Paton continued gracing the archipelago with his presence and receiving the tributes of his adoring fellow-missionaries (who dedicated the old Iririki hospital to him—Paton's name thus features on my birth certificate).

Now, as mosquitoes formed a whining curtain around my bed, I recalled the catastrophic consequences of measles here. (Some sandalwooders deliberately put infected men ashore.) Flu, later, had the same impact; indeed, they combined so devastatingly my father had nightmares about being summoned to the deathbed of the last New Hebridean—triggered, perhaps, by the story of Truganini, the last-but-one full-blooded Tasmanian aborigine, whose final plea to *her* doctor in 1876 was "Bury me behind the mountains." (No such luck; they rendered down the bones and hung her small skeleton in the Hobart Museum where it remained, an object of curiosity, until 1947.) I found myself thinking about the last member of a native American tribe who, said Lévi-Strauss, lived in the vicinity of large towns, "still chipping stones for the arrow-heads with which he did his hunting. Gradually, however, all the animals disappeared. One day the Indian was found naked and dying of hunger on the outskirts of a suburb. He ended his days peacefully as a porter at the University of California."

After breakfasting off tea and tiny purple eggs I boarded a Toyota Tony had borrowed from his father—a senior *yeremanu,* or chief, who owned the White Grass complex, and spent much of his time in Vila on political matters. The dirt roads of Tanna, bad enough during my visit twenty years earlier, now resembled scoured river beds. There were wall-of-death gradients, deep culverts and cambered trenches, potholes a man could hide in. I imagined the roads turning into white-water rapids during the rains, and Tony's shrug indicated this was, in essence, true. "Tourists come for volcano, but if vehicle roll, they not happy."

Jif Niva's village was smaller, meaner and poorer than I recalled, its gallery forest replaced by cracked earth frazzled by solar radiation. A child rushed off, and moments later Niva appeared, carrying the big signed Prince Philip picture and two new colour portraits given—said Tony—by American well-wishers. Laying them carefully on the ground he invited me to admire them. He had grown white-whiskered and bony, a naked old man with big flat feet and livid blemishes signifying scabies, or "scratch"; the penis gourd which caused such a stir in Britain (it briefly enjoyed a vogue as a fancy-dress accessory) looked thread-bare. All the old buoyancy and certainties had gone, only his watchfulness remained. I spoke of the day long ago when Jones and I disrupted his pastoral routine, but he looked blank. Tony said other journalists had since visited, film crews also; for a while he had been Tanna's most popular man.

"I'll bet." I'd personally done very well out of Niva, talking about him on radio and television, earning money and recognition ("Saw you on *Newsnight!*"), while the British media depicted him as a symbol of the Anglo-French divide: Auberon Waugh wrote a piece in the *Spectator,* the *Guardian* ran an editorial; and, following the usual circuitous, non-attributable route, word filtered through from Windsor that Philip himself had been "entertained."

But had Niva done well out of us? I vaguely assumed all the fuss would lead to better things, that he would prosper. So where, I asked, were Philip's girls? He shrugged: all grandmothers now. How were things at the school? School closed. And hadn't there been a clinic?

Closed also. I realized a chief who chose to live like his most distant ancestors wasn't interested in publicity-driven marketing opportunities. *Jif* Willy, on the other hand, would have had topless "brides" welcoming tourists to a thatched palace complete with throne, marriage bed and jokey petition begging Philip to quit England and fly south. Looking at Niva, I wondered how many centuries back he had travelled since our last meeting. And had the airmailed copies reached him, had he actually seen himself as a famous cover star? No; he shook a head full of strong mana. And I, aware my own head contained many memories of those days, knew I was trapped in the past almost as firmly as he.

Niva had been exploited by us all. (I had since learned the signed portrait was presented by a British resident commissioner interested only in putting French noses out of joint.) Ashamed, I handed over some stick tobacco, wished I had brought pigs or kava roots. Yet a light came into his bloodshot eyes as, suddenly animated, he asked after the Duke. In a few months they would hold a custom feast with an all-night Toka dance dedicated to him. Philip had sons who could take over his duties in *Inglan,* so he should come soon. Nothing had changed. The old man gave me a soft handshake and sent me on my way.

*

Tony had an appointment at a tiny clinic at Yapgersip, a forest village where outpatients waited on a mossy log. He said he recently broke both arms in a car crash and his father, bypassing Tanna's two derelict government hospitals, had rushed him here. After administering an anaesthetic infusion of leaves the doctor, Jack Numupen, cut around the fractures with a piece of razor-sharp bamboo. (I saw the scars.) He stuffed crushed herbs in the wounds, closed them with bamboo hoops and applied bamboo splints.

"Did he use disinfectant?"

He shrugged, and I thought about all the contagiums on this unsanitized island, anything from jungle rot and yellow jack to tsutsugamushi scrub typhus—perhaps even the rare Torrid Zone condition known as Kew Gardens spotted fever.

After three weeks on a *fiximap* remedy distilled from forest products, he was pronounced cured. His neck, though, still hurt and today he had come for medicine. Dr Jack, bent and white-stubbled, hobbled up and tenderly took Tony's hand—good clinical practice, since the symptoms of every known condition eventually present themselves in the fingers and palm. In the course of a conversation containing many sleepy silences I learned that during World War Two the Americans had invited Dr Jack to join them at Vila Base Hospital. To work on the wards? "No. He dig air raid shelters."

Now patients from all over Vanuatu visited his busy practice. "He can fix headache, fever, stomach, heart attack. Ya know? Fella came from Santo; he gone deaf."

"Jack cured him?"

"Sure. Give medicine, cut his back, soon he hear good."

"*Cut* his back?"

"Small cut only." Lumbar incisions with bamboo scalpels were routinely inflicted, the island equivalent of bleeding. As he spoke, sun filtering through leaves produced the lutescent glow of yellow medieval glass (glaziers achieved this by mixing antimony metal oxide with pure gold) once regarded as a manifestation of divine light. Each tree seemed to possess its own glittering armature, and I wondered if the shine of a tropical morning had somehow reassured the early missionaries.

A woman appeared, wiping a beer bottle on the hem of her dress. Smiling without quite meeting my eye, she handed it to Tony. He took a swig. "Want to try?" His analgesic was astringent, with a gritty residue of ground bark and an aftertaste of turpentine. She joined Dr Jack and took his hand. We left them, sitting motionless as figures engraved on a church window.

*

"Now we see tourist village," he said. "They dancing."

We came to a compound shaded by banyans. High in the branches naked young neophytes awaiting circumcision lounged outside their tree cabins. Forbidden to see females of any age (required, indeed, to disperse them with conch blasts before they scrambled to the ground), they now kept their gaze averted from five vacant-eyed, bare-breasted girls who shambled and hopped to the rhythms of a catatonic-looking drummer.

Yet, grinning down, they made sexually explicit gestures at a blonde woman standing near me. She, her husband and two fretful children

were the tourists for whom the girls danced today. I spotted Ed, squatting on his heels talking agitatedly to a guide. He walked over. "How
about this? Wayne there, from Sydney, just wants to get the hell out—
doesn't even want his money back. But the guide says if we leave early
we'll be *beaten*." He gave a kind of yelp. "With *clubs!* They're pretend-
ing this crap is sacred."

"It's all about mana," I reminded him.

"Christ, no, it's all about Aussie dollars." He pointed up into the
trees. "See those kids? Totally illiterate! No school, no teachers, no
future, just a one-way trip back to the Stone Age."

One began playing his Pan's pipes. The notes, carried up to the
canopy by heat convection, were barely audible, and it took a while
to realize he was mocking us with a reedy, discordant rendition of
"Waltzing Matilda." Even Ed allowed himself a smile. Tony intimated
that since we were not signatories to the dance contract, we could slip
away. *"Ciao,"* I said. Ed said, "I blame your missionaries, chum." And
he wasn't joking.

*

My missionaries are blamed also for the emergence of Jon Frum.
On Tanna there is uncertainty over the date of his arrival—he may
even have been around in the 1930s—but none about his origins.
Frum was, indisputably, American, and most islanders I talked to swore
he showed up soon after Pearl Harbor. (One said he landed from a
destroyer, another said it was a submarine, both agreed Jonfrum came
from Arkansas and wore a broad-brimmed black hat.) In 1941, evidently, he promised eternal life to everyone and *attacked the Presbyterian
work ethic.* Shrewdly couched in the same high-minded tones the
Presbyterians themselves used, the Frummers' own Good News proclaimed that, since work made you sick, people should leave their jobs,
lie on the beach, sleep a lot—not even trouble to eat, for Frum would
teach them the American trick of keeping one's stomach full without
lifting a finger. And, since they would have no further need for white
man's money, anyone possessing it should spend it.

Obediently they emptied the stores, slaughtered their animals,
bought kava by the ton and threw parties that lasted for weeks.

When word spread that a US Navy Catalina carrying Frum's sons,

Isaac and Jacob, had landed on Lake Siwi, the missionaries surveyed their empty churches and, unsure what to do, called the British police. They, equally confounded, made fifty-six random arrests. After that people threw away their Bibles and put up red crosses; these, once displayed in the hope of gaining free American medical treatment, now became symbols of defiance.

By war's end social order had broken down. (Recreation in many villages took the form of rampant "sexual dancing.") Midway through 1954 it was rumoured, falsely, that a Frum emissary, Captain World, had arrived. The two thousand followers who had flocked to see him gathered again, at Sulphur Bay in 1957, to welcome Frum himself. His failure to appear hardly mattered. By then he had inspired a full-blooded independence movement.

A key element of its manifesto was the expectation of "cargo." Some day America would send ships and planes laden with war-surplus materiel. (Though I met a whispery old couple who thought consumer items might be included too; paging through yellowing fifties magazines they pointed wordlessly to ads for golf clubs, garden furniture, porcelain bathtubs, goose-down pillows and shiny Studebaker saloons.)

Wharves were built and airfields hacked in readiness—some featuring life-sized bamboo aircraft arranged, like decoy ducks, to assist the inbound pilots. Dummy radios made from string and bully-beef tins would pass on landing and docking instructions.

It's easy to mock them. I've certainly dined out on Tanna's aspirations and, amid the laughter, noted that the comfortable London houses in which we sat were absolutely stuffed with cargo. And we, busy accumulating our treasures, talked prices, discounts, bargains and deals. Yet for the Tannese such things had no intrinsic value. They saw them in natural terms, like unexpected dry-season rain, or a bountiful harvest of yams.

*

Yasur, with its dedicated car park, lay on an eastern ash plain. As I arrived magma spurted from a vent in a three-hundred-and-thirty-foot-deep crater, and a bang made the ground wobble and lobbed boulders way up into the atmosphere. Ascending through dirty smoke, spinning slowly around the cloud base, they lost their momentum and headed back. I ducked, of course—periodically these things bombed the viewing area and killed people. The whole island, beneath its membrane of soil, seemed to be a raging pressure furnace seeking out weak points. Dig a well, plant a tree, make a hole anywhere in Tanna and, whoosh! you'd be vaporized.

Cook, aboard *Resolution,* grew fascinated by the "prodigeous colums of Smoak and fire at every erruption; at one time great stones were seen high in the air." After breakfast on Sunday 14 August 1774 he set out to obtain "a nearer and better View of the Volcano." A mile inland, coming upon a patch of steaming ground, he took its temperature, noted its appearance and texture, even placed some on his tongue. "The Earth in this place was a kind of Pipe clay or whitish marl which had a sulpherous smell and was soft and wet, the upper surface only excepted which was crusted over with a thin dry crust, on which was Sulpher and a Vitriolick substance which tasted like Alumn." But the volcano, he soon discovered, was off-limits. Finding the path to Yasur blocked by "a young Woman with a Club in her hand" he returned to the ship wondering why, "contrary to the Opinion of Philosophers, which is that all Volcanos must be at the summits of the highest hills," this one was so low and squat.

It was also, I noted, entirely unsupervised; Tanna's premier tourist attraction had no guard rails, no attendants or hard-hatted safety officers. I saw a kid approach the crater carrying a fish—did he plan to throw it in?—when a magma surge made him stumble and fall only yards from the rim. Heart in mouth I watched him scramble back to join an amused, handsome, youngish man who cuffed him lightly about the head. I asked what the fish was for. "It's supposed to be our lunch," said the man. He and his son were tourists from Vila, staying with a grand-uncle—a Frummer who, he smilingly confided, would approach American yachties saying, "You people got *samting* nice for me?"

*

One morning, on a bush path, I was stopped by a near-naked teenage boy who wanted to know my age and country of origin. Then, shyly scuffing his toe, he asked me to buy him a cow.

*

"The wearing of coconut armlets, the decking of the head with flowers by young women and girls, the cooking of food on Sundays, and the singing of purely innocent secular songs, have been denominated 'offences' and proscribed as 'heathenish' and 'works of the devil.' " These words were written by an angry young Englishman named Wilkes who landed in 1912 and found a degree of repression that would have gratified old John G. Paton. Mission courts enforced mission laws at mission trials, while club-carrying mission police mounted regular horseback patrols. Tanna had become a tyrannical, self-regulating feudal autocracy, and finally the Vila government felt obliged to act.

They abolished the Presbyterian judiciary, made Wilkes the Condominium Agent and ordered him to establish a Condominium court. There he and four native assessors—two of them heathen—faced the jeering missionaries and mission mobs who crowded in to disrupt proceedings. Wilkes, appalled by such a "defective and brutal" regime, sided unequivocally with Tanna's outcasts.

Down the years a two-tier society had emerged: the converted, who wore clothes, and the pagan subversives, who didn't. Yet these "sons of perdition," continually abused and menaced by the mission police, were also subject to Presbyterian law. (Any caught collecting wild honey on the Sabbath, for example, faced months of hard labour on the roads.)

Outraged by Wilkes's support for the dissenters—who, covertly, revived banned customs such as teaching young men the techniques of sexual intercourse—the Church leaders invented a series of wild charges, and sent details to influential people in Sydney and London. He stood accused of flogging women, of allowing the roads to go to ruin by lax sentencing, of encouraging the Tannese to open brothels—even of running one himself.

London and Vila, thoroughly alarmed, agreed to sack Wilkes; he, though, saved them the trouble by resigning to fight in the Great War. In his place they appointed the chief engineer of the British Resident Commissioner's yacht, a man so enervated by rum and lassitude he was happy to leave the Presbyterians to their own devices. A generation later Jon Frum arrived with his millennial cult and the evangelists were booted out, for good.

Pinned to the wall of a village store I came upon an ironic footnote to the Presbyterian occupation. It was a faded photograph showing Santo's first Jonfrum MP, bony, wispily bearded, making his maiden speech to the Parliament in Vila.

And he didn't have a stitch on.

*

When, in 1952, Dr Schweitzer won the Nobel Peace Prize, at my school in Melbourne we drew pictures of the inspirational, shaggily moustached old German. (I depicted him, at his leper colony in Lambaréné on Gabon's steamy Ogooué River, with a bone through his big Habsburg nose—and got a detention from the teacher.) Schweitzer could be a martinet, but we respected such people; they got things done, and I too planned a career in mission medicine.

The dream faded as I learned how the Presbyterians treated their own. When my mother, in Vila, required life-saving surgery in Sydney, my father begged for an advance on his miserly stipend. The Church refused ("You must learn to stand on your own feet") but promised to include Mrs Frater in their prayers. A Tonkinese moneylender came to his aid, while I turned my back on God and, eventually, embraced journalism instead.

*

Over a Friday dinner of stewed flying fox Otto said, "This is the Frummers' holy day. Tony says there will be a service."

"Where?"

"Near the airport. Under a tree."

We took torches. The moon was hidden by scudding cloud, a warm, salty wind blew off the sea, muffled noises came from dense bush flanking the road. "Wild horses, maybe." Otto sounded uneasy. "They have them here." A man passed carrying a lamp and a dead shark. *"Gud naet!"* he called. Moving through the heavy, damp air, getting a whiff of the shark, I recalled a passage in Lévi-Strauss's *Tristes Tropiques* which stated that fish perceived odours in terms of light and dark. Otto, when I told him, enquired, "So how would a rose smell to a fish?" I said its heavy fragrance would probably be perceived as shadow. "What about sweet peas? Or marigolds?" As I surmised that a marigold's carrion odour might, actually, dazzle a fish, I noted his smile in my torchbeam and, irritated, moved on to bees. They classify luminosity in terms of weight: dark is heavy, lightness bright. Seeing the night as a bee might, its dense folds pressing around me, I found myself instinctively slowing.

Otto said, "You are walking too fast," and paused to adjust a sandal strap. He'd had a bad week. No one knew anything about his ancestor, and mosquito bites on his feet had turned septic. Then, from a hillside off to the left, we heard singing, found four guitarists and a sizeable crowd sitting around a fire as a dozen women danced. They wore Mother Hubbard dresses and moved slowly, eyes closed, expressions dreamy. From beyond the fire Ed's American voice cried, "Yo, Alex!" He had a lady in tow—black, good-looking and at least ten years older. I had last seen her checking in at Vila airport. "This is Nelly."

"Pleased to meet you, Nelly," I said. "How's the pig?"

"*Pig?*" said Ed. "I'll have you know that was a pedigree Arizona saddleback."

She smiled. "It was a present for someone."

French accent, sinewy build, an adamantine glitter at her throat, more jewels on her fingers. I introduced Otto who, blinking through his fused quartz spectacles, gave a vague nod.

"Nelly's looking for her granddaddy," said Ed.

I almost laughed.

"He worked on the family plantation somewhere round Sulphur Bay."

She said, "His name was Ezekiel, he was a village boy. My grandmother was sixteen at the time. Her parents had a plantation, Le Croix de Sud. When she got pregnant they sent her back to France. The baby was my mother, so I am the granddaughter of Ezekiel."

"You will not find him here, madame," sighed Otto. "People have no memory, Jon Frum has wiped the past from their minds."

She shrugged. "He would be about sixty. Is that so old? And, if he is dead, maybe there are people who remember him. A friend in Vila gave me the address of a teacher, Mr Sunday; he is helping me to look. For him I brought the pig."

Ed, watching the Frummers, murmured, *"Hey, they're singin' hymns about America,"* and went to talk to a youth in an NYPD T-shirt. Nelly asked what I was doing on Tanna. When I mentioned my book she gave me a cryptic look. "All my life I have had tropical dreams."

"Oh?"

"Most are bad."

She described a couple. The first was about being denied access to Ezekiel's village which, guarded by lions, lay in a valley where the women wore bowler hats, the second—often recurring—had her alone in a drifting boat. It turned out to be her own motor yacht, a gift from her husband (it featured three luxury en suite cabins and a rosewood bar). The boat took her into an empty zone filled with blue. "The most *intense* blue, like space. And it has no gravity; I am weightless, and on the point of death."

"But you never die?"

"I wake just before." She shook a cigarette from a pack of Gitanes. "My shrink thinks Ezekiel is the problem: Melanesian and French blood make bad chemistry. Once he even put me in a lunatic asylum. There is such a thing as tropical madness, you know."

"Le coup de bambou."

She blew a perfect smoke ring. *"Exactement."*

I slipped off to listen to the singers and, through their slurred vocalizing, made out certain place names: Texas, Pennsylvania, Georgia, Chicago and JFK—waypoints, I guessed, for a pilgrimage or, more likely, a mass migration. "Correct," said Ed. "It's their stairway to heaven. The US is where all good Frummers want to go when they breathe their last." He pointed to a skeletal old man who sat with his chin propped on a stick sprouting tiny green leaves. "That guy's a Dolly Parton fan."

I said, "Tell me about Nelly."

"Nelly? Oh, she's loaded, got houses in Geneva and London. There's a husband back home in Marseilles, I'd say he was in organized crime: some *very* interesting commodities come ashore in that town." He grinned. "Quite a lady, huh?"

"Absolutely." I saw Otto yawning; I too had suddenly had enough of the Frummers and their cock-eyed ideas. We said goodbye to Nelly, who grandly extended her hand, palm down. I gave it a perfunctory shake, but courtly Otto *("Küss' die hand, madam")* brought it to his lips.

As we walked I told him about a party of elderly Japanese I had once come across on the island of Nauru. Each morning they filed off into the bush carrying bushknives and spades, each evening I found them back in the hotel bar, seated at tables heaped with human bones. Sipping whisky, they carefully wrapped each in brown paper, tied it with pink string and placed it in a worn army knapsack.

He peered at me. "So?"

"So we have something in common. They were there to find old friends from the war, we're here because of our forefathers."

"What forefathers? I don't even find bones. This has been a waste of time, your tropics have nothing to do with me."

"At Lake Turkana, Richard Leakey found bones that were 1.9 million years old. *Homo erectus,* the first evidence! From Africa we moved on, we *all* come from the tropics—and I think in every human there must be a dormant tropical gene. A sleeper. Don't we all yearn to return to our roots?"

"My roots," he intoned, "are in the Bundesrepublik Deutschland."

Some day, I thought, when GPs are able to call up a patient's DNA profile, they will note the curious chromosome; I imagined my grandson's doctor looking at his screen and thinking, "Wow! Better keep an eye on this feller." I told Otto, who growled, "Yes, he might want to go off and write a book."

Halfway home his torch went out. As, cursing, he banged it on his knee, there was a violent crashing in the bush and a wild stallion, gleaming black in the moonlight, burst across the road. For a few seconds we stood amazed, smelling the animal's sour sweat, almost rocking in its slipstream. Otto spoke first: soft, sibilant High German articulated very fast. Then, flat batteries and sore foot forgotten, he gave it to me in English. "Mares may follow!" he yelled, and began running.

The Garbage Dump at Millionaire's Point

At Espiritu Santo's airfield I watched a Toyota taxi with a small white-stubbled man at the wheel trundle by at 5 m.p.h. and hit a wall. The dull percussive thud made me flinch—yet the driver hopped out smiling. *"Gudmoning!"*

What I'd witnessed had been a small problem with the hydraulics, he had it under control, we'd proceed with care. Yet, once under way, the speedo registered so little forward motion I urged him to go faster; accelerating sharply, he began road-testing his brakes with such violence I begged him to slow again. This whiplash progress occurred all the way into Luganville, and I recalled a Vila friend saying that, probably due to the war, many Santoese were congenitally strange in the head.

The Boulevard Higginson, main street of the only town on Vanuatu's largest island, was lined by low-rise tin-roofed buildings and sidewalks left acutely angled and tilted by earthquakes. Vine-covered Quonset huts and discoloured slabs of concrete were the only signs that a vast army of occupation had once passed through. Further evidence—entire shiploads of discarded materiel—lay strewn over the bed of the Segond Channel: aero engines, trucks, tractors, jeeps, bulldozers, even crates of Coke, all now gaily clad in polychromatic rainbow coral.

The world first became aware of Santo when, in May 1942, Lieutenant Colonel Ritchie Garrison of the US Third Island Command arrived from Port Vila aboard a chartered junk. As Japanese forces streamed out across the Pacific he came looking for places from which they might be stopped, at Luganville found an obscure hamlet containing a few houses, a trading store and a rutted forest road. "Once in a while," he reported, "a small, ancient car would be seen," but mostly the heavy silence was disturbed only by an ocean breeze that fitfully clattered the palms. After a cordial French District Officer had shown him around, he made his decision—and, at the Pentagon, Santo became known as Base Buttons.

Within months army engineers had built forty cinemas, five airfields, four military hospitals, a first-class highway system, a dockyard, a torpedo-boat base, harbour-defence systems, wharves and accommodation for a hundred thousand personnel. Offshore they created moorings for a hundred ocean-going vessels, inland had their conscripted Iowa farmboys start work on the market gardens. These, according to US records, soon yielded stupendous crops of squash, eggplants, bantam corn, Chinese cabbage, Swiss chard, okra, beets, lettuce, string beans, black-eyed peas, carrots, radishes and cucumbers—countless tons of vegetables for the half a million Americans who would eventually pass through.

One, a thirty-seven-year-old writer named James Michener, found himself stationed at Luganville's army personnel office. His time there inspired *Tales of the South Pacific,* a Pulitzer Prize–winning collection of short stories read with interest by a New York song-writing duo; their stage adaptation became a blockbuster movie, soon the entire civilized world seemed to be humming the tunes. "Rodgers & Hammerstein's SOUTH PACIFIC," proclaimed the 20th Century Fox billboards. "IT'S ALL HERE! Romance . . . songs . . . laughter and spectacle!" Yet, even as Rossano Brazzi anticipated some enchanted Santo evening, and sassy Mitzi Gaynor vowed to wash him right out of her hair, and sailors—dancing by the Segond Channel—swore there was nothing you could name that was *anything* like a dame, their government had changed the quiet, enigmatic world of Michener's Bali Ha'i forever. In 1946, with the detonation of the first atom bomb at Bikini Atoll, they turned the region into a nuclear testing site.

*

The Hotel Santo, cool and airy, had a shady garden and a bar where, each evening, the expatriates congregated. I found half a dozen seated before their beers in reflective mood. Ed, a spiky, tattooed little Brit, told me he was in financial services. Everyone laughed.

George, a scholarly Australian, was in Santo prospecting for gold. "It's here all right, silver too—but no diamonds; geologically the Pacific islands are too young."

Jim had a fishery business, Pete repaired motor vehicles trashed by Santo's dreadful roads. "They bugger your headlight filaments so I get a lot of night-collision business." Nat, a Kiwi who raised pigs, had just returned from Vila and complained about the cost of eating out. "That place over on Iririki, they charge like a wounded bull. I heard they once gave Michener dinner there—but I'll bet they never showed him the fucking bill."

"Michener was in Vila?" I asked, surprised.

"Michener was *here*," said Pete. "Turned up a few years ago with a television crew. Nice old feller, very frail but happy to chat. Told us he'd never been over to Ambae so, obviously, we wanted to take him. But he reckoned it would spoil the dream."

"What dream?"

George said, "The volcanic smoke from Ambrym forms a mist that can blot out Ambae for weeks; some of the Yanks in transit to the Solomons never even knew it was there. Then along comes a front, the mist blows away and it suddenly appears over the water, shining in the morning sun—one of the most beautiful islands you'll ever see. That's what happened to Michener. He got out of bed, looked out the window and saw Ambae for the first time. He didn't know its name so he made one up: Bali Ha'i."

I'd always believed Iririki had been the inspiration for his resplendent isle; being born on Bali Ha'i easily constituted the most glamorous part of my personal history and now, privately confounded, I heard Jim say that the draft-dodging Rossano Brazzi character in the movie had been a French planter called Alfred le Bolle. "Had a place up round Turtle Bay and fell for an American nurse at one of the hospitals. Bloody Mary was a Eurasian woman, Madame Gardelle, she ran a small restaurant at Surunda."

"Mate, she ran a *whorehouse*," said Ed.

George said, "Michener made her a Tonkinese. But there's also supposed to be a lot of Aggie Grey in Mary."

I'd heard that, too. Aggie, Western Samoan daughter of a Lincolnshire-born chemist named Swann, made a fortune running an Apia speakeasy during the years of wartime prohibition; Michener, briefly based in "unutterably dull" American Samoa next door, dropped by regularly. (Today the multi-storeyed, package-tour-thronged Aggie

Grey's Hotel, like the speakeasy before it, plays a key role in Apia's economy.)

I sipped my beer and imagined this place in Michener's day. Japan, having grabbed the Solomons, planned to grab Santo next. They saw the New Hebrides as the stepping stone to the greatest of all prizes: Australia. By the end of 1942, a year after Pearl Harbor, the US had moved a hundred thousand men from Santo up to the Solomons—equal to half that group's indigenous population—for a violent, protracted campaign. As the Marines took Hell's Corner (once Honiara's pretty Chinatown) and won the Battle of Bloody Ridge, Santo-based aircraft engaged the Imperial Fleet in the inconclusive Battle of the Eastern Solomons. Near Iron Bottom Sound—once known as Sealark Channel—the shambolic, ninety-minute Naval Battle of Guadalcanal was fought in total darkness. (Two admirals were among the US dead returned to Luganville.) On a moonless night in August 1942 an Allied armada sailed through the Slot into a maritime ambush and the Battle of Savo Island. Australia lost the heavy cruiser *Canberra,* America so many ships US military historians later described it as one of the most catastrophic defeats suffered by their navy.

Gradually, however, the tide turned. In June 1943 Japan launched sixty bombers with fighter escorts for a final all-out attack on Guadalcanal; of the hundred fighters from Santo that engaged them, only six failed to return. Virtually all the Japanese aircraft were downed, and the greatest air battle of the Pacific War marked the beginning of Japan's retreat.

George told me that only one Jap bomber ever made it to the island. "He killed a cow. But quite a few Americans crashed here. The wrecks are turning up all the time."

I was directed to a framed newspaper clipping hanging by the bar. It described the hunt for the remains of Wayland Bennett, a twenty-year-old fighter pilot from Texarkana, Texas. Keen and high-spirited, he joined Major Gregory "Pappy" Boyington's elite Black Sheep Squadron and early in 1943, returning from a routine patrol in his gull-winged Corsair, vanished while approaching Luganville. In 1990 Dr Dan Bookout, a Texarkana chiropractor and family friend, arrived to organize a search party; in just three weeks they found *eight* previously undiscovered US crash sites—but not that of Corsair No. 02608.

It finally came to light four years later, located by men—perhaps looking for wild honey—in a densely jungled gulley. Yet, to this day, nobody knows how, or why, the kid went down.

"They reckon the most common cause was human error," said Pete. So, I reflected, but for a momentary concentration lapse, young Wayland (like those other skeletons still lying unrecovered in the hills) might now be a seventy-seven-year-old pensioner living in Florida, enjoying his great-grandchildren and, perhaps, a little gentle foreign travel. Ed said, "Don't know about gentle, the vets we see are tough old buggers. Last year a survivor of the *Coolidge* turned up. He was eighty-three—and he dived on the wreck three times."

Now we talked about Santo's greatest asset and finest war prize. On 26 October 1942, the 22,000 ton troopship *President Coolidge*—previously a fast, well-appointed liner on the LA to Yokohama run—arrived with five thousand Marines bound for Guadalcanal. Entering the Segond Channel she struck two friendly mines and, despite the efforts of her master, Captain Nelson, to park her on a nearby reef, sank with the loss of three lives.

Nat said, "In 1946 the owners sold the wreck to the New Hebrides government for $10. Their condition was that it would never be raised but, Christ, who'd want to do that? It's our biggest tourist asset by far, divers come from all over the world. The thing about the *Coolidge* is you can swim inside; the hold's full of jeeps, trucks, guns and so on. You dive, Alex?"

"No, I don't."

"Well, low tide at Millionaire's Point, you won't even have to get your feet wet. After the war the Yanks had thousands of tons of stuff surplus to requirements. They offered it cheap to the Condominium government who, of course, wanted it even cheaper—and got the price down to eight cents on the dollar. But when they still stuck out for more the Yanks lost patience and chucked *the whole lot* in the sea."

The talk grew general. On Saturday, at the Polo Club, there would be a match against a team of hard-riding, big-drinking Aussie girls down from Vila, Pete recalled a duck-racing derby he'd attended during a holiday in Sumatra ("You start a duck by sticking a finger up its arse. It goes *'Qwaarrkh!'* and takes off like a bloody rocket." "Probably heading for a quiet pond in the hills," said George). And Ed told me of a man who once visited Santo to teach touch-typing to a mixed class of Anglophones and Francophones. "Normal keyboards make English letters, so I asked him if the Francophones needed different ones. He said, 'No, mate,'—and here everyone grinned expectantly—*'mine can make French letters too.'"*

The Voyage of the Portuguese Grocer

My chief reason for coming to Santo had been to visit Big Bay. George, who had been there looking for gold, said the place now had a small resort offering basic accommodation and discounted weekend breaks. "And they throw in a driver."

Preparing for my trip I popped into the Lo Chan Moon store for biscuits, dried fruit, torch batteries and, on impulse, a bottle of "CAPT QUIROS NUMBER ONE RUM Prepared and Bottled by Tropical Nectar of Port Vila."

At the check-out desk I bumped into Pete, buying cans of white emulsion. He said, "That grog's fifty-eight per cent proof, it'll take the fucking enamel off your teeth."

"But it's dead right for drinking a toast to Quiros."

He handed the yawning cashier some money. "Quiros, eh? Why would you want to drink to him?"

"Well, really he should have been up there with Columbus and Cook."

"Mate, he was a loser." He counted his change. "Santo's first; the place has always attracted deadbeats like him."

*

A 4WD Daihatsu, driven by a silent, displeased-looking man, collected me early next morning. A mile or so out of Luganville the blacktop road gave way to washboard track. Yet it ran past landscapes—lush meadows, stately trees, fine views—possessing the ordered pastoral beauty that English aristos had spent centuries imposing on their estates. Next came spick-and-span Japanese plantations where sleek cattle grazed under the palms, then mile after mile of dark, unimaginably dense primary forest. A European in a rusting blue ute, speeding towards us on the wrong side, slalomed wildly; his swerve became a spin that instantly liberated a ton of billowing red dust. As he vanished I glimpsed a shadow—high, equine, prancing—bearing down through the murk, heard a whinny and an awful thud, yelled, "Christ, we've hit a horse!" The driver, blank-faced, hurtled on; each time I shouted for him to stop he seemed to go faster. Giving up, I took comfort imagining the horse's owner (a mad hippomanic bushman) waiting with loaded shotgun for the driver's return.

Finally, far below, I saw the enclosed immensity of Big Bay—a vast natural anchorage, reaching to the distant Cumberland Ranges, which had hoodwinked Quiros into thinking he had found Australia. As the Daihatsu lurched down a rutted arroyo (the rains would turn it into a river) I wondered if the obdurate, migraine-stricken *descubridor* had actually been the fool we all took him for. Maurice even made him into a verb: to "quiros" was to be mulish, or go wilfully barking up the wrong tree. As for my father, he claimed he had been the ideal founder of an absurd little island nation which, established amid controversy, rancour and confusion, had never once deviated from those principles.

But when I came upon the Hakluyt Society's superb two-volume account of the voyage, I arrived at other conclusions. He may indeed have been a seagoing Don Quixote, yet he organized the greatest maritime expedition ever carried out entirely within the tropics.

At the Big Bay Lodge, by the village of Matantas and just a few yards from the beach, the driver left me with barely a word. I found half a dozen bamboo huts managed by a sturdy, good-natured young man named Walter. "Anyone else staying?" I asked.

"Not so many people come."

A rubberized bag, with a tube and sprinkler head attached, hung from a hook in my coral-floored hut. "Solar shower," he said. "You just fill it from the tap and leave it in direct sunlight. But be careful, the sun can heat that water to one hundred and twenty degrees Fahrenheit, it can cook you alive."

In the airless little dining room, as he fixed a cheese omelette and strong Santo coffee, I asked about Quiros. Had he based himself here, at the Matantas end of the bay? Walter shrugged. "I think so. But tomorrow you should talk to *Jif* Moses. He is very old now, but he can speak all day about Quiros. He will tell you everything."

I wondered how an elderly, unschooled fisherman could possibly know about such matters; Walter answered my question without me having to find a delicate way of putting it. "He can *remember*."

I set off around Big Bay towards the River Jordan. It was a sunny afternoon, the shore lapped by small waves that rattled the shingle like coins. Two youths emerged from the trees and began tracking me. Keeping a wary eye on them I wondered how their ancestors had felt on that fateful April day in 1606. Then the Spaniards, in boots and armour, came crunching along this same shingly beach, picking fruit, shooting ducks—and, most certainly, mulling over the astounding possibility that they might actually be walking on Terra Australis Incognita itself.

As the youths, losing interest, wandered off I found a fragment of cow bone, elegantly sculptured by the sea, and put it in my pocket. (Weeks later a grim-faced official at Auckland's airport would take me aside, thinking it was human.) After two hours the Jordan and its mouth seemed no closer so I started checking the coastline for the fabled port of Vera Cruz. Seeing no sign of it, and taking comfort from the fact that Captain Cook hadn't been able to find it either, I marched back for a solar shower and a dinner of rice and stir-fried beef. A flickering hurricane lantern threw deep shadows as Walter, lounging on a bench, told me he was a sea cook trained in Tahiti; until recently he'd worked on a container ship captained and officered by Indians—his best years ever. "I had my own cabin with video machine, and always people to talk to."

"Not like here."

"No." On Gaua Island, nearby, he owned a small stretch of beach with a waterfall in one corner; some day he wanted to put bungalows and a restaurant there. In bed I lay listening to Big Bay's night noises. There were flying foxes foraging for wild apples, wild pigs crashing in the forest, rats scurrying through the thatch, overripe tropical fruit thudding to earth, the steady wash of surf and the constant glassy clink of pebbles being displaced. These sounds, I knew, hadn't changed since Spain's lost armada, with its mad, misguided commander, had dropped anchor almost four hundred years earlier.

*

The only certainties about the early days of Pedro Fernandez de Quiros are his place and date of birth: Évora, Portugal, in 1565; after that his life has no discernible beginning or end. But the recorded central section is a remarkable tale of ambition, nerve, politics (courtiers and cardinals glide in and out of the narrative), famous expeditions, high adventure and ultimate success; he becomes the greatest, most glamorous living *descubridor.*

Quiros first stepped from the shadows in 1595, aged thirty, and cut such a dash the Spanish king, a mere decade later, charged him with finding Australia—a challenge, in today's terms, pretty much like leading a mission to Mars. But during a voyage intended to place him among the immortals he underwent a major personality change. The humourless zealot (who probably never consciously cracked a joke in his life) grew so loopily eccentric he is now remembered as one of exploration's most enduring comic characters. As his career began to unravel he was dragged, raging—he loved being centre stage—back into the margins of history. Finally the shadows reclaimed him; we know he died aged fifty, but we don't know how, or where, or why. It's a very rum story.

There is no surviving portrait or likeness. Robert Graves in *The Isles of Unwisdom,* a novel based on the Mendaña Voyage, writes, "the Chief Pilot . . . was a fine-looking man, above the usual height, slim but muscular, with clear grey eyes and a short, curly beard; he was then in the thirty-sixth year of his life." Graves made that up; in fact he was thirty, and a vignette supplied by an anonymous contemporary states he had "a bronzed complexion with a mole on his right nostril." It is the only physical description to be found in the barren Quiros archive.

He possessed a quick, often violent temper; once, when the Viceroy of Peru declined him a favour, he roamed around Lima yelling threats at the top of his lungs. Articulate and quick-witted (remembered by one acquaintance as "a great talker"), he used his rhetoric to sway popes and kings. They probably assumed they were in the presence of just another garrulous geographer, yet he longed to be seen as something else: subtle, strong, clever, dangerous: a cloak-and-dagger character. Indeed, he confessed as much in a revealing letter to Clement VIII. "I am, Most Holy Father, a man of cloak and sword."

He was also insecure, sensing conspiracies around every corner. And, in a profession where men were supposed to be tough as teak, he suffered from violent headaches and bouts of illness. He was an obsessive planner. He made lists. He found it difficult to delegate. He had constant problems with money—claimed, indeed, he had been *muy pobre,* poverty-stricken, since childhood. And he had a chip on his shoulder put there by Madrid's patronizing nobility. Since Portugal had been overrun by Spain, any Portuguese competing for Spanish patronage stood at the back of the queue anyway, a supplicant from the provinces. So Évora-born Quiros—a provincial even in Portugal—was seen by the Spaniards as a rustic twice over, strictly lower deck. It always irked.

Yet Portugal had produced Prince Henry the Navigator, Bartholomew Diaz, Ferdinand Magellan and the great Admiral of India, Vasco da Gama himself; thanks to them a small European kingdom once controlled half the known world. Da Gama, who unlocked the secrets of the monsoon wind and sailed home with a fortune in spices, built a palace in Évora just forty years before Quiros was born. His grandparents must have seen him around town, friends and neighbours— some personally acquainted with the old pirate—would have told him da Gama stories. Meanwhile, that huge, plunder-filled house sent its message to every Évora schoolboy: find another India and you can have this too. At the end of the sixteenth century maps were already depicting continents shaped like those familiar to us now. There remained, however, an enormous void in the regions below the equator.

Australia first emerged as a metaphysical idea in the minds of Greek geographers. If the world was round, they reasoned, then to compensate for the weight of the northern hemisphere's known lands, an equivalent land mass must exist in the south. It was a simple matter of balance. Terra Australis Incognita became the subject of intense scholarly speculation—ended abruptly in the Middle Ages when Rome declared the world was flat.

After Rome grudgingly accepted the possibility of curvature, the Austral Lands theorists imagined a single great continent stretching from the Antarctic up to the Torrid Zone. But when Diaz rounded the Cape of Good Hope, and Magellan stumbled upon the Pacific, they revised their estimates and split it in two: one a polar region, the other—somewhere tantalizingly to the north—Terra Australis itself. For a *descubridor* it was the last great prize.

There is a reference to a youthful Quiros loitering in the Rua Nova dos Mercadores, a Lisbon street frequented by unemployed sailors, then the trail goes cold. He almost certainly talked his way into a job as a pilot's apprentice, later found work navigating galleons to the Indies and South America.

In 1567, when he was two, the first Australia-bound expedition sailed from Peru, commanded by the Spaniard Alvaro de Mendaña. He expected to discover his "southern continent" just six hundred leagues, or eighteen hundred miles, off the South American coast, but fetched up instead among a chain of lush tropical islands lying 6° south of the equator. Naming them for King Solomon, convinced they would some day yield prodigious wealth, he arrived home vowing to return with colonizing Spaniards—and try again for Australia. The arrangements took half a lifetime. Finally, in 1595, his four-ship armada set off carrying three hundred and seventy-eight settlers and a youngish, ambitious Portuguese chief pilot with a mole on his nose.

They never found the Solomons, certainly got nowhere near the Austral Lands. Quiros made some serious navigational errors (the first premonitional shadows loom, the first questions get asked), yet the fault wasn't entirely his; Mendaña's failing memory kept playing tricks. They came upon, and were enchanted by, the Marquesas Group then, many weeks later, arrived off a large wooded island which Mendaña named Santa Cruz. Yet, even as he planted the Spanish flag, his mutinous companions announced this would be the site of their colony. They refused to go further.

Within two months fever, feuding and skirmishes with natives had wiped out all but a hundred of the settlers; two ships had sunk with all hands, a third simply vanished. After Mendaña himself died Quiros put the survivors aboard the remaining vessel and brought them safely to Acapulco—where, after relaying the dismal news from Santa Cruz, they spoke only of Quiros. And what a story they had to tell! He'd dodged hurricanes, waterspouts, tidal waves, hidden reefs and war canoes. Crossing uncharted waters he performed feats of seamanship that earned the respect of even the Spaniards. Now all doubts seemed quashed; a proven deep-sea *descubridor,* his claim to make the next attempt on Terra Australis Incognita could not be contested.

In Lima he sent memorials to the Viceroy requesting forty sailors and a sixty-ton ship so he could head west and "discover the lands which I know to exist." The Viceroy, aware the plan would need royal approval, directed Quiros to Madrid to meet the King. But Philip III was out of town so Quiros, in pilgrim's robes, sailed off to lobby the Pope. In Rome he had a stroke of luck. The Duke of Sesa, Spain's Ambassador to the Holy See, took a shine to him ("The majority of pilots and sailors," he explained to the Spanish Secretary of State, "are generally rough and uncouth folk"). Invited to join his household, Quiros spent the next seventeen months writing letters, drawing maps and inventing a clockwork instrument for determining latitude and an engine which would make sea water potable. And he had several meetings with Father Clavio, a Bavarian Jesuit celebrated for his work on gnomonics, or the measurement of time by sundials. Clavio, and a committee of Vatican geographers, assured Quiros that the Austral Lands would be found between 36° and 40° south—prescient enough; this turned out to be the location of New Zealand's North Island.

The Duke fixed an audience with the Pope who, intrigued, asked Quiros back for several more. He told Clement about the Marquesans, some "very fair or blond, others of a tawny colour" and, by and large, the most "well-disposed" people he had ever known. Without a shred of evidence he had concluded they came originally from the Austral Lands yet, even as he described Terra Australis as a verdant country aglitter with precious metals and populated by exceptionally sweet-natured blonds, Quiros remained businesslike: in return for patronage and Letters Exhortatory he would take in a party of missionaries.

Clement promised six Papal briefs and a supply of Agnus Dei, or personally blessed wax discs embossed with the figure of a lamb. (Tossed overboard by stormbound mariners they functioned like spiritual oil slicks, miraculously calming the roughest seas.) Quiros, writing elatedly to tell Philip he now had papal support, included an embarrassing assessment of his own qualities: anyone joining the expedition would discover he possessed "the resolution of Caesar, Hannibal, Alexander, Columbus, Gama, Magellan, Pizarro and Cortez." Swaggering, he makes his first move into the realms of comedy.

Philip, defending his far-flung empire against the predatory English and Dutch, hadn't the resources to guard a new possession in the southern ocean. Quiros didn't deny that. Instead, he painted a rapturous picture in which his *misioneros* expanded Philip's domain until it embraced the entire globe—with him enthroned at its centre. "I desire that the undiscovered dwellers of the antarctic region be brought to pasture," he wrote, "and that Your Majesty may be the lord, known, obeyed and served from one pole to the other." For the King this—and the notion of millions of reformed cannibals saying their prayers in Spanish—proved a heady prospect. He signed nine royal *cedulas,* assigning to Quiros two ships in "excellent" condition and the crews to man them.

A frigate bringing him to Curaçao sank, in Panama a balcony collapsed as he stood on it viewing a procession. In Lima, still limping, he began assembling his armada. Though Philip had specified two vessels, he purchased three: for his flagship or *capitana,* the well-found 150-ton *San Pedro y Pablo,* then a 120-ton *almirata,* the *San Pedro,* and a small *zabra,* or launch, *Los Tres Reyes,* which had recently rescued a shipwrecked crew from the Galapagos Islands and would, after the discovery of the Austral Lands, race home with a message for the King.

The three hundred personnel signed up included ten monks, a couple of slaves, three Chinese servants and thirty *aventureros* travelling at their own expense. Spain's sixteenth-century navy boasted exquisite gradations of rank, privilege and precedence; captains, chief pilots, pilots and second pilots serving aboard first-rate vessels occupied the upper deck and dined in the admiral's gallery. Below lived the seamen and steward, the caulker and carpenter, gunners, grummets (*grumetes,* or ship's boys), page boys and clerical personnel: the accountant and the notary *(escribano).*

Quiros chose his officers with the Viceroy of Peru at his elbow, and the political bias of this professional bestower of patronage possibly accounts for the wrong-headedness of certain appointments. Juan de Bilbao, a Sevillian, signed on as the fleet's chief pilot—despite Quiros's certainty that he would cause trouble. (He did; having charged him with inciting mutiny, Quiros, in mid-ocean, exiled him to the *almirata.*) Yet his replacement, Gaspar de Leza, proved no better; a shadowy, subversive figure, he got a spell in the stocks. And Manuel Noble, master of the *capitana,* though loyal, suffered like Quiros from chronic headaches and spent much of the voyage in his berth.

Yet he made the Breton Luiz Vaez de Torres captain of the *almirata* and admiral of the fleet. (After the bewildering sequence of events six months later, this exemplary officer, transiting the seaway south of New Guinea, came within a whisker of achieving Quiros's objective by passing only eighteen leagues—fifty miles!—from Australia. In 1766 the British geographer Alexander Dalrymple decreed the seaway be named for him: Torres Strait.)

Quiros then provisioned his fleet, compiling his own list of requirements while requiring everyone else to make a list also; finally collated, these became his great List of Lists. For "the natives" he loaded 90 falcon bells, 60 pairs of Roman buckles, 120 Bohemian knives, 170 wooden combs, 440 glass medallions, 390 pairs of glass earrings, 5,000 gewgaws of imitation gold and silver, 213 coloured hats, 42 tunics and vests of silk and 59 suits of trousers. (Since some would be used for barter, he sought advice from Lima's archbishop. "There is the question of the exchange of things of lesser worth for those of greater." Was it permitted, say, to swap a hat for a horse? The cleric thought that a fair trade.)

The *capitana* carried enough ecclesiastical gear to equip a country church: one gilded wooden cross, one decorated wooden altar, four chasubles of Chinese grogram with three stoles and three maniples, two silk-lined choir copes, two surcingles of linen, one painting on canvas of the image of Our Lady, one hassock, a few corporals with their burse, one iron platten for making Hosts, four snuffer scissors and four small bells for the service of the altar. Since several men intended keeping journals, twenty-one quires of best-quality paper and a hundred and fifty writing quills went aboard too.

They also took Mexican axes, iron harpoons, moulds for lozenge-shaped arquebus bullets, twenty Peruvian gunpowder jars, four bronze culverins and ten *arrobas* of oakum. For his medical requirements Quiros carried twenty dozen rings of alchemy, two bundles of sarsaparilla, a set of lead spoons and a hundred and sixty ear cleaners. And he demanded certain items of an exotic, even theatrical, nature: vials of gold dust, tinsel in leaf, Chinese garnet and twenty ounces of glass beading for embroidering cloaks.

The King made him a general.

He scarcely seemed to notice, obsessively went on writing instructions to his captains. He required them to treat subordinates with kindness, yet if any man cursed or blasphemed—this edict must be nailed to each mainmast—he would go without food for a day. Cards and dice were forbidden, but backgammon allowed; should a game lead to fights, however, the board must be thrown into the sea. At dusk all would kneel and recite the "Salve Regina," an ancient breviary anthem said aboard the ships of Columbus. Each morning Torres would come up to the *San Pedro y Pablo* and wish all aboard a good voyage, each afternoon repeat this manoeuvre to ask for the watchword. All, daily, would receive one and a half pounds of biscuit, one pound of meat, two ounces of bacon, one ounce of chickpeas and a pint of water. On Fridays the ration would include a spotted dogfish. Lighted candles were not permitted below unless enclosed in lantern glass.

To every officer he sent a document describing the signs of impending landfall: heavy rain, thunderclaps and lightning flashes in quick succession, coconuts drifting in a greasy sea, the presence of shrimps, turtles and seals. Ducks, hawks and flamingos circling a ship for galley scraps indicated the presence of land, boatswain birds did not. "Boatswain birds are wont to fly where they will," he noted grimly. (They had fooled him before.)

Once they arrived in the Austral lands lookouts must be posted day and night. The natives, "great swimmers and divers," were likely to cut moorings, or even sneak aboard. Ashore, moving through open country, the Spaniards risked being ambushed by warriors hiding behind trees, or lying motionless in long grass; in steep defiles rocks might be rained down on them. "Do not underrate the natives, for they are quick with their hands and good runners, and when an opportunity arises they are quick to recognize it and quicker still to take advantage of it."

Yet he insisted they be respected. Under no circumstances should their fruit trees be cut down, and "None is ever to be ill-treated; nor may you break your word or any pact you have made." Though both would be broken routinely, their stern publication in Standing Orders probably helped cool the Spaniards' bloodlust. By and large his preparations proved satisfactory. Men and ships stood up well, and the only thing destined to fail Quiros—apart from certain key officers—would be his nerve.

*

The small armada sailed from the port of Callao at 4 p.m. on 21 December 1605. Noisy crowds came from Lima to wave them off on the flood tide. Manuel Noble, master of the *capitana,* embarked with a severe *agonia en la frente,* or migraine, and went straight to bed. Three days later, having established that his ships were set safely on a WSW course, Quiros came down with one too.

They made good time, and late in January began finding small islands, uninhabited and of no particular interest. On 2 February they encountered their first hurricane. The ships ran with bare masts and their crews knelt in torrential rain as Fray Martin de Munilla, Chaplain and Vicar of the Royal Fleet, threw four Agnus Dei into the sea. "It was a miraculous thing," he wrote, "when at once was seen the power of God's blessed medallions. The weather abating, we made way that night with some difficulty."

Munilla's journal is the best account of the voyage we have. Little is known of him other than that he was a Castilian friar who, in 1580, volunteered for the Franciscan mission in Chile. An old man when he embarked on the *San Pedro y Pablo,* he maintained a punishing schedule. Respected for his sagacity and firmness, he acted as chief mediator between the wardroom and lower deck, but also heard the confessions of Quiros and the *capitana's* senior personnel, supervised the work of his nine subordinate friars, directed the page boys as they recited, daily, the Fourteen Articles of Faith, the Ten Commandments, the Seven Sacraments, the Corporal and Spiritual Works of Mercy, the Theological and Cardinal Virtues, the Seven Capital Sins and the Last Four Things, and at sunset took the service when the Salve was said.

Then, each evening, he laboured over his journal—a detailed, entertaining, often gossipy document done with a fine descriptive flair: his deep-sea entries are shot through with salt and creaking timbers while, ashore, he got the strange, silky beauty of the tropics just right. And nobody chronicled the growing extremes of Quiros's behaviour with more relish than his old father confessor.

The General began displaying signs of stress several weeks into the voyage. He took to staring wildly about and crying, "Show us, O God, in this sea just one man—for of a certainty there are millions of them." He and Torres had calculated that on reaching 26° south they should steer due west, and within ten days his continent would begin looming. (That course would, in fact, have led them direct to Queensland, and a spot known today as Noosa Heads; a famously chic beach resort, it commands some of Australia's highest real-estate prices.) But tantalizing cloudbanks on the western horizon kept turning into shadows fashioned from dew; no thunderclaps sounded, no reassuring flamingos circled.

Quiros's behaviour now gave serious cause for concern. He grew increasingly eccentric, flew into rages, sighed and mumbled to himself. Then, one fateful morning, he summoned the pilots to his gilded great cabin and abruptly announced the fleet would head WNW. "We shall plough the sea with great sweeps until we find the land or lose our lives in the process."

What he actually lost was an assured place in history. The course urged by the Vatican geographers—now also rejected—would have given him New Zealand, then, lying massively across his path as he followed Philip's orders and headed north for the Philippines, Australia itself; a great house in Évora could have been his for the taking. Torres, sensing the proximity of land, knew their calculations were sound. "Keep on!" he pleaded.

Quiros began a long, aimless sweep south of the Marquesas, altered tack and went looking for Santa Cruz, where Mendaña founded his ill-starred settlement. The crews, growing restless, mocked him for his obsession with stores, took to calling him "the Portuguese grocer"; indeed, a shortage of food and, most acutely, water led to the first mutinous mutterings. Munilla records the men saying that "it was a dream; that no land existed; and that he had deceived the pope and the King."

On 25 March, Quiros, feverish, rose from his sickbed, summoned the pilots and raged at them for going the wrong way. There had indeed been some deviation from the prescribed course since it was plainly taking them nowhere, but Quiros arrested Bilbao, his chief pilot, and told Torres to lock him up aboard the *almirata*. Bilbao's friends rallied; Juan de Iturbe, the accountant, deplored this treatment of "a fine sailor and a man famous in his art"; mutiny seemed imminent. Quiros placed the execution block in a prominent position on deck, went to his cabin and prayed. Next morning they came upon a small island running with sweet water—yet, back at sea, an air of simmering rebellion still centred on the jailed chief pilot. Quiros summoned Torres alongside and, using graphic sign language, indicated that Bilbao should be strangled. Since the command wasn't in writing Torres ignored it, hoping something would come along to distract the old man.

Something did. On Sunday 30 April 1606, Quiros discovered Santo.

Notes from the Lost Continent

Jif Moses, an earnest, grey-stubbled old man, was seated so close to his crackling breakfast fire that, periodically, he seemed to become a spectral voice speaking from within its smoke. Walter had contacted Steve, a local teacher, who brought me to the *Jif*'s *nakamal* at 7 a.m. sharp. Now he and I sat with Moses watching a young, very beautiful woman boiling slabs of beef in a big black pot. "His wife," mouthed Steve. "That cow meat will give them meals for a week." A child wandered in and threw a corncob on the fire. Moses peered at me distractedly, wondering what I wanted, so I mentioned Quiros. He instantly sat up. *"Quirroshh!"* he went, and began talking in a fast, up-country Bislama I couldn't possibly follow. Steve picked up a twig and, idly drawing on the sandy floor, began translating what Moses had to say.

"Quiros come inside Big Bay first time at two o'clock in the afternoon, weather not so good, there was rain, a wind was coming, but they sail on and drop anchor at four o'clock. Three ships—one big, one not so big, one *smol smol*. Soon the wind gets very strong and there are big waves. The ships are rolling badly and Quiros is very afraid. He dashes about on his ship. He shouts. Soon he tells them to leave Big Bay. They do this, they go back out to sea. But next afternoon, also at two o'clock, they come back and anchor again. The sea is calm, there is no wind."

Staring at Moses, and recalling that no portrait of Quiros had survived, I asked what he looked like. The answer came instantly: "Big tall feller, very handsome. He had bright eyes and yellow hair. He had a big moustache. He had no belly. He wore a jacket of silver metal. He was very strong. He had a big voice—he liked to sing! He smiled a lot but he always knew what he wanted. You wouldn't want to mess with him."

"Did he have a mole on his nose?"

"Yes."

176

"How do you know this, Moses?"

"When my mother was a kid she stayed with her grandfather. *His* mother had told him about Quiros."

Ancestral memory meant that, having no other means of recording history, and with those hours of darkness to kill before sleep, the elders passed on the tales they themselves had been told. I seemed to be getting a contemporary eyewitness account of events on the beach.

"What happened when he came ashore?"

"First he went to Warewake village. All the people were hiding, there was nobody around. But he found footprints, then he found a garden. In the garden there were yams, bananas, *kumala* and pawpaw. As he inspected the garden, the Warewake people summoned other indigenous people from the area and made a plan to *test* Quiros. They came with bows and arrows and they shot the arrows above the heads of Quiros and his men. They soon ran away. They went back to their ships and sailed down to Nunumeia village. It was on the other side of the Jordan, and they arrived at half-past four in the afternoon."

"But they only anchored off Warewake at two o'clock."

"That was the previous day. There was a heavy swell at Warewake so they could only come ashore next morning, at eight o'clock. When they reached Nunumeia people were strolling on the beach. They ran away, but Chief Pun stayed, along with a man called Peter."

I said Peter was a European name.

"We have forgotten his real name. Quiros was nice to Peter and Pun, he gave them muskets, pipes and stick tobacco. But Pun became suspicious, he wanted to run away. Quiros said, 'No, no, my friend, you stay here, I will go to my ship and bring you more presents.' So Pun stayed. He sat on the beach and smoked his pipe."

What came next caused Steve to whistle softly. "Moses says Quiros and his men came back after dark. They shot Pun, they killed everyone at Nunumeia—men, women, even babies—and took the bodies back to the ships. They sailed out of Big Bay, to the sea, and threw them over the side."

In the silence the beautiful young wife began peeling yams. Moses stared grimly at his big black callused feet as Steve worked on his sand drawing—a series of intricate circles and rectangles taking the form of a bird. I felt uneasy. This story bore absolutely no relation to the expedition's own accounts, but a sense of real outrage lingered in the air. To defuse it I told Moses that a few months earlier I had visited Quiros's birthplace.

He looked up, interested. "His village?"

"Well, it's a town, actually. In Portugal."

"You were there?"

"Yes. I went looking for him."

As, again, he dematerialized briefly in a billow of smoke, his disembodied voice enquired, "You meet his family?"

*

Shortly before leaving for Vanuatu I spent several days working in Lisbon. Learning that Évora lay just two hours away by car I set off one Sunday morning and came upon a neat, contained little *cidade* on a hill sixty miles from the Spanish border. Behind the mustard and whitewash facades lay Roman walls and a pillared Roman temple; Évora had been old even in Quiros's time and I doubted it would yield much to me. In the Praça do Geraldo, resonating with brassy music from a shop selling bullfight tickets, I found a tourist information centre and asked the plump official for an Évora phone directory. It listed only one Quiros—an engineer at Ave Herois Ultramar 87. I explained my interest and begged him to call the number; it was a long shot, yet families descended from even the most obscure *descubridore* might have their mementos and stories. But there was no answer. "So what you say this Quiros discover?"

"Vanuatu."

"Uh?"

"It's an island group. Out in the South Pacific."

"*OK!*" He jiggled his heavy hips. "Hula hula!"

"That's right. Look, is it true da Gama had a house here?"

"Da Gama? Of course. But no more."

Handing me a town plan he pointed to where the house may have stood. I set off up steep, cobbled, empty streets, and at the designated spot found the Tropical Cocktail Bar. Oddly cheered, I climbed on, and opposite the elegant remains of Évora's Roman temple came upon the Convento de São João Evangelista, *fundado em 1485* and burbling with doves. Da Gama would have known this place—Quiros too.

Now, under new management, with three Mercs and a Paris-registered Porsche parked outside, it had become the luxury hotel Pousada dos Lóios. Studying the luncheon menu ("partridge broth, stewed hare with turnips, pot stew of eels, convent sweetmeats") in a lobby heaped with fresh-cut flowers, I was joined by two sleek, middle-aged Lisboetas who I guessed were married but not to each other. They considered my question. "I have not heard of him," said the man, "but we have a cyclist Quiros." The woman said, "Oh, Bobo, Quiros is a *golfer!*"

In Évora's dim thirteenth-century cathedral I found a gilded statue of an overweight madonna. A young man with a nervous tic came winking up to practise his English. Had I noted the madonna was pregnant? In the old days, he said, mothers with sons in the armadas prayed to her. I knew with absolute certainty that Quiros's mother had once stood on this spot—though when I asked about the General he looked blank. "Many Évora men joined armadas. This was very poor area, still poor today." He spoke of the poor local cuisine: thin soups, small snails and such a reliance on dried cod they had devised three hundred and sixty-five different cod recipes. At the market I met a vendor of bent hickory spoons who complained about Évora's wretchedly poor wood, inside the Restaurante Mr Pickwick I learned that Évora was the cork capital of Portugal.

"I suppose the cork is of poor quality?" I ventured.

"It is tip-top, the best."

"Is Évora a poor town?"

"No, is very rich town."

I drove home past the showroom of Évoracar (VW and Audi dealers) and the gaunt new three-star Évora Hotel. This was the way young Quiros would have come, through shady cork groves and hazy acres of wild lavender that ran right to the horizon and, this evening, on up into a matching lavender sky. (Now there were eucalypts too, ironic imports from the land he almost found.)

In Lisbon I visited the Jeronimos Monastery. It contains da Gama's tomb, resting on carved elephants so misshapen the sculptors plainly worked from wildly conflicting descriptions (they had problems visualizing the trunks). Then, by the Tagus, I came to the triumphalist *Padrão dos Descobrimentos*—a gleaming Soviet-style monument featuring the towering figures of Portugal's old maritime heroes—and knew that, but for his moment of madness, Quiros's giant marble likeness would have been up there too. A few yards downstream lay the exquisite little riverine tower on which Portugal's kings once stood to farewell their fleets, and where men hoisting sail for the New World strained back for a final glimpse of home. Here I had, for the only time, an odd sense of his presence—just a feeling, but strong enough to make me glance around. Then, a second later, it was gone.

*

Moses, through Steve, said, "A ghost? But it wasn't Quiros."

That took me by surprise. "Why not?"

Steve spoke with certainty. "Because it lives here."

My heart sank. When Melanesians start invoking ghosts you know it's story time. Fact and fiction become scrambled; there is artifice in the air. Sometimes they seem merely to pull your leg for the fun of it, at others their deceit takes on a sharper, angrier edge—stemming, probably, from the days of colonial chicanery and land theft. (It was Europeans who taught them to dissemble in the first place.) Now I guessed that everything Moses had said should be taken with a pinch of salt; his anecdotal history was probably little more than a ragbag of misreported facts garnered from visitors to Big Bay (next time he might even feature Quiros's mother).

Suddenly I needed fresh air and coffee. Having repaid his tales with one of my own (the duty of a conscientious guest) I now felt free to leave. Politely I thanked Moses—who turned his back on me. But when I thanked Steve he scuffed a foot through his exquisite sand bird and shrugged as if to say: on your head be it. Maybe the best is yet to come.

*

The fleet entered Big Bay on 3 May, anchored that evening within two musket shots of a shore where wild orange and lemon trees grew to the water's edge. Men who had been under way for a hundred and thirty-three days saw their mirrored ships fragmented by the fiery swirl of a sunset tide. "It was like sailing in a river," Munilla wrote, "bordered by thick groves in which day and night numerous birds sang, and it seemed as though we were in a delightful orchard." Quiros, on his knees, gave thanks.

In the morning it rained. In the afternoon he went ashore with forty arquebusiers to determine a site for his stockade. As he paced the beach they shot pigeons and ducks, harvested almonds "bigger than those of Castile, with a shell that has a most delicious smell of pippins," mangoes—"peach-like fruit"—and, probably, soursops or "the custard apple, which is very good and from which the negroes of this bay make their wine." Natives spotted walking their pigs meant fresh pork to come.

Torres knew they hadn't reached the Austral lands, Quiros believed they had. Big Bay, he noted elatedly, was "so capacious that it could contain more than a thousand vessels. The bottom is clean, and of black sand. No shipworm have been seen." He spotted four mountain ranges, several cloud-dappled peaks—6,195 foot-high Tabwémasana was first climbed by an Oxford University expedition in 1933—endless jungly blue hinterlands and the Yora River teeming with "herons, rushes and reed-mace." (One morning, meeting two startled men while exploring its estuary, he dressed them in silk trousers and left them "very pleased.")

A traveller who crossed the Yora in 1876 compared it with the Thames at Isleworth. Quiros, though, had arrived during the wet season when, according to another visitor, it could look like the Danube in flood. Santo was conspiring against him.

Having come to all the wrong conclusions, he announced his new continent would be named La Austrialia del Espiritu Santo—that first *i* inserted to ingratiate himself with King Philip (whose ancestry was Austrian). It would be formally claimed for Spain at a high mass; the Yora, henceforth, would be known as the Jordan, Big Bay as the Bay of St Philip and St James. Leading his officers along the beach Quiros pointed out the site of New Jerusalem, a city which in time would be grander than Lima. They, like Torres, guessed Santo was merely a large island but, too weary to argue, listened to his plans for a Ministry of War and Marine (which would clear the bush and erect a fort) and a New Jerusalem Town Council responsible for building and administering his metropolis.

Quiros, who spent most days aboard the *capitana*, displayed little interest in events ashore. When the natives realized some form of settlement was being planned they began cracking the intruders' skulls with their hockey-stick clubs—semi-sporting, mettle-testing affairs impelled by curiosity as much as anger; they took them for ghosts, kept stroking their victims' flesh to learn what they were made of. But when they discovered that ectoplasmic, or astral, shit smelled like terrestrial shit, and that a bang on the head produced a yelp of pain, uncertainty vanished; they embarked on a series of brisk little guerrilla skirmishes.

These stocky, black, pugnacious, woolly-haired people bore no relation to the charmers Quiros had encountered in the Marquesas. Here the women wore only a single leaf suspended from a string, the men bark penis gourds which kept the member permanently—and to Quiros, offensively—erect. They bleached their hair with lime, ate their enemies, strangled widows and unwanted children, buried their dead with head and hands protruding above the ground. Witchcraft flourished; rain-makers, sunshine-makers and disease-makers held positions of influence, ancestral spirits—dwelling in stones by day, roaming free by night—were exorcized by rattling bags of nuts. People belonged to tiny tribes which spoke mutually unintelligible dialects and squabbled endlessly over pigs—the mainstay of Santo's economy. Ownership of a mature boar, with its tusks grown agonizingly back through the head to contrive a double circle, conveyed such wealth and status it became an object of love, valued almost above life itself. To the Spaniards, though, it just meant meat.

At first they proceeded cautiously, observing the rigorous laws promulgated by Philip II (the King's father) regarding the treatment of natives encountered on expeditions. The Santoese, for their part, never killed indiscriminately; their wars followed strict, ancient rules. But they proved irritatingly clever opponents and the Spaniards soon lost patience. And wherever the soldiers went the priests—unmoved by the slaughter—went too. Munilla kept a grouse-moor tally. "We fired a few arquebuses, killing one native. The rest fled into the bush. Our men hung the dead man in a tree."

Relations deteriorated further when they shot a chief and a pig, both capital crimes. Now Quiros too began suffering losses; his blundering arquebusiers often found themselves outwitted. But clubs, in the end, proved no match for guns, and scores of islanders died. Occasionally the priests recalled their vows; once, after a fleeing mother abandoned her baby, "the child was baptized and left for her in one of the huts." Later the soldiers went hunting for swine but "found no herds whatsoever." Their prudent owners had driven them into the hills.

As New Jerusalem grew in Quiros's imagination—where it was destined to remain—reality ceased to interest him. Not a brick had been laid, yet he had already appointed a Municipal Council (its Public Trustee a gentleman adventurer named Don Diego de Prado y Tovar), Municipal Magistrates, a Royal Police Force and a Royal Treasury. His men nursed their wounds, sweated through fevers and wondered what else the grocer might have up his sleeve.

On 13 May they awoke to find they had become Knights of the Holy Ghost. Munilla, summoned early to Quiros's cabin, found him sitting on the floor cutting crosses from bolts of blue silk. In boisterous mood he said he had created a new Order of Chivalry to celebrate the discovery of his new continent. Handing Munilla a crudely scissored silk scrap, he explained the insignia were to be worn on all knightly robes; he must stitch his to his habit.

Munilla, reporting this to his incredulous fellow friars, reminded them of worldly vanity. As Franciscans they rejected all adornments yet, prepared to help out, agreed to wear crosses of plain wood instead. Munilla entered the General's cabin, next to his own, and broke the news.

Quiros grew so violent Munilla hastily retreated, then, to muffle the expletives coming through the bulkhead, covered his ears. Later he scrawled in his journal that the General bawled "things that cannot be set down with ink on paper."

Quiros raved for much of the night. His language, though, moderated enough for Munilla to record it. " 'So those shavelings refuse to wear the knightly insignia I am conferring on them! Well, whether they like it or not, I will make them.' On hearing this the Father Commissary [Munilla] jumped up and hastened to the stern-cabin where the General was, and told him to . . . mind what he was saying, for neither he nor all his forefathers together were enough to make the religious of St Francis commit so great an absurdity." As Quiros blustered, Munilla played his trump card: though every lay member of the expedition would wear a blue Knight's Cross the General himself—offering no explanation—had chosen not to. Munilla, turning on his heel, left him sulking.

Yet he soon perked up. This, the Feast of Pentecost, would be the day he formally took possession of his continent, and stepping on deck he magnanimously freed two Negro slaves who didn't belong to him (and who, immediately reclaimed by their owners, were sent back to fixing breakfast). As the men, sporting their wisps of silk, headed ashore even Iturbe, the humourless accountant, marvelled at their spirit of raucous "amusement." Quiros, smiling, ordered the ceremony to commence.

A chapel woven from saplings housed the portable altar and two brass swivel guns. At 7 a.m. platoons of arquebusiers fired a ragged salute as the bare-footed Quiros, re-enacting Christ's agony, staggered through the surf beneath a giant cross fashioned from Santo orangewood. Everyone cried "Long live the King!" then Iturbe intoned Quiros's plans for appropriating virtually all that remained of the southern hemisphere. "I take possession of this bay named San Felipe y Santiago and its port of Vera Cruz, and of the site where the city of Nueva Jerusalem is to be created, and of all the lands which lie before my gaze, and of all those parts of the South as far as the Pole, which henceforth are to be known as the Austral Region of the Holy Ghost, together with all its dependencies and appurtenances, for ever."

Munilla sprinkled the banners with holy water then said low mass, high mass and, later, an auxiliary mass for those who had missed the other masses while standing guard. After the ship's boys served drinks to scores of boisterous men in blue crosses Quiros, standing "on the banks of a cool stream," formally named the officials who would administer New Jerusalem. (Here Munilla allowed a note of irony to intrude. "It was a marvellous thing," he wrote, "to see such a diversity of knights. . . . here were sailor-knights, grummet-knights, ship's-page knights, mulatto-knights and negro-knights and Indian-knights and knights who were knight-knights.")

As Quiros returned to his ship, Torres led eighty men inland, and chancing upon a native feast, stole a dozen pigs. Next day a raiding party took fifteen more, together with three weeping boys, the eldest aged eight—a fact Munilla noted briefly in the course of a scholarly dissertation on the chestnuts and nutmegs that grew in the forest. When Quiros let it be known the children would be exchanged for even more pigs the Santoese responded with despairing charges into the guns, their dead and wounded leaving "the grass stained with blood."

On 18 May an earthquake jolted the Spaniards. "Our men ashore were terrified. On the ships it was also felt noticeably, for it lasted more than two Creeds and the ships shook violently." On 25 May they celebrated the Feast of Corpus Christi. After Munilla said mass in a palm grove, ten page boys, in costumes of Chinese silk hung with silver bells, danced for the congregation. Quiros inspected his pumpkin patch, planted to demonstrate the value of seed crops to the natives and coming along nicely.

Three days later the fleet sailed "to pursue its discoveries"—Quiros determined to prove he had located a continent comparable in size even to South America. But, near the entrance to Big Bay, the men dined off bad fish. "Some had acute nausea with vomiting and gastric trouble, and others had aches in all their joints. We were in a sad plight because, out of eighty people who were aboard this *capitana,* not eight could be found to work the sails."

They blamed the natives for having "cast poison into the river." Quiros ordered his fleet back to the anchorage. None of the men died, but two of the ships' cats did, howling.

*

They convalesced for a week, many with festering sores that refused to heal. Ashore, the fathers of the boy hostages blew conch shells and requested a meeting. Quiros stated his terms: thirty pigs per child. The fathers, incredulous, said no one had such wealth, but Quiros insisted: ninety pigs for the three—though, as a gesture of good will, he would throw in a couple of goats as well. *Goats?* Since the Santoese had never seen such creatures, two were rowed in and tied to a tree. The children stood ringed by arquebusiers as each father led out his most prized boar, one for each boy. Quiros rejected them just as they rejected his goats—which accompanied him back to the ship.

Early next morning he returned but the natives, done with talking, attacked. Munilla believed Quiros had no intention of releasing the boys. He reported that when the sobbing eight-year-old pleaded with him, the General snapped, "Silence, child! You know not what you ask. Greater benefits than the sight of heathen parents and friends await you." The ships put to sea.

*

Rolling wildly, unable to make headway, they turned again for the sanctuary of Big Bay. But the shifting trades wouldn't let them in; it took three long days for the launch and *almirata* to make it back to their anchorages. At dusk, as the *capitana* idled along behind, a sudden squall almost blew her into the forest. The crew worked wildly to reduce canvas then, with only the spritsail set, found themselves hurtling back the way they had come. By dawn they stood well beyond Big Bay's entrance and there they stayed, a howling force five shutting them out like a giant gate.

Torres hung lanterns to guide his flagship home, then in the morning sent boats to search for wreckage, and men to the hilltops with spyglasses. The *San Pedro y Pablo* had vanished without trace, and rumours began circulating that she had been sailed away by mutineers.

An anonymous crew member later would assert that mutineers had indeed taken over the ship as Quiros slept. (When he emerged at midday, as was his habit at sea, and demanded an explanation "he was told to shut his mouth and go to his cabin." This he promptly did, the door being locked and sentries being posted outside.) Munilla, though, never mentioned such an apocalyptic event. The *capitana* certainly contained souls who, according to a Quiros loyalist, "watched his doings with an evil eye"—and, in many respects, he certainly behaved like a man no longer in command. Plagued by depressions, migraines and illness, he took little interest in his ship's swift progress to Acapulco. Indeed, Quiros seems to have spent much of the voyage in bed.

*

On the evening of the meeting with Moses, as tropical rain sheeted down on Matantas, Steve stopped by the Lodge. I had just drunk a whole tumbler of neat Capt Quiros Number One Rum, and focused carefully as I shook his hand. He said, "You left us suddenly"—meaning, you displayed bad manners.

"Oh, come on," I blustered, "that wasn't history he was telling, it was bedtime stories."

He shrugged. "Who is to say which version is true?"

It was a fair point; Moses or Munilla—both would put their spin on events. "Care for some grog?" He shook his head. Ushering him to a chair, I lurched and sent the chair crashing to the floor. Retrieving it,

I knocked over another chair, and setting that up (then trying to sit on it) recalled a question I should have put to Moses regarding the armada's chaotic departure. Was it really possible the *wind* had stopped Quiros getting back into Big Bay?

He said, "South-westerlies can blow off the island at maybe sixty knots—sometimes for two weeks. Even with an engine you can have problems, often the copra boats have to wait."

"OK." Engulfed by a shuddering yawn, I asked, "And where was New Jerusalem?"

"Right here. At Matantas. It's obvious, check the evidence."

"And Vera Cruz?"

"Here also, it was the port for New Jerusalem. But, of course, there is no port, it was all a Quiros dream. It was in his head."

I looked around for my bottle. "Care for some grog?"

"No, thanks."

Walter walked in as Steve walked out. They glanced at me and exchanged winks.

*

Why did Quiros abandon his fleet? He would argue later he had completed his mission, and quote an ordinance—to which most *descubridores* turned a blind eye—that required him to sail home when half his supplies had run out. Iturbe, exasperated, wrote a furious remonstrance urging him to turn back and finish the job he had come to do—his harshest paragraphs being devoted to the expedition's hefty capital outlay and total lack of profit. (He had the remonstrance delivered to Quiros's cabin by the notary; Quiros quickly read it twice, made the notary read it aloud, sent him away, then summoned him back and read it again, this time very slowly. His appearances on deck became ever rarer.)

The voyage proved notable for two things. While running down the Gulf of California they struck a storm of such ferocity that the Agnus Dei, scattered like seed corn, proved useless; Captain Noble even contemplated chopping down the mainmast. Then, only hours afterwards, Fray Munilla died, aged eighty. Yet he kept writing almost to the end, and as the other priests gathered by his bed, recorded that fact in a final, wry marginal note.

At Acapulco, Quiros, suddenly in excellent health, quarrelled with the Viceroy of Mexico when he refused him two thousand pesos to go to Spain and see the King. The Viceroy, in fact, had written to tell Philip that several senior expedition members were demanding Quiros stand trial; Iturbe, in particular, claimed that "guided only by his own opinion" he was "a vain man of little substance." Quiros, in turn, portrayed himself as a victim of deceit and incompetence who, against all the odds, had established New Jerusalem, comprising *a church and four streets.*" His assurance took a knock when he learned that Torres, escorted by the tiny *zabra,* had gone on to make a famous voyage, but, responding in typically robust fashion, announced he would petition the King for a new expedition to find his elusive continent.

Philip summoned his advisers. Quiros, frankly, made them nervous, and they fretted about the consequences if he didn't get his way. The Cardinal of Toledo warned he "would become a source of mischief"; the Constable of Castile worried he might put himself "at the disposal of the King of England or other enemies." For seven years Quiros sat in Madrid, writing memorials, lobbying the King and talking obsessively to Doña Ana Chacon, his stoical, forbearing wife. Eventually Philip—who had developed a sneaking regard for Quiros—approved. He could, at Spain's expense, have another crack at the Austral lands and in April 1615, cock-a-hoop, sailed again for Peru aboard the galleon of the new Viceroy, the Prince of Esquilache.

At some point, late in the voyage, Quiros vanished. We know only that he was fifty, and that the circumstances surrounding his end remain as mysterious as those of his beginning; there are no records, letters, obituaries or tributes, certainly no marked grave. He would have hated that yet, posthumously, he found the recognition he craved. Inspired by his memorials—published throughout Europe—navigators like Cook, Bougainville and Tasman set out to find Australia for themselves. In 1699 the English buccaneer William Dampier made one of the first landfalls and, as a sign of respect, gave it the name Quiros had created (having first subbed out that fawning Austrian *i*). By doing so he bequeathed Quiros a tiny, but actually quite glamorous, footnote in history.

*

On my last afternoon I strolled along Big Bay, now pewter-coloured under leaden skies. In August 1774 James Cook had brought HMS *Resolution* in here. He wrote, "Every thing conspired to make us believe this was the Bay of St Philip and St James discovered by Quiros in 1606." His officers, not convinced, looked in vain for any sheltered haven that might have been the "port" of Vera Cruz. But Cook was content. "I found general points to agree very well with Quiros's description, and as to what he calls the Port of Vera Cruz [it] is undoubtedly the Anchorage at the head of the bay." The term *port* was, he informed his officers, "like many others used in geography," a vague one, and he urged them to apply general principles. So, having observed that "grass and other plants grew close to high-water mark which is a sure sign of Pacifick anchorage," they accepted his verdict. Big Bay and Vera Cruz having been identified, they took *Resolution* back to sea and headed off to discover the island of New Caledonia.

*

A young palm, growing strongly, had established itself on the beachhead. As, idly, I wondered where it had begun its journey—Bali? Borneo?—two boys riding a pony bareback emerged from the forest. Was I the man, one enquired, who had been asking *Jif* Moses about the old days? I said yes and, curious, asked how much he knew himself. Not a lot, it seemed, though he'd heard stories of the ghost. I sighed inwardly. Such as? Well, late one night some Americans, dynamiting fish further along the bay, had seen a bearded old European in an iron singlet—a cuirass, perhaps?—on their schooner's deck. "That's very interesting," I said, and turned to the other lad. "And what do you know about Quiros, sonny?"

"Captain Quiros is rum," he said.

The Tree of Life

That baby palm triggered memories of one I'd planted on Paama (my mother took a snapshot). It grew so fast you could almost hear the structural creaks, the running sap and papery crackle of unfurling leaves. Forty years later, on my first return visit, the elders led me back to that tree, now mossy and weathered but still, I noted with satisfaction, putting forth a decent yield of coconuts. An obliging child fetched one down and sliced it open. The milk and flesh tasted like any other, yet made me feel as if I was taking part in some kind of queer personal communion.

The palms have a lifespan not dissimilar to humans. By fifty or sixty they have retired from active work; most can expect to soldier on a while longer, a few even make it to a hundred. Back in London I often visualized "my" tree, and thought of the way we were growing old—if not together, at least in tandem. So news of its demise, scribbled on a Christmas card, made for an oddly unsettling moment, another intimation of mortality.

They are the tropics' finest adornment and most potent symbol. Commercial artists, say, doing posters with a Torrid Zone setting— for sun creams, canned drinks or whatever—merely work in a mature tall with its drooping, spiky fronds and, hey presto, they have instant recognition. And palms form part of the region's acoustic background; a puff of wind makes the leaves click and chatter, rain comes off them in an interesting tonal way. I've already asked my kids to ensure that my ashes are buried under a new sapling (and told them where). That would not only help nourish one of the world's most bountiful trees, but perhaps even allow me to wander eternally through the Torrid Zone. Coconuts are extraordinary travellers, and can go on voyages lasting for years.

Every navigator, Quiros included, was familiar with the migrating armadas which, since the last Ice Age, have been bobbing along the great anticlockwise currents of the tropical oceans.

Unsinkable, indestructible, impervious to water, salt or storms, a husk may travel thousands of miles before a high tide finally rolls it, mottled and wrinkled, back onto dry land. There, as it roasts in the equatorial sun, a low intelligence starts to stir; tendrils pierce two of its vacant, triangulated eyes and thread downwards, from the third a green shoot flags up. And it barely matters how sandy, alkaline or wretched the soil is, the new arrival will thrive—unless, like the lost Jamaica talls found forlornly trying to germinate along the icebound coast of Norway, it falls out of its proscribed orbit. (I'd be part of a giant super-nut crammed with endosperm and dynastic potential, ready to colonize a distant acre of warm, wet tropical littoral.)

Cocos nucifera has a crown of compound leaves set atop a slim, unbranched trunk. The fronds hang gracefully, in layered curves, while each lamina extends from its stem at an acute, very precise, angle. This mix of the voluptuous and mathematical makes for a thing of singular beauty; when stirred by a breeze its undulant green blades reflect light sequentially. Though the coco palm may look fragile it is, structurally, tough and whippy enough to survive typhoons and tidal waves—in high-risk areas it even puts out prop-roots to aid anchorage. And, of course, in economic terms, it's one of the world's most altruistic trees.

*

A coconut possesses as much protein as a quarter-pound steak; the mineral-rich milk (up to thirty-five fluid ounces per nut) is so aseptically pure it is also used, intravenously, to rehydrate victims of fever or cholera. While the copra—exported for its oil—keeps families solvent, it's the by-products that help keep them alive. In Java they say the tree has as many uses as days in the year: old nuts blend their milk and meat to produce a confection sweet as candy, young palms have crunchy, tender hearts that taste wonderful and are very good for you (cookery writers call them millionaire's salad). Juice bled from the flower buds can be boiled to produce a range of sugars such as jaggery, or left to ferment into high-proof liquors like toddy and arrack. The copra residue, known as coco cake, makes excellent cattle food. Leaves are woven into baskets, fans, fish-traps and thatch, the coir turned into doormats or mattress stuffing, shells and husks are burnt for fuel—smouldering husks repel mosquitoes. The palm's wrapper provides absorbent toilet paper, the central veins of its frondular pinnae can be fashioned into toys, whisk brooms, toothpicks, rat traps or bird snares. Rope is made from the trunk's fibrous core, houses and furniture from its hard, handsome, fine-grained timber; known as porcupine wood, it takes a high polish. The shells are turned into cups, ladles and bowls, often ornamentally carved. The root is chewed as a narcotic. In Sanskrit it's called *kalpa vriksha,* or Tree of Life. Marco Polo was the first European to describe it.

The oil, extracted from the copra with pulverizing machines and hydraulic presses (in Asia, historically, by mortar and pestle), goes into stuff like ice cream, margarine, glue, glycerine, epoxies, confectionery and cosmetics; its fast-lathering lauric acid makes it ideal for soaps and shampoos. The big plantation owners, during the period when the coconut was king, enjoyed fabulously opulent lifestyles. Then, in the 1960s, when it was overtaken by the soya bean, they trimmed their sails a touch (sold the Bentley, sacked the butler) and wondered anxiously if their munificent tree had any more tricks up its sleeve. Talk about a dumb question!

That doormat coir soon appeared in a product range that included high-quality sound insulation, marine cordage and, in Brazil, biodegradable seating for DaimlerChrysler trucks. (The moulded seats—each made from the husks of twenty-eight nuts—possess more natural springiness than plastic foam; also, coir's porousness reduces driver sweat.) Shell charcoal, or country cooking fuel, was reborn as a key component of industrial gas masks, and a purifying agent that scrubs airborne radioactive contaminants from nuclear plants. The homely flour milled from shells became a base for gunpowder and a detergent for cleaning jet engines. Even the root, liquefied, is marketed as mouthwash. Now there's talk of a laminate strong enough to make car bodies. If that works it may evolve into aeroplane fuselages; some day we could have coconut spaceships circling the stars.

I heard about Bernard Dolacinski from Ed over a beer at the Hotel Santo. He said a Bank Line ship, out of Hull, would call shortly to load copra. "That's if there's any copra to load; production's down, the price is crap." The others, talking copra too (they always got around to it in the end), spoke respectfully of a Frenchman working locally to regenerate the industry. "You should see him," said Pete. "He's a world authority."

Outside Luganville I found the Coconut Research Station occupying the site of an old plantation property. Its director, with his Gallic charm, neat fringe beard, keen blue eyes and gold-framed spectacles, could have been an actor cast in the role of a charismatic agronomist. Noting a giant world map behind his desk, I asked M. Dolacinski if there was any place the coconut hadn't reached. No; it enjoyed global domination. "Its oil products are used universally, also mankind has a sweet tooth; even in Outer Mongolia they demand the desiccated flesh." But when I suggested that no other tree on earth had so many practical applications he shrugged. "An ancient Hindu song lists the uses of its rival, the palmyra, *Borassus flabelliformis*. They stopped counting when they got to eight hundred and one—I think not even the coco palm can match that."

It comes in two basic sizes: tall and small. A grower won't even need a step ladder to harvest the pretty little Malaya Dwarf, yet talls like the Atlantics, Jamaicas and Pacifics—also known as Panamas—require a precarious climb of up to ninety feet. (Disease, such as lethal yellowing, is a constant worry; tetracycline injected direct into a sap vein provides some form of inoculation.) M. Dolacinski himself was a cross-breeder. "Marry the Giant and Dwarf Vanuatus, for example, and the nut yield jumps from seventy to a hundred kilos. But collecting that many nuts means a lot of hard labour so, by adding a tree from the Solomons to the equation, we've developed a super-hybrid that produces fewer, but bigger and better, nuts."

His work, it became plain, extended to the realms of human geography. "Copra production always rises when it's time to pay school fees. For months families have been harvesting the nuts, chopping them, sun-drying them, then scooping out the copra and putting it in sacks. It's back-breaking labour, worse even than cane-cutting. They take it to government centres for cash or, on the outer islands, they sell it to the boats. Most of these are Chinese-owned, and also carry goods for trade: clothes, medicines and so on, so much of the money handed over is then handed back. It's a strange cycle, but it works; break it and the rural exodus will continue, the crime rates in the towns will get much worse."

A youth brought in two glasses of pale, semi-opaque fluid and placed them, with immense care, on the desk. M. Dolacinski said, "Water from our new Solomons hybrid. You must try it!"

It tasted OK, with an interesting hint of effervescence. "Nice, eh? Every person in Vanuatu consumes between six and eight nuts a day, it's a staple food. Yet since independence in 1980 there has been no replanting; ageing trees mean poor diet, less money and more kids taken out of school. So what must we do? Well, we're urging everyone to plant, to fill their plots with palms. Problem is, they also put cows in there—and hungry cows *love* baby trees." He drained his glass. "Can you imagine Vanuatu running out of coconuts? We need government support. Coconuts must go right to the top of the political agenda."

The Philippines grow twelve *billion* coconuts annually yet, in August 2000, three million Scouts and Guides marked National Coconut Week by planting new hybrid saplings all over the country. Legislators and business leaders gathered at Makati's New World Hotel for the Coconut Industry Forum enjoyed a wide variety of coconut snacks, and coconut-themed songs performed by the Philippine Coconut Authority Choir. Then they called on the people to plant even more. "We can do better. There is still room for improvement."

*

We chatted about the Palmae family generally. The fruit of the betel palm provides the world's most popular masticatory, while raffia and rattan remain the most the enduring palm fibres. *Daemonorops draco* yields dragon's blood, a valuable resin, while tagua, another palm product, is used as a substitute for ivory. Yet it's the domestic versatility of the species that makes it so extraordinary; to a rural community it brings more benefits than electricity, and I found myself recalling Gourou's list of things the Fang people of Guinea did with their oil palm. The nut was used for cosmetics, the ashes of the male flowers as table salt. Broken calabashes were mended with its fibres, the leaflet veins bound into the fly whisks carried by chiefs. Leaf buds were boiled with red pepper to make a remedy for bronchitis, the juice from the frondular spine applied to cuts, the roots chewed as an aphrodisiac. A felled tree was invaded by the larvae of a beetle (*Rhynchophorus ferrugineus)* and these "palm worms" made a tasty, nutritious snack.

Eve, if the subsequent needs of mankind are anything to go by, should never have chosen the humdrum apple. She should have handed Adam a coconut.

*

Surfing the net for coconut cures I came upon the curious story of Chris D, an AIDS victim from Cloverdale, Indiana. In September 1996, with only months to live, he prepaid his funeral, stopped all treatments and chose to take his last vacation in the jungles of South America. On 14 October the dying man began eating a daily dish of cooked coconut prepared by local Indians (who, according to Tom Mountford, author of this tale, themselves "ate cooked coconut every morning to help prevent illness"). Chris D gained thirty-two pounds and, on 27 December, feeling "great," returned home to find his HIV viral load had dropped to "non-detectable levels."

Mountford claimed that lauric acid, the lathering agent found in coconut oil—and mother's milk—is converted by the body into monolaurin, which causes "the disintegration of the virus envelope." He quoted a Dr Mary Enig who, having extensively researched trans-fatty acids, wrote that "some of the pathogens inactivated by monolaurin include HIV, measles, herpes simplex virus, cytomegalovirus (CMV), influenza virus and pneumonovirus, as well as several bacteria."

I showed it to John, then at London's Imperial College writing a PhD thesis on HIV antiviral drug resistance. He shrugged. "There could be something in it. Who knows?"

"So some day coconuts, conceivably, might be used to treat AIDS."

"Well, *conceivably*. But so might chicken noodle soup."

In Luganville I found myself queuing for stamps at the Post Office with a man I had last met in an early-morning *epot* (airport) queue. Now, looking drawn and distracted, he told me his uncle had been killed two days earlier.

"I'm so sorry," I said. "What happened?"

He sighed deeply. "A coconut fell on his head."

*

Around a thousand Europeans lived on Santo. Peter Morris, who looked like an ageing thirties matinee idol, was among the handful

born there. Tall and greying, with beautiful manners, he shared his
Luganville bungalow with Gabriella—young, gorgeous and black—and
their infant blonde-ringleted daughter Juanita. Over a breakfast of
warm croissants and excellent Santo coffee—"sixty per cent Arabica and
forty per cent Robusta"—he told me about a local function attended, long
ago, by his English grandparents. Realizing their oven-baked *laplap*
contained human remains, they decided Santo was not a good place to
raise a family and moved to a remote island up north. There, on the
beach, a wild-eyed man announced that passing Fijian war canoes had
recently depopulated the place; he was now its only inhabitant. Yet they
stayed. The grandfather, a retired blackbirder named Woodford, even
had a governess sent from Britain to supervise the children's education.

Peter's mother married a Santo planter who drowned soon after
Peter's birth. Her next husband, a French windjammer captain marooned
in Luganville after his ship went down, knew very little English. She,
governess-taught, spoke pretty decent French—yet she found it increasingly hard to speak it to him. Each syllable had to be squeezed out, and
eventually the effort became so great she stopped altogether. Then in
1943, marooned in a mute union, he had to watch as the US Navy,
needing gunnery practice, retrieved his lost command from the seabed
and blew it to bits. Later he moved to Epi. Walking home from a party
one night, he collapsed by the roadside and died. Peter never found the
grave.

It was a sad story, certainly, yet I wondered why the captain had
never bothered to learn English.

Peter said, "For my mother, actually, it was a matter of principle."

"Maybe it was for him too." Did the shadow of the Hundred Years'
War that hung over the New Hebrides also darken their marriage?
In a sense; his mother, it seemed, had sided with the three thousand
Vietnamese who then lived on Santo. He said, "We called them
Tonkinese; actually they were slaves brought by the French from Hanoi
and Haiphong as indentured labourers. They planted all our coconuts
and market gardens, but had no civil rights whatsoever—their kids
weren't even allowed to go to school. Well, the Americans changed all
that. They said: give them their rights, let their kids into the class-
rooms! But the damage was done. When Ho Chi Minh kicked the
French out of Indo-China, our Tonks supported him, after America got

involved a lot of Santo boys went off to join the Viet Cong; in the end almost all our Tonkinese were repatriated." He smiled. "Uncle Ho told them to bring all the consumer durables they could lay their hands on—which was why, for years, you couldn't find a sewing machine in these islands."

Musing on the irony of Santo boys killing the sons of the men who had insisted they must have an education, I realized that one of their mothers may have inspired—in part, at least—Michener's Bloody Mary. "Could she have been one of the people repatriated to Hanoi?"

He had grown up with the story. "Of course."

So, having helped create a character America took to its heart (the great Ethel Merman played her on Broadway), she might, in fact, have ended up chasing downed American aviators with a pitchfork. But his look said it was no joking matter, and I guessed when tourism eventually replaced copra as Santo's primary source of foreign exchange, *South Pacific*'s frothy fiction would become Santo's *Beowulf*, a true chronicle of its past—with special reference to the old plantation days. "Yes, a golden age. Copra was strong, we had beautiful homes, we gave fabulous parties. But with independence people began drifting away." He drained his coffee. "Now the homes are rotting, nobody collects the coconuts . . . well, you've seen it. One old friend, a chef who went home to Lausanne but always dreamed of returning, wrote asking what things were like now. I wrote back with the truth and, a few days after he got my letter, he died. You know from what? A broken heart."

Gabriella, who had taken no part in this conversation, gave a sad little nod. "Yes, it's true. His heart broke. Just like that."

*

Mary Jane was present during the events that came to be known as the Coconut Rebellion. Handsome and quietly spoken, she first noticed the New Hebrides (at home in Malawi) as an evocative name on the map. "I knew some day I must go—it seemed to promise such romance!" That was prescient of her. Staying at the newly built Hotel Santo she met, then married, its Vietnamese owner—one of a handful who had chosen to stay put. Now she managed the place.

From her I learned it was the British planters who had drifted away; the French clung on in the hope that Jimmy Moli Stevens might save them. A charismatic, flamboyant Eurasian with a heavy white beard and a theatrical limp, Stevens had driven bulldozers for the PWD before entering politics. Vanity drew him in, a dazzling talent for oratory took him to the top. (Whenever he addressed meetings his audience, spellbound, barely dared breathe.) Yet even as he dreamed of becoming a world figure, he took care to remain in touch with the electorate; each time he visited a village, for example, four local girls were selected to have sex with him, and all later recalled their union with such evangelical gusto his approval rating soared even higher. But Santo, while adoring its priapic silver-tongued son, never knew how stupid he actually was. Jimmy had a small, low-grade, bulldozer-driver's brain wholly unsuited to such ambitions—so some of the Quai d'Orsay's best, most duplicitous minds went to work on his behalf. And he always had money. A bunch of US millionaires saw to that. Ultra-conservative, calling themselves the Phoenix Foundation, they had at last found a tame nation state where they could practise their barmy libertarian ideas.

When Jimmy announced Santo would become a republic he had ranged against him the UN, Whitehall (wringing its hands) and Vanuatu's first elected government-in-waiting—an all-Anglophone affair led by a black clergyman, Father Walter Lini; France, denying complicity, remained neutral. Two months before it was due to happen, as tensions rose nicely, I flew to Santo to try to meet Stevens. Friends in Vila had arranged an introduction to one of his cousins. She and her family lived on the beach in a tent, and invited me to stay. I spent a happy couple of days catching my meals straight from the sea and talking about Moli Jimmy. The cousin said, "The last time I saw him his kitchen table was piled with gold and silver coins, all shiny and *heavy*, with his head on them. He said, 'Help yourself, take all you want!' He is generous—but he can be moody."

She gave me directions and, early one morning, as spies in the treetops used birdcalls to signal my progress, I drove to his plantation house. On the lawn his naked Stone Age army cooked breakfast over wood fires and did rifle drill with saplings; a radio somewhere was tuned to the BBC World Service. A fat Eurasian carrying a baseball bat waddled to the gate and told me to bugger off; when I started arguing he took a violent, two-handed swing at my head. Later I was waved down by Santo's British police chief, a red-faced Londoner who had raced up from Luganville to find me, and could barely conceal his anger at what I had done.

Yet, I told Mary Jane, the most interesting thing about my flight up from Vila had been the presence, on Air Melanesia's daily Focker, of the French Resident Commissioner. A tough old ex-rugby league player, he insisted to me he was merely coming to see friends. She laughed and led me to a window. Across the road stood a big World War Two Quonset hut. "The friend was Jimmy, and they met in there. He promised one hundred per cent French support for an independent Santo—while, back in Vila, his colleagues were saying the exact opposite."

When Stevens finally seceded, few people even knew where Vanuatu was. (Correspondents arriving to report on its "Comic Opera War" and "Coconut Rebellion" sent home some very droll dispatches.) The metropolitan powers, still apparently acting in tandem, each dispatched a hundred troops to Santo. "Britain sent the Paras. They were billeted at the Relais Bouganville Resort and were absolutely charming. They spent their days on the beach or diving on the *Coolidge*, at night a lot came here for dinner and to romance the girls. They were always well dressed, and had lovely manners. The French were staying somewhere else, we hardly saw them."

"And the rebels?"

"They were still in control. But there was a lot of drunkenness and looting. Jimmy hadn't a clue what to do next—and neither did London or Paris. It was a stand-off: both armies had orders to stay put on the beach, while in Vila Father Lini was going crazy. Finally he asked New Guinea for help. We expected real trouble, but those Papuan boys behaved impeccably. And, of course, they were the ones who finally arrested Jimmy and stopped the rebellion."

Stevens died, virtually forgotten, several years later in the Port Vila jail.

*

Lesley Bianchessi bought the Hard Rock Café from a young Chinese man who, daily, closed for lunch and drove home to eat with his mother. She renamed it the Natangoro (which means sago palm) and now, doing a roaring lunchtime trade, had turned it into one of Luganville's busiest restaurants. The adopted daughter of a footloose American doctor who practised all over the Union, Lesley married a nomadic Italian, Pierro, who did sailboat charters all around the South Seas. That, I suggested, made her exactly the kind of person most likely to finish up in Santo: "Rootless."

She said, "I'm here because Pierro docked one day and fell in love with the place. He applied for a plantation, and now he's living out his dream, he's right where he wants to be." Red-haired and green-eyed, with an easy American manner, she had mixed feelings about Santo. "Sometimes I adore it, others I'm ready to pack up *this minute.* There's so much corruption—like it took three whole years to get our plantation lease extended? If we'd paid the bribes it would have been done overnight—but go down that road once and they'll run you ragged. And there's too much social bickering and backbiting. When you throw a party you need to know exactly who, at the moment, is *not* talking to who."

She meant the whites. While they met at clubs dedicated to yachting, golf and polo, she and Pierro attended the Alliance Française—which, unlike the others, had an excellent library.

One afternoon, out at the Polo Cross Club, I found several dozen white families watching a match in which the hardest, loudest, most combative riders were white women. I chatted to Shane Egan, an Aussie in a stockman's boots and Akubra hat, his good-looking French wife, Pascale, and their two small, blonde, exquisitely mannered children. Shane built Vanuatu's first abattoir and piggery, and now had a plantation at Shark Bay dedicated to copra, cattle and thoroughbred Appaloosa horses. "At home Pascale speaks English to me and French to the kids. My French is lousy, so I talk English to them and they talk to each other in both. It's funny; in a two-minute conversation they'll switch back and forth maybe six or seven times."

"What about Bislama?" I asked.

"They are forbidden to speak it in the house."

There was a flurry of hooves and a wiry blonde, scowling, whacked a ball into the net. Shane yelled, *"You beaut! "* and strode off. Mary, aged five, wore ear studs shaped like dolphins. When I told her how pretty they looked she whispered, "Thank you." Pascale asked if this was my first visit to Vanuatu. I said I'd been born in Vila's British hospital and she smiled. "I was born in the French one." It was probably the French cadence that brought it back—a rush of prejudice I'd forgotten I ever had. Atrophied brain cells, flickering back to life, told me I shouldn't be talking to this bright, likeable lady; I felt my parents' displeasure, and heard the censorious voices of my High Tory tribe. We all knew that while both nations had been profitably exploiting the tropics for centuries, the British, at least, continued to spread enlightenment while the Frogs, with their dreadful manners and anarchic, obstructive ways (and weakness for native women), were out to grab everything they could get. And what kind of example did they set the locals? Pétain's craven capitulation—though our Frogs, to be honest, had supported De Gaulle—had demeaned all white men.

The moment passed, leaving me dismayed. Had she noticed anything? Evidently not; cheerily she waved over her own parents. As her sparky old father, having established we had Vila friends in common, told a story about one which scandalized his wife and made his daughter whoop with laughter, I realized that not a single French kid had ever been invited to our house; all were judged to be morally unsuitable.

Yet, viewed from a distance, they seemed to have a much better time. Our birthday parties, for example, were strictly supervised affairs intended to prepare us for social occasions we would attend as grown-ups. (After the Loyal Toast, drunk in Rose's Lime Juice, someone would cry "Three cheers for the King!") The French, by contrast, threw long, exuberant, tantalizingly unrestrained parties and now, in late middle age, I felt a weird kind of sadness at having missed them.

Their food was almost certainly better than the bread thinly sprinkled with hundreds-and-thousands we'd had, while the idea that any of their girls, sophisticated enough to wear lipstick and rouge, might want to talk about Mr Churchill or the Varsity Boat Race was ludicrous. I knew nothing of their culture and barely a word of their language; "French lessons" was a phrase that made our adults snigger. Regretting these lost opportunities, envying Pascale's children their diglotic wizardry, I realized she was speaking to me. "Alex, this is Justin, he came out from Switzerland a year ago."

A croaky, stringbean adolescent, Justin told me (in an amused, wryly European way) how his father had arrived home from an overseas business trip raving about a place called Santo—then resigned from his job and announced they were moving there *toute suite.* "So it was bye-bye, Switzerland!" Two men joined us. One, affable and over-weight in a Polo Cross Club shirt, was Santo's Mr Telecom. "He's been here for ever," said Pascale.

"Well, twenty-six years," said Mr Telecom.

The other, a retired Qantas pilot with an aloof manner, was cur-rently looking at a place near Hog Harbour; he could settle down there, no problem. Then Justin, surprisingly, spoke up for the children of the fathers (it was rarely the mothers) who, pursuing some Arcadian dream probably stemming from their own dysfunctional childhoods, uprooted their families and took them off to sweat in the tropics. "My dad still hasn't got a project, my mum works in a souvenir shop. I study by cor-respondence." Most of all he missed his friends—and the Alps. "The skiing, the beautiful scenery and cold frosty mornings . . ."

Mr Telecom shuddered. "Not for me, son. My metabolism needs heat and rain just to keep ticking over." Wondering how they felt about the tropical region in general, I learned from the pilot that it came in two categories: in one logging and mineral rights were there for the taking, land was cheap, governments obliging (and everyone wanted telecommunications), in the other you had over-regulation and exploita-tion, hopeless corruption and a woeful lack of social organization. Men-tion of those corners of tropical Africa where people kept killing each other brought an exasperated sigh. "It's because of too much carbohy-drate in their diet," he explained. *"Africans don't eat enough fruit."*

*

Back at the hotel a morose, gold-chained Greek yuppie, checking in his calfskin luggage, grumbled about a wet weekend he'd just spent on Tanna. I said, "Cheer up, in the Bay of Bengal they average thirty-six typhoons *in the month of May alone.*" Buoyed along by his look of loathing I went to the bar and found Pete. When I mentioned I would be heading off to Gaua next morning he said, "Interesting little island, it's got a lake that once confounded modern science."

I bought him a beer. "Confounded how?"

"It used to put on live video shows."

The Miraculous Reflection

Light deprivation is a common cause of depression among tropical exiles in wintry latitudes. One solution is to try to visualize water-dazzle at noon. Closing the eyes, thinking of a hot sun shining on seas, rivers, paddies and ponds, should conjure up enough glitter to lift the spirits—perhaps even produce a figurative moment of dazzle-blindness.

Gaua's brightly reflective Lake Letas is exactly the kind of place we might evoke. Yet when officials from French state security (who had doubtless never heard of it, let alone seen it in their heads) learned the lake could *see them*—in real time and full colour—they set about jamming its strange oscilloscopic powers. Today the matter remains shrouded in mystery and controversy.

Letas lies 1,640 feet above sea level. Oxbow shaped, lapping around an active volcano, these days it mirrors nothing more interesting than drifting clouds of volcanic smoke and superheated steam. People cook fish in its geothermal springs or, at the more temperate ends, scoop up eels, prawns and, in season, ducks made stupid by sex; thousands fly in to breed.

But once all that was just ground clutter.

Since France closed the show in 1973 I am obliged to freewheel a bit here, and invent a yachtie who calls at Gaua in, say, the sixties. He wants to see the sights so his guide proposes a hike to the lake. As they reach it the guide points to a twelve-inch-long, two-dimensional ship right there in the water, and tells him it's actually a 12,000 ton Thai freighter making for Honiara—but the image is fuzzy, and the idea so crazy it makes his visitor smile. The guide points again: this time it's a baby tanker making smoke, next some breaching whales all sardine-sized, finally a silvery little Cross of Lorraine so pretty you could wear it around your neck. (It turns out to be a DC3 on its way to Sola.) Still the visitor puts it down to tricks of the light, or exhaustion from his climb. Then, in very sharp focus, he sees a miniature steamer gliding towards him leaving a threadlike wake.

A fish jumps through the steamer and the picture shatters; up here, he notes, the fish leaps, down there a ship disintegrates. But the ripples subside, things slip back into focus, the splintered steamer is reassembled—and the visitor perceives his own sloop, now reduced to a bathtub toy, moored exactly where he left it.

Incredulous, it dawns on him the lake is a giant screen carrying live images from all around Gaua. So where is the box of tricks, who's hidden the camera? The guide says, "There is no camera." Yet, even as he speaks, clouds appear and the lacustrine display begins to flicker and fade. "But it needs sunshine."

"What does?" our visitor implores. "*What* needs sunshine?"

The guide says, "The Magic Stone," but will tell him no more. The matter is *tabu*.

Many years later, at Wongrass Bungalows, my landlord spoke of a mysterious crystal that sat somewhere on the lake bed. In 1973, during a burst of extreme volcanic activity, the French evacuated Gaua's population and, finding they had the island to themselves, located and raised (*"Stole,"* said Francis) the Magic Stone. Now, locked in some Parisian bank vault, it remains the subject of an ongoing dispute. Official protests are lodged from Vila but the French, he alleged, refuse even to discuss the matter.

"How did it work?" I asked.

He didn't know. But next day at Teuvrat I came across a handsome old man with pitch-black skin and perfect white teeth who, seated on a bulldozer eating peanuts (a ten-cent bag was the price of our interview), explained that Letas had once been radioactive and sensitive to light: the "picture" was formed by signals bouncing off the volcano, rare chemicals produced a kinescopic membrane on the water—the "screen." But the crystal remained the key. "Like radar."

It sounded like surreal nonsense yet, later in Vila, I met a retired US Navy captain who had called at Gaua in his big high-tech catamaran, and kept describing the lake in radar terms: false echoes, trigger pulses, precision focusing, three-pointing and so on. Someone had told him it could pick up sea-clutter and do storm-tracking—once its luminal equipment had even jammed the radar of a passing British warship.

"What utter bullshit," I protested.

"OK. But I tell you, something truly weird must have been going on."

Today the French government sends baby food, vitamin supplements and powdered milk but, so far, not the one thing everyone wants. Gaua without its miraculous reflection is, they claim, like a man without eyes. It has been blinded.

*

Norm Sanson took me there. As I queued for a sandwich at Luganville's airport his large, heavy hand fell on my shoulder. "So where are we headed today?" After establishing we were both, in fact, headed the same way, I found myself back in the cockpit of Noriega's Twin Otter. Last time he'd talked about gravel; now, barging through heavy turbulence, the theme was air crashes. Having pointed out the locations of various wartime incidents, he steered over Big Bay towards the jungly hills and plunging ravines of the Cumberland Peninsula. Here we encountered thermals so violent I looked back to see if anyone else looked as anxious as I felt. But small-plane travellers in the tropics know a quiet sky is likely to contain as many hidden crossflows and currents as a calm sea; most dozed, while a young mother, unable to breastfeed her screaming baby, offered it a finger instead. Norm spotted another important disaster site and took us bouncing along a densely wooded ridge. He frowned. "That's funny! You can't see it."

"See what?" Wind shear sent us soaring a hundred feet.

"An Islander went down here a few years back, no survivors. It was carrying forest rangers and took three days to find." Now, doing a tight turn, he began *hunting for the wreckage.* "The search party had to abseil down from a helicopter."

"Is that so?"

"The spot must be hidden by those trees. What are they? White cedars?"

"Could be."

"See what happened? He entered a dead-end valley and didn't have the height to climb out again. The pilot was a young Pom."

"Right."

"Good-oh!" He gave the site a final scan and, moments later, we found ourselves in quiet air out over the wide blue Pacific. "Before

I forget, there's a bloke on Gaua called Mark; first-class chap, worked for me back in the days when I did logging. I sent him home with a chainsaw, and now he's the number-one timber man there. He could tell you stuff, so remember the name."

Gaua, roughly circular, packed some eye-catching terrain into its hundred and thirty square miles. Pondering the forests swarming around its hulking, smoking volcano, I saw the only habitable region was down along the coast. Today clouds obscured the lake which had tracked Quiros's fleet when it called here before blundering on to Santo. The present population, Norm said, was about eight hundred; I told him the General had estimated it at two hundred thousand. He shrugged. "They must have had high-rise flats."

On the ground a man wearing a "Dept of Customs and Taxes" badge directed me to Wongrass Bungalows. "*Smol* walk, not far."

A trim yard contained two neat huts and a big yellow rain tank with its tap secured by a padlock. Prowling, I spied movement in a frangipani tree; a tiny black girl in a red dress slithered lizard-like up into its branches and lay there, staring intently. When I said, *"Alo, missi, wanem nem blong yu?"* she blinked, when I explained, *"Mi stop lukaot managa"* (I'm looking for the manager), she gave a faintly amused smile.

Then, puffing hard, the manager appeared. Still in his thirties, beefily built, with doughy features, discoloured teeth and big, splayed, muddy feet, he had the lapsarian look of a once-fit man who had developed a craving for fried food and sugar. He didn't like what he saw either. In Vila they'd told me that ambassadors and other grandees occasionally came here to go bush walking; I was not the high-roller he'd hoped for and, after a cursory handshake, he said, "I am Francis; voucher, please." I passed him a chit which entitled me to bed and breakfast on *Toste, Fraede* and *Satede,* plus three dinners. It got a cursory glance. "You have not paid enough."

"I settled everything in advance."

"But this not correct."

"Can we go inside, please? The sun's very hot."

He grunted and produced a bunch of keys. I waved to the child in the tree then entered the finest village accommodation I had ever seen. My hut contained a snug sleeping area—its bunk beds, I learned later, *gifted* by the Government of New Zealand—and a kitchen with a Calor-gas stove bearing a gold-starred Communauté Européenne sticker. He said, "You must give me money for one dinner." On the wall, pegged to a square of pigskin, hung the Lord's Prayer, while a sealed door led to a room boasting a phone that had never worked. Yet he spoke of it with pride. "There are only four telephones in all Gaua." Then we got back to business.

"I paid for all the dinners in Vila."

"You pay for two. One is not paid. It cost five hundred *vatu*."

That came to $4. I said, "Tonight I'll cook my own," and idly opened a cupboard. A tide of cockroaches swept across the floor. Sighing, he blitzed them with a Mortein Roach Bomb, then kicked their twitching, clattering, carapaced corpses into a corner. I handed him his money. He said, "Jungle trek is extra."

"I'm not doing any jungle trek."

"OK, you can tour to the lake, see volcano and megapod birds. Or the big *nabanga* trees—for this we are world-famous."

"All I want to do right now is fill the kettle."

He gave me a baleful look and walked out to the tank. I asked, "Why is it locked?"

"On Gaua we have water shortage." He banged the tank with his fist. It gave off a dull boom indicating there wasn't much in it. "No rain."

"But Letas is a freshwater lake. And a big one."

"It has sulphur, make you sick."

Grudgingly, like a wino sharing out his dregs, he half-filled the kettle. I reminded him I also needed to wash, and his sigh said: if I don't (he smelled rankly feral) why should you? Yet he dribbled a pint or two into a tin basin and placed it on a tree stump by the bamboo privy. This, badly storm-damaged with giant rents in its walls, had no roof, no door and no privacy. Wondering about that, I glanced up at the frangipani. But the child had gone.

After dark he brought me a plate of cold *laplap* served with a hard-boiled egg and a few spoonfuls of bully beef. When he returned to fetch the plate I said, "Can't you get some fresh meat?"

"All our meat is from tin."

"There must be cattle on Gaua."

"Plenty, but no butcher."

"How about fish?"

"For fiss I must send out fisserman to sea."

"Well, can I have some bread? For breakfast?"

He was fast losing patience. "I must tell baker tonight."

"OK. You tell him."

"What is time now?"

"Seven o'clock."

"Too late! He close."

I asked where I could get a beer. He said Gaua was dry. I thought: Dry? No booze, no water, no precipitation, probably not even a sprinkling of morning dew: it's bloody *parched*. Yet it was Gaua's prohibitionists who actually brought us together; as I maligned them—sensing in this the dead hand of the Presbyterians—he suddenly confessed to a subversive dream of, some day, opening a tavern for sailors. So I confessed to being here with pen and notebook, on the lookout for interesting stories. Stories, eh? Well, he could tell a few. It was then I heard about the Magic Stone.

Next he moved on to the tale of Quiros's cows. The General, in benign mood, put a dozen ashore (though no cattle were ever listed on his manifest). The Gauans, who had never seen such extraordinary beasts, ran for their lives, while the cows made for the hills; their descendants still roamed wild today, rarely seen, never caught. "I have more tomorrow," he said, and wished me good night *("Swit dream!")*. He had, evidently, appointed himself my information officer; that could certainly be useful—but what was it likely to add up to in supplementary costs?

*

Soon after sunrise I made my way to the ruined privy, tore aside its drapery of spiders' webs and positioned myself, gingerly, over a dark, stinking pit buzzing with blowflies. A dog trotted up. It had an oversized head, powerful jaws and scarred, scrawny hindquarters. I said, "Sod off!" and it began snarling. Jesus, I thought, it's going to bite me. When it lunged at my ankles I yelled and struck out wildly. Two women loomed into view and sent it packing with a few casual whacks of their hoes—but remained rooted to the spot, staring. I shouted

"Gowe! Gowe!" and finally, with the easy, loose-limbed gait of Melanesian females—fingers touching, bumping together companionably—they drifted off, their laughter audible for moments afterwards.

Breakfasting off a ripe pawpaw picked in the garden, I heard a tap at the door. A young thickset man said, "Are you Alex?" He had a confident manner and sharp, quizzical eyes. "My name is Mark. Captain Norm sent a message you were here. If you like I can show you some places."

I remembered. Mark ran the timber business.

He also ran Gaua's taxi. A rust-pitted old Land-Rover now parked outside, it was one of only two Gauan motor vehicles in working order. "Two cars for nine miles of road." Waiting at the head of a gradient I watched the Highway Department's bulldozer busily rearranging the road—gouging out new furrows, excavating new craters—with no apparent purpose other than to keep both Gaua's motorists on their toes. A churning bow wave of rocks and heavy red clay clunked off its blade as it passed (with a cheery thumbs-up from the driver), leaving us to careen down a new mudslide.

A tiny village clinic, built on stilts, was run by a vivacious, pretty nurse who turned out to be Mark's girlfriend. As we sat on the steps, chatting and sunning ourselves, I became aware of a noisy meeting being held outside a house nearby. "They are talking about water," she said. A spry old man left the group and hurried towards us. "And I think the chief wants to talk to you."

The agitated *Jif* told me the pipes connecting his village to the regional tank had broken. Could I find him new ones? I said I had no access to pipes; Mark muttered a few words and the *Jif* departed. "He thinks you are British High Commission. He laid his pipes the wrong way and cracked them. Stupid! So now all water must be carried." For the women this meant a daily four-mile trek across rugged terrain—also for an emaciated Peace Corps volunteer who wandered over to join us. The first middle-class, college-educated American I'd met who appeared to have scurvy, he put his condition down to exhaustion. "Any idea how much a gallon *weighs*? Back home the best thing in my apartment won't be my computer any more. It will be the kitchen tap."

Yet just a glance up at Gaua's cloudbound Gothic interior showed how, over the centuries, people had tamed and organized the coast on which they lived. Moving on, we passed well-tended plantations, healthy cattle and neat villages—some with meetings in progress. "Are they talking about water too?" Mark said, "They could be talking about anything." The highway ended in a bush clearing. As we abandoned the vehicle he added, "On Gaua people meet at the drop of a hat, we love the sound of our own voices." A fast-running creek (slippery boulders serving as stepping stones) and a flooded tea-coloured stream (crossed by a wobbly two-log bridge) mocked the shortage. "Smell the sulphur? Can't drink that. There *is* good water on the island—but it's over on the wet side. We just have to manage it better."

A house stood at the end of a long, deserted beach. It looked like a big holiday bungalow but was, in fact, a school; kids played by the sea as several dozen adults held a meeting on the veranda. "That's not about water, that's PTA." A portly man leaning on a furled umbrella asked if I had come to fix the fax. Mark, taking his hand, told him I was out from London, a friend *blong* Norm. To me he said, "This is my uncle. He also thinks you are British High Commission! See, they gave a fax to the school, it's the only one on Gaua. So every day this is where the businessmen come."

The uncle assumed a look of comic despair and took my hand too. "But first we must wait until the teachers have finished. They have all gone into business too."

*

That afternoon, strolling, I met an old man half-blinded by cataracts who was prepared to talk about the Magic Stone. But when I asked how it came to be in the lake in the first place he said, "Because God made Gaua on the First Day, and it had a special place in His heart. So an angel brought it down."

My own guess was that Gaua, along with the tropics in general, had been left till last. Having positioned the ice caps, and elegantly rounded off the cool, temperate regions in which most of His followers would dwell, God wondered what to do about the rest. Before Him lay a jumble of leftover options too volatile for the more favoured hemisphere: extreme weather, geological instability and a whole host of ghastly afflictions. I reckoned that late on the Sixth Day, in a mood of deepening pessimism and uncertainty, He finally dumped them all in the Torrid Zone.

That night, when Francis brought my dinner (cold *laplap* and a mess of small, sharp chicken bones), I asked if he believed in the First Day theory. But, in fractious mood, he grumbled distractedly, "I don't know. A European and Japanese woman have come."

"What? To Wongrass?"

"No." That seemed to be the problem. And they weren't staying with him because, as I discovered next morning, they had brought their accommodation with them.

Beyond the deserted *efil* a path brought me to a beach where a man, drinking from a tin cup, slouched outside a big blue tent. He wore his hair in a pigtail and when I approached, glanced around with evident annoyance.

"You've found a good spot," I said.

"Yeah."

"I'm Alex."

"Hi. Nick." The voice was British.

Slightly built, in his late twenties, he had the delicate features and wide, luminous eyes of some arboreal leaf-eating creature, a bushbaby or marmoset. And, for somebody living rough, he looked surprisingly clean—spotless white shorts and short-sleeved white shirt. I asked, "Where do you get your water?"

"From the village back there—but it costs."

There was movement in the tent and an Asian girl stepped out. She wore a red floral sarong and gave me a smile and a strong handshake. "I'm Hazel. Would you like some tea? No milk, I'm afraid, it's black. And the sugar's brown, with ants in it."

"OK. Thanks. And just a little sugar."

A muscle jumped in Nick's jaw; he badly wanted me to go away. "So what brings you to Gaua?" I asked.

She said, "Nicko needs peace and quiet. He paints." Nicko made an odd noise that seemed to disconcert her. "Actually, he's just starting out. But you'll be reading about him some day."

Entering into a conversation he didn't wish to have, he told me he had, until recently, been designing web sites in the States. Hazel boasted, "Last year he won an award from a cultural foundation in Osaka. The site was called Crazy Janet's Porno Planet and it got millions of hits."

Her accent was cut-glass, just one beat away from a parody of ruling-class English, his the faintly cockneyfied estuarine vernacular that denoted an expensive private education. And, just as I wondered if they had met in the course of his job, she said, "I'm not one of his Asian Nympho Babes, you know. I've got a geography degree. From the University of London."

"She just missed out on a First." Nick, unexpectedly, sat up and began taking an interest. "Haze comes from Burma. She's a princess, actually."

"*Actually* she's a glorified switchboard girl in a City bank—or was until she agreed to come along on this . . . adventure."

Old photographs I'd seen of the Burmese court showed tiny, brittle women hoisted erect by their poker spines. Hazel, though, looked more like one of the palace cooks: sturdy and broad-faced, with fleshy shoulders, she had a sweep of black hair that fell to her waist and cheeks faintly pitted by, perhaps, childhood eczema. "If the royal family still existed I'd be way down, *really* minor."

I said if some form of democracy still existed in Burma it would be my favourite country. She said, "Don't get me going on politics, that place is . . . unspeakable." Then, sipping her tea, she told me she had left it, aged ten, to live with an uncle in Putney (an NHS hospital doctor who trebled his salary by gem-dealing) and had returned just once, to try and bring her parents out. "But they wouldn't come. They're retired now, and set in their ways." She added, "Daddy used to be a riverboat skipper."

Nick grinned. "Yeah, *and* the rest, Haze. Tell the truth." To me he said, "I've seen photos of their house!"

With a hint of pride, she said, "Well, he smuggled a bit."

"A bit!"

"It was his way of defying the regime."

"Daddy ran a coke boat! He was Captain Narco!"

"That's ridiculous." But she was smiling.

I stared. "Was he on the Irrawaddy?"

"What other river do we have?"

Some years earlier I had taken a ship downstream from Mandalay. It had been an old creek steamer carrying passengers and freight, and according to a Ministry of Home and Religious Affairs official, my companion and I had been the first Westerners to sail all the way to Rangoon since Burma became independent in 1948. "That trip changed me," I told her. "I still dream about it."

"Hey, steady on. You'll make me homesick."

She collected the cups and strolled down the beach. Nick, watching her with lips slightly parted (bushbabies use their teeth for grooming), gave a tiny sigh and asked, uninterestedly, what I was doing here. I said I was getting some stuff for a book. "Yeah? About what?" When I told him, he gave me a look so sharp I wondered if he might even be exploring the same territory in paint. "The tropics, uh? Cool." Then, picking at his toes, he began chatting in a random way. His American job, it seemed, had earned money for an odyssey that would take them from the South Seas to Brazil via South-East Asia. (Hazel had said no to Africa.) He gave himself two years. If he hadn't begun to be noticed by then he would return home to Surrey and join the family business. "Antiques," he said. "Overpriced crap, actually."

"They're the kind of countries that interest me."

"*We're* interested in hot places and cheap living. That's the big picture!" At art college he'd won prizes for his nudes, and down on Tanna, Hazel persuaded some girls to sit for him topless. They'd had fantastic skin tones. Hazel too, she was great to paint. I suggested that fantastic skin tones was a characteristic of many tropical women. "Yeah, right." I learned he had problems with hands—but so, it seemed, did Gauguin. Then Hazel returned and said to him, "Well, my poppet, what shall we do? Want to wander round the village a bit? I need things from the shop."

I wished them luck, thanked her for the tea and, trudging on along the beach, heard him say, "Should we ask him to dinner?" She said, "Absolutely not." He said, "I think he heard that." I didn't catch her reply, and did not look back.

At Wongrass Bungalows the tiny girl in red waited in the frangipani tree. I said, *"Alo, yu oraet?"* and looking at her with an artist's eye—the colours of dress and skin, the sinuous way she lay along a branch, luminous green eyes peering through yellow-yolked blossoms and shadowy leaves—wished, for the first time ever, that I could paint too.

That night Francis brought boiled yams and Portuguese sardines. "You're surrounded," I said, "by billions of bloody fish and you get these from Europe in a *tin?*" He chuckled, and told me another story—this one about a Japanese sub fleeing from a US destroyer in 1943. It found sanctuary in a massive underwater Gauan cave and, after spending many hours submerged, sneaked out at the dead of night. "But Uncle Sam is still waiting, he shoot depth charges. Boom boom! *Sayonara,* submarine!"

From the locked room next door we heard a startling sound.

The phone was ringing.

He had the door unlocked within seconds. In the darkness it burbled on. He lit his torch and stood, open-mouthed.

"Well, answer it," I said.

"No. You answer."

I picked it up and winked at him. "Sports Desk."

From far away, across the crackling ether, a woman's voice said, "Is that the Irrawaddy Flotilla Company?"

"The *what?* Excuse me?"

The voice laughed. "Hi, Sports Desk, it's Hazel, we're down at the school with the fax, Nick's trying to send something home. A guy here told us where you were staying."

I said, "This is the first time this telephone's ever worked."

"Really? Sometimes I have that effect on machinery. Look, my dear, I hear you're a writer interested in, um, is it *les tristes tropiques?* Yes? How riveting! Well, anyway, the boy Rembrandt wants to pick your brains, or bounce some ideas off you, or perhaps he just wants you to write about his fabulous talent; he is entirely without shame. The thing is, we've managed to get hold of a chicken—now *there's* a story—and I'm going to cook it on our camp fire. Beach barbie. Care to join us?"

This was an invitation from a woman who had just lost an argument. I told her I'd already eaten and was dog-tired. Her voice brightened perceptibly. "Oh, *shame!* Well, of course, we understand. Nick says hi, by the way. See you around."

"You bet."

"*Ciao.*"

Francis, snatching the phone, yelled, "Hullo? Hullo? Hullo?" But she had gone, and left the line so dead it didn't even offer the consoling hum of a dialling tone. He slammed it down, locked the door and left without another word.

Big River Blues

Lying in bed I recalled there had actually been two roads to Mandalay—one the main highway running direct from Rangoon, the other a meandering, pastoral route which shadowed the course of the Irrawaddy. We chose the latter. Before taking passage aboard our steamer we wished to get the measure of the river at the points where the road careered precariously along its crumbling banks. Ever since reading Norman Lewis's magisterial *Golden Earth* I had dreamed of getting waterborne in Burma myself, so when the *Observer* charged me with commissioning a series on the world's great rivers, I selflessly chose the best for myself and shared the rest out among my favourite writers. (Theroux went down the Yangtse, and Chatwin the Volga; Piers Paul Read took the Danube, Lewis himself accepted the Nile.) Thus early one morning in Rangoon, with my old Santo associate Colin Jones—whose own riotous magazine assignments with Lewis somehow completed the equation—along to take pictures, I boarded a Toyota van manned by two drivers and a mechanic.

Pushing through the antique Vauxhalls and Rileys we went first to a crowded roadside shrine where our drivers, bearing ropes of jasmine, knelt with the congregation of praying truckers. They sought luck and blessings for our journey.

The previous day I had been caught in a stupendous traffic jam supervised by battalions of whistle-blowing, baton-waving cops. Someone said, "General Ne Win is going to play golf." At that time Aung San Suu Kyi was still a young Oxford housewife and the General a local thug much influenced by Stalin; though the seedlings of corruption were already sprouting, Ne Win had yet to gather in his great harvest. I watched the motorcade (including a chauffeured Merc for his caddy) go howling through a metropolis unable to find the paint and plaster needed to mask the ulcerous, spavined decay which disfigured it. It reminded me of Lévi-Strauss's theory—architecture being cited as a prime example—that the tropics weren't so much exotic, as out of date. While cool-climate civilizations moved forward, those in the Torrid Zone seemed to slide back. Rangoon, once the smartest city in South-East Asia, was now one of the sleaziest; and, not for the first time, I found myself pondering the paradoxes and contradictions that consti-tuted Burma's uniquely idiosyncratic brand of socalism.

There was, for example, her bureaucracy. During the two years Burma's Ministry of Home and Religious Affairs took to consider our applications many letters were exchanged and questions asked (were *either* of my grandfathers Buddhists?). I had made repeated visits to Burma's small, silent embassy in Charles Street, London, even invoked the help of Britain's mission in Burma. Eventually the Ministry prom-ised permission and visas then, just twenty-four hours before we were due to fly out, cabled, "Permission withdrawn, visas denied." On a crackling line from Rangoon the British Ambassador said, "Oh, *God.* Well, come anyway; I'll have another chat with them."

Our final leg, a fifty-minute flight from Bangkok, had been spent filling in forms. There were new visa forms, immigration forms, cus-toms forms and currency forms, but on touching down at Rangoon's Mingaladon airport and trooping into the hot little terminal, more confronted us. You wish to use your American Express card? Fill in a form. You have a camera, a pocket calculator? Fill in a form. You are wearing a wristwatch? Fill in a form. You are—what's this—a *journal-ist?* Fill in a form, fill in a form! But the appropriate form could not be found. The official, forehead seamed with worry, suddenly grew bored with his search and, demonstrating the ingenuity Burmese display when taking on the system, amended an existing form. Smiling faintly, he let us into his country.

Everywhere Jones and I met with tolerance and courtesy. At Rangoon's echoing Strand Hotel, where Kipling drank pink gins and you could get lobster thermidor for a under a pound, the staff attended us like courtiers. And when we called at the Inland Waterways Board to confirm our passage, the managing director himself elected to deal with the matter. From a dim, lofty office lit by sunbeams bouncing off dusty mirrors, this austere, whispery-voiced old master mariner ran the largest fleet of river steamers on earth—six hundred ships dispersed around the country, carrying 1.36 million tons of freight and fourteen million passengers annually.

"You are the first Westerners to make the journey since 1948. It will not be too comfortable, the ship is not equipped to Western standards." The ceiling fan rippled papers on his vast teak desk, a clerk brought freshly squeezed lime juices. "Also, the water levels are low and we are compromised by sandbars. There is a strong chance you will run aground. I urge you to pack plenty of books." He added, "I, personally, never sail without a chess set."

Our drivers returned and, refreshed in spirit if not in body (both would soon contract gastroenteritis from tainted water), took the Toyota down the road to Prome. Prome stands right on the Irrawaddy—unlike Rangoon, which is served by a tributary—and it was there that I caught my first glimpse of that broad and stately waterway. It came in from the north, gliding past the little bluff on which the town stands and mirroring the pale hot-season sky above. The Irrawaddy, I soon saw, was a built-up area crowded with villages, townships and settlements—while only a few miles away on either side there were few signs of human involvement. If an astronaut passed over when the evening lamps were lit the river's thirteen-hundred-mile course would be marked in lights, a curving, radiant track reaching from China all the way to the Bay of Bengal.

It took two days to reach Mandalay. I had always taken this to be a place where people lived in pavilions of sandalwood and put up uncut rubies as collateral for their elephants. But we found unswept, potholed streets, the stench of rotting fish and gangs of kamikaze monks on bicycles. The hotel clerk, handing me a key, said, "You are in one three eight, that is *tit nit shit.*"

At the Zegyo Market, eating noodles at a lamplit food stall, Jones remarked, "Even if you live to a hundred you'll always remember the number of your Mandalay room. Am I right?"

A hundred is *tar ya.*

Mandalay may be the nation's cultural epicentre—and last royal capital—yet it only took root in 1857. Then King Mindon laid it out on an American grid system, his centrepiece a mile-long walled and moated enclosure surrounding a palace decorated by Venetian craftsmen. During World War Two the Japanese made it their HQ but in

1945, as General Slim and his 14th Army drove them up the Irrawaddy and out of Burma, Allied bombers flattened the palace. The Burmese have not forgiven this "vandalism" and Britons are advised to approach the subject warily. As for Kipling, the man whose poem conferred a kind of immortality on Mandalay (though he never bothered to visit), few had ever heard of him.

Three covered stairways ascend a seven-hundred-and-seventy-five-foot rock plug named Mandalay Hill. They pass holy places and pilgrims at prayer, so must be climbed in bare feet.

The view from the temples at the top was very fine. On the eastern horizon stood the hazy indigo battlements of the Shan Hills (still governed by rebel warlords) while Mandalay, with pagodas proliferating like bus shelters, resembled a Buddhist theme park. The glittering sweep of the Irrawaddy, where the wakes of ships looked like fragments of looping Burmese script, formed its western boundary. This is the river's true hub.

It flows from a glacier inside China's border, splits into a pair of alpine streams, comes together again at a great rock basin called the Confluence then runs south, through dense jungle, past Myitkyina and Bhamo—a town populated mainly by smugglers. Steamers ply between Bhamo and Mandalay all year round, negotiating two defiles where the river narrows and quickens. One is of interest because it passes the mines which produce the world's finest rubies, the other because it is spectacular and, on occasion, very dangerous.

Here the Irrawaddy, a mere three hundred feet wide, runs turbulently between towering cliffs lined with wild bee hives. Close to the entrance stands a large rock, shaped like a parrot's head and painted green and red; it is this the captain consults first. If the water touches the tip of the beak it means a fast, difficult ride ahead. (If the beak is submerged he steers for the bank and waits for the level to recede.) Racing down the defile he heads straight for a rock wall at its foot—a tiny pagoda stands, limpetlike, near the top—then, at the last moment, puts his helm hard over, skids out of the defile and into safer waters. A day later he docks at Mandalay.

Walking down a staircase on Mandalay Hill I came to a landing where a stout, balding monk sat by a gong and brassbound money box. I dropped in some kyats and he tapped the gong lightly. But as I turned to continue my descent I heard a shout and a single thunderous clang. On the step below—coiled just inches beneath my bare, hovering foot—a pretty little krait waited with raised head. Orchid-hued and shorter than a pencil, it inflicts on its victims several minutes of unimaginable agony followed by death from cardiac arrest. As it turned and flickered away the monk, wide-eyed and on his feet, gave a long, low whistle. After I'd emptied my pockets of currency—US, UK, Thai, Burmese, every coin, every note on my person, went into his box—he grinned and sent me on my way with a soft gong roll, rapid, rippling jazz percussion that seemed to float me all the way to the bottom.

*

The Inland Water Transport Board is located at the end of 26th Road. Dusty trees straggled along the stone embankment, a line of ships lay moored by the muddy shore far below. Both sidewalk and embankment were broken by the earthquakes that regularly rattle the town. The Mandalay quakes are seldom serious, just brisk tremors that rearrange the paving stones and leave the trees tilted at interesting angles.

A man emerged from the Transport Board's warehouse-like offices. His bearing was military, his gaze direct, his shirt and *longyi* neatly pressed, his English fluent and idiomatic. He shook hands and said his name was Maung Maung Lay, but that we were to call him David. "I'm the Board's Marine Officer here at Mandalay," he said, "and I've been delegated to come with you on the steamer tomorrow as far as Prome, three days' sailing. At Prome you will catch another ship for the final leg down to Rangoon. I was a steamer captain on the Irrawaddy myself, so I hope I can make some sense of the river for you. That's your vessel down there. You want to look her over?"

She was a creek steamer, small, double-decked, iron-hulled, built for service in the tortuous tidal waterways of the delta, now assigned to Burma's Blue Riband run because the few remaining paddle steamers—monsters with decks like tennis courts—had been converted into freighters. "This is a T-class vessel," said David, "given by the Japanese as war reparations in 1947 and still going strong. She can carry sixty tons of cargo and up to four hundred passengers, and she's powered by Kelvin diesels with automatic transmission. Her advantage on the

Irrawaddy, specially at this time of the year, is that, unladen, she draws only four feet six inches. Even so, we'll still probably run aground. She arrived this morning from Prome and, on the way up, got stuck twice."

She was called *Tainnyo,* or "Dark Clouds," and passengers were already claiming deck space, placing mats, food and baskets on either side of a high metal grille. "That's the panic barrier to stop people rushing from side to side and turning the ship over. They do that when storms blow up, we've lost half a dozen T-classes that way. They roll badly even in a one-foot swell."

"When is the season for storms?" I asked.

"You can get some interesting ones right now."

We found the ship's only cabin on the upper deck, built over the bows to catch the breeze. Though intended for monks—we would move out if any turned up—for a small surcharge we could use its table and chairs, wooden sleeping platforms, wash basin and giant teak lavatory. It all seemed very satisfactory.

Departure was scheduled for five thirty next morning. At the black market I bought rum and pineapples, back in my room imagined doing this a century earlier: an early night in Mandalay followed by a voyage to Rangoon organized by men from Glasgow. On a treacherous waterway in febrile, snake-infested Burma, generations of nineteenth-century expatriates—all tenacious, fiercely focused, profit-driven Presbyterians—created, and ran, the greatest riverine fleet on earth. It was an awesome achievement, and I found myself comparing them with some of the Brits I'd met working for big overseas enterprises today—neatly besuited executives who flew business class, stayed in the best five-star hotels and kicked up a fuss if their mini-bars weren't properly stocked.

The Irrawaddy Flotilla Company's Clyde-built flagships—the three-hundred-and-twenty-foot Siam-class steamers, then the largest river craft afloat—were able to accommodate four thousand two hundred deck passengers and forty more in opulent staterooms. Their triple-expansion engines raced them *against* the current from Rangoon to Mandalay (barges carrying two thousand tons of freight lashed to their sides) a full day faster than our unencumbered T-class boats would do the same six-hundred-mile trip in reverse. The crews were Indians from Chittagong, the masters and officers mostly Scots. Photographs show them, with beards combed and moustaches waxed, seated ramrod-straight before paddle boxes emblazoned with huge gilded coats of arms. Their social standing was so unassailable one Mandalay shop sported a sign saying "Silk Mercer to the King and Queen of Burma and the Captains of the Steamers."

It was still dark when we reported to the Mandalay Shore. Two ships, tricked out in lights and moored side by side, were thronged with shouting, shoving people; the air reeked of diesel, sweat and anxiety. Aboard the first I asked a corpulent old monk which one was bound for Prome. He glowered, then yelped and menaced me with his staff, almost driving me onto the horns of two wild-eyed water buffalo tethered amidships.

In the bow of the second, beside a windjammer-sized wooden wheel, a kneeling figure prayed, softly but urgently. An iron vase bolted to the prow—standard issue on all Irrawaddy steamers—contained fresh flowers. A betel-chewing colleague leant on the wheel, lips stained a womanly crimson. "Are you going to Prome?" I asked.

He nodded.

"You're the captain?"

He pointed to the praying man. "Him captain, me pilot."

In the monks' cabin I found David sitting at the table, preparing to dispense cups of green tea. He accepted a cigarette, touching the inside of his right wrist with the fingertips of his left hand, the formal Burmese gesture of thanks. "We have finished loading and will cast off any moment now," he said. "The first few miles are difficult, due to the number of wrecks around Mandalay. Over there, under the far bank, there are ninety-six. Downstream there are many more, several hundred in this stretch of river alone. They are buoyed, of course, but still a hazard to shipping."

Those wrecks were nothing less than the mortal remains of the Irrawaddy Flotilla Company. In 1942, as the Japanese surged north, the fleet was summoned to Mandalay where, the Allies had decreed, a stand would be made. But when it became clear the city must fall, John Morton, the manager, and his staff went down to the river and, firing Bren guns into hulls thin as sixpences, sank the lot—Siam-class paddlers, express vessels, creek steamers, even the pusher tugs and buoying launches. Now, though, I'd heard, plans were afoot to raise

them and put them back to work. David smiled. "If you can't afford
new ships you dig up the old ones. Improvise! Improvise! In Mandalay,
you know, we have men who can build Land-Rovers from 7-Up tins."

At five twenty, as the bow flowers trembled and Kipling's dawn
turned the sky pink, we got under way. Mandalay was a city full of early
morning shadows; up on its hill the gilded pavilions began to glitter
and flash. We hissed along, staying well clear of black-flagged bamboo
buoys marking the graves of the old steamers, now bending like reeds
in the current. The Irrawaddy, almost a mile wide, proceeded unhurriedly beneath the Sagaing Bridge—erected in 1931 and still the only
way a pedestrian can cross. The river keeps rearranging Burma, moves
large areas in liquefied form from north to south; shortly after comple-
tion, it had irretrievably silted up eight of its ten spans. While dredgers
struggled with the remaining two the Flotilla Company had to chop
the tops off its Siam-class funnels—yet even then, during high water
in August, captains squeezed under with whitened knuckles and
quickened pulse. Now just a single arch remained open and, waltzing
through, we saluted a train passing overhead with a long blast of our
siren.

Sagaing, with its rounded hills, had once been the royal capital.
Others—Ava, the City of Gems, and Amarapura—lay only a few miles
upstream; more—Pagan and Prome—lay downstream. All, like
Mandalay, adorned the banks of the Irrawaddy. The Burmese kings
cherished their river; as courtiers fawned about their Golden Feet they
travelled it in gorgeous barges shaded by giant silk umbrellas. Their
generals and scholars made war and taught the scriptures along its
length, their subjects traded up and down its every mile. It was, and is,
the artery which nourishes the nation, and without it, Burma would
perish.

Sagaing's jewel-encrusted hilltop pagodas flickered like fireworks as,
with engines geared down, we nosed into a tiny dock to load potatoes
and monks' begging bowls—Sagaing's major manufactured product.
We were carrying two hundred and forty passengers and sixty tons of
cargo: onions, rice, livestock, cheroot wrappers, bales of wet and dry tea
leaves and polished teak veneer for temple facings. David reckoned our
draught was just over five feet.

Under way, the skipper stood in the bows with folded arms, reading the water ahead like a musical score. It was flecked with eddies, the diameter of each indicating the depth beneath: thus a twelve-inch eddy meant the bottom was only four feet away, a five-foot diameter signalled a comfortable twenty feet. The pilot sat with bare feet resting on the wheel's lower spokes, one hand clasping a truncheon-sized cheroot, the other a tin bowl for the ash. There was little conversation between the two men. "They are listening to the bow wave," David explained quietly. "When it grows soft it means the water is getting shallow. When it vanishes altogether, you're in trouble. And he is using his feet on the wheel because the steering on these old T-class ships is so heavy you need the full power of your leg and thigh muscles."

Aboard an acre-sized bamboo raft a woman lit a breakfast fire. Two men smoked outside a thatched hut, a small girl knelt at the edge, washing her face. "Teak. Under the bamboo chained logs are drifting down to the sea for export. You also see plenty of jar rafts—bamboo platforms built over thousands of clay cooking jars. The trouble with them is when they go aground the jars break."

The Irrawaddy was beginning to bustle. Old country craft laden with cargo and driven by ancient, thumping engines lumbered by, trailing veils of blue fumes, a massive pusher tug shoved a barge of crude oil up to Mandalay, a local ferry cut diagonally through the traffic carrying a lorry and two oxen and, all over the place, fishing skiffs ran before the breeze with patched sails billowing like iridescent butterfly wings. Now the breeze blew fitfully but, at any moment, might grow into a gale-force wind. These high-sided steamers could be capsized by the impact so skippers had to keep an eye constantly peeled for telltale spirals of dust approaching across country. If you spotted one the rule was simple: run for the nearest bank and get your passengers ashore as fast as they could be urged to jump. There had been an incident only two weeks earlier. The ship survived, but the wind went on to rip the roof off the Mandalay fire station.

The light had lost its early radiance and become flat, white and hard. At the stern there was a food stall run by a handsome woman with fine eyes and a teasing smile. We drank tea, ate delicious sweet cakes—kept tied, with a plastic bag of sugar, to the ceiling out of the way of ants—and a savoury snack of wet green tea leaves, salted and mixed with nuts. From an antique teak dresser worth a small fortune at a London auction house the manageress also sold soft drinks, green bananas and single cigarettes, and rented out a selection of comic books.

In the cabin the temperature reached 105° Fahrenheit. On deck the passengers, sprawling listlessly, sat up only when, as regularly as a country bus, we stopped to load and unload. If he lacked a landing stage the captain simply beached the ship, driving it hard up onto mud; then regiments of women with trays of cheroots, sweetmeats, fruit and roasted chickens balanced on their heads clambered aboard like pirates, yelling for custom.

In the early afternoon we steamed past the confluence with Burma's second great river, the Chindwin, which empties into the Irrawaddy through several giant mouths. Then at sunset, miles from anywhere, we ran aground. I was sitting on the roof, watching for the dolphins that often chase the steamers hereabouts, when all at once there was a sustained grinding noise from below. The engines stopped and the "Dark Clouds" began listing from side to side as her passengers moved anxiously about.

I looked for marker buoys but couldn't see any. There are eight thousand between Rangoon and Mandalay but the ones on this stretch had probably been pinched by someone needing bamboo for building purposes—a perennial problem on the river. I recalled that grounded ships often remained stuck for several months, and that the masters were obliged to remain aboard until their vessels had been refloated. (Though the skipper who put one of King Mindon's little Italian stern-wheelers on a sandbank was beheaded on his own foredeck.) Our man, prodding at the bottom with a cane, ordered the engines full astern. The steamer trembled violently as a cloud of frothing, cocoa-coloured water streamed away past her bows. Then he rang up full ahead and, creaking, the ship inched forward. Back and forth we went, painstakingly digging our own trench and, within an hour, he had got us out of there. It was a performance of consummate skill and, under way again, we proceeded cautiously through a long stretch of shallows with hardly any bow wave audible and those telltale whorls only the size of dinner plates.

Despite repeatedly hitting bottom—hard enough to spill a criminal amount of Mandalay rum—we kept bouncing clear, and as darkness fell arrived at the little town of Pokokku and tied up beside a cargo flat. Two itinerant monks had claimed our berths and no space remained on deck. Jones and I took our sleeping bags to the flat and laid them out amidst consignments of onions and coolie hats. On a nearby perch sat a magnificent fighting cock, its plumage lustrous in the dim light of our kerosene lamp. Three hours later it sensed a false dawn and began to crow. Awoken from bad dreams and a heavy, rum-induced sleep I jumped up and clouted it repeatedly with my pillow, sending it spinning round and round on its pole, wings flapping, squawking furiously, until a small boy slipped in and, giving me a deeply aggrieved look, bore it away as tenderly as a puppy.

Before dawn we pulled into the deserted gunmetal river and made for the ancient capital of Pagan, at 7 a.m. ran onto its beach to discharge passengers. We had called there in the Toyota and now, during a twenty-mile run downstream, saw again the five thousand temples stretching along the foreshore like a setting for some stupendous Asian opera. The Burmese claim there were once thirteen thousand here, and that the missing ones had succumbed to earthquakes and pillaging armies. But many had been miniatures—exquisite little pagodas not much larger than wedding cakes—which doubtless now graced the distant, cold-climate gardens of foreign invaders and collectors.

Ashore we had met farmers and lacquerware artisans who claimed that Burma's true identity belonged in Pagan. The first king, Anawrahta, arriving with thirty-two white elephants bearing the sacred scriptures, was enthroned here in the eleventh century. It remained the royal capital for more than two hundred years, only falling when a monarch named Narathihapate, "the swallower of three hundred dishes of curry daily," murdered an emissary sent by Kublai Khan. Fearing retribution he abandoned the city and fled down the Irrawaddy; Pagan, never regaining its old eminence, was destined to become one of the most fabulous ghost towns on earth.

Anawrahta, I reflected, had turned up here with his albino elephants at much the same time as William arrived in Kent with his Normans. Why was there such a discrepancy between what their respective nations had since accomplished? (I blamed it on weak rulers and the iron grip of the monks; Jones on chronic, climate-induced inertia. Both were probably right.)

The last pagoda vanished around a bend and "Dark Clouds" steamed on cautiously, still wary of shallows. David was in high spirits. "The current is faster now and we should be able to jump any sandbars. But on this river you can never be sure. It changes its configuration every hour, every day. You might have a fifty-foot channel over there at dawn. But by dusk it will be gone, silted up, and a new one will have opened on the other side of the river. That is why our pilots concentrate on just one section, maybe fifty or sixty miles, and why that section is handed down from father to son. Between Mandalay and Prome we use no fewer than seven pilots, and at every stop, you will hear villagers advising them of changes since they last passed by. The Irrawaddy engages anyone who sails on her in a running battle of wits. Our buoying launches are going up and down all the time, putting bamboo markers along the new channels. The buoying skippers often suffer from nervous troubles, and are the only masters allowed to have their wives along for solace. You want some music?"

On a portable cassette machine powered by a couple of old car batteries he played his favourite tapes, including one by a rural monk who went to the top of the Burmese hit parade with an anthology of sermons, songs, homilies and jokes. But, while still enjoying his royalties and star status, the monk was murdered by five men who tied him to a tree and drove a jeep into him. A more orthodox pop song took my fancy for the pain the female vocalist managed to convey. Her anguish had a kind of Wagnerian resonance and, David, beating time, told us the title: " 'Mummy, My Car Has Broken Down.' "

Ordinary Burmese girls didn't own cars, so this one clearly had to be the daughter of a drug smuggler or black marketeer. David shrugged. "I can't deny that both activities go on, even aboard the steamers, though most of the drugs go down the Salween, which is close to the Golden Triangle. The contraband we get is mostly towels and painted enamelware from China, and from India—coming first down the Chindwin—talcum powder, bed linen, gents' neckties and machine tools."

Lunch was terrible, a chicken curry consisting of blackened fragments of beak, crop and claw. Afterwards, at a dusty halt marked only by a solitary tree (where we loaded consignments of cradles and crimson ceremonial drums), David spotted a woman selling a solitary egg.

"An egg! An egg!" he cried, leaping ashore to secure it. He returned, beaming, and promised that we should have it, scrambled, for breakfast.

A blistering afternoon wind, abrasive with sand from the plains, roared across the ship, the grains pattering against the superstructure and forcing deck passengers to cover their heads. Columbus, in the tropics, claimed he encountered heat so intense his water and wine casks exploded, his grain stores ignited, the dried meat began spontaneously roasting and his men feared they would be burnt alive. It was his defence for sailing past Brazil without noticing it and, back in Spain, the grandees mocked him for such hyperbole (though Quiros, another misser of big countries, may have drawn comfort from it). But right now I was inclined to believe him.

Leafing through the Inland Waterways Handbook I noted it was forbidden to load dynamite from junks in the rain, and that a surcharge must be paid for the carriage of books and feathers. David appeared and offered me the loan of his fan. But it merely rearranged the air in scorching little gusts and, handing it back, I told him a joke I'd heard in Bali. A man goes to a shop where the fans cost a hundred, fifty and ten rupiah. He buys a flimsy ten-rupiah model, an hour later returns with it in pieces. The shopkeeper says, "No, no, this fan must be held in front of your face while you shake your head from side to side." David sighed, "That is also a Burmese joke," and fell into a doze. Actually, it was probably a staple of comics all over South Asia.

Lévi-Strauss called South Asia "the martyred continent" and blamed its plight on overcrowding: one quarter of the world's population inhabited just 8 per cent of its exploitable surface; dense, squashed-in pockets of humanity scratched a living from tiny parcels of over-cultivated substandard land. He was writing in the 1950s, before South Asia produced its revolutions, yet now, pondering the arid country sliding by, and the wretched peasant families packing our decks—such people were *always* on the move—Burma seemed as hopelessly out of date as ever.

In some respects, though, Lévi-Strauss had got it wrong. For centuries, in other South Asian states, enlightened minds had been considering how all the figures swarming through their landscapes might best coexist; the ideas they came up with—social, cultural, technical, political—produced civilizations infinitely superior to any found elsewhere in the tropics. Latterly, of course, that same organizational genius re-emerged to humiliate America in Vietnam, then to devise an economic onslaught that shook the West to its foundations. Looking elsewhere in the tropics for a bold technological response to South Asia's tiger economies, I recalled the Zambian space programme.

I'd heard about it back in the seventies, from friends who had been on a game-park holiday and expressed concern for the trainee astronauts—brave young men who learned about the stresses of blast-off by squeezing into oil drums and being bounced down hillsides. (And straight into hospital; soon Zambia's dream of Bantu-speakers on the moon was quietly abandoned.) It was a classic African catch-up solution, a confused, wrong-headed attempt to make a mark on the late twentieth century; the Burmese, with their sophisticated sense of the absurd, would never have devised anything quite so barmy.

Sometimes I imagine a mildly narcotic vapour drifts across the Torrid Zone. Evanescent as laughing gas, created by decaying vegetable matter, it's borne along by the trade winds and causes a kind of stupefaction in its victims. They develop short attention spans, find concentration difficult, grab at any distraction. I've seen workers suddenly come alive as raindrops slide down windowpanes, or tea is poured into a cup containing ants. (Which drop will reach the bottom first? Which ant will drown last?) South Asia, having created its tiger economies, then grew distracted and lost them; that wafting cataleptic gas may have been partly to blame for the crash (which wiped 30 per cent off the value of my pension). It was, after all, one of the more aggressive tigers—Malaysia—that gave us the word *amok*.

As the sun waned we paused at Yenangyaung in the lee of shadowy, biscuit-coloured cliffs. Here, centuries earlier, the Burmese struck oil— today the same twenty-four families still hand-pump the wells and sell their crude along the river. In 1795 a British army captain named Michael Symes called at Yenangyaung on his way to establish diplomatic relations with the Golden Feet. Shown what this strange combustible stuff could do, he sent a string of urgent dispatches back to HQ in India. There, after a cursory reading, they were filed and forgotten.

And at Yenangyaung, moored by a trio of country boats with high brass-bound rudder posts, we swam. It was like plunging into warm bouillon and, as "Dark Clouds" loaded straw mats, tamarind seeds, kapok and wrought-iron plant stands, I soaped myself beside a small raft dressed with bunting like a ship-of-the-line. It carried a life-sized golden Buddha which surveyed my ablutions with a faint smile. Then, as I went to work on my grime-encrusted scalp, an eddy swung the raft about and, sharply, he turned his back on me.

Under way again, we drank our rum neat and watched the dusk turn the river into the colour of lemons. Trees had begun to appear, misty blue hills loomed out of the eastern horizon. "There used to be monkeys along those banks," said David, "until the army ate them. We lost a T-class near here several years ago, sunk by a flash flood from a *chaung*. A *chaung* is a dried-up stream. Only last month a dance troupe was performing for a village in a creek bed when a cloud burst caught them; everyone was washed into the river and, days later, we were still picking up bodies dressed in silk. Every one of these *chaungs* is a potential menace. They make a roaring noise and that is something a master must always listen for, because if one strikes his ship broadside on there is nothing he can do. The T-class was steaming at night. It caught him at 4 a.m. and that ship vanished entirely. We know where it went down, and we went looking with metal detectors, but it was buried under thousands of tons of sand."

The skipper switched on his spotlight. Flickering over the banks and black water, it picked up the tin reflector discs nailed to buoys, also giant gaudy moths and shadowy flying foxes. The lights of the Siam-class steamers (which could pinpoint a high-flying aircraft) needed twin motors to rotate them, and though ours was puny by comparison, it safely plotted our passage and turned the occasional crystal-studded riverside pagoda into a ripple of summer lightning.

Talk of the *chaungs* had made David morose. He spoke of a great flood when, since there was no dry land for burials, the dead were wrapped in mats and launched upon the Irrawaddy, bobbing corpses through which he grimly navigated his side-paddler; then, very loudly, he played "Bad Moon Rising" on his cassette machine. We docked at Magwe and, after a meal of fish soup prepared by a mad-eyed, half-naked cook ashore, got ready for bed.

The ship's cockroaches massed to meet us. They seemed as large as lobsters and came scuttling across the deck in waves. "The Thais *eat* those," David said. I already knew that—but only after they had milked, from the insects' glands, a famous relish which, while costing a king's ransom, was so pungent a single drop would transform a family sized dish. Once I awoke to find cockroaches trekking across my face, by the dawn's early light watched a lame brown rat hobble off through a hole in the bulkhead.

That afternoon an overweight colonel, grumpy and sweat-stained, commandeered our best chair. After exchanging ages—a standard courtesy between strangers—he announced that much of Burma was in flames. "The combustion is *spontaneous*." As a consequence he had combed the region to check hoses, rehearse procedures and supervise drills. Recently he spent an entire day preparing the citizens of one township for the eventuality of fire, and what happened next? It burned to the ground. An estimated three hundred perished, including a batch of prisoners locked in the jail. He sighed windily. "They are hopeless, *hopeless!*"

After putting him ashore at Thayetmyo—where, in 1883, the British built an eighteen-hole golf course—we passed a side-paddler which, somehow, had evaded the Mandalay sinkings and now laboured upstream with barges of cement. Boasting giant boilers and a steam-driven rudder, she had been Clyde-built half a century earlier. The captain, reclining in a chair on the bridge, lifted a teacup in salute while his great seven-bladed teak wheels thundered away inside their boxes. The countryside was changing, the sandy wilderness giving way to low green hills, fields of millet and plantations of toddy palms. We saw country-boat slipways hidden in groves of flowering plum trees and, everywhere, pagodas. Some indicated lazy monks and shiftless congregations, but most were lovingly tended and a credit to their villages.

The first part of our voyage was almost over. That evening we would disembark in Prome and wait for a ship to take us on to Rangoon. "Dark Clouds," after discharging cargo, would return with David, to Mandalay. But at the village of Kama the sky turned black and raindrops came whanging down like dumdums. "Ah, the mango rains have come," said David, relishing the sudden chill, but this was no seasonal shower putting a bloom on the fruit. When a wind sprang up the skipper ordered the fine-boned women loading onions and charcoal to quit the ship. Dust whirled by as, with engines full ahead, we ran for open water, the pilot complaining loudly that he had sand in his eyes and couldn't see. Canoes and country boats slipped past in the murk, while on the hills above, the pagoda bells were wild and clamorous.

"Dark Clouds" plunged and yawed among steep breaking waves. David yelled at the captain to get to the bank. He needed no urging and hit it at such speed he buried his bow in streaming red earth. Then, abruptly as it had come, the storm receded, leaving behind the washed pink skies of evening.

We made good time to Prome. A following breeze lent the water a curious bounce and energy. David, who had become our friend, talked with a particular intensity about his relationship with the river. He had run away to it as a child and signed up as a ship's boy; shortly afterwards his elder brother drowned in it; his mother detested the Irrawaddy. His wife had gone into labour aboard one of his own steamers and their first son, after a difficult delivery in the forward cabin, arrived stillborn. Many babies were lost off the ships; carelessly positioned by their parents at night, they rolled under the guard rail while they slept. "In an emergency," he said, "we must cope by our-selves because we are not equipped with radio. It can be two or three days before help arrives."

As we docked he pressed a small package into my hand. "It's noth-ing," he shrugged. "Open it later." Prome, at dusk, looked homely and welcoming, but having said our goodbyes we found ourselves travers-ing muddy streets filled with growling dogs and the jangle of bicycle bells. At the People's Hotel a wedding was in progress. Music blared and grinning drunks shook our hands as we made our way upstairs to squalid, windowless cubicles with graffiti-covered walls and filthy con-crete floors. I opened David's package and found an old opium weight, a tiny crested brass duck made shiny by handling—today one of my most valued possessions.

Aboard the ship cockroach bites had caused my feet to swell; now they were half the size of footballs. Showering, I noted that when the room had last been whitewashed, an empty beer bottle left on a corner shelf had been whitewashed too, leaving the wall behind untouched.

Our mentor for the final stage met us for breakfast. Ko Kyaw Win was thin and watchful; while we tucked into coffee and sliced pineapple, he chose a poached egg with a dollop of strawberry jam on top. We passed up a swim in the Heavy Industries Pool and a visit to the Japanese rubber-ball factory, called instead at the Shwesandaw pagoda, reached by electric lift (all rides paid for by a local businessman hoping to gain merit), where priests chanted the scriptures into microphones, their tinny voices audible all over town. A buoying launch had been put at our disposal. There, attended by the master himself—decidedly jumpy after a spell deciphering the course of the lower river—and his gentle, reassuring wife, we bathed. Later they pressed palm toddy upon us, along with barley sugar, movie magazines and savoury snacks wrapped in leaves. The surface was glassy, the current treacherous; and the bottom felt like warm porridge.

Browsing through the black market, not much refreshed, I found that a bottle of Johnnie Walker Red Label, brought down snake-infested jungle trails from Thailand on a smuggler's back, cost only slightly more than at my London off-licence. I took one aboard the *Taing Kyo Saung*, or "Patriot"—a T-class too, her monk's cabin dusted with anti-cockroach powder in which my feet left prints like rhino spoor.

The captain, a bald old man wearing broken spectacles, brought fresh fruit and tea in his best pot. Such courtesies are routine in Burma and he withdrew shyly, nonplussed by our thanks. Moments later we were under way with the promise, after two hours' steaming, of a wonder to come.

Carved into Ghautama Hill, a three-hundred-foot-high cliff extending for one and a half miles, are hundreds of images of the Buddha—some done in relief, others set in niches, many painted and gilded. At the time of the kings this was known as Tax Point; here ships paid tolls before being allowed to proceed. The statues had been commissioned by devout, excise-rich local royalty.

The first day's run was quiet. At the stops we swam, noting the urgency and vigour of the current; entering lower Burma, the river seemed to feel the tug of the sea. We tied up for the night beneath a deserted mudbank that reared high above the ship. Darkness brought a heavy silence, broken only by the murmur of the captain saying his prayers. Shortly before the lights went out I idly shone my torch along the bank and found it crowded with spectators—scores of them watching intently as we scrubbed our teeth and prepared for bed. They were mortified at being caught and, as one, fled up the bank as though running from a tidal wave.

We had entered a region boasting the world's biggest mosquitoes, and as I lit a candle and settled down to my notes they began bleeding me. But when fleas began dancing on the page, I suddenly recalled that fleas can give you bubonic plague and, shivering, jumped into my sleeping bag.

Daylight brought more changes. The river flowed between high, commanding banks, the pilot did slaloms around the sandbars. Everything now looked lushly tropical, the bamboo groves had a neon sheen, flights of mallard appeared in every quadrant of the sky. And with Rangoon just over the horizon, the people had changed too. Gone were the earnest, inflexible courtesies we'd encountered upstream. The villagers who met the boat now cracked cheeky jokes and showed a bit of swank.

In the afternoon we were joined by an old scholar who wore, in the buttonholes of his white silk shirt, rubies the size of chickpeas. He had been appointed, he said, by the Minister of Home and Religious Affairs to collect and collate classical Buddhist texts. It was an immense undertaking, and he now spent his life moving from one ecclesiastical library to the next.

A hundred yards of river bank fell into the water. Perhaps a thousand tons of earth vanished beneath the boiling surface, yet it was such a common occurrence we barely gave it a glance; each year whole villages vanished this way, indeed, for days, I had watched the river casually devour the countryside and flush it away to the Bay of Bengal. But this time waves rocked the ship.

I wanted to ask the scholar, who spoke agonizingly slow and fractured English, about the Tibetan Book of the Dead, but he only wanted to talk about Tottenham Hotspur. British football was his passion.

The sun sank unnoted behind massing banks of cumulus. The rains were imminent, and not a moment too soon. After dark there were fireworks. Burma, as the colonel claimed, was burning all right, and the eastern sky flickered redly. Was it crops? Stubble? Villages? I asked the pilot, who neither knew nor cared. Yet, even as he shrugged, the first heavy shower swept across the river.

Then, abruptly, he quit the Irrawaddy and made a sharp left turn into the Twante Canal—an artificial cut that links it with the Rangoon tributary. Our great waterway now lay astern as we prepared to enter the vast, creek-veined swamp that is her delta. We motored on through the rain, overtaking lumbering country boats at a speed befitting an express steamer concluding a mainline run.

The golden finger of the Shwedagon Pagoda appeared on the horizon, and eventually city lights shone blearily through the murk. We docked at 4 a.m., and clambering into a 1947 Buick taxi with a leaking roof I glanced back at the old ship to say goodbye and realized I couldn't see her. Well, I wasn't going to lose any sleep over that. I was glad to be off the river. My feet hurt, I had contracted some kind of fever and lost a stone in weight.

An embassy couple invited us home for a dinner of grilled English sausages, bacon, fried eggs, chips and beans—washed down with cold, creamy Guinness, and so good we had it again. The talk turned to Burmese artefacts; were we interested? We said—Pass the ketchup! Where's that mustard?—you bet, then, later in the kitchen, watched incredulously as a man entered, upended a sack and tipped, onto the table, an exquisite load of antique jewellery, reliquaries, Buddhas, palm-leaf texts, *pongyi,* or monk, figurines and several model *chinthes*— the mythical lion-dragons that guard pagodas. Our host confirmed that most had been looted from temples. "Which means it's all genuine— and the prices are a joke." But wasn't it forbidden to export religious artefacts from Burma? "No problem, it goes straight to London in the diplomatic bag." Knowing it was absolutely the wrong thing to do, yet suddenly seized by a collector's sweaty-palmed greed, I chose a beautiful miniature Buddha's head in bronze.

Sure enough, back home a couple of weeks later, I got a call from a crisply spoken woman who said, "Mr Frater? This is the Foreign and Commonwealth Office. We have a package for you. I am sending it over by courier." Today my dreaming little Buddha, surrounded by his force field of serenity, has become a focal point of my life. I justify my crime on the grounds that—well, there are no grounds, and occasionally I tell myself that some day I'll put matters right and take him home again.

Who's kidding who? I have learned to live with my conscience, while he has learned to live with me.

*

I called on Nick and Hazel early one morning (kettle already steaming on the Primus stove) to tell them I would be heading off shortly, and say *tata*. But, really, I wanted to talk about Burma. "Oh, Gawd," said Hazel, as she saw where the conversation was headed. Nick, though, ceased yawning and perked up. "She hardly ever mentions the place. What was it like?"

What was it *like*? Well, nowhere else had I ever felt so utterly perplexed; Burma, with its urbane people and languorous social conventions, its eclectic mix of Diamond Sutra metaphysics and discredited socialist dogma, seemed to exist in a separate universe. Recalling a cigar-smoking citizenry who combined lordly Buddhist detachment with a wicked fondness for jokes (novice monks were the worst), I said, "We had some laughs."

Hazel gave me a shrewd glance. "Be honest, it was like a love affair you never got over. And ever since you've been travelling to find it again. I've met your type before. It usually grabs the chaps; it's the boys who love Burma. No offence, Alex, but you're getting a bit long in the tooth for all that." This, unexpectedly, irritated Nick. "Jesus, Haze, give him a break, the guy only went on a trip." Yet she was right. You didn't need spatio-temporal geometry to find the place I'd been looking for, in fact it wasn't even the old Burma I wanted back, but a younger, less-damaged version of me; Burma had just been a place where I'd got on a boat and gone down a river. Though it couldn't compare with, say, the birth of my children, it had nevertheless become one of those waypoints when life seemed charged with unusual promise and possibility.

I told them about Jones who, travelling more for fun and profit, had used the occasion to set up his personal pension fund. One morning, in a Mandalay shop, he spotted several dozen faded postage stamps from the Japanese Occupation and, acting on impulse, bought the lot. Back home he learned the history, studied the catalogues, read the literature, got to know the dealers, traded shrewdly and, within a decade, had acquired such a high-value array that a leading London auction house referred to it, respectfully, as "the Colin Jones Collection."

One of Britain's most eminent photographers, a drily funny man who married a beautiful model (they dined with rock stars), would protest, "I'm only doing this for my old age," then talk about going back. New philatelic opportunities may have been on his mind yet, years on, he too remained bewitched. From time to time we, "old piss-artists" both, would meet over a drink to hatch our plans but, inevitably, end up squabbling over the Burma conundrum: was it better to boycott the regime, or to fly out and report on what was really happening?

Hazel remained silent. I mentioned the writer John Hatt who, after meeting Aung San Suu Kyi's husband in Oxford, launched a vigorous stay-away campaign among the British media. For a while I backed him then, growing restless, and without even telling Jones, furtively faxed a Rangoon shipping agency for details of the run from Bhamo, on the Chinese border, down to Mandalay. They never replied but, weeks afterwards, a letter came with Burmese stamps and a Yangon postmark; containing no sender's address, and erratically typed on flimsy airmail paper, it said:

Dear Mr. Frater,

I understand you have been making enquiries regarding permission to visit the Upper Irrawaddy. I have it on good authority that some people at SLORC wish to talk to you. You understand what this means?

Yours sincerely,

A Well Wisher

I told Nick, "It's their KGB. State Law and Order Restoration Council."

"To whom human rights are about as comprehensible as rocket science," said Hazel. "So, of course, you never went." Suddenly she seethed, "Those names! *Myanmar* sounds like some dodgy import-export operation—drugs, arms, any old shit. And Yangon is a real *noodle*-town name. Daddy says, apart from the SLORC morons, absolutely everyone still says 'Burma' and 'Rangoon,' and fuck the Generals." The woman who liked to affect the manner of an old Roedean hockey captain had become a furious, gimlet-eyed Oriental revolutionary. "That debate of yours—it wasn't just confined to bloody journalists, I know about your John Hatt and I'm right behind him.

You were wrong to even think about going back. Wrong! Wrong! Quite out of order!"

"I agree. Absolutely."

The kettle began bubbling. She gave a little sigh. "You take sugar, don't you?"

"Nothing for me, thanks. I've just had breakfast."

As, silently, she made tea, I reflected that the Generals had not only expunged Burma's name from the map, they had also somehow altered its spiritual centre of gravity. And, by moving it away from the ecliptic, or tropical parallels of latitude, they had in effect made winter a Burmese season.

Nick, as I turned to go, said, "By the way, you heard about the lake here? How it used to do these weird reflections? Well, I'm just about seeing an idea for a picture but . . . the damn thing keeps kind of slipping out of focus."

I knew the feeling. "Really? Look, we'll chat next time; I'm running seriously late."

One unrecognized aspect of the tropics (the evidence to date remains largely anecdotal) is the way it attracts coincidence; some synchronic lodestone keeps pulling utterly random factors together with a frequency unknown in the temperate areas. Cool-climate people don't like too many surprises, here we're disappointed if a day goes by without one. "Hey, haven't we met before?" or "Well, I'll be damned!" or "This is quite amazing!"—such exclamations are heard routinely. So, when I assured Nick our paths would cross again, I meant it. (In fact, it was the last I ever saw of him.)

Back at Wongrass, Francis checked for any breakages which might require a cash settlement. As I waited, the child in the tree slid down and, while still not acknowledging me, joined us for the short walk to the airfield. Francis and I had become friends, and he worried that I hadn't learned enough about Gaua. "I think your mind was not here." That was shrewd of him; for the last couple of days, actually, it had been several thousand miles away, hovering over a terrific sweep of river reflecting a rubescent dawn sky. We watched the plane come banking over the sea and, suddenly, the child squeezed my hand. *"Au revoir,"* she said, and went skipping off down the road.

In the Doldrums

The Irrawaddy left me with such nostalgia for tropical rivers that whenever I happened to be in the vicinity of one I tried to get afloat. Also, I read a bit of science and asked some questions. Somchan, a young Mekong boatman with a shambolic private life (three marriages, four kids, two pregnant girlfriends), simply urged me to use my eyes. So for the first time I paid attention to such matters as the behaviour of rain—not just the way it sluiced off gradients and dripped from every leaf and grass blade, but how, seeking the steepest, shortest routes—depressions formed by the intersections of slopes—it kept rushing in all directions while making, inexorably, for the same destination.

I learned that a river achieves perennial, or historic, status through erosion, and that erosion is caused by a combination of volume and velocity ($e = vo + ve$). Velocity, though, depends not just on the water's speed and weight, but also the frictional resistance of the bed. Only after hard usage has polished a bed, and smoothed its contours, will aeons of additional vo + ve turn it into a perennial. In South America, on Suriname's torpid, winding Commewijne, Captain Balradj, a Hindustani commanding a fifty-year-old ferry (three hundred tons of stratified rust, with new blooms growing vigorously among the old), explained that perennialism is achieved when a river runs deep enough to be fed by groundwater. At base level—where depth starts inhibiting forward flow—it expands sideways, cutting laterally to create sinuous loops and meanders; out on the coast, meanwhile, it lays down alluvial fans and cones, deltas, flood plains and channel bars.

In Hué, Vietnam, tiny Miss Dieu, who paddled me down the Perfume River in a basketwork coracle, said that waterways always deal with problems in a practical way. If, for instance, a sluggish meander slows up a mature river, the river digs a channel across the meander's arc and isolates it. It turns the arc into an oxbow lake. (*Osbo rake.*) Miss

Dieu spoke grammatically perfect World Service English and wore a conical hat which, held up to the light, revealed a poem—woven into the straw—about Hué's bridge. When I asked how she knew so much about rivers, she in turn asked me if I liked Vietnamese girls. I sneezed, and she wagged a finger. "Now you are thinking of your wife!" Charmed, I continued my studies.

Should a young, rain-laden system need to expand, it may break into a neighbouring drainage basin and divert, or steal, its water. (Scientists call this "piracy," and in the tropics such muggings are commonplace.) If, during its formative years, a river is sent plunging over escarpments, hanging valleys and so on, it will resort to actual thuggery: its instinct, when interrupted by a waterfall, is to demolish it. Gnawing away at its lip, or cap rock, steadily eroding the bed above, it gradually *moves the whole thing backwards* (Niagara, so far, has journeyed about seven miles). As the fall regresses, it loses size and height, in time is reduced to rapids which, continually battered by the river, then vanish altogether. The Irrawaddy, before it became a placid perennial, boasted plenty of cataracts and tumbling white water.

As a child in Fiji I was almost killed by a waterfall. During a family picnic nearby I'd hauled myself thirty feet up a tangle of roots to the top. Once there, mesmerized by the silky, soundless way the stream slid over the lip, I decided to walk across. At that point everything went blank; all I know is that a passing wood-cutter fished me unconscious—a rock had caught the point of my chin—from the pool below. Today, from time to time, it returns as one of those plunging-down-a-liftshaft dreams where, if you hit bottom, your heart stops.

That may explain why I never bothered with any of the big tropical falls until, not long ago in Guyana, I flew to Kaieteur, deep in the rainforest and five times the height of Niagara. The views from the top were so vertiginous I gulped and hung back. Sheila Alleyne, the waterfall warden and weather girl, cried, "Best way is to crawl to the edge on ya tummy." So, just inches from my nose, I watched the tea-coloured Potaró River plunge silently into a gorge, become partially vaporized during its seven-hundred-and-forty-foot descent, then roaringly reconstitute itself among rainbows. These shone with such intensity they lit up flocks of parakeets barnstorming through the spray. (Later I learned they weren't parakeets at all, but common swifts replumaged by that high-voltage iridescence.)

Sheila, black and talkative, said the falls created their own climate. "When the cloud and mist come down I must call Mr Fernandez in Georgetown on my UHF." What did she think of the Kaieteur turning, some day, into just another set of rapids? The idea made her laugh. "I am Met Office–trained, and fall specialist, so I guess Fernandez will have to find me anudder one. Ya know, in Guyana we also got King George the Sixth—almos' twice as high as Kaieteur; and in Venezuela they got the mighty Angel."

That tumbled three thousand two hundred feet down the sheer wall of Auyán-Tepuí. It was the world's tallest, while the Guaira, on the Paraná between Brazil and Paraguay, carried its largest flow. "You in South America now. We got de biggest and best. And ya know why? Because we got de *rivers.*"

Ah, yes, the rivers. She had reminded me that before I could start on this book, I had one more journey to make.

*

Frank Clarke once took a *gaiola* down the greatest river of all, doubtless jumping off to do business with any Tupi-speaking congregations crazy enough to build their churches along its unstable banks. The high point had been a visit to a giant American plantation where jungle rubber was grown for auto tyres and the expatriate managers enjoyed the best facilities: fine houses, schools and shops, a first-class hospital, a comfortable hotel. And it was there, when a chapel was being added, that he met up with an irascible old man to whom, after protracted negotiations, he sold a set of tenor bells. "Frank swore it was the boss, Henry Ford himself," my mother recalled, "and he always referred to that type of tenor bell as his Model T." But what most interested me was Frank's claim to have seen, somewhere along the river, a mermaid drifting quietly on her back as she breastfed her baby.

What he almost certainly spotted had been a bottom-feeding aquatic mammal distantly related to the elephant. Indeed the manatees, found on both sides of the tropical Atlantic, often became mermaids in the imaginations of lonely seamen; adult females have a pair of mammary glands on the chest, and while suckling a pup, float on the surface clasping it in their flippers. (Columbus, sighting three, reported, "Although they were not as beautiful as they appear in pictures, their round faces were definitely human." Yet his expectations may have clouded his eyesight; these quarter-ton sea cows have big blubbery heads and large fleshy lips—the upper cleft into twin lobes—thickly strewn with bristles.)

Frank, though, had offered such a wistfully appealing hint of the Amazon's possibilities that when, at the *Observer,* we matched writers to our great rivers, I was torn enough to toss a coin. It came down tails so Ronald Fraser took it on instead, and came home with a story that, in less able hands, could have been overwhelmed by the immensity of what he set out to describe. Though, at three thousand nine hundred miles, it isn't the world's longest—the Nile beats it by two hundred and sixty—the Amazon and its eleven hundred tributaries transport one-fifth of the world's fresh water supply, produce one-fifth of its oxygen and sustain half its tropical forests; in a lakelet the size of an Olympic swimming pool, scientists have found eight times more fish species than in all the rivers of Europe, while any random two-acre bush tract may yield up to three thousand separate botanical species—many still unclassified, some containing yet-to-be-discovered wonder drugs. Fraser's river was a global locomotor powered by gravity and fluid dynamics (including plenty of Andean snowmelt). I knew that at some point, I too would have to board a *gaiola* and check out this tropical life force for myself.

Years later, having taken no further action, I happened to mention it to a London friend over lunch. He said, "I know about those *gaiolas,* you just hang in your hammock going crazy with boredom. For *days.* And they're crewed by criminals. Some night they'll nick your money, cut your throat and dump you over the side. Don't P&O go up the Amazon? If it was me I'd be on to them like a shot."

So, head still filled with the uproarious fumes of an estate-bottled Australian Tarrango made by the talented Brown Brothers (with whom I had been at school), I called a lady who handled PR for P&O. A beacon of competence and enthusiasm in a profession markedly short of both, she confirmed that the company, just once a year when the water was high, cruised a thousand miles up to Manaus; a berth could be arranged. Sheepishly I said such a trip really wasn't for me; travel writers, after all, are supposed to suffer. "Soft beds and four-course dinners? On the *Amazon*? I'd never live it down." She said, "*Six*-course dinners, there are a dozen bars, and you can smoke to your heart's content."

"I see. All the way to Manaus, eh?"

"And back. Also of course, since you'd be writing about it, we'd bear the cost, you just pay for drinks."

I said, "I'll have a think," and, minutes later, still quite drunk, called her back. "Why not? Count me in."

*

I had gone on deck hoping to hear the *pororoca*—a collision between river and ocean triggered by the full moon and likened to the crash of siege guns—but our skipper, mindful of his 1,460 sleeping passengers, stayed upwind. At 4 a.m., moving dead slow beneath blazing equatorial stars, *Arcadia* slipped past the Amazon light vessel and began her fifteen-mile transit of the bar with only three feet between seabed and keel.

Every eight hours a million tons of silt are dumped on the bar, every fifty days the Amazon discharges enough to form an adobe Everest as wide as it's high. The bar, therefore, remains in a state of constant agitation. I waited for the bump and shudder that would signify we had touched bottom, yet the largest liner ever to enter the world's greatest river finally heaved her 63,534-ton bulk across and picked up speed.

The mouth is a hundred and seventy miles wide, and though a succession of giant trees—mahogany, araucaria, various exotic hardwoods—came wallowing past, it was midmorning before we saw smudges of land. Meanwhile, the ship settled into its routine: line dancing—"Yeeha! Buff your boots and mosey along to the Palladium"—a Rotarians' get-together in the Oval Bar, a Masonic meeting in the Horizon Lounge, whist in the Conservatory, holistic therapies (featuring shiatsu head massage) in the Canberra Room, the Arcadia Bridge Teams Championship in Trumps, golf chipping in the nets, shuffleboard, a tango class, the Morning Singalong . . . Then came a bridge announcement: "At 3 p.m., after boarding our pilots, we shall cross the equator." A woman pointed to an opaline butterfly with the wingspan of a swallow. "We really are in the tropics!" I noted we also now seemed to be in a river—though the banks remained so far apart they seemed like the shores of different continents.

Over an excellent Goan fish-curry lunch I tried to imagine the incredulity felt by Francisco de Orellana, a one-eyed Portuguese who, two thousand miles upstream on a Sunday morning in 1542, went searching for cinnamon in a small wooden boat. Emerging from a tributary, he and his men encountered a phenomenon which "came on with such fury and with so great an onrush that it was enough to fill one with the greatest fear." They arrived at the mouth seven months later, telling tales of female warriors even more barbarous than the mastectomized man-killers of Asia Minor. The Amazon was thus named for a Greek myth compounded by Orellana's own feverish imagination.

At Santana, a sprawling, leafy town with a scattering of high-rise buildings, we anchored a mile offshore to collect our officials. As preparations were made for the arrival of King Neptune and his Court—an excuse for the kids to beat up unpopular members of the entertainment staff—a purser told me about the rapacious Rebelli brothers. "They were the first Amazon pilots to realize the kind of money they could make from cruise ships; pay up or you don't move. Even today the skipper has to hand over $55,000 US *in cash.* They also want a big chunk of the takings from our shops and bars. If it goes on like this we may stop coming altogether."

Few liners visit anyway. A circular from the tours office explained why P&O, selling around a hundred cruises annually, offer this only once. "As one of the last frontiers in the world, life in Amazonia is very different from life as we know it in Europe." It warned of bad roads, poor transport, inadequate guides and—carefully seeking the right phrase—"varying degrees of poverty." Yet ships have travelled it for a hundred and fifty years. Clipper-bowed and brig-rigged, built from live oak, locust wood and hackmatack (double-planked and strapped with iron), they even had string quartets and champagne bars; chandeliers went twinkling along the Amazon.

It descends in a series of sweeping parabolic curves, the force of water around the outer rims scouring channels so deep we swept along at oceanic speeds ("Seventeen knots over the ground," reported a gratified officer of the watch). At times one bank remained a wisp on the skyline as *Arcadia,* hugging the other, put us within yards of macaws and troupials, blizzards of white egrets, orchids half-smothered by strangler vines, blossom-decked trees taller than Nelson's Column, tiny whey-faced monkeys scampering through a banyan's canopy. Someone even heard a whippoorwill's call.

Leafage thick as thatch neutralized sunlight, made the forest's interior dim and smoky. At dusk a few clearings appeared—each containing a shack where rubber-tappers or distillers of rosewood essence sat by their supper fires. Peering with voyeuristic intensity at them I wondered what they made of us—shining white, fourteen decks high, humming with wealth and privilege—and was tickled to note that most barely even glanced up; we were of less interest than a passing canoe.

Chlorosis, or green sickness, is a condition that makes the faces of young women viridescent; after hours of tree-gazing I had it in the brain. Yet by moonlight the forest became metallic, almost blue. It was a formal night aboard, the men wearing black ties and tropical tuxedos, the women gowns from Bentalls and the House of Fraser. Strolling on deck after dinner we heard, from far off, a barking, yowling chorus which caused turbulence within the inner ear. Gradually it turned into a dreamy tribal chant, ending almost in a sigh. The distant songs of the howler monkeys, soothing and rather beautiful, seemed an appropriate way to conclude the day. Or, rather, conclude it for me. The Pacific Restaurant, "transformed into a Chocolate Lovers' Paradise," was about to reopen for the Chocoholics' Late Night Buffet.

*

I was rather enjoying the ship. Indeed, lying there as we steamed up the dark Amazon, I liked being tucked up in a well-run, efficiently air-conditioned bubble of comfort and security. Here, far from home, I could look forward to early-morning coffee served in my cabin, freshly cooked eggs and fresh-baked bread for breakfast, new-release movies each afternoon in the Festival Theatre and a choice of evening diversions (including a dreary, self-regarding Irish comedian who, apparently, had once been on British TV). We even carried a well-equipped little hospital which charged Harley Street prices and had the only twenty-four-hour cardiac-response team and intensive-care unit for a thousand miles in any direction. From a hundred-and-fifty-foot-high observation deck (within easy strolling distance of several shipboard bars) I looked down at the triple-decked, swaybacked *gaiolas,* waved to their villainous crews, and felt not the remotest wish to join any of them.

Yet one of my assigned dinner companions, on his maiden cruise, called the ship *"Titanic"* and hated everything about it. Jerry Catchpole, a retired Hackney tobacconist and sometime Labour Party activist, had a weeping eye and a whippet-thin body squared off transversely by giant red-framed David Hockney spectacles. Finding we were both smokers, and socialists from a discredited era, we sat together; thus I learned that, acting on advice from his cousin Ray (Finchley-based, owner-driver of a black cab), he had booked a cheapo inside cabin shared with three strangers. On arrival he bagged all the coat hangers, mixed up the towels, dumped his clothes on the floor, farted a lot, drank vodka in bed, used obscene language, even accused the man in the next bunk—a football-mad grocer from Watford—of being gay. Sure enough, first morning at sea, he was summoned to the purser's office and, at no extra cost, allocated single-berth quarters, with porthole. "Bad manners get good results. It's Ray's Upgrade Law."

We became friends, then, confronted by a class enemy, political allies. Each night a youngish, self-regarding, zealously anti-smoking Blairite couple who had made a fortune in property development regaled Table 121 with tales from the world of fast-build, hard-sell, low-cost, high-priced executive housing, or sighed about the burdens of wealth. (When moving between various holiday homes they had to charter a separate plane for their *dog.*)

Afterwards Jerry and I usually went to a bar to vent our spleen in drink. One evening, peering through lenses so opaque his eyes were wobbling pools of light, he told me he'd have preferred to have seen the Amazon from a *gaiola.* "At least there'd be some laughs." That brought me up short. Laughs, no question, were in short supply on this ship. I'd had plenty on the Irrawaddy yet, recalling it now in an idle, disinterested way, it finally dawned on me that Burma no longer mattered; it was history. I assured him he was better off here, comfortably sipping his malt. A widower, ten years my senior, he gave one of his rattling emphysemic coughs. "You must be getting old, mate," he said.

*

Being "in the doldrums," meaning entrapment in a depression that can be either climate-related or personal, dropped out of common usage with the invention of the steamship. Known also as the Equatorial Belt of Calms, the doldrums lie at that tropical junction where the northern and southern trades collide and adopt a vertical flow. What they leave behind is, famously, a breathless vacuum in which quiescent sailing vessels could—like Coleridge's painted ship—drift for weeks. (These days only round-the-world yachties know how the Ancient Mariner felt: "There passed a weary time. Each throat / Was parched, and glazed each eye. / A weary time! A weary time! / How glazed each weary eye.")

Yet here the world's hurricanes are hatched. Starting as tiny cones of depression around egg-sized zones of calm—each creating as much breeze as an electric fan—they're coddled and nourished by massive doses of equatorial solar radiation. High humidity and low pressure are common, squalls and thunderstorms cause grumbles aboard transiting cruise liners.

Arcadia was in the doldrums now. The Amazon's flow approximately follows the doldrum line and, at Santarém, I found a population mooching around their broken streets, radiating hostility and aggression. Though the town, set on a tributary fifteen miles wide and shallow as a pond, possessed a university and a pretty little eighteenth-century cathedral, it was really just a toehold in a wilderness reaching all the way to the Mato Grosso. Suffocating heat and a sense of isolation characterized Santarém on a Sunday morning—yet I enjoyed being ashore in Brazil and, disembarking behind a stout Geordie woman (who hailed a taxi with a cry of "Take me to the jungle, pet!"), dragged Jerry past a clutch of pubescent whores in hot pants (*"Phoar!"* he went) at the dock gate.

Strolling along the waterfront we noted that people looked either through us or past us; I bought postcards from a woman who didn't see me: sullen eye-contact-avoiders shouldered us off pavements. A mulatto youth peddling porcelain statuettes wanted money to go to America. The statuettes, of black gynaecologists peering earnestly between the legs of grimacing black women, were interesting, but he could tell us nothing about them. Instead, we learned of the Southern Confederates who, fleeing the Civil War in 1867, founded a colony in Santarém; after a few years those not killed by fever or local violence hitched lifts home aboard a US lumber barque. "I am descended from one of the families," said the mulatto. "I must go to Texas and find them."

In a cafe a child with a withered, grotesquely misshapen upper body sidled up and asked for a cigarette. A waiter, chasing him off, said he was a victim of the mercury used by wildcat *garimpeiros* when prospecting for gold. (An ore-amalgamating toxin leached into the river, and poisoning the food chain, it would take centuries to wash out.) A bright, personable young man ("It is my ambition to study astronomy"), he bore a striking resemblance to Ossie Ardiles, the legendary footballer. Yet when Jerry pointed this out, he glared at us and stalked off. I said, "Maybe it's because Ardiles is Argentinean."

"Or because he's probably a grandad and ready for his pension." He sighed. "What's wrong with these fucking people?"

"They're in the doldrums," I said.

*

During the sixteenth century ships regularly brought Brazilian produce to France. (In 1531 the frigate *La Pèlerine* carried three thousand leopard skins, three hundred monkeys and six hundred parrots—many of the latter already speaking a few words of French.) In 1558, when famine struck a vessel with a similar cargo, passengers and crew ate the monkeys, then the parrots—though an Indian woman demanded a cannon before handing over her talking birds—and finally the mice and rats, which changed hands for four écus each. Those people were, plainly, trapped in the doldrums too.

*

The property developers had once met Tony Blair at a business function. He had, they claimed, taught them it was OK for the rich to get richer, because they would inspire the poor to work hard and get rich too. "He has made us aware that being successful brings its own responsibilities," said the man. "Because of him we have become better, more caring, people."

Jerry asked, "So how does Tony feel about smokers?"

"He'd probably have you all lined up and shot."

*

He refused, on principle, to join any of the shore excursions: the shuffling, sheeplike compliance of the queues, the hectoring guides and Tannoy announcements appalled him. I went on a half-day look at "Amazonian Local Life" which took in an airless little "hammock factory" and a stinking "old-fashioned rubber factory" where chunks of latex were fed into a thunderous machine before being turned into tyres. A wistful employee told me that once the factory had made condoms and surgical gloves, and he seemed to miss the refinement of those days.

But Jerry made an exception for the forest. It was, he said, the only reason he had come on the cruise at all.

Just outside Santarém, in 1876, Henry Wickham, a British adventurer, collected seventy thousand wild rubber seeds, *Hevea brasiliensis,* wrapped them in banana leaves, placed them aboard a chartered freighter and smuggled them off to Kew Gardens (where he woke the curator, Sir Joseph Hooker, at three in the morning). It was all pre-planned, of course, and Wickham spent his £5,000 reward on the purchase of an Australian tobacco farm; utterly forgotten elsewhere, he's still known to every Brazilian school kid. They call him "the Executioner of Amazonas."

Joe, our guide, told the story as we headed for Amazonia's Green Hell aboard a shiny new Mercedes bus. "In those days all our rubber grew wild; his criminality caused us great suffering. We could not compete with your big British plantations in Malaya and Ceylon." Young, black and intense, he offered a few tips for today. "Ask before you touch. There are beautiful flowers here that will put you in the cemetery."

Access to the jungle was through an ornamental garden gate; inside a few acres had been fenced off, de-snaked and sanitized. I followed a widowed Glasgow doctor who told me about the great ant-eater, or *tamandua,* which, if approached by humans, hauled itself up against a tree before choking them with its forepaws. It was steamy and breathless in there, with diffused sub-aquatic light and unexpected sound effects—exploding rubber pods scattering their seeds, raucous birds and such heavy rustlings that Jerry and I kept a nervous lookout for jaguars. The choice of a rubber tree for our first halt was political. Using a *seringueiro*'s curved knife Joe made a delicate descending "flag" incision, caused a few droplets of milky fluid to dribble into a zinc cup. "This is the forest's wealth," he said, moving us on to the forest's food: heavy cannonball capsules stuffed with Brazil nuts, nourishing *araçá* and wild cocoa fruit, raspberry-flavoured pineapples, leaves from which you could brew cashew-flavoured beer, a *soveira* tree which, when its trunk is incised, yields more milk than a cow, trees holding gallons of potable water, rotting stumps crawling with fat, buttery, coconut-flavoured *koro* worms.

Building materials lay to hand: palms like the *accashy* made good thatch, the *caranda* strong walls, cradles and baskets. (Joe plucked a frond, slit it with his thumbnail, tied a few knots then held up a winged bird that could nod its head: "Indian toy.") Swatting at the stingless, sweat-drinking bees known as *lambe-olhos,* or "lick-eyes," that flew direct for your tear ducts (and made strong, pungent honey), we came upon plants used against malaria and depression, learned the forest Indians had identified at least fifteen female oral contraceptives, that shrubs containing revolutionary anti-AIDS or cancer compounds might be growing only yards away. "Or maybe the last such plants were burned yesterday," said Joe. Each year developers burn a region the size of Belgium; now the Amazon smoke cloud (which causes chronic respiratory problems and routinely closes local airports) has reached Antarctica. Experts agree that the burning of Amazonia constitutes the greatest incineration of living matter in history. Gilberto Mestrinho, a sometime governor of Amazonas State, believed in "a chainsaw for every voter." Responsible for flattening a million square miles of rainforest during his terms in office, he declared, "I like trees, but they are not indispensable."

Joe spoke of high-level corruption, of huge areas due to be flooded for hydro-electric schemes, of the long-range, heavy-lift Russian helicopters soon to start plucking the most valuable trees from places previously protected by their remoteness. "Come back in a hundred years," he said, not altogether joking, "and Amazonia will be golf courses."

Jerry, reckoning the morning had been worth two weeks on the *Titanic,* said he might even display a Save the Rainforest sticker on his Mondeo. A high point had been learning that the Indians had a profound fear of stars. "I know what they mean, it's like the M25 on a bad Friday night here, millions of stationary headlights all on full beam. Then you get the shooters, *whoosh!* Honest, sometimes you almost got to duck. Me, I prefer those friendly little sparklers up there in the English smog."

The first time his mum went to visit his brother in Australia, he added, she became increasingly apprehensive. "After a few days the old gel worked out why: she was upside down. And these stars scare me the same kind of way, I feel *just like the Indians.*"

I didn't tell him that here I sometimes felt the same; in the doldrums, at the geographical centre of the world, the weight of both hemispheres can seem to bear down on you.

*

One morning *Arcadia* passed a hamlet set on a high clay bluff. In the shallows a dozen people standing waist-deep watched a man in a blue beret seize a grey-haired woman, push her under then bring her up again, spluttering; everyone spontaneously began to sing. A burly old Scot standing with me said, "A baptism. I'd like to see them try that in the Clyde."

Approaching a fork where both arms, unbounded by horizons, simply flowed off into the sky, I remarked, "It looks like the edge of the world. But which one's the Amazon?"

"I should know that, really—been up here often enough."

A retired ship's engineer, he had once done the Liverpool to Manaus run. "Coming home we always carried Brazil nuts, plus a dozen nut-trimmers—men who kept them turned and aired; filthy job, but Brazils need constant attention. Once we got stuck on a mudbank for ten days and some Indians appeared with their canoes full of fruit. The lads yelled, 'Take that away! Bring us women!' and, sure enough, they were soon back with a load of naked girls. The Old Man, well, he went bananas; and bananas, in the end, was all we ever got from those Indians."

A tributary's mouth slid by, wider than the Thames at Westminster:

such streams were ten a penny—one, never noted before, had recently been spotted by satellite. There was a village here, its soccer pitch half eaten by erosion; soon its pretty blue church, neat blue school and blue houses would be devoured too. Though dense forest surrounded it on three sides, most shoreline trees had already departed for the South Atlantic, leaving a few stragglers tilted at acute angles. But the women doing their laundry in the soupy red water (which somehow washed whiter than white) waved cheerily.

Tiny elliptical canoes, carved from mahogany and looking like salad bowls, went bouncing across our wash; foaming corrosively along the banks, it shaved off a few more tons of earth. Now, up ahead, there was a flash in the sky and a third river appeared. This one, brimming with light, looked large enough to carry the US Sixth Fleet all the way to Argentina. "Good gracious," my friend muttered, "now what is that?"

Talking my way onto the bridge I put the question to Luis, our smart young pilot. He said, "Just another tributary. Now we have three choices—and here the Amazon is the narrowest. But it changes all the time, and very fast; if I am away for just one month I start to lose the picture, and then my confidence. On this ship I have satellite navigation but often I will use the old methods—lining up trees, following ripples and drifting vegetation. This lower region we call the Occidental Amazon; it's not so bad. But upstream, beyond Manaus, the Oriental Amazon starts, there it can be so unpredictable we often need aquasounders."

He pointed to a neat, solidly built wooden house under a mango tree. "A characteristic dwelling. It has a floor that can move up and down; as the flood rises you crank it higher and higher until"—he bent double—"you must walk like this." I wondered how much further he could take *Arcadia*. "All the way to Iquitos in Peru, two thousand two hundred miles from the sea; a smaller ship I could get quite close to the Andes; the source is there, fifteen thousand feet up in a glacier." Our British navigator muttered, "I'm doing a fix every three minutes but, according to the charts, we're crossing dry land."

"That is absolutely typical," said Luis.

Moments later the air grew dark then seemed to liquefy spontaneously; rain made the water foam. We moved into a dense black wall, dead slow, siren blaring. Luis said, "Our problem is the *gaiolas,* they keep up top speed—their crews are so ignorant; there is no money for education in Amazonas." The sun reappeared and vaporized the cloudburst. "Ladies and gentlemen," said the navigator, broadcasting to the ship, "if you look for'ard now you'll see we're about to sail right through the middle of a rainbow."

Luis grinned. "This river! She can be a real old drama queen."

*

I know of a man once employed as navigator on a thousand-ton gin palace owned by a French industrialist. During an Amazon cruise, not far from Santarém, they were boarded by an armed gang who made everyone lie face down as they grabbed jewellery, money, liquor and electronic items. After a while the industrialist, unable to contain his rage, jumped up and threw a fire extinguisher at a man stealing a chandelier. He was saved from execution by his cook, who offered the pirates fresh-baked cookies and Blue Mountain coffee; this calmed them and, after taking a little refreshment, they hopped into their speedboat and departed.

*

One morning, rounding a bend that could have contained half Manhattan, we came upon Boca do Valerio. A hamlet of a dozen high-stilted houses, it now played host to *Arcadia*'s invasion force. As we trampled through their homes some inhabitants posed, in cloaks of iridescent feathers, for a dollar a picture. Others peddled crude souvenirs; a Scot asking for shrunken heads (miniaturized, he explained, by removing the skull then packing the skin with hot sand) got wry smiles from the Indians. P&O's printed *Port Guide* said we might haggle ("Bartering is possible") and I watched a City banker doggedly knock fifty cents off a wooden bird carved by a slash-and-burn peasant. In the end the peasants always gave in. Indeed, part of the charm of the transactions lay in the fatalism of the traders; ultimately, you could almost name your price.

Back aboard I wondered what such a tiny community would do with the wealth it had acquired that morning. A deck officer pointed to a satellite dish half-hidden in the trees. "Last time I came here they were watching Man U. versus Chelsea." He added, "But it's causing tensions ashore, the chief has even asked us to stop other villages getting in on the act. And there are, uh, *cultural* implications. Have you noticed what's going on aft?"

A flotilla of canoes clustered beneath the stern. Indian women, some holding parasols and suckling babies, gazed up as female crew members tossed down lipsticks, eyeshadow, blusher and nail varnish—all taken, by the Indians, with expert one-handed catches. "It's a sisters thing," a lady purser told me crisply.

Approaching Manaus, *Arcadia* passed the tributarial line along which the inky Rio Negro meets—but does not mix with—the mustard-coloured Rio Solimões. Beyond the floating ice factory, capping a spring in the river bed, lay a giant floating dock built by a Scot in 1902 and able to adjust, seasonally, to forty-six feet of fluctuating levels.

Best known for an ugly little neoclassical opera house (where José Carreras is said to have charged a million dollars for a night's work), it's a foetid, chronically disorganized city with a chemical edge to its ozone, a sullen citizenry and some of the worst slums in Brazil. Yet it offered access to the *igarapes,* an intimate wetland of creeks, bayous and half-submerged woodlands. One morning two hundred of us, hurtling through a drowned forest in fast motorized punts, came upon a lone fisherman waiting in a canoe. Our drivers, in a bit of exquisitely choreographed watermanship, slewed around to contain him in a perfect circle.

Then, midway through an ovation for the graceful way he cast his net, the fisherman quickly paddled away. During a further halt, for a symposium on Amazonian grasses, we understood why: the river, inverted, began falling out of the sky—not rain in the usual sense, more a spell of severe localized violence. As it crashed over my skull I blearily glimpsed, glowing like Chinese lanterns on the punt ahead, an eruption of multicoloured pac-a-macs.

Ashore, in hot sunshine again, the punt's occupants told me they came from Sussex where, at certain hardware stores, their monsoon gear was available for £1.50. A florid-faced Sussex magistrate (still in his dripping primrose plastic) seemed ready to have me up for indecent exposure. "You're so wet I can see right through you, you're a bloody X-ray." His wife said, "Not quite an X-ray, darling, we all know which side he dressed this morning."

They were booked to do a route march with Brazilian army jungle-survival experts; I went to dry off at a small waterside hotel where, over a glass or two of cachaca, or white rum, I got talking to a retired school-teacher. His home was tied to a tree on the far side of the cove—a lopsided raft bearing a small, mossy house with a rusting tin roof, walls of worn crenellated timber and a smoking tin chimney; a garden planted in pots caused the raft to tilt. Hens and a goat, he said, supplied him with eggs and milk, his surroundings with all the fish he could eat ("They deliver themselves to my door"). Even after he had bought rice, sugar, coffee, cooking fat, paraffin, soap, matches and so on, his pension still left enough for certain "luxuries." He remained indifferent to seasonal river levels, paid no rent, rates or taxes, and had no fixed address; when he grew sick of one locality he hitched a tow to another. Lean, with humorous eyes and flecks of white in a sparse ginger beard, he was beholden to no one.

We swapped stories. Named Milton by his Anglo-Brazilian mother, he had taught English in various Manaus schools, and when young—driving hundreds of miles in his own boat, providing his own slates and chalk—spent every vacation teaching riverine Indians to read and write. Now his wife had left him for a builder in Belo Horizonte, his grown-up kids had also moved to distant cities. All remained satisfyingly far away and out of touch.

He thought Britain's pensioners were rich—the reason so many kept turning up on cruise ships. I told him the British state pension actually required one to live very frugally. Yet when, on the back of a damp envelope, I converted it into rials, it seemed a huge sum. He whistled and sipped some rum. "This is strong," he pronounced, "but not the strongest. In Iquitos there is a rum so phenomenal it fills the eyes with blood."

Lévi-Strauss, charmed by the Amazonians' "fondness for superlatives," described a rubber cultivator who, living deep in the forest, also made gramophones and five-star brandy. Though things often went wrong—his horse kept being attacked by vampire bats, in Manaus his family once went on a shopping spree that left him destitute—thanks to an "ever-fertile imagination" he remained largely content.

Milton told the story of a nineteenth-century Manaus heiress who, interested in the principles of flight, built kites of unusual beauty.

Those that did not easily get airborne she destroyed, those that broke free were retrieved by trained macaws working like gun dogs. (The kites, displayed in her mansion like heraldic shields, could be seen by the public on Monday afternoons.) To celebrate the birth of a grandson she created one in gold—gold leaf, gold-plated wire, gilded silk, yellow topazes on all the pressure points. Launched in blustery conditions on the day of the baptism, it cut loose and, evading the macaws, went floating off, apparently lost for ever. Yet it carried the usual reward note and, months later, a claimant got in touch from *Belgium*. What did I make of that?

I said it obviously got tangled in the rigging of a Belgium-bound ship moored in the river. The idea that it was somehow blown over there was, like his macaws, too silly for words. But thinking about winds, I suddenly remembered the doldrums and, half-joking, asked how it felt to live among them. Milton seized on the idea. "I am a citizen of *the* Doldrums!" he chuckled. "Like *the* United States. Well, we must have our flag also! I think, actually, it would show the golden kite. It would be our symbol. It found a good wind and broke free."

Then he told me that in 1954, on his only trip abroad, he visited his mother's family in Lincolnshire. The locals (their raw-boned, weather-flayed looks carefully described) puzzled over this exotic Amazonian "jungle man." He wanted to talk about Dickens and Thackeray while they, after a few drinks, wanted to talk about cannibalism. How many people had he eaten? Where was his blowpipe? Could they see his body tattoos? As—shivering theatrically—he described the way the cold got into his bones, I wondered where all this was leading. "You see, they were poor peasants," he said. "Their life was hard. I think they also could never find the good wind."

A harpy eagle flapped by, its huge, tapering wings almost touching at the apex of each beat. He meant the doldrums had a global reach, and could catch up with you absolutely anywhere.

*

Whenever the Ship's Bore—with his regimental tie, panama hat and opinions on every subject under the sun—approached, people scattered like chickens before a fox. One morning, as *Arcadia* headed back down to the Atlantic, and I had a pretty little capuchin (usually seen with a tin cup, soliciting coins for organ-grinders) focused in my binoculars, this solitary, rather tragic figure sneaked up behind. "So what," he twinkled unctuously, "have we spotted today?"

"A mermaid," I said.

"A mermaid!" He gave a thin smile. "Well, well! And is she shagging a monkey?"

Turning smartly on his heel, he never spoke to me again.

*

The Amazon, largely empty and lifeless, made me nostalgic for the crowded rivers of Asia—in particular a labyrinth of sacred caves high above the Mekong. There several thousand gilded Buddhas gazed over a landscape of shimmering, scrubby hills which, though apparently empty, stirred with energy and application. In the reed beds people hunted for edible crickets, in the marshes they panned for gold. Tiny waterborne figures paddled after giant Mekong catfish worth 4,000 kip (£1.40) in the market, on a beach a father and daughter, sweating over a charcoal fire, distilled rice whisky for river travellers. ("Rocket phuel," the man called it, offering me a mouthful in a dented mug.)

Downstream, there had been reminders of Laos's recent past: rusting US gunboats half-sunk in the shallows, an assault barge hauled up on the bank then filled with earth and planted with green beans—typical Asian improvisation, plus a nice touch of Asian irony. From the mouth of one dim, statue-filled cave, I watched an ark-hulled Mekong freighter labour by with gunpowder trans-shipped from China, from another I looked across giant whirlpools towards a furious commotion of carp. Standing beside an exquisite "Calling for Rain" Buddha (hands extended downwards, exuding calm), I watched a dozen men expertly trap the carp within a ring of closing canoes; the moment seemed to combine centuries of spirituality and robust human progress. The Amazon, by contrast, was a void.

Yet the Mekong, interrupted by falls and rapids, and only partially navigable, belongs near the bottom of the First Division of tropical rivers. The Irrawaddy lies near the top, along with the Nile, Zambezi and Zaire—whose Kisangani to Kinshasa ferry, made up of four double-decker barges lashed together, features an on-board brothel. That the Amazon remains eternally at number one is due, primarily, to its role in the well-being of nations; without that supply of good air (20 per cent of the oxygen in every breath we take is Amazonia-generated) we'd be left gasping—perhaps, in time, even choking our way to extinction.

On our last night at sea, in the Oval Bar, Jerry was in buoyant mood. At dinner our property tycoons had finally blown their New Labour cover; after a bottle each of £20 Chardonnay it emerged that cop-killers should be hanged, welfare cheats flogged, and rapists . . . well, a silence fell before she murmured (delicately touching a napkin to her lips), "Actually, I'd have them castrated with a blunt knife."

Furthermore, in just a few hours we would disembark at Barbados and fly home. "Fancy a Glenfiddich?"

"OK. Just a small one."

A waiter brought the whisky and a jug of faintly discoloured water. Jerry said, "You get that from the Amazon, son?" The waiter huffed, "Certainly not, sir," but the whisky's glints and reflections started a train of thought, and I found myself telling Jerry about the Mekong. He gave me an exasperated look. "What *is* it with you and rivers?" I said rivers were perfectly calibrated to the requirements of travel writing; each, with a beginning, a middle and an end, had its own narrative flow. "The story keeps unfolding willy-nilly. A novelist can get stuck for days, I just poke my head out and see what's around the next bend." He muttered, "Which turns out to be as boring as the last." I conceded that might be true; it depended on the quality of the information picked up along the way. River folk all had their tales: family stories and histories, local scandals, personalities from the past . . .

A smiling young man from the purser's office, professionally affable and probably gay, stopped by our table. "Evening, gents! Last drinks, eh? Well, hope you had a good time."

"The best part is yet to come," said Jerry.

"*Yet* to come?" He frowned at us, suddenly anxious. "So what's that going to be?"

Jerry finished his whisky. "Jumping ship," he said.

How to Be Boss: Politics in a Hot Climate

One warm, thundery morning in Port Vila, at the urging of friends, I went to see Barak Tame Sope, Vanuatu's newest Prime Minister. Told he was young, charismatic, clever, accessible and—it mattered—a good Presbyterian, I found him installed at the handsome old French Residency high on the hill behind the town.

Of the hundred and eight nations set wholly or partly within the tropics, no fewer than seventy had moved from colonial status to self-rule in the course of the past half-century; seventy new flags were run up (usually at midnight, local time) and seventy new anthems sung. Vanuatu had been the latest, and I hoped Barak Sope would have something to say about how parliamentary democracy was introduced to an electorate whose hundred languages contained not a single word for "vote."

Arriving in good time for my 10 a.m. appointment, I was told I'd have to wait by the PM's watchful white secretary. "He's got a list of meetings as long as your arm." I joined a dozen other supplicants on a deep veranda; periodically she would call a name and someone, moving unhurriedly, would follow her indoors. Sitting there, I ran through Vanuatu's present political landscape. Ranged against Sope's Melanesian Progressive Party were the Republican Party, the National United Party, the Our Land Party, the Union of Moderate Parties and, located down by the wharf in a padlocked tin shack, the *Leba Pati.* (I wanted to make contact, but a passing woman saw me knocking and, much amused, cried, "Nobody there!")

It was a wonder Vanuatu had managed to create any coherent political structure at all. In 1914 the Vila-based British barrister Edward Jacomb described a colonial occupation destined, over the next seventy years, to grow ever more shambolic. "There is as much fundamental difference between an Englishman and a Frenchman as there is between a Turk and a Chinaman . . . Whatever enthusiasts or politicians may say, a real 'entente cordiale' between Britain and France . . . is an absolute impossibility. It is *contra naturam.*" A key factor, he noted, was that "Frenchmen are too fond of politics. It is one of their national failings. One of the first things which is done in a nascent French Colony is to found a local newspaper, and given the excitable, impulsive Gallic temperament, it soon becomes filled with columns of mingled abuse and scandal. The columns of the *Neo-Hebridaes* . . . constitute one of the most remarkable collections of scurrilous matter that has ever been published anywhere."

But sometimes the two sought common ground and, in 1905, they established the Joint Court. Here Jacomb worked, appearing before a president and a public prosecutor appointed by the King of Spain. The President, a wheezing twenty-stone lawyer from Seville who wore heavy crimson robes and rode to work on a mule, supervised a British judge, a French judge and a registrar from Holland. (The President spoke neither English nor French, his Spanish Prosecutor knew a little French, the Dutch registrar a little English, the French judge no English and the British judge only a smattering of Hindi and kitchen Swahili. None of them knew Bislama, the language in which native plaintiffs complained about the wholesale theft of their land by white settlers.)

At midday, a smallish, chubby, scholarly looking man walked out, got into a shiny black Mitsubishi Galant with a flag on its bonnet, and was driven away. "Is that the PM?" I asked a woman seated nearby. She nodded, and told me she was here because her son had been arrested in Australia. An hour later he returned and hurried to his office. "Can I go in now?" I asked the secretary. She said, "Not yet!" and, when I sighed, snapped, "Remember, he's got a country to run." As men in cars came and went a young black aide wandered out for a smoke. He wore a T-shirt proclaiming "I Is At The University of Life" and said, "His Excellency has to see various officials before Cabinet tomorrow."

"I had an appointment for ten o'clock," I said. "That was four hours ago."

He gave me an amiable smile. "Don't hold your breath."

The trick, in fact, was to slow your breathing, to clear the head of all notions of punctuality and time. Idly I recalled telling some Javanese villagers that I lived not far from a famous laboratory in London where the atomic clock had been invented. But when I boasted, "It loses only a second every million years," their incredulity quickly turned to laughter. *What was it for?* I was on the verge of sleep when finally the secretary summoned me. In a dim, shuttered room the Prime Minister seemed dwarfed by the giant polished table at which he sat. "Ten minutes," she muttered. He seemed preoccupied, dealing with my questions in a cursory way, fiddling with my card as he spoke. Then, suddenly focusing on it, he frowned. "Frater? There used to be some people here . . . Do you have a connection with us?"

"Well, my parents were on Iririki for ten years."

"Dr Alec? He was your father?" He said his father, also a physician, had been trained by mine. "And my grandfather knew your family too. Pastor Sope."

I stared. "Pastor Sope christened me."

We were still talking animatedly when the secretary returned. "The Santo chiefs are waiting," she said. He shook my hand. "Come back tomorrow. We'll do a proper interview, no, let's have lunch." I told him next day I was leaving for the Cook Islands. He said, "Well, be sure to look up Tom Davis. Ask him about the astronauts! If you're interested in tropical politics he was unique, a prime minister without parallel."

*

Sir Tom, in visored helmet, drove through his gate on a shiny Harley-Davidson bike then, removing the helmet, revealed the face of an eighty-one-year-old Polynesian. I noted deep-set eyes checking me over with the absolute, bred-in-the-bone assurance you find among the island nobility, became aware too of a fierce intelligence, and recalled being told—my informant's hands delineating an object the size of a *coco de mer*—"He's got a really *huge* brain." It was encased in a squarish, broad-browed head thatched with thick white hair and set atop a burly frame. Moving briskly, he led me indoors, said he had just popped down to the offices of the *Cook Island News* to deliver his Saturday column. "Dunno why they keep running it. Bores the pants off everyone, I bet." I said I enjoyed his column and he gave an amused little grunt. "We journos must stick together, eh?"

Today Sir Tom—known also as Papa Tom—Davis was in reportorial mode. He could, just as legitimately, have spoken as an ex-premier, physician, novelist, seaman or pioneer NASA expert in space medicine. Here in the remote Cook Islands, fifteen of them strewn randomly as coins (small change mislaid a few degrees below the equator), I had just met the most remarkable man in Oceania. Cook Islanders are honorary New Zealanders. Happy as a box of birds, they move in and out of the country more or less as they please. Yet, seated in Sir Tom's living room, I wondered whether he, as a leader, ever felt politically intimidated, or culturally swamped, by New Zealand's looming presence.

He said, "How many generations can you go back?"

"Me personally?" I knew my great-grandfather lay in a Scottish graveyard but, beyond that, the trail grew cold. "Three with any certainty," I said. "And you?"

"With any certainty, one hundred and sixteen. Two thousand years before Christ our navigators were trading with Asia. *New Zealand?* We found it four hundred years before Cook did." In 1350, he said, a fleet of fourteen giant double-hulled canoes, each driven by junk-rigged matting sails and twin banks of thirty paddlers, headed south from Avana Harbour ("Very popular with yachties now") on the Great Migration. Seven survived the perilous journey, and New Zealand's seven great Maori tribes are named for those canoes. I thought historians were ambivalent about which Polynesians actually got there first, but Sir Tom had no doubts. "Look at our languages," he said. "Kiwi and Cook Island Maori are kissing cousins. White Kiwis may share the richest islands in Polynesia with us, but they're leaseholders. We own the freehold."

He wrote a novel, *Vaka,* about the 1350 voyage and, to ensure the details were right, built two replicas of the Great Migration canoes and sailed them all the way from Tahiti. "We used traditional navigation— stick charts and sextant gourds which let you find the zenith of a star. It was damn hard work; no wonder the old navigators had apprentices. But we proved, unequivocally, that those craft could sail dead into the wind."

He also built this cool, shadowy house, helped by shipwrights who knew how to work tropical hardwoods. Books and pictures crammed the ground floor, a staircase led topsides to a minstrels' gallery that looked like a quarterdeck. Growing up on a lamplit island where conch shells summoned him to school and church bells warned of approaching cyclones—a society still adrift in the nineteenth century—he developed an interest in space travel: could man actually survive out there? "It was just an extension of what my ancestors had done. Those big covered canoes were, no question, life-support systems." Studying medicine in Auckland, he designed his first space capsule, refined it during a spell back home as Chief Medical Officer, embarked on a new design while doing a postgraduate degree at Harvard (typically, he rejected the offer of an air ticket, preferring instead to head for the US in a leaky old yacht). There a mysterious new agency named NASA, allegedly dedicated to celestial mechanics, headhunted the bright young Polynesian and put him to work on a project so secret— he claimed—not even the White House knew about it.

Most Americans remained sceptical about the notion of surviving without gravity or oxygen. To enlighten them he wrote a piece for the *Atlantic Monthly* announcing the imminent arrival of the space age. The editors ran it, tongue in cheek, as science fiction.

Three months later Gagarin flew. "All at once things really hotted up. They were extraordinary days—the early Mercury flights, then the Apollo programme. In Houston I virtually lived with the astronauts: Alan Shepard and Virgil Grissom who did the first sub-orbitals, John Glenn, of course, Buzz Aldrin, Michael Collins, Deke Slayton, Wally Schirra; fine, brave men who became dear friends."

Then, in 1963, a committee of chiefs summoned him home. "I had a fantastically interesting and privileged life in the States, but I'm Polynesian, and when the chiefs tell you to come, boy, you come." They simply wanted him back at their hospital, but in 1980, after Prime Minister Sir Albert Henry had been charged with electoral fraud, asked their favourite son to clear up the mess. (Henry—later stripped of his knighthood—secured a general-election victory by placing a ballot box at the airport and offering free flights to all New Zealand–based Cook Islanders prepared to fly in, spend a few days with their families, vote for him, then fly out again; 445 made the trip, and the taxpayers picked up the tab.)

Under Sir Tom the Cookies had their first contact with the laissez-faire theories of Adam Smith. *An Inquiry into the Nature and Causes of the Wealth of Nations* (pub. 1776) became his all-purpose guide to economics. "Encourage self-interest! Remove all constraints! Keep gov-

ernment interference to a minimum! I gave private enterprise its head
and, quite soon, agriculture increased ten-fold, and manufacturing
twenty-four-fold; when Gorbachev was mulling over his free-market
ideas he used to get in touch; and, from time to time, Ronald Reagan
would call up for a chat."

Sir Tom's pastoral electorate, however, didn't want to be a dynamic,
freewheeling tiger economy, and in 1987, they finally voted him out.
Yet he remained their senior statesman, and no local politician made a
move with first consulting him.

An arthritic mongrel wandered in and collapsed at his feet. I put
away my notebook. A widower, Sir Tom had recently lost his son in a
New Zealand traffic accident and, suddenly, looked bone-weary. Yet at
the hospital there were still patients to be seen, and he had begun work
on a new novel which, unsurprisingly, would be set in the Southern
Pacific. Then, courteously, he saw me out and lifted a hand as I drove
away.

*

Riding a bus into Rarotonga one day I noted men on the road
sweeping up leaves. "That's the Beautification Team," said Lou, a
chatty woman seated next to me. "We've also got the Public Health
Team, who inspect every house four times a year. Once they left me a
note saying 'Weed your garden.' Huh!" Near the airport a ramshackle
bungalow built for construction workers now housed the Cook Islands
Parliament (the Prime Minister, she said, had his office in a front bedroom). I heard about Apenera Short, the Queen's Representative, who
liked to prefix his speeches with "My name's Short, so I'll keep it brief."
In a recent referendum, she added, 90 per cent voted to retain the
British Queen as Head of State. "She's a kind of paramount chief—
though we didn't like it when Short spent our tax dollars to fly himself
and his mates to London to get his knighthood. Back home the *Cook
Island News* asked if he had any message for his people. 'Tell them,' he
said, 'the car drove me past the sentries and through the gates *and right
into Buckingham Palace!*' "

Lou, who wore a coronet of flowers (and called England "the land
of roses"), said her dearest wish was to jump on a plane that, so far
as she was concerned, could be going anywhere. "We all got itchy feet,

lots of us are mixed blood—my husband's descended from the House of Orange, I have an Irish uncle in Golders Green. We hop around so much there's an MP who just looks after all the Cookies who are some place else." Since these postal-voters were scattered throughout Australasia, America, Canada and a dozen European countries, the Overseas MP, a wealthy Auckland-based doctor, possessed the largest constituency on earth. It was touching the way he kept a fatherly eye on them when they moved—like a priest worrying about their souls in the next world.

*

Once, driving through the Serengeti, my guide suddenly exclaimed, "That is our MP!" and jumped out. As the politician stood frowning over the engine of a broken-down Datsun Bluebird, several women in bright cotton dresses loitered in the shade of a fever tree. One, a wrinkled granny (whose name, in Swahili, meant Loveliness), asked for water. I handed her a bottle of Sweet Spring Kilimanjaro and, in return, she lent me her fan. The MP, a slim, mild-mannered man in an oatmeal safari suit, said he represented the Ngorongoro and Serengeti districts. "That's pretty exotic."

He shrugged. "I am one of the few politicians who can number two million wild animals among his constituents."

*

It was my old friend George Kalsakau, a retired Port Vila policeman and famous teller of ghost stories, who invented the name Vanuatu ("Our Land"). Thanks to him, the nomenclature given to the islands two centuries earlier by Captain Cook was consigned to history. At a stroke—and confounding cartographers everywhere—George removed the New Hebrides from the map.

But who had removed Zanzibar?

A presidential diktat, it seemed, issued in Dar es Salaam, the capital of Tanzania (formerly known as Tanganyika). It decreed that the place known as Zanzibar would henceforth be called Unguja, while a new Indian Ocean administration zone comprising Unguja, Pemba and the Latham islands would, in turn, be named Zanzibar. Stone Town, Unguja's ancient, intricate heart, was built by Arabs who had painstakingly carved every splinter of exposed wood, dressed the doors with copper and brass, mixed their plaster with milk and eggs to give it a crushed pearl finish. From the air it's like a gorgeous Caravaggio yet, on the ground, you realize that the canvas is, so to speak, in urgent need of restoration.

One evening, out strolling with an elderly Scotswoman who had visited many times, I learned that Zanzibar's present sultan now lived, in permanent exile, near Bournemouth. His father had owned a red MG which, on Sunday afternoons, he liked to drive around Zanzibar's cratered roads at high speed—followed by a lorry which transferred everyone he'd knocked down to the One Coconut Hospital. His great-great-grandfather kept a harem of a hundred girls and slept with them in strict rotation—six girls a night, seven nights a week—till the day he died. "The secret, apparently," she said, "was Gentleman's Relish, spread on ship's biscuits. He was a cruellest, most autocratic of the Omani despots."

During the nineteenth century, arriving in dhows blown from Muscat by the monsoon winds, Omani Arabs turned the island into a major producer of cloves and slaves. When the first African President, Abeid Karume, came to office, he authorized the slaughter of their descendants (a Stone Town bookseller—not unduly troubled by the memory—told me the Omani dead, in their white djellabas, floated off the coast like discarded bed linen) before giving his attention to matters such as accommodation for the proletariat. But blocks of flats designed originally for Ukrainian tram drivers found little favour with the pastoral Zanzibaris and, years later, I found the buildings rotting and semi-derelict, piles of rusting iron and discoloured concrete set among the palm trees. As for Karume, he became obsessed with the notion he would be assassinated by enemies who had turned themselves into leopards. Having hired white hunters to shoot every leopard on the island, he was assassinated anyway—by gunmen appearing in human form.

*

A weird surrealism also surrounded the end of Guyana's President Forbes Burnham—not his actual demise, but the rumoured loss of his body by Cuban embalmers in 1985. Having been paraded around

Georgetown under a roasting sun, it was flown to Havana where, some allege, decomposition was so advanced much of it vanished down the drains. Whatever really transpired, the whereabouts of the head of state who outlawed the potato (smugglers grew rich running illicit King Edwards from Suriname) remains a mystery. I saw soldiers guarding the mausoleum said to contain his remains but, plainly, their hearts weren't in it. And, I guessed, he wasn't either.

The sun, a key factor in tropical politics, can cause anything from lethargy to outright anarchy. (Indian party bosses would never dream of going to the polls just prior to the monsoon's burst; during that sweltering period people grow tetchy and irrational.) Torrid Zone legislators know all about seasonal volatility, so those in Madagascar were probably less surprised than I when, during a month of intense heat, dissident troops captured Antananarivo's radio station. Shortly after they had taken to the air, accusing President Didier Ratsiraka of "impoverishing" the nation, loyalist commandos appeared. The station stood opposite my hotel, and afterwards one of the rebels was carried into the lobby with gunshot wounds to the chest and stomach. A handsome lad barely past his teens, he died quietly there on the carpet, watched by two shocked Austrian businessmen waiting to pay their bills.

*

Any tropical country, having gained independence, was expected to try on a variety of new constitutional clothes. Thus the well-tailored Westminster or Washington outfit might, in time, be swapped for a more austere garment from Moscow, Cuba or Libya—which, in turn, could be discarded for something ethnic and home-made. During all his years in office, Zaire's ruinous President Sese Seko Mobutu (known to quiz addicts for banning the use of Christian names) rarely appeared without his leopardskin hat. Malawi's President-for-Life Hastings Banda, remembered chiefly for banning all opposition (also banning Simon and Garfunkel's "Cecilia" since it happened to be the name of his mistress), was never seen without his trademark fly whisk. Yet, whenever Dr Banda came to London for a Commonwealth Prime Ministers' Conference, he bought several £50, off-the-peg Marks &

Spencer's suits (and had his teeth fixed free on the NHS). The suits, made by Third World workers, were ideologically sound and, having been worn to meet the Queen, assumed a special juju for his people.

Before being elected Prime Minister of Ceylon, Solomon Bandaranaike, a British-trained barrister, had swapped his wig and gown for a Buddhist's saffron robes. When he was assassinated—by a Buddhist monk—his widow, Sirimavo, succeeded him and later created a stir by rechristening Ceylon: Sri Lanka is Sinhala for "resplendent land." (I once met Mrs B. at a party in Colombo and, though I haven't a clue what we talked about, I do remember a plump, clever woman who kept perspiring through her heavy make-up.) Then she was gone too, expelled for "abuse of power." On and on it went, the amazing merry-go-round of the post-colonial era. Yet, good or bad, each leader had to be practical: there were parliaments to be housed, ministries to be created, civil services recruited and trained. At the end of the day it was the power of their visions that counted, and the force of their personalities. Also, they had to know how to improvise.

I once saw France Albert René, President of the Seychelles, arrive at a decision—spontaneously, it seemed—he knew would cause uproar. It happened one wet afternoon at the opening of a new children's playground in Mahé. René, a well-fed figure in a safari suit, stood beneath a crimson golf umbrella haranguing dozens of fidgeting kids in pantomime costumes. If anyone had reason to complain about the country's scandalous shortage of playgrounds they did, and now, for them, he announced a major playground-building programme. But he never said who would pay, and that evening, without consulting a soul—and wholly unconcerned by the outrage their fathers would feel—announced that the price of beer would be raised by fifty cents a bottle.

Hammer DeRoburt's nine thousand people consumed eight million cans of imported beer annually yet, had he raised the duty, not a voice would have been raised in protest. Ruler of the phosphate-rich, mid-Pacific republic of Nauru, he ran it like a personal fiefdom. (At his wife's birthday party I watched guests pin so many large-denomination banknotes to her dress that, as the evening progressed, she began to rustle like a small tree.) When, in 1968, Nauru became one of the

world's smallest democracies—just eight square miles of ossified guano—
his main preoccupation was investing all that revenue in overseas trust
funds. Thus his advisers came not from Beijing or Havana, but the
Melbourne stock exchange.

DeRoburt faced no opposition I could discern—though, on the
beach one day, I met a subversive young Australian backpacker who
had dreamed up a plan to wreck Nauru's economy. Since Nauru's phos-
phate reserves were fast running out, its colourful postage stamps, sold
to collectors worldwide, had become a key source of foreign exchange.
His idea was to apply a toxic adhesive to the stamps that would kill
anyone who licked them. "A sap-based poison like curare," he said, "or
the venom you get from Brazilian tree frogs. One day old Hammer
wakes up to find he's wanted for global murder. What do you reckon?"

I reckoned, actually, that he had a big future in international ter-
rorism. But what had he got against the President?

"Aw, look, this is a man with his own international airline—but
have you seen his hospital? It's a disgrace, you'd be lucky to get an
aspirin. Everyone here's obsessed with money and bird shit. And, Christ,
don't they just love outsiders; I've never had so many doors slammed in
my face. This is the republic from hell, mate, and I'm out of here
tomorrow. Air Nauru, of course. How long are you staying?"

"A few more days."

"Ah, well. Send us a postcard. And don't forget the stamp!"

*

The tropics were once plagued with absolute rulers, suzerains and
sovereigns who had never faced election. Colonialism saw the end of
most (the French, for example, deposed Madagascar's King Andrian-
ampoinimerinandriantsimitoviaminandriampanjaka, while Britain
shipped both the King of Uganda, and Prempeh, King of the Ashanti,
off to exile in the Seychelles). Today only Thailand and Tonga have
retained their constitutional monarchies. In the latter, the subjects of
Taufa'ahau Tupou IV seemed contented enough—though it was sometimes hard to tell: inertia pervaded, phones went unanswered and
appointments unkept; the big, slow-moving Tongans appeared
weighed down by their own body weight and ancient, implacable class

system. Deeply conservative, they had no problem with Victorian edicts that forbade them, on the Sabbath, from climbing trees or crying "Sail-ho!"

In 1997, along with the King's baker—a New Zealander clutching a big boxed cake—I flew into Nuku'alofa, its capital. On the road to town a banner said "Happy Birthday Your Majesty May God Be With You Always Tonga Water Board." Our bus driver confirmed the King would turn seventy-nine on Friday; a beauty contest and a rugby match against the Cook Islands were included in the celebrations. I found the Cook Islands team at my hotel: giant Polynesians playing guitars, ukuleles and spoons around the swimming pool, all harmonizing nicely as they sang a number called "Coconuts."

I had requested an audience with the King, and to my surprise he granted it. One morning I turned up at the wooden palace, prefabricated in New Zealand a hundred and thirty years earlier and looking vaguely institutional, like a minor boarding school. I knew he was descended from Finau, a nineteenth-century warrior who united Tonga by attacking secessionist elements with English naval guns mounted on canoes (often, allegedly, he directed operations from a throne placed at low tide on an adjacent reef). I knew also that Tupou wasn't a monarch in the European sense. He was even grander, the highest of Polynesia's autocratic high chiefs, commanding subjects for whom obedience and servility were bred in the bone.

He came shuffling in on sticks, a huge, weary old man who, sighing, heaved himself onto an elevated chair engraved with his coat of arms. I, in a lesser chair—everyone must sit below the King—put my questions. Some he answered, some he appeared not to hear, occasionally he would go off on a tangent such as public health. To inspire Tongans to join his anti-obesity crusade he had slimmed down from thirty-three stone to twenty, attending a gym where, as he laboured on an exercise bike, two bodyguards kept an electric fan trained on their sovereign.

During my first visit, a decade earlier, there had been a Happy Hour rumour that he kept in shape by running up and down the palace stairs in lead diving boots. I didn't like to ask about that (or, indeed, the story that, when the country's constitution went missing, frantic courtiers found it under his bed). Instead, I learned that 58 per cent of the kingdom's females, and 40 per cent of its males, were clinically obese. "A typical Tongan adult consumes over 12,600 kilojoules a day—twice the normal intake in the West. To combat heart disease and diabetes we have placed scales in banks and offices. People *must* weigh themselves."

Turning to the economy, he said, "The Tongan pumpkin, better known as butternut squash, has proved extremely popular with the Japanese, yet now we are about to market something even better: natural gas made from sea water." Tupou is known for his eccentric entrepreneurial ideas (like offering to burn thirty million used tyres from Washington State—four million tons of rubber—to fuel his generators, or selling Tongan passports at $20,000 a time to twitchy international fly-by-nights like Imelda Marcos). But this one, proposed by a bunch of Koreans thought to be Moonies, was pure alchemy. When I said so he gave a gurgly, whiffling laugh.

"We estimate the market for natural gas is worth six billion dollars in the Pacific alone."

"Do you know the scientific formula?" (Did *anyone*?)

He shrugged. "The Koreans know it."

Out in the garden his royal geese honked. He wore a gold Rolex on either wrist and, occasionally, would glance at both to indicate I was asking dumb questions in two time zones, or lapse into one of his famous transcendental silences. I said I had once met his mother. He nodded. "She composed songs, you know. Many are now classics." He likes to be woken by an army brass band striking up outside his window, and plays guitar, electric organ and a Greek bouzouki.

His son, the rather engaging Crown Prince, plays the piano and, at Sandhurst, had a band called Straight Bananas. I met him at the beauty contest where, leaping from his private air-conditioned London taxi, he told me—in Gussie Fink–Nottle accents—he was developing a series of Tongan Murder Mystery Weekends. "Stay in touch!" I watched nervous, beefy girls wrapped in ceremonial mats, shoulders gleaming with coconut oil, parading shyly down the catwalk. Miss Good Samaritan Inn was placed first, with Miss Pleasant Tongan Holiday Tours and Miss Made of Earth Leather Gear close behind.

At 5 a.m. Whitechapel bells woke everyone for the big day. Arriving at his birthday parade, Tupou climbed slowly from a stretched black Cadillac as, all around, his subjects dropped like flies. (I dropped when an obese lady cop snapped "Down!" and clubbed me across the shoulders with her truncheon.) That evening an educated young Tongan told me that within a decade they would have a revolution. "The King stifles us." But a New Zealand airline executive laughed when I mentioned this. Deference was so ingrained, he said, that whenever the royals flew, they had to be smuggled onto the plane and placed in a curtained-off section at the front. "Otherwise all the Tongans aboard would get out of their seats and sit on the floor."

*

The Comoros consists of three south Indian Ocean islands which, in 1975, formed themselves into an Islamic republic. Moroni, the largest town, is the world's smallest capital, with a Chinese-built parliament, a couple of embassies, a ramshackle hospital, a market and a Friday mosque; even in rush hour Moroni can be transited in two minutes. (During my visit the Assembly was debating the installation of its first traffic light.) Yet I found a nation of great political complexity, with twenty-nine different parties and a voodoo-obsessed president. What made it unique in the annals of parliamentary democracy was the decision, soon after independence, to hand it over to a council of teenagers. They lounged around their ministries eating pizza, listening to music, smoking spliffs, talking about girls and travelling to Cabinet by skateboard. When the economy collapsed—helped on its way by a sex-mad chancellor who counted on his fingers—the army suddenly found itself being led by one of those shadowy figures who figured in the development of several tropical democracies: the European mercenary.

Colonel Bob Denard, a Frenchman, had arrived fresh from triumphs in Yemen and the Congo. During his time in the Comoros one elected president was shot dead and another blown to bits by an anti-tank rocket fired through his bedroom window. Denard denied responsibility yet on his return home was found guilty of fomenting coups and murder. Set free with a three-year suspended sentence, he now lives somewhere in France, at peace, with his pretty Comoran wife.

One morning I went to meet Mohamed Mchangama, a London

School of Economics graduate and President of the Assembly. A stocky, pleasant man with a quick and fluid mind, he spoke of the obstacles confronting the Comoros. The French, after an occupation lasting a century and a half, had left nothing but a vague historical dependence on Europe. "We know all about Paris and Provence, but nothing about our brothers in Dar es Salaam or Nairobi. Our education has made us a small country culturally marooned in Europe. Clearly that must change."

Flowers would feature in the new economy. Earlier I had stopped at a ylang-ylang distillery where at harvest time truckloads of blossoms were boiled in silver drums. Here they produced ylang-ylang essence for the French perfume industry, and traces of steam seemed to linger in the air like a luscious narcotic. "Once we sent over hundreds of litres a year, it was our principal export, but now the same smell can be made much cheaper with chemicals."

Smiling faintly, he said he had no interest in the supernatural. The President might, but he hadn't the time. "And voodoo, I assure you, plays no part in the collective decisions of this government."

Later his chief aide, the Directeur de Cabinet, said gravely, "Will you sign the Golden Book?" A charming young man with a degree from Glasgow University, he showed me a pamphlet just received from Whitehall. It was titled *Debates: How Parliament Discusses Things.*

"I wrote off for it," he said, "and I am sending it to the President of our Law Commission. I think he will find it useful."

*

Anguilla's dyslexic, inverted, back-to-front revolution famously contravened the whole spirit of post-colonial history. It began during a beauty contest at the Valley Secondary School on the night of Saturday, 4 February 1967.

Midway through the show's opening item—a rendering of "My Grandfather's Clock" sung by the dramatist Cromwell Bowry—a crowd of disaffected islanders started throwing stones and bottles at the building. Its occupants fled, some taking shelter in the cemetery of nearby St Mary's Anglican Church. One, a fire-eating magician and limbo dancer named Tunka Abdurama, was hiding in an open grave when a young woman fell on top of him. "Where am I?" she cried. Tunka said, "In heaven, darling," and they had a laugh—though, elsewhere, less amusing things were happening.

The police fired revolvers at the rioters and Claudius Lake took a bullet in the leg. Turning to his companions he said, "Boys, I get shoot," so at John Proctor's shop in the Quarter they poured cask rum on the wound. Several others suffered minor gunshot injuries, and Fred Fleming had an encounter with tear gas.

That evening's beauty-queen brawl was no flash in the pan. It marked the beginning of a stubborn campaign which in the course of the next two years would seriously embarrass Whitehall and provide the British electorate with some high-class entertainment.

The Anguillans didn't want independence. They had been offered it in conjunction with the neighbouring islands of St Kitts and Nevis, but insisted on retaining their imperial relationship with "Mother England." A campaign of civil disobedience was only abandoned when Britain's exasperated Prime Minister, Harold Wilson, sent in three hundred Paras and—storming the beach with whistles and truncheons—a detachment from London's Metropolitan Police.

In the end Anguilla won. It got its governor back and returned to the sleepy obscurity that had characterized it for three hundred years. The seven-thousand-strong population on their scrubby sixteen-mile-long island fought to retain a colonial yoke that had brought them full employment, six foreign banks, three radio stations, a digital telephone system (they were the second nation in the world to get one) and, puzzlingly, the promise of a sophisticated radio-paging network. They had no income or corporation tax, and no exchange controls. All Anguilla lacked was a decent cricket team.

During my visit two important events were taking place. First, the Antiguans were playing at Ronald Webster Park, their fast bowler Hungry Walsh rattling Anguillan wickets at such a rate that Radio Anguilla's match commentator, a Rasta with dreadlocks and a beard down to his waist, was unable to keep the pain from his voice. (Radio Anguilla's first broadcasters, back in 1969, had been seconded from Customs and Excise.) Second, a teenage youth named Andy Otto was standing trial on a charge of raping and murdering two vacationing American lesbians at Windward Point, a remote beach on the east coast. The crime outraged the islanders; before the trial even began an elderly churchgoer wrote to the Governor offering his services as hangman.

Over dinner at a crowded outdoor restaurant, Emile Gumbs, the Chief Minister, told me, "We are God-fearing people born with the highest moral scruples. One year the Mafia turned up wanting to build the world's biggest casino, and we just threw them off the island."

A tall, trim, greying man, he was the scion of Anguilla's most influential family. There were scores of Gumbs in the phone book, ranging from heroes of the revolution like Emile and his cousin Jeremiah, to a Gumbs who unloaded the Cessna from St Maartens (five minutes' flying time away) at Wallblake Airport. Another, Lionel, was the one of the first black policemen to join the Met.

"He would have been one of the Slough Gumbs," said Emile.

More Anguillans live in Slough than in Anguilla itself—so many, indeed, that some claim they are colonizing Britain through the back door. But why Slough?

"Why not?" said Emile. "Perhaps the first went there because it was close to Windsor and our dear Queen. More followed and the community just grew. But they can still vote, and when we have elections here all candidates *must* campaign in Slough. Lots of Slough money comes to the island, when our retirees return home the Slough DHSS sends out their pensions every week. This is one place where you don't make jokes about Mars bars."

Before entering politics he had been master of the trading schooner *Warspite*. "She sailed for close to a century and survived two sinkings. That is because of how she was made, the sweet way those men could spile the planks. The only metal used was the gudgeon and pintle and, of course, the nails; they were dipped in shark oil before being hammered home. This used to be an island of master shipwrights, famous for sloops and schooners built of white cedar." He smiled. Being Chief Minister was all very well, but there were days when he longed to be back at sea.

He urged me to call on the Governor so, next morning, I did—and found, to my astonishment, that we had met in Port Vila. Geoffrey Whittaker, an affable, youthful-looking Englishman, had been one of the Foreign Office whizzos sent out to prepare for independence.

(Though I preferred drinking with the Quai d'Orsay crowd, who were all terrible gossips and much funnier.) Sitting on the balcony of Anguilla's modest Government House, we sipped pink gins and talked about his job. Responsible for defence, external affairs and internal security, on big occasions he still wore the flamingo-plumed hat— "Made by an old chap in Sackville Street"—a general's Mameluke sword, and the £6,000 governor's uniform tailored by Gieves & Hawkes of Savile Row (who have been making them for two hundred years) boasting collar and cuffs sumptuously hand-embroidered with precious wires. And islanders still turned up to reaffirm their loyalty by signing the Book, kept in a tiny shed by the garden gate.

*

Ben Higgins was a retired London printer who, widowed in his sixties, had moved to Cuba. A spry old socialist with a deeply seamed face and thick white hair (a dead ringer for Spencer Tracy in his senescent years), he had a particular interest in the politics of colonialism. One morning, over coffee, I happened to mention my family's involvement in those murky times. He went "Ha!" and plucked a book from his sagging shelves. "Here's what Bacon had to say about the role of the church: 'It cannot be affirmed, if one speak ingenuously, that it was the propagation of the Christian faith that was the adamant of that discovery, entry and plantation; but gold and silver, and temporal profit and glory; so that what was first in God's providence, was but second in man's appetite and intention.' "

He closed the book. "So first you stole their wealth and land and ravaged their settlements, then you enslaved them, *then* you made them Christians . . ."

"Oh, come on, Ben! We never ravaged or enslaved any . . ."

". . . *then* you insist on making them democrats—while they get no choice in the matter. Why?"

"Eh?"

"That's the last part of the equation. Finally they get freedom—but only on your terms. What makes you think democracy's right for them? What kind of Western conceit is that?"

I shrugged and repeated E. B. White's "recurring suspicion" that democracy was merely more than half of the people being right more than half of the time. "They're not great odds, but they're better than most."

"And what are these people so right about?" Down the ages, he lectured (peering over his half-moon glasses, wagging a finger), nations had prospered under other systems which, occasionally, produced rulers infinitely wiser, more far-sighted and humane than many elected officials he could mention today. "Take a man like the Emperor Asoka. I'll bet you can't name one Indian politician around at the moment who accomplished even half what he did."

"Those other systems also produced their share of bastards."

"And democracy hasn't? Dear me, in America they've even had a president *impeached*. A leader of the free world who turned out to be a shabby crook!" He grinned. "Want to take your coffee outside?"

The balcony of his ramshackle apartment contained a garden planted in pots, while a purple trumpet vine curled up the rusting wrought-iron balustrade. (Daily, he said, a pair of hummingbirds called for sugar.) And, if you leant out far enough, the coruscant dazzle over to the right was Havana Harbour. The sun on my back, I said, "I'll bet you miss Teddington."

"I miss good newspapers and, at my age, the NHS. The medics here are brilliant, but they're always battling shortages."

I sipped my coffee. "So will Cuba ever be democratized?"

"Of course. Everyone has a great hunger for dollars. Maybe they'll even turn themselves back into a Yankee playground, with whorehouses and crack dens and cocaine as easy to come by as cigars. Mind you, if that happens, a new Fidel may emerge. Don't forget it took Europe a thousand years to sort out its ideas, none of these new republics—your old colonies—have had time for the big questions we've been thinking about for centuries."

He listed a few: the nature of justice and morality, the relationship between the state and a citizen, and between the state, a citizen and his god or, if the state happens to be Marxist, between it, a citizen and his economy.

I pointed out that the voters of the tropical Third World often acted a lot more responsibly than voters in the First. For them a general election really was democracy's holy communion, and they might trek for miles, even days, to reach their polling stations. "Unlike us.

Half the time we can't even be bothered to jump in the car and pop round the corner."

"But maybe their needs are a touch more fundamental, like food for their kids. Or maybe they just want to get rid of the bastard who's causing them so much grief. Remember the rigged Zimbabwe election? Those *queues*?" He shook his head. "Actually, I find Mugabe quite interesting. He's a dinosaur, the last of the old African freedom-fighters, still clinging on through brute force and intimidation: there's no attempt to sweeten the news, no nerdy young men in Harare with focus groups and demographics and *empirically validated* computer models. He reminds me of the way the imperialists used to behave when they were threatened: round up the troublemakers and shoot a few if necessary."

"I seem to recall a few of Africa's first leaders did that."

"Of course. Those colonial governors were their role models. But back in those days Mugabe was one of the good guys, like Kenny Kaunda (I once met him—*what* charisma!—buying fish and chips in Clapham). And Nyerere. And Kenyatta—now there was a wise old bird. But Robert's turned into a sad example of what happens when you've been in power too long. And it's not just Africa. There's a bit of Mugabe in plenty of Western politicians."

I laughed.

"Watch them when they're being contradicted. The tiny flicker of rage in the eyes? Suddenly you realize they really do believe they're masters of the universe. It's a Mugabe moment."

"And Fidel doesn't do any of that?"

"Oh, Fidel. He *bores* you into submission."

*

Yet I wondered about those people whose civil rights had depended, latterly, on the whims of foreign officials, before that on power-of-life-and-death tribal rulers. Then, virtually overnight, they acquired the freedom—as Samuel Johnson noted—to "put little balls or tickets, with particular marks, *privately* in a box." That must have taken an extra-ordinary leap of the imagination. In Port Vila, however, I learned it also involved education.

At the Wan Smolbag Theatre, located in an abandoned warehouse on the airport road, a score of young Melanesians were preparing for yet another tour. Lucy, a breezy English producer wearing a frangipani in her hair, said, "We go to seventy islands and put on plays about social and environmental matters—AIDS, dental hygiene, dengue fever, unsustainable logging, save the turtles, improved pit latrines (we did a song about that actually, it was a big hit on Radio Vanuatu), disability and blindness . . ."

"What about elections?"

She laughed. "Oh, boy! For the last one we wrote a special play. It was about the rights of voters, and seven groups of actors went out and performed in *hundreds* of villages. Afterwards we had discussions. They were pretty interesting—we heard loads about bribery and coercion and corruption, plenty of people told us they wanted absolutely nothing to do with any of it. But seeing the play changed their minds. We got a lot of them to the polls! So that was good."

I reflected that Vanuatu, the youngest of the tropical republics, seemed to be up and running. Yet, two whole decades after independence, extreme volatility remained a feature of the post-Condominium arrangement. On that hot Vila afternoon, as I said goodbye to its dedicated young Prime Minister, Barak Tame Sope, neither of us could have guessed that, within a year, he would face a vote of no confidence and be thrown out of office.

The Fragrant Isle

On Erromango, to mark the birth of her baby, a provident mother plants a *sendewud* which when mature will pay for its education. (Should her ambitions for the child go as far as college—teacher training? *law* school?—she merely plants more.) Yet these treasure trees are nothing much to look at: the scraggy little *Erromango santalum,* growing in the rain shadow of the south-east trades, is low-forked, short-boled and unbuttressed. Forest botanists describe the bark as greyish brown with discontinuous vertical fissures, the twigs as glabrous and the leaves as narrowly elliptical. The tiny flowers are an insipid green, the sapwood white and valueless, the fruit an inedible, purplish, pea-sized ellipsoid mainly dispersed by birds. It's the yellowy brown heartwood that is of interest. Found only in the squat lower bole and main roots, *sendewud*—scented wood—brought Erromango to the attention of foreigners when, in 1820, visiting American whalers noted stands reaching as far as the eye could see.

Sandalwood has been in use since at least the fifth century BC. The Egyptians, Phoenicians and Assyrians all prized it (John Masefield's Ninevan quinquereme loaded some at Ophir—along with consignments of cedarwood and sweet white wine). Almug, mentioned in the Bible, was probably a red species from India. And Buddha, who died in a sandalwood grove, was cremated on a pyre of sandalwood logs; along with aloes and cloves, it remains one of the three incenses specified for Buddhist ceremonies.

Erromango lay to the south of the Vanuatu group, and as I hitched a ride from its hilltop airfield in its public truck, people said, "You going to William's place?" I said yes, and down at Dillon's Bay, in a neat, sloping garden by the sea, found a one-roomed hut with a doorstep on which, when the concrete was still wet, someone had inscribed, "Welcome to Dream House."

William, wiry, grizzled and watchful, his left cheek oddly lifeless as if key nerves had once been cut, asked what I thought of it.

"Very nice."

Palm fronds had been set around the door, hibiscus strewn across the bed and "Good Sleep, God Bless You" embroidered in scarlet thread on the pillow. A gold wall clock formed the room's centrepiece. Shaped like a crescent moon, its pendulum was a glittering pumpkin coach swinging between a snowy medieval town and an isolated castle on an alpine peak.

"It's a Cinderella clock!" I said.

He frowned. "This is a Citizen quartz clock from Mr Yoshioka, my agent in Tokyo. He was here, a nice man. He called me Honourable William. He gave me hugs! Yoshioka has had my wood lab-tested. The quantity of oil is a little less than Indian wood, but the quality is much, much better—he says the best in the world. He is going to build a house from Erromango sandalwood and give it to the Emperor."

"How much will he need for that?"

"Plenty. This year me and Joe are sending twenty tons; the contract is signed; next year we send much more."

Joe, the eldest son, was stocky and quietly spoken, with two small children and a slim, beautiful wife named Margaret who had a gliding walk and an air of serenity that seemed, at times, almost transcendental. Yet she also had a faintly mocking smile and, no question, a touch of subversion in her nature. Beneath the clock, for example, a roll of Red Spot Chinese toilet paper had been set on a big white porcelain dinner plate and crowned, ironically, with a single red flower. Margaret had done that.

"We will start shipping next month, after the wedding."

I said, politely, "Oh. Who's getting married?"

"Joe."

I stared. "*Joe's* getting married?"

"Yes. To Margaret. They are living together. They have been *cohabiting*." William was distressed by that—and distressed also that the ceremony would mark the first time in ages that Joe had set foot in a church; he hardly ever picked up the Bible any more, was always busy with his music. Music? What music? Looking oddly bashful, he said, "His songs. You know? On Radio Vanuatu they play him all the time."

"They do?"

"Sure. He has many fans."

"*Fans?* What fans? How come?" Gradually, after much prodding and persuasion, it came out.

Joe was a rock star.

*

Though Erromango, jungly and declivitous, covers an area of three hundred and fifty square miles, it has only fourteen hundred inhabitants; of these four hundred and fifty live at the main settlement. A quiet village that starts by the sea then meanders up a small river, it's named for Peter Dillon, an Irish adventurer who, having heard the whalers' tales of a large, hilly island clad in sandalwood, called to see for himself. In China it fetched £50 a ton—a stupendous sum—but in Melanesia it was used only for burning on chilly nights (*sendewud* gives off exceptional ambient heat). Thus a ton would routinely be swapped for an axe, or a set of silver buttons, yet Erromango's chiefs, too stupefied by cannibalism to make even the most basic deal, waved Dillon back to his ship. Thus the first European to come expressly for sandalwood sailed off bearing scarcely a twig.

Others, though, had met the talkative whalers, and the island's fate was sealed. Unaware the invasion would last forty years, regarding it more as an incursion, the Erromangans at first avoided pitched battles. They favoured bushwhacking—quick ambuscades followed by kava parties when they feasted off their prisoners. The Europeans countered with crude biological warfare: Santo men showing symptoms of measles, mumps and venereal disease were deliberately infiltrated into communities and left there, living time bombs. Gradually the "treacherous" Erromangans (their reputation for mendacity would remain with them for a century) grew more confrontational, dispatching skirmishing parties and even attacking shipping; war canoes being handier than schooners, they settled a few scores out beyond the reef. Yet still the Europeans swarmed ashore, mad for the aromatic timber. When it wasn't produced fast enough teams of Tongan woodcutters were drafted in; those not captured and eaten—they were big, unusually meaty men—felled huge tracts of forest. By 1860 the island had been picked clean. With no more trees to fell, the invaders kidnapped the remaining able-bodied males and shipped them off to Queensland's sugar plantations. When the first sandalwooder arrived the population had stood at ten thousand. By the time the last blackbirder sailed away, according to a contemporary census, it was just four hundred.

*

The Dream House had a narrow, vine-covered patio where, in the evenings, William liked to drop by and chat. For twelve years, he said, he had been a teacher; milking and baking were his specialist subjects, and though he loved the work, he kept having sandalwood dreams. "It was all I talked about with my family. So one day I think: time to stop the talk and get a boat. I bought a twenty-footer—with a very high transom, like a mission launch—and went up and down the coast, buying for cash. Now Mr Yoshioka has spent ten million *vatu* putting Erromango sandalwood on the Internet. We are big time!"

They produced the yellow variety; you tested a tree, he said, by cutting into the trunk and sniffing the oil. When judged ready it was ripped, fully rooted, from the ground, and left where it lay; white ants and termites devoured the unwanted sapwood while leaving the heartwood untouched. Then it needed only to be sawed, weighed, packed and shipped off to Yokohama or Tokyo Bay.

I laughed. "It sounds so easy!"

He admitted God did most of the work—but he had all the worry.

My research revealed that the oil, extracted by steam distillation, contained high levels of active fragrance compounds (though they don't remain active for ever; fifteen years ago in Hanoi I bought a carved monk figurine which today smells less interesting than oak). Perfumiers, who speak of its warm notes, floral sweetness, smoky, leathery texture and balsamic overtones, can boost these properties by adding castor oil, or oil distilled from cedar chips left over from the manufacture of lead pencils.

William spoke of its importance to human health. The claims made for the remedial powers of sandalwood are indeed remarkable, with supporters pointing to its effectiveness against cardiac fatigue, gonorrhoea and gleet (or chronic gonorrhoeal urethritis). Mixed with benzoic and boric acids it is prescribed for cystitis, two drops of oil on a sugar lump assist in the treatment of chronic bronchitis and persistent coughs. Herbalists recommend it for sciatica, haemorrhoids, asthma and impotence. Its antifungal properties, allegedly, repair damaged skin. It may increase the production of white blood cells and stimulate the immune system, and is variously described as an antiseptic, a sedative, an antispasmodic, a decongestant, a diuretic and an expectorant.

"Scalp tonic, too," said William.

Scalp tonic was on my list.

"Barber's rash."

"Yes. Also bladder infections," I said—adding that some doctors prescribed massages with warm oil.

He cocked his head. "Massage which part?"

"The, uh, sexual organs."

Watching him stiffen—and suddenly beguiled by the idea of a bladder clinic staffed by lady masseuses who all looked like Margaret— I did not mention the tantric ceremonies in which males were anointed from head to toe with sandalwood oil. (Females had it applied only to the thighs, but spikenard was rubbed in their hair, jasmine on their hands, patchouli on the neck and cheeks, amber on the breasts, musk on the abdomen and a dusting of saffron applied to the feet.)

*

One evening we talked about an Erromangan fish, caught only half a mile from where we sat, which caused a stir in Victorian Britain, and an Erromangan child named Elau who, in 1831, became a minor London celebrity.

In 1829 the British barque *Sophia,* having disembarked a hundred and twenty-nine Irish convicts in Sydney, delivered a party of Tongan woodcutters to Erromango. George Bennett, her surgeon—young, pushy and ambitious, recently elected a Fellow of the Royal College— saw himself more of a scholar-explorer than a humble ship's sawbones, so when sailors found a pearly nautilus floating in Dillon's Bay (looking, they reported, like a dead cat) he claimed it for science. Though the shell had been damaged, the fish inside was intact and, perhaps anticipating the interest it would arouse in England, he pickled it in a jar of preservative.

Then he had a further stroke of luck. In the forest a party of

Tongans came upon cannibals about to strangle three boys and a girl they had orphaned moments earlier. The children were rescued and brought to the *Sophia*'s captain who, preparing to sail for England, proposed dropping them at the safe island of Rotuma; there, however, his shore transfers were interrupted by a violent storm. Hurriedly putting to sea with the six-year-old girl, Elau, still aboard, he told Bennett the child would now accompany them home; he, furthermore, must be her guardian. Bennett's first act was to measure her. She stood three feet four inches tall, the length of her sternum, and breadth of her thorax were four and a half inches, the circumference of her abdomen twenty-two and a half—while her pot belly was caused by tympanitis, or gas in the peritoneal cavity (later attributed to worms).

In England, Bennett settled Elau with his sister in Plymouth before hurrying to London with the "living fossil" from Dillon's Bay. There, for reasons we cannot fathom, he entrusted its dissection to an opportunist friend, Richard Owen. Owen, aware it was the first specimen ever seen by scientists, gave its remains to the Royal College of Surgeons' museum then, in 1832, brought out a surprising little best-seller, *Memoir on the Pearly Nautilus*. If Bennett felt piqued, his protests were lost in the clamour that followed. As a debate raged on the origins of man (Darwin would not publish for another twenty-seven years) many believed that Erromango's cephalopod mollusc, descended from a genus that flourished two hundred million years ago, might hold some answers.

(The nautilus fish, found only in tropical oceans, occupies a silky, graceful Art Deco shell that undergoes constant enlargement; as one chamber is outgrown, a new, more spacious one is prepared. Buoyancy comes from filling those vacated cavities with gas, and momentum—a nautilus swims backwards—by jetting water through a funnel.)

One evening Bennett took Elau to a "conversazione" at the Royal Institution in London. How would a child from a savage, lawless island half a world away respond to such cosmopolitan glitter and fuss? Bennett, observing her always with a clinical eye, wrote, "Although it was the first time she had ever entered a large room splendidly lighted and filled with company, she did not for a moment manifest the slightest shyness or fear, but left me and mingled with the crowd." Mingling, she met and charmed Michael Faraday. The man who devised mass-produced electricity lifted Elau onto a table where, though "highly amused at the interest she excited," she stood patiently as the eminent ethnologists present examined her head and pronounced it "remarkably well formed and the brain quite up to the average."

At smart London parties she met actors—Bennett had a passion for the theatre—and artists who wanted to paint her; Frederick Tatham draped her in a necklace of human teeth and called his picture *The Young Cannibal,* while the author Mary Howitt (who first translated Hans Christian Andersen into English) told her story in a new book.

At home in Plymouth, bright as a button and unfazed by all the attention, her "mental powers excellent, her perception quick, her memory retentive," she studied hard, learned to read, went to church and acquired the attributes of a well-mannered, middle-class English child. "Her needlework," we learn, "was neat and clean, her dancing very graceful."

Then in 1834, aged ten, Elau died from intestinal tuberculosis. Bennett asked a friend to perform the post-mortem, but scrupulously wrote up the results. "On incision the body was almost bloodless . . . the muscles pale, flabby and soft . . . mesenteric glands greatly enlarged . . . heart pale and flaccid." He buried her in a Plymouth cemetery which, damaged by German bombs in 1941, was later redeveloped; Elau, today, lies somewhere under the Plymouth Civic Centre. As for Bennett, he settled in Australia where he practised as a surgeon and joined the ranks of the great and good. A founder of the Sydney School of Arts and the New South Wales Zoological Society, he was also appointed Inspector of Abattoirs and, maintaining his interest in natural sciences, became a noted authority on the platypus.

*

Today thirty-three nations possess tropical rainforests. The oldest biomes on the planet, they first took root a hundred million years ago (most temperate woodlands have been around for only a few thousand) and represent one of the most sublime acts in all creation. Since the first organism emerged from the primordial soup, ten million separate life forms have evolved—half of them, it's estimated, flourishing in the forests of the equatorial region. Their diversity is staggering; *thousands* of species may exist in a moist, shadowy plot no bigger than a suburban garden. Such munificence caused Mr Dass, a part-time musician and long-time member of the Sundarbans Launch Association, to say that a forest enabled us to "understand the mind of God." But this steamy place was also home to India's largest population of Bengal tigers and, worried that God might be minded to arrange a meeting between an awesome specimen of *Panthera tigris* and a knock-kneed, round-shouldered, chain-smoking specimen like me, I took little notice.

Veined by bewildering networks of tidal creeks, the Sundarbans supports three hundred thousand forest families—though none were visible now. From Mr Dass's boat I saw dim galleries lit by torch ginger and luminous epiphytes; when a mouse deer appeared on the bank a waterlogged palm trunk, twitching, became an estuarine crocodile; the deer, without bending its legs, sprang back, a precise clockwork jump. The forest gave off an odd smell of rotting books. There was compost and carrion too, but the bookish smell predominated—whiffs of sodden paper and rancid glue at times so strong that somewhere in there entire libraries seemed to be in a state of advanced decay. Sweat pouring off me, I told Mr Dass I was producing as much moisture as a small tree; he joked that soon it would evaporate and form a small cloud. I recalled, once or twice, a slightly salty taste to the rain in heavily populated cities like Calcutta, and wondered if it might be partly due to human transpiration. When he cut the engine we heard hoots and squawks from creatures high in the canopy. The thousands of species up there had nothing to do with the thousands down here; separate lives, different agendas, other predators to deal with.

Late in the afternoon, over glasses of sweet Assam tea, I recalled his "mind of God" analogy. It was a good one yet, to me, a tropical forest seemed more like a human brain: bewilderingly complex, almost infinite in its possibilities—and as little understood. Nodding agreement, he spoke of brain damage, meaning that done by man, and the famous hundred forest species which, daily, are supposed to be irrecoverably destroyed. "Many are gone before they are even being noted. They are like passing thoughts."

I liked that. "And you hardly even know you've had them."

"But you do know! There is spark! And you are wondering: hey, wait a minute—was that the secret of life just on the tip of my tongue?"

*

Along with its tribes of tigers, the Sundarbans also boasts the world's largest mangrove forest. Stands of this tangled, tidebound evergreen hardwood—good for wharf pilings—grow like hedges around countless tropical coasts. They're so widespread the eye barely heeds them, yet mangroves play a key role in the control of water flow, sedimentation, fish-stock regeneration, the upkeep of habitats used by aquatic mammals and migratory birds, the general health of the local littoral.

In Honduras peasants once cut them for firewood, or made a few lempira by stripping tannin-rich bark from mature red trees for the local tanneries. Then, around the Gulf of Fonseca in the 1980s, speculators burnt big stands of mangroves to make way for shrimp farms. The effect on the region's hydrology was predictable. Water flow and purity suffered (exacerbated by shrimp-farm effluent—which also contaminated estuaries and mudflats), and, worst of all, the seasonal lagoons silted up. Full of fish after the rains, they traditionally fed the poor; multitudes came with lines and nets. Now, though, they had become a perfect habitat for shrimp, so the farmers grabbed the lagoons for themselves.

Meanwhile the inter-tidal land, historically accessible to anyone wanting wood, tanbark or shellfish, was found to be perfect for shrimp *ponds*. Various politicians and generals had a financial stake, so steel fences went up with armed guards patrolling them. Meetings between the hardline National Association of Honduran Shrimp Farmers and an environmental group famed for its strong principles and marathon-length nomenclature—the Committee for the Defence and Development of the Flora and Fauna of the Gulf of Fonseca—were rancorous but non-violent; in the streets, though, there was rioting. By 1987 the shrimp industry employed 11,900 people (most of them women). As communities turned on each other, any anxious, disfranchised peon knowing a bit of botanical terminology might have reflected, wryly, on one of the species at the centre of the trouble. A stunted, ill-nourished, poor-flowering little tree, prone to insect-borne diseases and banished to the outer fringes of the growing zone, it's called the stress mangrove.

Years ago, on London's District Line, I found myself seated next to a dentist from Tegucigalpa, the Honduran capital. I knew he came from the tropics before we even spoke. Though it was a mild May evening he wore a woolly hat and heavy topcoat; like many hot-climate inhabitants, he seemed to believe that in temperate England hypothermia, frostbite, even snow blindness, lay around every corner. Middle-aged and slimly built, with rather aristocratic features, he needed help deciphering the Tube map on the carriage wall. He was the first Honduran I had met, so until he disembarked at Kew I kept him talking, asked about the 1969 Soccer War against El Salvador which, beginning with crowd trouble at a friendly, blossomed into a bloody military conflict that lasted five days. "I was baby then," he shrugged, and spoke instead about the privileges we Londoners took for granted: free health care, free schooling—in Honduras 40 per cent of the population remained illiterate—and an awesome public transport system. His enthusiasm for our near-ruined Underground became credible when I learned the only railroads in his country were built to carry bananas for the American fruit companies. Honduras, he said, needed a road and rail network expressly for its citizens and, until they got it, his outlying patients would continue to visit him by mule. "Many years before Columbus, the Mayans have a fantastic civilization in Honduras. But if they see Honduras today, I think they might, how would you say, smile and die."

Die laughing, we would say.

*

In Dakar, Senegal, I once met a leathery old Englishman out there to buy timber. That day he and I, independently, had both been robbed, and over a beer we grumbled about this rackety, charmless city and its roaming gangs of pickpockets. After forty years of doing business around the tropics he thought many of its inhabitants were, essentially, dysfunctional. "It's as if they can only cope with consonants and odd numbers. Something's missing."

When I suggested he check out some of the UK's own literacy and numeracy data, he explained, "I'm talking about a particular mentality." This had a familiar ring—decades earlier, at the Fiji Club, ageing expats like him had sat over their gin swapping yarns about the eccentric nature of tropical people. And, sure enough, he launched into one now. It concerned a Guinea-Bissau football ground with portable bamboo goalposts which a keeper, if dazzled by the sun, could pick up and place elsewhere. I'd heard it before—the ground had been somewhere in Central America—and knew it not to be true. But he wasn't done yet. At a hospital in southern Borneo he claimed to have seen doctors, overcome by the heat, order patients onto the floor while they commandeered their beds for a snooze. In the Society Islands he had played a board game named Missionaires where the pieces were multicoloured jelly babies; when you captured one, you ate it. As he began recalling a Burmese golf club which penalized you if a wild animal took your ball, I said that in Patna—an Indian city even more evil than Dakar—I had actually seen a crow carry off a ball belonging to an army colonel; such things happened, each country had its own hazards, sporting or otherwise. Disappointed in me, he shrugged and drained his glass.

A friend once asked, "If you were put in charge of a UN tropical secretariat, what's the first thing you'd do?" (Free education and healthcare, I said.) Now, curious, I put the same question to him. He never even hesitated. "Plant trees."

That was surprising. "Save the world, eh?"

"Save my job," he said.

*

This was how Columbus recalled his first walk in a tropical forest. "The trees were so high that they seemed to touch the sky; and, if I understand correctly, they never lose their leaves; for I have seen them as fresh and green in November as they are in May in Spain; some even were in flower, while others bore fruit . . . Wherever I turned, I could hear the nightingale singing, accompanied by thousands of birds of different species."

*

Sunday morning dawned fine and sunny, with a fitful south-easterly trade making small whitecaps on Dillon's Bay. Yet William, collecting me for church, seemed scratchily out of sorts. Earlier I heard him remonstrating with four women in billowing dresses who, obviously planning to skip worship, passed his gate on the way to the beach then hopped into a canoe. Now, seeing them far down the coast, paddling with Olympian power and precision, he muttered, "They are going to Happy Lands. Their gardens are there."

"Happy Lands?"

"Once it was called Umponyelongi. But an elder decided it must have a new name—and straight away the devil came. He is still there, and the people are very sad. Where is your Bible?"

Airily I told him I had no need of one; I knew it by heart.

"Oltesteman? Niutesteman?" he murmured, amused by the epic scale of the lie. *"Jenesis, Eksodas, Sing Blong Solomon? Matiui, Mak, Luk* and *Jon?* All that, uh?"

I said, "Yep, all that," then realized, too late, I'd just baited my own trap.

He pounced. "Then you must preach today."

Bloody hell. "Well, perhaps just a little talk. To say hi. Five minutes."

"Twenty. And you must start with something from the scriptures; they will expect it." He added, "You can speak after we have prayed for the government."

"Right."

"I will tell the pastor." Then, frowning, he retrieved, from beneath a croton bush, a quart bottle containing a fluid ounce of rainwater and some mosquito larvae. The label read, "McBrewsters Fine Old Whiskey Vanuatu's Own." *"Grog,"* he muttered, and contemptuously tossed it into a ditch.

We were approaching the church. "Why do you pray for the government?"

He said, "We must ask God to make them work harder."

A big sturdy structure built in 1879, it contained an animated congregation; the hum as we entered made this seem more like a social event. Behind the pulpit hung a cotton tableau of the Last Supper imported from some ecclesiastical discount store, and a giant gold wristwatch, over a foot in diameter, suspended from the buckle of its gold bracelet. Then I noted the Victorian portraits, in heavy black frames, set above the pews. Erromango had been known as the Martyrs'

Isle, and this was the Martyrs' Church; those rigid, zealous faces belonged to the missionaries—five men and a woman—who had been devoured by cannibals. The most celebrated, John Williams, was dismembered with such ferocity the axe grooves are still visible in the rock—across the Williams River—to which they'd pinned him. (Later his bones, sucked clean, were taken to Western Samoa and buried in Apia's Taimane o le Vasa Loaloa, or Diamond of the Wide Ocean Church.)

When, finally, proceedings got under way, the pastor did little actual work but, like a talent-show host, simply sat back and smilingly introduced the various acts. As the first, a reading from *Dutronome* got under way, I started worrying about my talk. With no idea of what I should say, I knew only that I would need biblical grounds for saying it. Then William's mention of the *Sing Blong Solomon* brought to mind a Yemeni queen, famously strong-willed and beautiful, who packed a camel train with gifts for Solomon and drove it, over twelve hundred miles of desert terrain, to Jerusalem. One of her offerings came, like sandalwood, from a small tropical tree, unremarkable in appearance yet containing gum worth its weight in gold.

Reputed to spring from solid marble, frankincense in fact emerges from a kind of Gro-bag, packed with local variants of lime and mortar, that attaches itself to marbeloid rock. A longitudinal incision in the trunk yields milky sap which hardens into a yellow crystalline tear. Once valued for its medicinal qualities—Pliny prescribed it as an antidote to hemlock—it's still used in rural China to treat leprosy. The kohl with which Egyptian women paint their eyes is mixed from charred frankincense, while winter braziers in Egypt are sprinkled with frankincense pellets. It remains the only incense licensed by the Church of Rome and, given its blue-chip status at the time, was an obvious choice of tribute by the Three Wise Men. (Myrrh, also harvested from a plant native to Arabia Felix, is today used in toothpowders and mouthwashes, and a veterinary remedy known as Horse Tincture.)

As a woman in a green dress began recounting the parable of the sower, I recalled my father saying that church attendance should be educational—always give a congregation something to chew on. Well, I would give them Yemen and its legendary trees. They could be shown to have close parallels with Erromango, since deforestation had cost both places immeasurable wealth and opportunity. That settled, I sat back and tried to remember what had most struck me about a country I visited some years earlier.

It possessed, for a start, the most improbable tropical capital I had ever known. Standing 7,500 feet up on the roof of Arabia, flanked by cinnamon-shaded mountains, Sana'a had an oasis-like intimacy. Its quirky buildings, fashioned from mud and limestone, were like gingerbread houses; whitewashed geometric patterns divided the floors, kaleidoscopic arrangements of coloured glass dazzled in the fanlights. Locals claimed it had been founded by Noah's eldest son, Shem. This would make it the oldest city on earth, and until they struck oil—the latter-day frankincense—it was certainly one of the most obscure; for centuries a strict purdah had warded off all worldly contamination.

A few foreigners were allowed in and they, awash with money, were responsible for the creation of a new industry. I first got to hear of it when during my stay Haynes Mahoney, director of the US Information Service, was abducted on his way to a Thanksgiving dinner at the American Embassy; twenty-four hours later, after payment of a ransom, he was returned safely. Today kidnappings are so common that no foreigner may venture into the countryside without his own personal truckload of troops. And since Islamic terrorists have entered the equation, there is no guarantee that hostages won't be sent back with their throats cut.

Though there is not a shred of evidence that the Queen of Sheba actually existed, her Yemeni name, Bilqis, popped up all over Sana'a. At my hotel, I ate Scottish sirloin in the Bilqis Grill, washed my hair with Bilqis shampoo, at the Bilqis Pharmacy noted displays of special-offer Bilqis Flower Essence, bought *Newsweek* at the Bilqis newspaper kiosk and awaited my flight out in the airport's Bilqis Lounge. Her smouldering beauty remains a key part of the mythology. In the 1959 movie *Solomon and Sheba* Gina Lollobrigida played a Bilqis so sultry she seemed ready to lap-dance for King Solomon (Yul Brynner, looking troubled in an ill-fitting wig), and I wondered how people perceived her now. "She was *ekdum* (very) pretty," said the Sheraton concierge, revealing himself—despite his Sheik of Araby costume and bejewelled *djambia* dagger—to be an Indian migrant worker. My Yemeni guide, Fatah, saw her as the epitome of womanly perfection yet, as we headed for the desert in his jeep, admitted she'd had one blemish: her legs were

hairy as an ape's. Solomon, rejecting razors, had ordered that a depila-
tory of gypsum paste be applied then, on her final night in Jerusalem,
seduced her.

"They make a baby, a boy, Menilek."

I knew about Menilek, who took the Ark of the Covenant to
Ethiopia and founded another tropical dynasty there. (Haile Selassie,
keen to have his descent from Solomon and Sheba formalized, actually
wrote it into the Ethiopian constitution.)

On Erromango, after a prayer for the murdered missionaries, the
pastor made some routine announcements. As he reminded the *Kristin
Yut Felosip* to bring teapots to their Thursday meeting, my mind drifted
back to Yemen, whose *yut* were more interested in firearms—an estimated three guns owned by every citizen. Fatah had promised to show
me the At Talh Saturday souk where, if you had dollars, you could buy
anything from Kalashnikovs to Scud missiles and a scary assortment of
bombs. It was, allegedly, the world's largest arms bazaar, but a British
diplomat warned that only legitimate buyers could safely visit. "The
dealers don't like browsers, they can get very flaky; a month ago someone got shot."

A trip to the interior was proposed instead; having realised that
some crumbly, latex-like stuff in the market was, in fact, frankincense,
I asked to see a frankincense tree and, from Fatah, learned that our
expedition would take us deep into frankincense country. At Wadi
Dhar, eating melons in a chocolate-coloured palace set atop a plug of
ochre rock, a dozen spirited Chinese women approached ("We are
lady tailors from Beijing!") wanting their picture taken. Through their
viewfinder the Empty Quarter's huge horizons sprang into focus while,
from above, came the sporadic rattle of small-arms fire. "A wedding,"
said Fatah.

At the head of a precipitous track the parties of the bride and
groom occupied adjacent cliffs. On one cliff listless men danced in
circles, a hawker with an eagle on his shoulder sold paper flowers and
a youth peddled runny sulphur-coloured ice cream from a bucket.
Forty guests squatted on the cliff's rim, gazing blankly at the horizon,
or idly blasting their Kalashnikovs at the sky. On the bride's cliff, by
contrast, many of the women were rock climbing. I watched them,

veiled and dressed to the nines, balancing on crags with arms out-stretched and calling gaily across the void. Though my heart was in my mouth nobody, on the groom's cliff, appeared to heed them at all.

"Why are they here?" I asked.

The Yemenis, he said, were a cliff-loving race inhabiting a land blessed by many such escarpments. They enjoyed the views, and gath-ered at places like this to socialize. "I think it is the same in England? The White Cliffs of Dover? You like to go there with your friends."

When I said England's white cliffs were crumbling into the sea, he announced they were obviously collapsing under the sheer weight of their visitors; also, it was God's punishment since many, being British, would doubtless be drinking alcohol and having sex there. Islam's tropi-cal inhabitants, I reflected, possessed moral certainties unknown to the Erromango Christians. I told him a story I'd heard about Alaskan grizzly bears—a species that so love panoramic views they regularly meet on mountain vantage points to enjoy them. But he looked offended, as if I had attributed certain brutish characteristics to the Yemeni people.

We began passing men striding along with AK-47s slung across their backs and small polythene-wrapped trees in their hands, moments later entered a village where the shrubbery was being sold from the backs of Toyota vans. Fatah grunted "Khat!" and stopped the jeep. "Here they have tip-top quality; it will make you happy." He thought I needed cheering up.

Khat releases a substance similar to amphetamines; adrenaline is produced and blood pressure increases along with the pulse rate. It's an upper and downer, excitement followed by lethargy and appetite loss (and in the US, where it's banned, perhaps a prison sentence). A boss-eyed old dealer seized my hand and patted it. "Stone the crows!" he kept murmuring. After some confusion it emerged that I was the spitting image of Mr Pepper, a Scout master in the southern port of Aden back in the days when it had been a desolate sun-blasted British colony. Under Mr Pepper's tutelage the dealer won badges for Astro-nomy, Knotting, Radio Construction and Swimming—the latter, it seemed, gained nude in the Gulf of Aden; Pepper liked to take the boys of Goose Troop skinny-dipping. "He tickle our balls!" Wistfully, he insisted on giving me a discount.

Fatah, back in the jeep, began tearing the leaves from his tree and stuffing them in his mouth. "You not swallow, just chew." Mine tasted like privet clippings, and very soon I spat them out. He, cheek bulging, drove dreamily past miles of verdant, well-tended khat fields as I reflected that half Yemen's arable land was given over to its cultivation, while every family spent a third of its disposable income on the stuff— and this in a country that once amassed fortunes from its agricultural exports; after frankincense, they discovered coffee: Al Mokha had been Yemen's principal port.

So where would we find frankincense today? Fatah pointed ahead. From far off, Tulla looked like smoke. Drawing closer, it acquired a curious opaline radiance, as though small fires were smouldering inside. Later, it became a towering granite mesa with a fortress teetering on the top, and at its base, a little town made up of ascending diagonal gradients. In the alleys women covered their faces when they saw me, by the door of the mosque a frightening assortment of automatic weapons had been left by worshippers, at the Alwhada "restaurant" someone crept up behind, covered my eyes and planted a damp, thunderous kiss on my ear. I went "Whhaaa!" and sprang from the chair. A stooped old man stood there, grinning. Fatah, slightly irritated with me, said, "He is the owner. He is just making you welcome."

Shibam lay on the far side of the sandy plain, set below a mountain range. At a walled village a thousand feet above the town, tiny veiled girls with hennaed hands tried to sell me silver Maria Theresa dollars. In the late afternoon we returned down a plunging track that unravelled like a streambed, all whorls and meanders and wicked little currents of pebbles that set skates under your shoes. During our descent the sun began descending over Arabia, firing up the sky, causing its serrated mountains to cast huge, swooping shadows that crept forward like the onset of sleep.

I said, "We still haven't seen a frankincense tree."

"They have been all cut down," said Fatah, lying.

In the Martyrs' Church the pews had become so sticky with sweat we made squelchy, embarrassingly flatuous sounds as we shifted position. A bearded man strumming a blue guitar led us through a clapping hymn, an elderly couple in matching plastic leis sang quaveringly and drew warm applause. The pastor's Prayer of Intercession for the *gavman* sounded more like a list of complaints against a lazy, incompetent landlord. Waiting, half comatose from heat, I now planned a short talk on Sheba's distant queendom and its legendary tree. And while no one in Yemen had seemed bothered, here surely it was time for a major sandalwood replanting programme—both to celebrate God's munificence, and the willingness of the Japanese to pay $40,000 per ton for the stuff.

After that, a few words on forest conservation: a hope, for example, that Mr Yoshioka's fragrant Imperial house would teach the Emperor's subjects—who turned one quarter of all tropical timber into disposable chopsticks—more respect for forest products, and perhaps a warning that the Panama Canal (their main seaway to Europe) was at risk due to the activities of loggers in its drainage basin. But then I thought, oh, bollocks, just tell a good story. The one about Alaska's forest-dwelling, view-loving grizzlies would at least get people smiling and, trying to think of an ursine scriptural reference to keep William happy, recalled the child-massacre passage from II Kings in which bald Elisha was taunted by a crowd of boys—forty-two of whom were then torn to pieces by slavering she-bears lumbering from the woods.

But when, finally, the pastor beckoned, the congregation were on the verge of sleep. Heads lolled, eyelids drooped, palm-leaf fans ceased their agitation and dropped into warm, damp laps. So, with relief, I resorted to a few pleasantries about Dillon's Bay and its historic old church: great to be here, thanks for having me, cheers and God bless. The pastor, who seemed to be the only one listening, smiled gratefully. "That was really interesting," he said.

*

Next morning, as I shaved on my little patio, Margaret drifted languorously by. "Hi, Frater," she said. "Seen William?"

"Afraid not."

"Well, if he shows up, you remind him: boat tax!"

Later, in the village, a man fell into step beside me. "I am Eddie," he said, taking my hand. "I was also born in the Iririki hospital—but a long time after you!" In his forties, heavy set, with black skin, a bright pink tongue and the bouffant hairstyle favoured by Fijian cops, he seemed to be implying that coming from the same labour ward gave us kinship. "At church yesterday the pastor said you are a writer. But what kind of writer? Fiction? Non-fiction? Are you writing about Erromango?"

Yet he interrupted my answer to tell me about himself: here visiting a married sister, otherwise—his shrug implied—what would a *Sydney-trained* Vila secondary school teacher be doing in a dump like this? I learned he had a wife and two sons and, though social studies was his subject, politics was his passion; some day he might even stand for parliament. Also, he read "avidly."

"That's very interesting," I said and, aware our sweat was comingling, carefully withdrew my hand from his. "So who's your favourite author?"

"Oh, Paul Theroux, I think. Right now he is my number one. For *The Happy Isles of Oceania* he came to Vila—but I only found out much later! You know it? A classic!"

Theroux, paddling the Pacific in his collapsible canoe, had explored some dangerous coasts, and battled against tides and currents that would have terrified me. It was a brave, funny book—with plenty of curmudgeonly Therouvian moments—yet not, I reckoned, one of his best. When I said so, however, Eddie frowned, as if doubts had been cast on his own judgement. "But I think he is more famous than you."

Ow! "No question about that."

"So I think you don't write as good as him." He spoke almost regretfully.

"You're thinking on the right lines, Eddie."

"The tropics, uh? That is your subject."

So he had listened after all.

"But your generation is colonialist—imperialist, actually."

Actually, I told him, my generation had put an end to all that. Shaking his head, he challenged me to name a corner of the tropics that hadn't been colonized by Europeans.

"Thailand."

"Thailand is *still* colonized by Europeans. Sex tourists."

"A lot of them are Orientals. Who apparently tell their wives they're going on golf holidays."

He wasn't interested. To cheat and steal was in the European nature, we couldn't help ourselves; look what we'd done here in Erromango. For centuries the tropics had brought out the worst in us; even those who were law-abiding citizens at home underwent big personality changes out here. What he called "God's abundance"— meaning the weedlike exuberance with which items of great commercial value grew—made us venal, mendacious and, often enough, plain murderous. I couldn't fault him.

The light dazzled; I had forgotten my sunglasses. He talked on, blaming everyone's problems on colonial exploitation. Now, look— I might have said—these days the exploiters were often indigenes. African and Malagasy bush dwellers, clearing forests with fire, had created deserts, fuel-wood requirements in the Himalayas annually triggered catastrophic floods in Bangladesh, loggers in Malaysia caused rice production to drop by a quarter, in the Philippines they fished with dynamite and in Kalimantan wrecked streambeds by using them as roads. Canopy mosquitoes, which once bit only canopy animals, at ground level now bit humans; logging spread disease (Brazil recently posted the world's highest number of new malaria cases). Over a six-month period researchers in Bangkok's Sunday market counted 68,654 native birds—most of them protected forest species—for sale. Who should be blamed for that?

But it was too hot; I couldn't be bothered to say a word and, anxious to be on my way, merely pointed out that Europe's guilt about the past was reflected in the size of its Third World aid budgets.

Eddie said, "They still use Mercator."

"They *what?*"

"Mercator's projection. His map."

Why, I wondered, were we standing beside a sluggish little South Seas river discussing a sixteenth-century Flemish cartographer? Apparently because his projection, devised for European sailors, so enlarged Europe and the Northern Hemisphere (he'd made Greenland bigger than Africa) that the closer you got to the equator, the smaller the countries became; Mercator's dwarfed tropics, proportionately reduced to nothing like their real size, diminished the self-esteem of all its member nations.

I said these shrunken countries had been portrayed that way due to the curvature of the earth. To regard it as some kind of political downgrading was absurd; at the time, indeed, many hadn't even been discovered. Also, Mercator's Southern Hemisphere loomed just as large as his Northern one, it was merely a matter of balance. "And today it's still the best way of . . ."

"It is not! The A. H. Robinson projection shows every country in true size. Even the US Geographic Service use it! I have told my head-master we must tear down Mercator's old colonialist maps and put up Robinson's, our children . . ."

"I'd have thought your headmaster would be better advised to get enough bloody books and pencils for the . . ."

"You boys arguing?"

William stood behind us, holding a loaf of bread. Eddie gave an easy smile. "No, no, brother. Alex and me, we are both Iririki kids, you know that? Just chatting, just chatting. That so, Alex?"

"Sure."

He shook my hand and, chuckling, walked away.

I sighed, and as we strolled on, suddenly remembered something. "Boat tax," I said.

*

At the Dream House, one evening, I was joined by William's chubby rock-star son. Clever, unassuming and very intense, Joe said his father had sent him to New Zealand to study theology, but in place of a preacher's degree he returned home with a battery-driven synthesized Yamaha key-board. Two aspects of life there impressed him: elevators and porridge—the latter so much that memories of it made him almost maudlin. "I try to describe it to people, but . . ." He shrugged. "You like porridge, Alex?" "No." He had grown up surrounded by fresh fish and fruit; how could such dismal stuff with its origins in some freezing, stormbound corner of the planet (Cape Wrath came to mind) have become his dream food? The Scots, I suggested, invented whisky to wash away the taste of boiled oatmeal, and smiling faintly he began talking about music.

His first album, *Remember the Children*, dealt with the problem of broken marriages and parentless youngsters. It sold six hundred—astronomic by local standards, but was easily exceeded by *Manis Ogis* ("Month of August"). August is the planting season, and this compila-tion celebrated island gardens, and the tradition that communities work together. His biggest hit single, regularly played on Radio Vanuatu, urged young people to quit the towns and return home to their families. Recently he had recorded a two-hundred-year-old *kastom* song—after tortuous negotiations with the *kastom* chiefs—about land; set to a rock beat, lending a disco glamour to the arcane laws, it had become Vila's biggest dance craze. I asked to hear a few bars but, perhaps thinking it would be bad karma to sing it to a whitey, he sang instead (voice very dreamy and tender, accompanying himself on the Yamaha) Stevie Wonder's "I Just Called to Say I Love You." Then, as he talked admiringly of Mick Jagger, his father appeared and pulled up a chair. "He an English boy?" enquired William.

"Old feller now."

All the tropical musicians I'd ever heard—ranging from steel-band and gamelan performers to pastoral players of gong chimes, bone bags, bell rattles, sheep-skull maracas, rain-wood marimbas, cow-horn flutes, ivory oboes, bamboo xylophones, army-surplus trumpets, one-string ground bows (a hole in the ground acting as resonator), two-string spike fiddles, lutes strung with civet gut, even bagpipes stitched from whales' scrotums—insisted their audiences get itchy feet. The question they would ask of anyone choosing to sit, inert, in a draughty, cold-climate concert hall, was likely to be: if the stuff you're hearing is so good, why don't you get up and dance? Joe's fans, while certainly doing that, were also persuaded to confront important social issues. They might laugh at what their preachers and politicians kept telling them, but they evidently listened to Joe; he had made thousands of young islanders take stock. It occurred to me that this unassuming man could be changing the thinking of a generation.

William, who had written some of Joe's songs—"He's got talent," said his son—picked up an Ed McBain paperback I'd been reading and idly riffled through the pages. A postcard fell out. Sent by friends visiting Moscow, it showed one of the twenty-nine Gauguins allegedly "lost" in Russia. *Te Arii Vahine* was a stocky, small-breasted nude reclining beneath a flowering tree, one leg propped over the other, a crimson fan stuck coquettishly behind her head. The date, 1896, meant it had been painted on Hia Oa, the model probably his child bride Marie-Rose—here depicted with a hint of a smile and a quick glancing look, as if something amusing had just been said. It was a curiously formal, courtly picture, yet William examined it with distaste.

"Beautiful, eh?" I said. "She's Marquesan."

"I don't like it."

"Because she's naked?"

"No. Not that."

As Joe examined it, without comment, it occurred to me I had never seen a painting of, or by, a Vanuatu native. He shrugged. "Not part of our culture, I guess."

Kastom again, I thought. The *jifs,* deeply conservative and cherishing the nightmarish, goggle-eyed deities created by their haunted, ancestor-driven old craftsmen, discouraged any depiction of the human form—in contrast to the Mbaya Indians, who had even turned their naked bodies into works of art. (When a European ship, the *Maracanha,* sailed up the Paraguay in 1857 the tribe, next day, appeared painted all over in anchors, their chief in an officer's painted uniform that included buttons, epaulettes, sword-belt and coat-tails.)

Kastom had made theirs a monochrome world; I wanted to ask about this, but William suddenly stood. "Time for *kaikai.*" As Joe followed him home across the garden, I reckoned their melancholy island could have done with some Mbaya exuberance and exhibitionism. (Western missionaries, remonstrating with them for spending so much time fussing over their make-up, were invited to strip off and join in. "It's fun!" the Mbaya men cried.)

A big surf sent ripples up the Williams River. I poured a covert whisky and imagined a synod of evangelists, nude but for their boots and celluloid collars, at prayer with their rainbow-coloured wives, all tricked out like totem poles. In Brazil Lévi-Strauss met a tribe whose women, using bamboo spatulas dipped in the colourless juice of the *genipa*—which gradually darkened through oxidation—covered their faces, even their whole bodies, with asymmetrical arabesques and delicate geometric patterns.

In Suriname, on the confluence of the Palumeu and Upper Tapanahoni rivers, I once visited an Amerindian village of forty houses set beneath giant banyans. The women teased cotton or made cassava beer which the men, lying in hammocks, drank from saucepans. In a doorway a grandmother sat painting the face of a young, pretty girl. Dipping a chewed twig into a mix of spit and vegetable dyes she applied mossy green to the lips and shaded the eyes a smoky lavender

blue. Green lozenges and voluted blue whorls were set along the forehead and down across the cheeks, fine yellow lines zigzagged up from
the chin. As the woman worked on, creating a kind of postmodernist
tartan, I became aware of the silence. Kids played, a dog barked,
sambas drifted from a radio tuned to Brazil, yet the forest somehow
neutralized and absorbed the sounds, made them magically diminish.
In the design, suddenly, I saw elements of leaves, sunlight and shadow, while the face became that of a forest child peering through trees.

Trees, unsurprisingly, featured on my last morning at Dillon's Bay.
Before I left him to catch the aerodrome truck, William showed me a
sandalwood sapling planted in his garden by a relative. It was a scraggy
little thing yet, some day, might make her rich enough to visit Israel.
"She wants to see the Bible places." We were joined by a neighbour,
a large, easy-going man who, constantly scratching at an itch on his
elbow, launched into a sudden attack on the Vila Forestry Department.
"They have been here, but they just plant pine and eucalyptus, foreign
trees that do no good. For five years they have promised us sandalwood—
but they are ignorant about it, they ask kindergarten questions, they
have made no research." He looked at William. "Not like Mr Yoshioka."

William nodded. "You can ask Yoshioka any question about sandalwood, *any* question, and he will give the correct answer. He has
studied everything. He *knows*."

I said, "Shame he's not running the Forestry Department."

Yet Vanuatu's government people were not as bad as, say,
Indonesia's, with their enthusiasm for logging, mining and grandiose
national parks. In Irian Jaya, I'd read, officials from Jakarta kept harass-
ing and bullying the shy, engagingly named Amung-me people who,
for centuries, had been meticulous and intelligent custodians of the
forest. If the Japanese had won the war, I suggested, a battalion of
clued-up, sandalwood-mad Yoshiokas would, long ago, have turned
Erromango back into the Fragrant Isle. They did not disagree.

*

In the *efil's* shabby, open-sided little terminal, a barefoot woman with
a whisk broom was sweeping up broken glass. Built years earlier by the
French, it now resembled a vandalized bus shelter. Strolling down the
runway (which needed mowing), I found it ended at a precipice; sea

glittered far below. The Twin Otter, flown by a tubby young Australian and running an hour late, dropped giddily off the escarpment— *aaargghh!*—then laboured back up over Erromango. My neighbour, a tall Santo businessman stooped in his tiny seat, said he had been checking out a site for a store at the village of Port Narvin, but had decided against it. "The people are poor, I would have to keep prices too low."

When he added that 80 per cent of a store's sales depended on food, I wondered aloud why they should pay any price at all. They had their gardens and a sea full of fish, anything else could probably be found growing wild.

He said, "Of course, some food they get from their gardens. But people like to shop, a shop is a social centre. Also, you know, this is the age of *convenience*." Quietly he added, "In England, do you have a supermarket in your town?"

When, in other words, did I last go scavenging for edible roots, or hunt a wild boar for its meat, or climb a tree in search of honey? Chastened, I recalled a bay on the tip of the Cobourg Peninsula, where Australia starts nudging into South-East Asia (Indonesia's outer islands lie just across the Arafura Sea). Here Rupert, a knowledgeable local ecologist, demonstrated that the tropical bush hereabouts had been a larder which, for millennia, supported vigorous human populations; walking me through a few acres he identified billy goat plums—the richest source of vitamin C on earth—and six species of wild yam. There were *nypa* palms yielding sugar and wine, conkleberries that cured warts and lower-back pain, stringybarks with antiseptic leaves, turkey bushes with bark which, made into an infusion, eased general aches and pains, termite mounds rich in kaolin—"Top diarrhoea remedy"—and large red ants with edible green tails; bitten off, they were sweet as candy. (I gobbled a dozen.) Under a salmon-coloured woollybutt gum we drank strong, eucalyptus-scented tea and listened to the drone of tiny native bees. "They make bonzer honey, very fragrant." From a freshwater pond where magpie geese ("Good tucker") were feeding, he snapped off a water lily. "Try the stem. What's it taste of?"

I took a bite. "Celery."

"But celery with *flavour*."

In a dinghy on Trepang Creek, walled by mangroves, he talked about oysters. "Out there in the bay they're wall to wall, the seabed's almost paved with the bastards. Delicious too, but we can't touch. The oysters belong to the Aboriginals."

"Do they eat them?"

"Never," he said. "But that's not the point."

In the foliage a bright golden snake went gliding by, its arrival registering as a sudden bright presence; down below a shallow trench leading to the water turned out to be a croc slide. He pointed to a trio of salties dozing on a sandbank, weathered as driftwood and, possibly, the craziest beasts in the equatorial region. "They can go from nought to sixty in about four seconds, that grin on the face of a charging salty is actually G-forces lifting its lips clear of the teeth." (Lacking any braking mechanism, a salty slows by sticking out its forepaws and hoping for the best; decelerating salties split rocks and flatten tracts of bush before sliding to a halt in whirling clouds of dust and leaves.)

As he started the outboard and puttered home, I asked about the future of this place in particular, and the tropics in general. He talked about erosion. A forest's dense, whippy, serrulated canopy acts as a giant windbreak; lose the forest and the soil—no longer stabilized by a rooted substructure—simply blows away. "Trees, through transpiration, help make clouds. Remember that old Searchers song, 'What Have They Done to the Rain?' That's going to be our anthem here at the Top End. As for the overall picture, well, if you multiply that scenario enough times, you're talking about something apocalyptic, worse than nuclear warfare."

The pilot turned and shouted, "Vila in ten minutes, folks!"

I wondered what kind of Torrid Zone my great-grandchildren would find when, in around fifty years' time, they too set out on their travels. This account of how certain parts seemed early in the century is, in a sense, intended for them. Would it still ring true, or would they be left puzzling over an arcane memoir—fetched down from the attic and pretty soon returned there—dealing with an area of the world they scarcely recognized? The Sahara, after all, was once populous grassland famed for its wheat and corn, its honey, almonds and barley beer.

The Elusive Turret Bell

If, ever, they got to Paama, I wanted them to hear the Whitechapel chimes. I'd been lax about organizing that and, one spring morning on the Whitechapel Road in London's East End, finally found myself at the Whitechapel Bell Foundry (its premises elegantly half-timbered and, according to its shiny brass plate, est. AD 1570). The nature of its business, anonymous from the outside, became instantly apparent as you entered. A spring-triggered bell pealed, a second had to be sounded for attention in the shadowy little lobby, three more set over a door clanged when, eventually, it opened to admit Richard Brewis, the works manager. Stocky, brisk, businesslike, with a direct East End manner, he looked and sounded like a change-ringer steeped in bell lore (and raised on such thunderous classics as "Oxford Treble Bob" and the "Grandsire Triple"). "We cast Big Ben here," he said, keen for me to know the kind of people I was dealing with. "That was back in 1858. It was a monster, thirteen and a half tons, our largest ever."

"Right." Having recently swotted up on my bell lore, I knew that its chime tune, the "Westminster Quarters," comprised the notes E, D, C and G in various combinations. It had been composed in 1793 by a Cambridge organ scholar, William Crotch, for a new clock in Great St Mary's Church and, until opportunist politicians hijacked it to Parliament sixty-six years later, was known as the "Cambridge Quarters." (St Paul's Cathedral rang the "Ting-Tang," a repeated alternation of two notes which, along with chime themes like "Turn Again, Whittington" and the "Holsworthy Tune," had been whistled by everyone; Frank, the old salesman, had doubtless coaxed both from our ruined piano.)

"Ben," said Mr Brewis, had been Sir Benjamin Hall, the elevatory engineer who hauled the bell up the tower's interior. "Tricky job, it took days, the nation held its breath." Here, also, they furnished the belfries of Westminster Abbey and Canterbury Cathedral, made the Liberty Bell and Bow Bells. "*And* St Clement Danes."

The oranges and lemons bells of St Clement's! Humming the tune in my head I reflected that Whitechapel had even chimed its way into the nursery.

He led me to a cosy panelled office warmed by a coal fire. "Vanuatu, eh? Where's that?" Yet, as soon as I mentioned the South Pacific, he knew; they also cast bells for the King of Tonga. The general location now clear in his mind, he began probing the requirements of my particular congregation.

How big was the church? Where was it located? Were there any adjacent buildings to baffle the sound? Any hills? Where did they lie? Were they wooded? Any beaches with surf? (Surf caused low-frequency interference.) How high would the belfry stand and how far should its peal travel? "Height equals reach," he muttered as he began mentally mapping Liro's acoustic contours. I said, "There's no belfry, and we're talking about quite a smallish bell."

"Hmm." I already knew about Whitechapel's towering reputation (in July 2002, for the citizens of New York—at a solemn ceremony attended by the American Ambassador and the world's media—they would cast a giant bell to mark the first anniversary of the Twin Towers' destruction). Bishops, or their millionaire benefactors, routinely flew in from all over the planet to sit in this very chair and, in some cases (he let slip), *book their bells by the score.* I cleared my throat and, feeling as if I'd gone into Aspreys to locate a tiepin among the tiaras, put my question: did they stock any cheap, off-the-shelf specimens? He frowned: a few *comparatively* cheap, ready-made ones were available— ready-made and kept mainly for any Africa-based missionaries who wanted a Whitechapel original. But enquiries about second-hand cast-offs earned me a frankly scandalized look. "*Redundant* bells? No, no." (You got those from scrap dealers.) Finally, having weighed up the evidence, he recommended "a melodious twenty-four-inch model in F."

"F being the note?"

"Exactly. You can have any from A to G sharp. Once we used tuning forks, but these days the bell resonates into a stroboscope set to one-hundredth of a semitone; that's perfect pitch, way beyond the human ear. The twenty-four-inch bell weighs three hundred and forty pounds."

I steeled myself. "What's the cost?"

"Three thousand, three hundred and forty-two pounds."

Blimey! "Plus freight, of course."

"Correct." And, his earnest manner indicated, worth every penny. He stood. "Care for a look round?"

The workshop evidently hadn't changed much since the firm arrived on these premises in 1738. ("Our original foundry was just down the road.") I saw corners swallowed by shadows, elsewhere a greenish light the colour of the coppery residue found on old bronze— even the dust motes seemed verdigrised by age.

Shakespeare was four when the company began trading, and by the time he reached London, Whitechapel's founder, Robert Mott, was making himself heard throughout the capital. I wondered if a passage from *Hamlet*—"Like sweet bells jangled, out of tune and harsh"— might have been aimed at him. Mr Brewis laughed. "Mott had plenty of competition. And anyone making duff bells soon went to the wall." Here the wall, which should have been strewn with cobwebs, was hung with blackened moulding gauges shaped like the rudders of veteran ships (Big Ben's gauge could have steered the *Titanic*).

It seemed to me that the thirty-two bell founders employed today were making exactly the same products Mott's men had once made; new technology merely streamlined a four-thousand-year-old process. He shrugged. "Bells change. The medieval ones were long and narrow, sort of tulip-shaped with a flared mouth. By Mott's time the modern look had already arrived, and we've kept developing that—today we've got a broader bell, waist shorter and more concave, the shoulder squared and the sound bow"—the band struck by the clapper—"thickened. And, of course, the firm's changed too."

Now their clappers were forged from ductile steel by specialists in Scotland, while their alloy came from the Home Counties—Australian copper and Malaysian tin alchemized into blocks of bell metal then trucked up to Whitechapel's furnaces. Yet I watched blacksmiths renovating cast-iron clappers forged during the time of Pitt the Younger, and tuners "skirting," or revitalizing, bells that had been rung after Trafalgar.

A man slopping mud onto a heap of broken bricks performed a task that would have been instantly recognizable to Mott. "This is Florian," said Mr Brewis, "and he's making a bell. Actually, he'll probably make yours." A grizzled, soft-spoken Romanian in blue overalls, Florian told me the muck in his bucket—he continued moistly slapping it on as we talked—was a mix of sand, clay, goat's hair and horse manure. Dried, it would form the core over which, eventually, the cope would be fitted; any inscriptions, stamped in reverse on the mould, then stood—"true and proud"—on the bell.

He had been creating them for thirty-five years—the last ten in England, where commissions from churches gave him particular pleasure. "In Romania they want bells for fire brigade and navy . . . for warship, not worship." And he liked the idea of creating instruments that might be heard by his great-grandchildren—even their descendants. "You know, it is a kind of immortality." When I told him about Paama he smiled. "OK, I do nice one for your island." That reminded me: should it be climate-proofed? Mr Brewis said it would be routinely primed with Galvafroid rust inhibitor but otherwise, for the tropics, no further steps were needed. "Bells are impervious to the weather."

I said that Liro's old one, cast by the Glasgow Foundry Boys' Bible Class, had been destroyed by the weather.

He frowned. "It must have fallen."

This was probably true.

"Well, then! You must never drop bells. Bells are brittle."

The carpentry shop lay up two flights of narrow stairs. Here, using steam-bent ash and air-dried English oak, craftsmen built the giant wheels that spun bells full circle for English change ringing. One told me there were ten thousand different peals in England alone, and that a mere dozen bells could, theoretically, ring almost four hundred and eighty million different changes. Late in the fourteenth century, said another, several English bell-makers had rung changes of their own, adapting their equipment to forge cannons. (The heaviest guns carried by Henry VIII's warships were cast in bell foundries.)

Bells, long credited with special powers, have been sounded to seed rain clouds, dissolve storm clouds, quieten volcanoes, drive off demons, purify pestilential towns and ensure good harvests.

The Sicilian Vespers were a peal which, in 1282, triggered the bloody massacre of the French living on the toe of Italy; more bells led to the massacre of France's Protestant Huguenots on St Bartholomew's Day in 1572. And in 1776, the Liberty Bell proclaimed America's Declaration of Independence. (The instrument which launched the most profound rebellion in Britain's imperial history had, ironically, been cast in its capital—even odder, in this very building.)

William the Conqueror's curfew bells, sounded at 8 p.m. in every English town, told citizens it was time to put out their fires and go to bed. If Hitler had invaded Britain every church bell in the land would have been rung to announce the fact.

Bell founding stems from the Bronze Age. (Bell metal, 77 per cent copper and 23 per cent tin is, in fact, bronze.) The first Christian bells were crude affairs, iron plates hammered and riveted like cowbells. It was the Chinese who pioneered the modern instrument. During the fifth century BC's Chou Dynasty they cast elliptical, sweet-toned temple bells with lotus-shaped rims and exquisite decorations achieved by using the *cire perdue*, or lost wax, process.

Now, in the carpentry shop, I mentioned that history's first chimes—Chinese "stone chimes"—were played on marble slabs suspended from ebony frames.

Mr Brewis nodded. "Indeed, and we've kept an unusual record of our own history." He pointed to a beam covered with intricate inscriptions. "Here our company motto—'Nothing is impossible for a man who doesn't have to do it himself'—has been translated into every language ever inscribed on our instruments." Among the scores there I noted Mandarin, Maori, Malay, Zulu, Catalan, Burmese, Basque, Norwegian, Estonian, Afrikaans, Korean, Cornish, Japanese, Slovak, Tongan, Maltese, Turkish, classical and modern Greek, Russian, Ethiopian, Esperanto, Gola and Kiswanahini. ("African dialects, I believe.")

Each Saturday morning, he said, groups of Americans came to White-chapel to see where, in 1752, their most sonorous national treasure had been created. "The Liberty was cracked *twice,* the second time during a politician's funeral when they were clocking it. To clock a bell you tie a rope around the flight of the clapper and pull—but hold it a split second too long and the sound bow resonates against the clapper and self-destructs." I made a mental note to pass the message on: no clocking.

Back in his office, now determined that Paama should have its own new, custom-made model, I consulted Mr Brewis's List of Particulars. Shipping charges, I reckoned, would add a grand at least to the recommended £3,342, twenty-four-inch, three-hundred-and-forty-pounder. Glumly picturing my incredulous bank manager ("You bought *what?*"), my eye came to rest on the smallest, cheapest, most freight-friendly model available—a £1,950 turret bell with swing chime fittings. "Actually, I think I'll have one of those." He said, "Right you are!" and told me that inscriptions in relief—true and proud—cost £1.89 per letter.

"Fine." We shook hands. "Nice doing business with you," I said.

Several days after I mailed my deposit a Job Sheet arrived.

PAAMA, SOUTH WEST PACIFIC—CHURCH BELL.

The Bell.

From copper and tin cast a 14 inch diameter bell accurately and
   harmonically tuned on the five tone principle to note F,
   and weighing approximately 78 pounds.

Inscriptions are required.

Drill the crown for supporting bolts.

The Swing Chime Fittings

Headstock of square section steel bar with ends turned in true
   alignment.

Self aligning, sealed ball bearings, in cast iron plummer block
   housings.

Insulation pad for fitting between the bell and headstock, together
   with supporting bolts, with nuts, lock nuts, and insulation
   washers.

Independent clapper staple fitted with stainless steel hinge pin.

Clapper of ductile cast iron, properly proportioned, and fitted with
   a resiliently mounted Tufnol bearing.

Pulley of polypropylene in an enamelled steel housing.

Bellrope of polypropylene, flax hemp in appearance, and with a close
   woven red, white and blue sally.

Its technical complexity startled me. An object I took to be simple and homely as a plough or a pillar box turned out to be remarkably intricate, a hand-assembled engine for raising the roof.

Delivery was promised for the first quarter of 2000. But that proved to be only the beginning of a complicated tropical saga that would move, inexorably, into the wilder realms of tropical fiction.

Confessions of a Beachcomber

On the London Underground, one hot, crowded August morning, I saw a middle-aged black woman in a T-shirt bearing the words "Send Us Your Tourists!" The name of the supplicant country was hidden by a bag on her lap, yet I knew it had to be in the Torrid Zone, and struggled to get closer. Then at Piccadilly she jumped off, leaving me to wonder which far-away, clapped-out, coconut-dependent economy had recently signed up to the biggest money-spinning idea since slavery.

The historian J. C. Beaglehole wrote that after eight months at sea, James Cook's crew were "imparadised" in Tahiti. While any visitor to a tropical resort will, hopefully, feel a similar degree of enchantment (with its faint whispers of promiscuity), they should note it was Cook himself who insisted that local sensibilities must never be offended, and local customs always shown respect. These remain good ground rules for today. Thus, if vigorous beach games are considered antisocial, don't play them. Or if, in noonday's heavy stillness, the natives fall asleep, the tourists should sleep too. Indeed, doing exactly what the locals do is the best way to gain the Zen-like peace that flows from torpor and lassitude. Tranquillity, in hot places, may be found in extreme indolence.

Visitor numbers to the hundred and sixty-nine countries and territories lying wholly, or partly, within the Torrid Zone are difficult to collate (try finding figures for the Îles Glorieuses). But a UN estimate showed that the Developing World, pre-9/11, received approximately 30 per cent, or around 200 million, of the 664.4 million tourists travelling annually. Post-9/11, the consequences of Muslim terror attacks in South-East Asia have yet to be measured; how far down the years will that Bali bomb echo?

Meanwhile, places choosing to throw their hats into the ring have so much in common—flora, climate, hours of daylight, post-colonial politics—they must first identify the attractions that will set them apart: what do we have the others don't?

Kenya highlighted its game parks, Kerala its inland waterways, Fiji its firewalkers, Singapore a shrewd mix of instant Asia and duty-free shopping. Vanuatu decided to promote its live volcanoes, *kastom* tribes and US detritus from World War Two (circling sharks, on some islands, would deter the beach-holiday crowd). Yet Ambrym, while possessing one of the biggest volcanoes of all, had something infinitely more intriguing to offer: magic.

Looming just over the water from Paama—a mere four-minute hop by Twin Otter—it is home to wizards who, beneath Mount Benbow's ash-smeared, wildly volatile hulk, are said to perform feats such as walking tightrope across threads spun by *spaedas*. This, plainly, had to be investigated.

At Craig Cove I scrambled aboard a tiny launch rigged with trawling arms. Its driver, Solomon Douglas, tall and fleshy, kept his thoughts to himself. "How far?" I asked. He shrugged. "Two hours." The sea had a bumpy chop that banged on the hull like a drum. Then, thirty minutes out and passing a series of deep, forest-clad canyons running to the sea, he spoke again. "Dip Point."

Up there the vaporized Presbyterian hospital once stood. This was the spot where, during Benbow's epic 1913 debouch (six vents erupting simultaneously), Maurice and the Paama traders had performed their famous rescues; those canyons had been bulldozed by lava. We motored on, halted when a canoe approached. Laden with firewood, a whippet-like dog trembling in the bow, it was paddled by a youth who, easing alongside, handed over three eggs. He received a cigarette in return.

The Solomon Douglas Guest House, at Ranon village, stood by the beach. Near my hut a cold-water pipe dripped among a tangle of flamboyants and pink cedar flowers, on an adjacent slope there was an earth closet with no door but sublime ocean views. Later, I found Solomon sitting under a breadfruit tree whittling a length of wood. "I am a carver, you know," he said. "This will be a small *tamtam*."

A *tamtam* is a slit gong sculpted in a quasi-human form and, now, he began hollowing out eyes round as saucers. "So, Alex," he said, "what do you want to do? Climb up Benbow? I can show you the ash plain."

"I'd like to see the men walking on spider's webs."

"It might be difficult. But we can try. The cost is fifty dollars. Cash."

I whistled. "Do they take *vatu?*"

"No. Their village is not far. We can go in the morning."

But in the morning sheeting rain formed a ground mist that swirled about our knees like smoke. We marched past glistening native gardens, through dripping plantations and tracts of primary forest, came eventually to a chasm a dozen feet deep, six feet wide, and floored with jagged rocks. Oh, Jesus, I thought. "Big jump," urged Solomon. Landing, I stumbled and began sliding, was abruptly gathered in by a small, bearded man, strong as a bear, who appeared from nowhere. He set me down, patted my shoulder then, effortlessly, leapt the chasm himself. As he vanished into the scud I saw he had a withered leg and club foot. "Who was *that?*"

"Just a farmer."

We entered a deserted village. The rain stopped, the sun shone. He called, and a magician stepped from a house. In his late teens, tall and good-looking with a supercilious, aristocratic air, he wore a Brazilian soccer shirt and carried a ghetto-blaster tuned to a voice I knew well: Andy Kershaw, the BBC radio star (he and I once knocked around North Korea together). Here, meanwhile, the news was not good. Solomon said, "The spider fellas are away. This is Esau. He will do some things."

"Can he walk on webs?"

"No."

I was getting the sorcerers' apprentice.

"But he is quite cheap. Also, you can pay in *vatu.*"

Esau, stifling yawns and moving very slowly, fetched a stick, dug a hole, tore a branch from a dwarf palm and planted it six inches deep. Finally he spoke. "Pull it out."

Solomon said, "This is a very good trick!"

Placing my hands around the stem, I found it studded with tiny thorns which drew blood. *"Ow,"* I muttered, noting Esau's fleeting smile. Then, grabbing at the fronds, I gave a sharp tug. It didn't budge. Even when I heaved and strained it remained fixed, seemingly shackled in concrete. Finally I stepped back, panting. "No can do."

Solomon chuckled.

Esau took the tip between forefinger and thumb and, pinkie minimus extended as if lifting a cup at a tea party, plucked it from the ground.

"Do not ask how," advised Solomon. "It is his secret. Next you will see the sticking coconut trick."

Now he slashed a nut in two and placed both halves, husk sides up, on his palm branch. He turned the branch over and they clung, limpet-like, to its underside. Even when the branch was waved and shaken, they remained in place. Solomon applauded.

"I'd like to take a closer look."

"No. He will be angry. But this last one is his best."

An elder appeared with a pile of giant fanlike kava leaves which Esau arranged on the ground, carefully overlapped to form a mat. A small boy was summoned, and lay face down on the leaves, clasping his ankles in a hunched, almost foetal position. The men stationed themselves at his head and feet, Esau muttered, "*Wan, tu,* tri!" Then, seizing handfuls of vegetation, *but without touching the boy,* they lifted him and his litter—its kava folioles miraculously fused—and shuffled both into the hut.

I was left open-mouthed.

Esau, emerging, accepted my congratulations with a mocking air. Handing him a pile of sodden *vatu* notes, I asked when I could return to see the spider men. He didn't deign to reply, but Solomon murmured, "You know, it is a special *kastom* thing. You should talk to the big *jif* at Fanla village. Maybe he can fix it."

Walking home, he spoke of magic being the catalyst that would build hotels along Ambrym's craggy coast, and fill them with wealthy foreigners. But would they come all this way to see what I had just seen? I pointed out that Europeans were accustomed to different kinds of tricks.

"Like what?"

I tried to think. "Well, a woman gets into a box, then the magician takes a saw and cuts the box in half."

"But the woman is not cut."

"Correct; she steps out smiling. And here's another. The magician has a hat. He shows it to everyone, and puts it on his head. When he takes it off again fifty pigeons fly out."

"Hmm." He reckoned they had nothing to fear from that. I agreed; the key, without doubt, was the web-walking routine—which, *if true,* would be an international sensation.

"Of course it is true!"

"You've actually seen it?"

"Many times."

I asked about the spiders. Some tropical species, huge and hairy as possums, prey on hummingbirds and small woodland animals, trapping them in high-tensile scaffolding of almost industrial strength. Perhaps Ambrym had monsters that spun man-bearing silk? No, their spiders were quite small. The problem lay with the magicians, who could walk only when *kastom* allowed—and *kastom* was strongly opposed to tourists. Ambrym might, after all, have to depend on the volcano to lure them in.

I said loads of islands had volcanoes. Anyway, what was the rush? Tourists brought drugs, crime, prostitution, AIDS and venereal disease; a new Ambrym underclass would be created.

"I think in the Caribbean they are doing OK."

"You really want to go down that road?" Armadas of cruise ships appearing each morning? Lines of coaches queuing for Benbow? Farmers abandoning food gardens to peddle trinkets on the beach, fishermen working as short-order cooks? Centuries-old tribal values sacrificed? And for what?

"Money," he said.

"Oh, sure. Well, obviously, but isn't . . ."

That triggered a flicker of anger. "I suppose you have a nice car? Electricity in your house, a fridge and so forth? TV? *Video?*"

I saw where this was going.

He continued, "You ever worry your kids die from malaria?"

"No, malaria's not actually a . . ."

"They get good education? Maybe go to university?"

"Yes." Mine had grown up—as he knew—in a country of such wealth and amplitude the chance was there for everyone.

"No one here *ever* been. And they travel, I suppose? Like you? Like you just buy a ticket and come here? Or maybe you say to your wife, 'Honey, let's go to New York.' So you go."

"Who's Honey?"

"Alex, I think deep down you don't really want us to change. There are many like you, you want to rough it a bit, get back to nature and so on." He spoke the next bit, unexpectedly, in authentic Australian. "Aw, it's just gorgeous, so peaceful, so *unspoilt*. Mind you, the sandflies bite like buggery, a week's about enough." Then he listed the amenities foreign capital could provide: power, proper hospitals and schools, roads, clean water, sanitation, public transport, jobs and pensions. And implicit in all this, I knew, was the self-respect that came with a First World standard of living. Their government could never afford anything like it—and neither could their faltering pastoral economy.

Walking through his quiet, beautiful island, scoured and shiny from rain, I had no answer. We continued in silence.

*

But Tofor, the old *jif* allegedly able to influence the magicians, shuddered at the mention of tourism. Bony and bearded, naked but for a frayed penis gourd, he accepted my gift of tobacco sticks then handed me a shell of kava. Seated in his hilltop village beneath a giant French Tricolour, a medium-sized Old Glory and a small, gaudy Vanuatu banner ("My flags"), he said it was entirely alien to *kastom* teachings. However, since Solomon had vouched for me, my request would be considered.

"Can you say when? I have to leave tomorrow."

He shrugged. "Maybe nex' year."

Woken at dawn by a shower pattering on the roof, I felt a small, furry creature snuggle up to my neck and, taking it for a kitten, turned sleepily; a plump brown rat erupted from the bed and vanished through a hole in the wall. But Solomon, as we breakfasted off sticky village bread and high-octane Santo Arabica coffee, merely shrugged. "It didn't bite? So it's not a problem."

"Jesus, if you want tourists here you'll really have to do something. People are squeamish."

"I know that. But tourist money would give us a public health department. With trained inspectors. *There would be no rats.*"

We were back where we'd started.

*

In Habana Vieja, the old quarter of Cuba's collapsing capital, much restoration work was in progress. The Hotel Ambos Mundos (Hemingway wrote *For Whom the Bell Tolls* in Room 511) looked pristine and sleekly pink yet, recently, had been a near-ruin. Nearby I watched cobblestones being relaid as craftsmen brought an intricate network of lovely squares and carriage-width streets back to their former glory—and all because Russia had stopped posting the cheques.

Once Havana had been subsidized by Moscow to the tune of one dollar per day per inhabitant. (Cuba's population was 11.4 million.) Then, struggling to fill the post-glasnost void, they turned to tourism. Now querulous, introspective, unattainable Cuba—great beaches, cheap rum, beautiful women, the world's second largest coral reef girding the Caribbean's most interesting island—beckoned us in; we were the solution. For us Fidel spent a fortune to make his nation shine.

*

Some nations, though, first had to overcome a xenophobic dread of foreigners, or social constraints (their women might be stared at), or protests from religious leaders or just plain inertia. Then—often for no apparent reason—the objections were withdrawn and, as mysteriously as if raised by the moon's gravitational tug, a new frontier would be declared open.

Oman, for a traveller, was always one of the hardest countries to get into. Periodically, as though tossing coins into a wishing well—and with about the same level of expectation—I would send off a visa application. But the Omanis never replied and, in truth, I would have been astonished if they had. Their shadowy, half-mythical desert kingdom, with its elegant little slave-traders' capital, would probably remain off-limits for ever.

Then, in 1989, barely credible rumours began circulating to the effect that Oman was admitting tourists. *Tourists!* Enquiries revealed they weren't admitting many (and all were carefully hand-picked) but the curtain was being lifted, and soon afterwards I managed to slip under. Before I went, though, an experienced Omani hand put the place in perspective.

"In 1970 it had ten kilometres of asphalt road, one hospital and virtually no education; there were thirty foreigners, and only the doctor was allowed into the interior. Oman was medieval—even wearing spectacles in the street was an arrestable offence. Today you'll find four thousand kilometres of asphalted roads, sixteen hospitals, thirty major health centres and two hundred and fifty thousand children in full-time education. If Sultan Qaboos needs something from Harrods he'll send a private jet—maybe even one of his 747s. Oil paid for all that, but now prices have dropped and they're feeling the pinch. That's why they're showing a cautious interest."

Yet, finally arriving in Oman, I kept wondering: where are the Omanis? Many of the cars on the fine new motorway to Muscat were driven by Europeans. Mine was in the charge of an Indian who identified the motorway maintenance teams as Sri Lankans, Bangladeshis and Pakistanis. The check-in clerk at the Al Bustan Palace Hotel was an Austrian. The man who took me to my room was a Palestinian and the girl who brought breakfast a Filipina. Apart from a gimlet-eyed female immigration officer at the airport (who may have been Egyptian) I had still not knowingly met an Omani after several hours in the country. All I had come across were scouts from Oman's huge army of hired help—which included nineteen thousand Britons there on lucrative short-term contracts.

For a tourist it was interesting enough. Wadi-bashing one weekend I found myself in a vast, sun-blasted place dominated by the Jebel—an apparently unscaleable mountain range displaying, high on its stony flanks, smudges of green. "Peach gardens!" said the driver. "Walnuts! Pomegranates!" (Arabian leopards too; the last eight on earth were said to be somewhere up there.) The town of Salala possessed frankincense groves, a pretty corniche, and a souk selling eight different kinds of date—though I preferred the souk at Bahla, located in the shade of a haunted tree and famed for its walking sticks. Yet I came across few tourists and, back in the capital, an official explained why.

No visa could be granted until Muscat had issued an NOC, or

No Objection Certificate. And they wouldn't do that until satisfied the applicant was middle-aged and prosperous. Budget or gap-year travellers—indeed, anyone under the age of twenty-eight—were rejected on the grounds of a probable drugs or alcohol dependency or, worse, "immodest" dress. ("It's terribly important," said an Irish teacher who made me swear not to mention his name. "Women not properly covered don't get their legs caned like they do in Saudi, but they must change and report to a police station for inspection.") Yet it seemed to me that penalizing the next generation of wealthy foreigners could bring its own problems; they, having grown into perfect NOC candidates, might in turn impose their own Oman boycott. I said as much to a charming Indian lady who interviewed me in Salala for local radio. Sighing, she switched off her recorder. "Oh, dear," she said, "the censor will never pass *that.*"

But on Ko Samui, a Thai island in the Gulf of Siam, you'd have once been hard-pressed to find a tourist aged *over* twenty-eight. I'd long known it to be a cult destination for the young—though in 1986, boarding a ferry with kids who would pay a pound a night for accommodation, I noted too a smattering of middle-aged couples toting expensive luggage. A Bangkok lawyer said they were "returnees"—a generation nostalgically revisiting a place where they'd once known "bliss."

"But they won't camp on the beach?"

He smiled. "For them we are building luxury hotels. It is very good for our economy; now plenty money coming in."

I thought of Oman: ignore the youth market at your peril.

We docked after dark. Na Thon, the tiny capital, echoed with young voices. It had a bank, a bee farm and streets crowded with Western kids on mopeds—many driving crazily, and without lights.

The lawyer said they had probably been eating omelettes.

"Omelettes?"

"Local speciality." He smiled. "Very nutritious."

I first needed somewhere to sleep. Finding a bed could be a chancy thing, and youngsters off the ferry had to tramp the beaches for a place to lay their heads. Most ended up in bungalow colonies with names like Lucky Mother, Maliblue Bill, Best Kiss, Joy, Big Buddha and Munchies. Sun Shine Cottages had a vacant "chalet"—more of a Wendy house, really—and, having claimed it, I went for dinner at an outdoor eatery set just above the tideline. A dozen young Australians were being served by a middle-aged, long-haired German in a dirty vest. "You want omelette?" he asked.

I wanted fish, and ordered shark fritters and giant prawns. When he came to fetch my plate he said, "Omelette now?"

I shrugged. "What have you got?"

The Aussies smiled. One advised, "Try the mushroom, mate. They're in season—and a bit, uh, special. You with me?"

Finally I understood. "OK. One of those."

The waiter said, "In the old days mushrooms are free, now restaurants must pay five hundred baht a kilo. So the hippies have gone. To other islands. One day I will perhaps go too."

Ko Samui had been "discovered" by a lone Swedish hippie in 1970—one of the Kathmandu pioneers who, fanning south from Freak Street, had fetched up in some interesting corners of the tropics. (I recalled a Dutch couple in Bali who made glove puppets and sold them at the Ubud market. They'd been strictly orthodox: burned incense, wore dragon tattoos, hung Tibetan Thangkas in their shack, smoked or swallowed anything that came to hand—mushrooms cooked with *eggs* would have seemed risibly bourgeois to them—yet were among the hardiest travellers I've ever met. When Qantas inaugurated a weekly service to Bali they slipped away to Flores, spoke of maybe catching a boat for Mindanao after that.) The waiter was right. The hippies moved on as others moved in. These people had come to eat the lotus—known to the police as narcotized fungoids—before heading home to solid jobs and big mortgages. I finished the omelette then, feeling mildly concussed, stumbled off to bed.

Ko Samui lived chiefly on coconuts. Two million were shipped to the mainland each year, picked by monkeys trained at a school near Surat Thani. The best-known Ko Samuian, Boon Ta, runner-up in a Miss Thailand contest, had a suicidally dangerous cliff named for her on Thong Yang Bay. This I learned next day from an ebullient lady named Patchree Vialatte, trained abroad as an architect but so infatuated with Ko Samui she had bought land and begun building. "Here there's a by-law stating that no man-made structure may be higher than a coconut tree. I'm certainly observing it, but I don't know if the big Bangkok developers will."

We were on our way to see her new hotel. The Village, at the luxury end of the market, had London stockbrokers among its guests; the social and economic balance of tourism on Ko Samui was already shifting. "Bet you don't give them omelettes," I said. She shrugged. "Last month a Danish girl at Best Kiss ate one then, on the beach, sexually assaulted an American chap *twice her size*. My people must be protected from such acts." (Yet I knew one or two City brokers who might enjoy having their braces snapped by an amorous little Scandinavian strung out on psilocybin.)

A structure of silvery, weathered wood appeared. "That's the buffalo-fighting stadium. Once the bulls took early morning gallops on the beach, before a bout special chants were sung; they had red ribbons and golden horns, and fought like crazy. But these days, for the tourists, they just stand and moo."

Later I saw a new luxury resort on Thong Sai Bay: Bangkok money, air-conditioned Spanish-style villas, security guards patrolling a landscaped hillside. In just two decades the hippies had been displaced by the budget travellers who, in turn, would soon be priced off Ko Samui by the £500-a-night crowd—few of whom, according to Ms Vialatte, were revisiting scenes of youthful enchantment. "Most of my guests had never *heard* of Ko Samui. Places like this are put on the map by people like me; we create the facilities and hope they'll come." She didn't need to add that, in those pauperized areas of the Torrid Zone blessed with the kind of magic they had here, there was just one thing to do: exploit it.

Yet the economic benefits could be double-edged; even on Ko Samui I heard tales of misfortune. A family's good sons traditionally inherited the valuable coconut plantations in the hills, its bad sons the low-grade places down on the coast. Now, with coastal real estate fetching up to £50,000 an acre, the bad sons were baht millionaires while the good ones sat wringing their hands.

Throughout the tropics tourism remains the subject of a continuous, often rancorous debate, with academics, intellectuals and religious leaders often opposing development plans. In Sri Lanka, for example,

I found the brand-new Kandalama Hotel—set in country so remote that leopards had left their footprints in the wet concrete—a centre of intense controversy. Local Buddhists didn't want it there and, in a dogged, subtly subversive Buddhist way, were fighting it tooth and nail.

The Dambulla cave temple, nearby, consisted of five caves set atop a three-hundred-and-fifty-foot-high rock face and crammed with carved likenesses of the Buddha. In the Fourth Cave a guide pointed to a two-thousand-year-old statue and said that, recently, a German female in shorts and a bikini top had been photographed sitting in its lap. Next morning the picture appeared on the front page of the *Sunday Observer* in Colombo, and caused such uproar the statue had to be scrubbed with holy water—plenty of which, handily, dripped from the roof of the cave next door. At the Kandalama I talked to one of the managers, a Catholic, who claimed the scandal had been organized by monks. "It was done to discredit the hotel," he said angrily. "They think tourists will lead to corruption and a loss of cultural identity, and have been against us from the start. Who took that picture? How did it get all the way to Colombo in time for the first edition? They will stop at nothing!"

Yet, in Colombo, I saw a *Daily News* headline which made it plain the monks had strong grounds for objecting. It said, "GERMAN TOURIST, SIX ACCOMPLICES IN COURT OVER BOY PROSTITUTION." Reporting yet another instance of "sex perversion by foreign visitors," the paper said police had arrested Gunter Platzdasch of Stuttgart, and six local men. It continued, "Mothers who flocked to the Ambalangoda police station were aghast . . . Their sons had been enticed into a vice ring under the promise of gifts like bicycles, foreign chocolates, ballpoint pens, stickers, T-shirts and cash. They admitted their children had been making excuses for being away from home at odd hours."

The poorer regions of the Torrid Zone have long been hunting grounds for Western paedophiles—their activities even leading foreign governments to repatriate citizens arrested abroad for trial and public shaming at home. But in Penang, Malaysia, a young Muslim lawyer told me custodial sentences were not enough; such men should be sent to the gallows. "We already hang tourists who import drugs. This is an even graver offence, and I would like to see a mandatory death sentence for anyone convicted of sexually abusing minors."

*

"Victims" was how a Swiss friend described the citizens of an East African town now swamped by "neo-colonialists," or foreign holiday-makers. I thought of her soon after arriving at a small Muslim hotel in Stone Town, Zanzibar (where my room contained a broken gramophone with a 78 called "Bom Song"—by the Egyptian Musical Club—on the turntable). A young Indian brought saucers of jasmine then went to check the taps. "Yesterday," he explained, "we are having no water."

"Oh?"

"Two cruise ships were here. They fill their tanks, they take *so* much there is nothing left for us."

"You mean they sucked the town dry?"

"Yes, nothing left for cooking, not even ablution for moskey."

I looked at him incredulously. "But that's scandalous. And nobody complained?"

"Sir, only my wife." He smiled shyly. "And she only to me."

After dark, in a Stone Town alley, I found a tiny restaurant, the Chit Chat, run by an exiled Goan printer who cooked me fresh crab in coconut milk. At the next table a handsome young Omani all a-glitter with gold—gold Rolex, rings, chains, bracelets and ear studs—grumbled about the "primitive Marxists" running the island; what kind of people named their hospital One Coconut, their cigarette factory the *Good Habit*? Yet it wasn't just branding that got up his finely chiselled nose: it was also indifference to the benefits of tourism. "They are so *lackadaisical.*" That made me laugh. Where had be learned a word like that? King's College, London, he said. Wincing, I asked if he was a tourist himself. Certainly not. He worked for a developer who planned to build a resort here. "I am having a look-see, chatting to people."

One of these turned out to be the Admiral of Zanzibar. Earlier I had seen the old seafarer, wobbling along on a bicycle, and learned now that his flagship, a rust-streaked little steamer named *Revolution,* had been taken off coastal-defence duties to operate a regular tourist service to Dar.

"You can have the Presidential Suite for ten dollars US. The rich young Americans will go for that. They love bargains."

"Or perhaps," I said, suddenly angry, "it should be out chasing the bloody cruise boats that stole all the water yesterday."

He scowled. "Listen, in places like this, tourism can succeed. But first"—a zealot's gleam lighting his eye, he thumped the table—'SACRIFICES . . . MUST . . . BE . . . MADE."

Next morning, passing the old British Consulate, familiar to Nile explorers (Livingstone organized his first expedition in a potting shed on the roof) and godowns crammed with cloves, coriander, cinnamon, nutmeg, lemon grass, chillies, black pepper and ylang-ylang—a distillation that made the senses reel—I came to the old English Club, now a sleazy hotel catering mostly to vacationing East Europeans. On a previous visit the manager had opened the Club library and showed me a thousand volumes that included first editions of Scott, Thackeray, Dickens and Kipling; this time, squinting through the keyhole, I saw only empty shelves. A barman said the books had been burned in the kitchen during power cuts. He winked. "When it happen our guests say the food taste of paper!"

*

Emerson was America's honorary consul on Zanzibar—no big deal, he insisted, since only half a dozen US citizens lived there. A sometime New York psychiatrist—"I treated disturbed children, mostly the kids of Fifth Avenue overachievers"—he'd once come on vacation and decided to stay. Stocky and gregarious, he owned a small exquisitely furnished hotel, and, in its wind-tower, was holding a lunch party. The rusted corrugated-iron roofs of Stone Town spread below, he talked about Chole Island, where he hoped to establish a marine park.

"It was the last place in East Africa where slaves were sold—an Arab market operated there until 1922. I'm involved because I want to help save the reefs of this country. You know people go after fish with dynamite? It sure as hell kills the fish, but it also kills the reefs, and occasionally the fishermen too. Now they've damaged the vacation villas of some ministers and, it's said, even broken the President's windows. So there may be action soon."

"That would be an asset for tourism," remarked a smart, beautiful Sudanese woman who ran a travel company.

"So what exactly *are* Zanzibar's assets?" I asked.

A list was compiled: Portuguese and Arab ruins, several beach resorts, troops of red colobus monkeys in the Jozani Forest, and a state barge in which Queen Victoria once reviewed the Fleet at Spithead. Gifted to the Sultan who accompanied her that day, it remained a thing of beauty (though in urgent need of restoration; earlier I'd seen a man heedlessly slapping white Dulux over intricate oak carvings once emblazoned with gold).

"And that's it?"

"Well, there is Stone Town," said the Sudanese. "It could be your next project, Emerson." She nodded at a pile of rubble, which until recently had been the house next door. "When places here reach a certain age they can't cope any more. So they just roll over and die. It's the climate. Unless something is done the whole town will collapse."

Emerson may yet save it. The tropics have a strong attraction for immigrants like him—many in the travel industry, some gay, a surprising number involved in community work. What they get in return is social tolerance, cheap labour, and, of course, weather to die for. Could he ever settle back in New York? "Sure," he said, "but I'd have to be even crazier than the kids I left behind."

*

Most West Europeans head for resorts like the one at Uroa Bay. There a young teacher, selling shells on his lunch break, told me about the purity of the Swahili spoken on Zanzibar. "It is classical, like Oxford English; people come from all over to study. We are the world *centre of excellence*. But how many tourists know?"

"Probably very few."

"I will tell you what I would do. I would make every tour group learn about Zanzibar: our history, culture, economy, et cetera—just a short lesson, one hour on first morning. If every resort did this the world might be a better place, people more understanding. I think visiting a new land, you should have some knowledge."

"What if they refused?"

He frowned. "It could be a police matter."

This was the kind of idea floated often enough in the tropics—chronically unworkable yet containing a grain of sense. So now, when I see a pale-skinned horde stewing on a beach, all interest in locality and indigenous affairs zapped by an equatorial sun, I think, Time for school! Ring that bell! Know the land you visit!

*

Tourists know the Galápagos, all right; there education has a high priority. Only an hour after boarding a vessel that would take us around the most stringently regulated territory in the tropics, we were summoned to our first lecture. A guide, distributing cotton litter bags to be worn around the neck, said, "Every scrap, even an orange seed, goes in. Orange seeds are very aggressive; just one could change the environment of an island. Do not take away a twig, shell or pebble; that will also change the environment. No smoking ashore. In 1985, sixty per cent of the island of Isabella—and much wildlife—was destroyed by a cigarette carelessly thrown away. Flash dazzles the animals; don't use it. No touching or feeding them; it will affect their social structure. If people off fishing boats try to sell you souvenirs made from tortoise-shell, black coral or sea lions' teeth, say no and tell them their practices are abominable." He frowned. "Is that clear?"

We nodded. He continued, "You are Cormorants, and I am your guide, Fernando. The Cormorants will go ashore together, stay together and come back together. Do not mingle with the Ospreys, Puffins, Shrikes and so forth. When I call 'Cormorants!' you must come to me." He picked up a life jacket. "This is a life jacket. Into these openings you must put your arms. People who put their legs in the openings will float upside down. You must always wear your jacket in the *panga*. A *panga* is the small inflatable which will take you ashore. Is that clear?"

That also was clear.

"Now the ship will set off. You are in good hands. Our commander, Contra-Almirante Penaherrera, is the most highly decorated officer in the Ecuadorian navy. He has twenty medals."

Yet the real stars of our expedition turned out to be the guides themselves. All zealous young science graduates, they had formed themselves into an eco-commando with powers to board visiting vessels and check permits. And they were an obdurate lot. When the government proposed offering guiding jobs to non-Ecuadorians, they occupied the islands' main administration building and stayed until winkled out by naval gunfire.

We knocked off two islands a day—saw blue-footed boobies and swallow-tailed gulls on North Seymour, turtles and herons on Bartolomé, finches, frigate birds and lava ducks on Tower, seals on Santa Cruz, more furred and feathered wonders on Isabella—while being constantly lectured, hectored and reprimanded ("Don't walk there! Keep your voices down! Stay away from that animal!"). On our final visit ashore I noticed a middle-aged Italian stop by a sleeping sea lion. He checked the guides were occupied then, after a short penalty taker's run, booted it hard on the rump. The beast didn't stir, but the Italian, turning away, was smiling broadly.

*

Vietnam's Ha Long Bay, six hundred square miles in area—the place from which many boat people sailed—is one of Asia's best-known beauty spots, a classic panorama widely celebrated by poets and painters. There I boarded a small ship so decrepit you could gouge holes in its decking with a fingernail. A local guide, Miss Thanh, said, "The book *World Wonders,* Éditions Hachette Paris 1950, states that Ha Long Bay is Eighth Wonder of the World. It contains six hundred islands which have names, and maybe a thousand which do not. If you want to give name to an island, you can. However, all must agree on name; *vote must be unanimous.* Later, after some, uh, formalities, it will be written on Ha Long charts."

That was a shrewd move. She had challenged the transitory nature of tourism by offering a territorial stake in the country, and her clients—many of them Swedes glassily transfixed by the scenery—grew animated. A rush of talk was followed by the sound of scraping chairs: canvassing had begun. A lawyer from Malmö wanted one designated for her daughter, a Göteborg builder for his mother, a smiling young Thai surgeon (with a startlingly beautiful wife) passed around three smudged words inked on an envelope.

For the reaminder of the trip everyone circulated the scribbled-on bits of paper that might, literally, put them on the map—and which clever Miss Thanh would binh the moment she stepped ashore. She knew it would be the highlight of their day, even, in years to come, the most enduring memory of their tour: did one of those islands ever get my chosen name?

Teasing is the most irritating aspect of Vietnamese humour.

*

But not half as irritating as the disinformation peddled by some tropical tourist boards. Legends or stories associated with certain sites may, for commercial reasons, be embellished, or given a bit of added zip and resonance. In the Seychelles, for example, I was told that the lovely island of Silhouette had been bought by Auguste Dauban, a handsome young French infantry captain who had battled for Napoleon at Waterloo. And the price?

A Stradivarius.

A what? It sounded like fiction dreamed up by Gabriel García Márquez, and deeply sceptical, I arranged to meet his grandson, Henri Dauban. A planter and boat-builder born on Silhouette, Henri once attended the London School of Economics and, at the Paris Olympics in 1924, threw the javelin for the Seychelles.

I found a tall, fine-featured, strong-voiced old man, aged eighty-nine and partially blind, lying on a couch having his portrait sketched. The artist, an English expatriate named Michael Adams, smiled when I mentioned the Strad. He had lived on Mahé for twenty years and knew all the myths surrounding the Seychellois. "One of my favourites is that they sleep with their boots on."

"Why would they do that?" I asked.

"Because the rats bite them in bed."

Henri, chuckling, said the Silhouette story was true—up to a point. Auguste, planting vanilla, rubber, citronella and patchouli, had been buying the island section by section. "Finally there was one bit left, right by the sea, where he wanted to build his house. The owner, an African, agreed to sell it for a sum of money—and a violin. But it wasn't a Stradivarius. It was a Madagascar bull fiddle—which the African played at his famous Saturday night parties. There he served bat curry and rum, and, accompanied by a man blowing a bamboo *maloumba,* he made it *sound* like a Stradivarius." He added, "You should go over. It's a pretty spot."

So, next day, a launch took me to a steep, beautiful island where, by the jetty, biscuit tins bearing the words *Liberté, Egalité* and *Fraternité* had been nailed to adjoining coconut palms. Beyond Le Grande Case, the palatial home Auguste built from local *tacamaca* wood, stood the Dauban family mausoleum. A miniaturized copy of the Église de la Madeleine in Paris, it contained the remains of Auguste, his Irish wife (a handsome, combative woman from the same clan as John F. Kennedy) and two daughters—all commemorated by worn marble tablets inscribed with meditations upon the death of Socrates.

*

In 2002 the Malaysian Tourism Minister, Datuk Paduka Abdul Kadir Sheikh Fadzir, accused Kuala Lumpur's taxi drivers of overcharging foreign visitors and proposed that offenders be executed by firing squad. Cabbie Muhammad Jamal told the *Straits Times,* "Most of us have a hard life, and are just trying to make a bit extra to feed our families. We don't need shooting, we need higher fares."

*

Back in the sixties I wrote a series of short stories for the *New Yorker* magazine about a tropical island called Tofua. It was an entirely imaginary place with a made-up name—until one of their fact-checkers found it on the map. "I have it in front of me," he said. "Tofua. It's actually in the Tonga group."

"Well, I'll be damned."

"And it's a lot bigger than yours. We estimate an area of about thirty square miles."

It became clear that the real Tofua, with its dense forests, lofty mountains and active volcano, bore little resemblance to the palm-fringed atoll I'd invented. Also, it turned out to be the place where the *Bounty* mutineers finally lost patience with Captain Bligh. "They dumped him right off the coast there."

"Good heavens."

"Uh-huh. Well, you learn something new every day."

After a couple of years I ran out of ideas; the series ended by mutual consent and I forgot about the place. Then, one evening in Tonga's down-at-heel little capital, I had a drink with the son of the King's bootmaker, Joe Ramanial. He pointed to a man sitting in a corner reading a newspaper. "That's Dusty Lee Rivers. Canadian feller, once a well-known Country and Western vocalist. He's moved here, and brought a little floatplane along. That's how he makes his living, flying tourists around. You should meet him."

Dusty was a wiry, fifty-seven-year-old chain-smoker with a shock of iron-grey hair who had now given himself a new name—Larry Simon. "Also got me a new life and occupation, came to Tonga 'cause there ain't no malaria. Brought the Beaver over for charters. It can take off from wet grass, it can land on the morning dew."

"Where's a really good place to go?" I asked.

"Well, Tofua's pretty interesting."

I laughed.

"What's so funny?"

"Nothing. What's it like?"

"Well, quite small, I guess. But with a big surprise."

"What kind of surprise?"

"Come along and you'll see."

He was free early the following afternoon and, if I cared to hand over a couple of hundred dollars, would be happy to take me.

Over the spot where the mutiny occurred dolphins threaded a flat sea with tiny, evanescent stitches of foam. Cumulus covered Tofua, leaving only its black beaches exposed; on one of these William Bligh, seeking water, had been chased by natives who had earlier murdered his quartermaster, John Norton. Larry found a path through the cloud, skimmed the smoking volcano's rim and arrived over an eighteen-hundred-foot-deep crater with a sheet of oily, discoloured water at the bottom. I stared. "Jesus! You're not landing on *that*?"

"Sure am," he said, and dived into the volcano's heart. Then, taxi-ing through wisps of steam and algae green as a cow pasture, he parked on a tiny pumice beach that crunched underfoot. The forest, floored by leaf-mould strewn over crumbling scoria, grew to the water's edge, its interior dim as a crypt. "You want to look around?"

"Yes, I do."

"Just be careful. It's easy to go astray."

Inside, I found the trees wrestling for space. Branches locked, limbs colliding, they were linked vertically by a tangled rigging of lianas, vines and aerial roots, and at ground level sent out lateral trip-wires and spiky leaves with serrated edges. A puddled, overgrown track ended at the volcano's base. Turning back, I became momentarily distracted by a tiny gemlike beetle, and strayed a yard or two: suddenly the track, when I looked for it, wasn't there. And which way lay the lake? After crashing about for an hour I finally acknowledged I was lost.

Aware I was going in circles I carved penknife crosses on trees then, trying to walk a straight line, kept revisiting them. It was hot and airless, with a smell of putrefaction. I fell and twisted an ankle, fell again and broke my glasses. I had scratched hands and a bad thirst, and imagined someone, years hence, finding my skeleton propped against a rock—strangler vines around the throat, parrots nesting in the skull. As, bleakly, I compared the homely, pastoral island of my stories with this awful place (the fact-checkers hadn't known the half of it), despair set in. I knew Larry had to make his Nuku'alofa landing in daylight; panic would come when, heading home, he passed low overhead. Shouting did no good; sounds were absorbed so efficiently that a fruit dove, pecking at berries nearby, barely glanced up. Then a thunderclap from the volcano, and a distant clatter of rocks, gave me my bearings. If the volcano lay that way, the lake must lie this. I went blundering off and, moments later, found him sitting by his plane, smoking peacefully.

He laughed. "Look at you! What happened?"

"Nothing much. Interesting spot, eh?"

"You been gone close on three hours. And it's gettin' late."

The Beaver left a track in that heavy virescent water like a furrow ploughed through grass. I examined my bleeding hands. "You got any Savlon?"

"No." Tofua, I reflected shakily, had been the obverse of the tropics familiar to tourists: a scary place governed by dark, transcendent forces. Over the coast we flew into sunlight. "No developers," I remarked, "are ever coming here," and he smiled. "Don't bet on it. Know what you're likely to find in a few years? Captain Bligh's Island Hideaway—with a Bounty barbecue restaurant, a Fletcher Christian coffee shop and, so help me, probably a goddam *Mutiny* Bar."

*

Port Vila, until independence, possessed just one hotel—run by ill-tempered, high-handed staff who served their guests jailhouse food and treated them with exquisite rudeness. In certain respects the transformation of Iririki, an island stripped out, sanitized and turned into a cold-climate tourist's vision of a castaway's tropical paradise, echoed what Richard Branson had done to his Caribbean hideaway. When someone told the shaggy tycoon about the British Virgin Islands—of which, allegedly, he had never heard—and suggested it might be cool for the head of Virgin to own one, he bought uninhabited Necker for £200,000 from an English lord—who, allegedly, had never been there—then spent a further £6 million dynamiting the island's 104-foot-high summit and replacing it with a Balinese long hut.

Balinese craftsmen spent three and a half years creating a dozen luxury en suite bedrooms, a living room the size of a parish church and, suspended from the ceiling, a library deck. Aside from the dining table (a three-thousand-pound slab of teak), the furnishings and décor were all authentic Balinese—though stamped on each wooden shingle cladding the terrace eaves was the gnomic slogan "Fuck Brazil." Had Virgin been refused landing rights in Rio? No; it turned out to be the name of the timber merchant who supplied the roof; Snr. Fuck had raided the rainforest for Richard.

After a lunch of quiche and champagne I walked around the island. A path had been laid, with shelters placed at strategic points—one, a lovely antique pavilion shipped over from the Morning of the World. I meant to pause for a minute but stayed an hour. The trades blew, an iridescent sea slapped drowsily against the rocks. Then a boat approached crowded with day-trippers from Tortola. As it nudged close the amplified voice of the guide said, ". . . exclusive haunt of the rich and famous. See the guy up in the hut? He's probably a rock star. Give him a wave!" But somebody had binoculars. The guide said, "Oh! Well, maybe he just owns a bank." Reassured, they waved anyway and I waved back, wondering about the moneyed tribe that kept mustering in this glitzy corner of the tropics. Just the previous day, in Antigua, I'd heard about a honeymooning Saudi prince who, on arrival, demanded a hundred-and-twenty-foot yacht, a helicopter and a submarine. The nearest available non-nuclear boat, somewhere in Florida, would have to be brought down on a specially converted 747. Yet after the huge costs and improbable logistics had been explained to the Prince, he looked puzzled. "So what's the problem?"

Don Reid, the friendly Canadian in charge, told me most guests were anonymous millionaires. From time to time, though, Richard's friends showed up: Sir Paul McCartney, Bryan Ferry, Phil Collins, Robert De Niro and Steven Spielberg—who brought Harrison Ford and Richard Dreyfuss—and the Princess of Wales, who had brought her mother and children. But something bothered me about Necker, and it wasn't just the mosquitoes which, undeterred by the ravenous mastiff bats (each bat consumed a thousand a night), came zinging out of the darkness. I realized it was the very quality for which the rich forked out their money—solitude.

The island was dark and silent. And, apart from a few of us dining on stuffed Cornish game hens up on the hill, it stood empty. It possessed no community, no customs or culture, no festivals, no social history, no store or trading post, no church, mosque or temple, no local eccentrics or personalities.

*

At the Senegalese village of Bargny half a dozen Americans had each paid several thousand dollars to work for Earthwatch, an environmental charity dedicated to halting planetary damage (much of it caused by the travel industry; on the same day I arrived, Peru announced plans to send cable cars up to Machu Picchu, its peerless World Heritage site). This was an eco-tourism project and, in return for an unusual vacation, volunteers worked on the very projects they were funding; ours was to record, in sound and video, a series of key cultural events.

One evening, as we lugged our equipment to a local dance festival, I recalled Richard Leakey's famous plea. The former head of Kenya's Wildlife Service believed the only responsible way to enjoy nature was to stay home and watch it on television. Jim, boss of a Maine insurance company, said that was exactly why we were capturing this fragile aspect of Africa.

The Sabar festival, noted for its clever, complex drumming and the exuberance of its performers, was enlivened tonight by the presence of an MC named Djibril Samb. He had soft intelligent features, wore a glamorous purple robe and exuded waves of warm, twinkly charm. Yet when Bruce—an orthopaedic surgeon from Oregon, back in Bargny for a repeat visit—introduced us, M. Samb led me aside and told me he was very short of money. "I work in the mayor's office, but every evening I must sell eggs."

"That's a real shame," I said, and forgot all about it. Next day, though, he appeared at my lodgings, and after a handshake—thumbs entwined, two resonating finger snaps and a murmered *"Ça va?"*— enquired, "What can I do for you today?" What he did was continue the Wolof lessons begun by Anna, my landlady's ten-year-old daughter. (Wolof is a minefield of baffling words and intonations: *sip* means hate, *fonk* is love, *xonq*—pronounced honk—is red, while *xanq*—pronounced hank—is entomological, a wasp.) Little Anna, exasperated by the way I kept sighing, *"Wuy walloo!"* ("Help!"), began muttering in Deep Wolof—classical, declamatory and *xoot* (pronounced hoot, and meaning old or archaic). Finally, she gave up.

Djibril, within minutes, did the same. "It's a waste of time." Then he said he was planning to open a shop. "You like to see?"

"OK."

In Bargny's main street, heaped with sand blown from the beach, we came upon a small three-sided breezeblock structure with an earth floor, but no roof or frontage.

"It will be butcher place," he said.

"Really?"

"But first I must buy a cow."

"Uhuh."

"So I need one hundred dollars."

Wuy walloo! "For a *cow?*"

"Top-quality animal."

"Didn't you tell me you sold eggs?"

"More money in beef."

I gave him fifty. He said, "Now we are partners," and asked for my address; a share of the profits, he promised, would be posted regularly. Then, over a celebratory drink, he spoke of the butchery empire he would create; I left him with an embrace, and a strong hunch it had been a sound investment.

Three months later I received a letter, scribbled in French. He sent felicitations to me and my family, emphasized our continuing friendship, said our joint enterprise was prospering, and requested $300 more. I sent another $50 note.

No word has reached me since. Yet still I toy with the notion that, in time, Djibril will announce a spectacular deal likely to make us both rich; major consignments of tender steaks and spicy African sausages air-freighted daily to, oh, let's say Harrods.

*

Close personal relationships are so important in the Gambia they contribute, in no small way, to its economy. Just a hundred and ninety miles long and twenty-two wide (with thirty miles of Atlantic beaches), the Gambia lies on West Africa's Fever Coast or, as malaria-ridden old sweats liked to call it, the White Man's Grave. In the seventies, dependent largely on peanuts, it joined the tourism race. Hotels bloomed by the sea, in the interior events like Forest Awakenings for Birdwatchers attracted busloads of excursionists. Yet the most interesting thing to emerge was the "strolling" phenomenon. Strollers are young men who walk the beaches trying to catch the eyes of female holidaymakers. If he makes contact, a stroller will engage his quarry in conversation. Top strollers have a working knowledge of Swedish, French, German and Dutch—English too, naturally—and great charisma. Disarmingly, in the course of that first chat, they may ask for nothing more than friendship.

If the women aren't responding they'll approach men also, mostly to cadge things. I was asked for pens, tapes, shampoo, any Salman Rushdie novel, shirts, shoes, and from an apprentice stroller—a small, worried-looking boy of seven—an atlas.

The only overt reference to money came from a crippled fourteen-year-old youth who dragged himself along on crutches, both legs bent at acute angles. He had been kicked by a horse during infancy, but recently a vacationing surgeon from Gloucester had offered him artificial implants as a gift; all the youth needed to find (and a letter from the surgeon, carried like a reliquary, confirmed this) was half the airfare. Tourists handed over their *delasi* notes because the story cheered them and helped dignify the strolling business. And it helped assuage our guilt at the economic chasm between us. Though, at the end of the day, they were selling sex, there was a courtly finesse about the strollers, a code of manners not evident in Banjul, the grubby little capital, where hungry people crowded around with outstretched hands crying, "Dash me a dollar!" That was the kind of edgy aggression found at resorts elsewhere in Africa.

*

Gum Air, owners of the single-engined Cessna that took tourists to Palumeu, insisted on weighing me prior to boarding in Paramaribo. The man operating their freight scales called the Palumeu people "lazy and primitive," and when I wondered what they'd make of intruders like me, rolled his eyes as if to say: foreign devils from a bad cactus dream. Yet their forest village, near Suriname's border with Brazil, was tranquil, the thatched camp on its outskirts run by a quietly spoken Creole who had once been a travelling librarian; Stanley Powers used to cart books—romantic novels mostly—around the riverine communities in a dugout canoe.

He told me the village had no school; its hundred and twenty-four Amerindian inhabitants were illiterate. "Before I worked in a region just as remote, but because of missionaries most people could read. Here I train my staff with picture books: how to place knives and forks, make beds, serve drinks and so on. And I explain about the tourists. Do not envy their money, I say; you have such freedom that, secretly, many will envy you."

He liked to take his guests on jungle walks. Most were either Dutch (curious about their colonial links with Suriname) or well-to-do folk up from Paramaribo. I chatted to a youthful grandmother who owned a waffle shop in the capital. She had never ventured so far inland, and was enchanted by everything she saw. "Isn't it beautiful?" she kept exclaiming. Then an Amerindian boy casually killed an armadillo as it cooled itself in a creek. Stanley said, "It will feed his family," but the grandmother had grown very quiet.

One night a village party was held, and by mid-afternoon all the Amerindians at the camp had left. Some began drinking early; I watched a man walk into a pillar, apologize profusely, then—still wearing his contrite, silly-me smile—walk into it again.

Guests were left to cope on their own, and at dinner everyone joined forces to cook, tend table, man the bar and wash dishes. I befriended an unshaven Rotterdam policeman, and a tiny Hindustani shipping tycoon from Paramaribo who had recently crashed a container lorry and broken his neck in two places.

The cop, a cheery, benevolent whirlwind doing the work of ten, provoked the only disagreement of the evening. Pointing to our flickering hurricane lantern, he claimed it had been invented in Sumatra by an eighteenth-century Dutch musician. "One day in a typhoon he put a candle in a glass jar; the wind could not blow it out. So he collected jars, cut their bottoms off, and put candles inside. He sold so many he gave up the cello and went into business; my granny told me about him."

But I happened to know his granny was wrong; the idea came from a Swiss, Aimé Argand, in 1784. Down the years his simple, affordable lamp—with its smoky adjustable flame and pop-up glass chimney—became the standard source of luminance for tropical people. Fuelled first by whale oil, then kerosene, its contribution to their well-being was on a par with the discovery of quinine—and, for those who could afford it, air-conditioning (invented in 1900 to keep US textile workers on their mettle). They remained perennial best-sellers, however, with Chinese firms like the Yangzhou Hurricane Lantern Co. Ltd pretty well cornering the market.

He shrugged. "A Schweizer, eh? Well, I do not give a fuck. You know what life is? I tell you, sure. Life is give and take."

"Import–export," murmured the tiny Hindustani.

"Rock 'n' roll!" cried the cop, and bought beers all round.

*

Back in my room I noted that the Amerindian maid had used a hammer—the timber behind was badly splintered by heavy, off-centre blows—to nail my towel to the wall.

*

At a lodge on the lip of Tanzania's Ngorongoro Crater the towels hung from gold-plated rails in gleaming marble bathrooms. From my private viewing deck I pondered, two thousand feet below, the floor of a perfectly imploded volcano which ranked with the Great Barrier Reef as the Torrid Zone's greatest natural phenomenon (and biggest tourist attraction). Its walls, sheer and unbroken, encircled sixty square miles of sunken country remote from Africa, yet containing all its classic elements: grassy plains, rivers, springs, swamps, a dense forest, thirty thousand animals, Maasai with cattle, tourists in Land Cruisers, even a few itinerant poachers.

I longed to get down there and, next morning at eight sharp, joined a traffic jam of 4WDs descending into the crater. Within that circle of shimmering grass animals ringed the skyline. We paused by a hare, its spinnaker ears up and trembling, motored past waterbucks and duikers, dik-diks and gazelle, herds of grazing zebra and wildebeest, a pride of lions breakfasting off a buffalo. Surrounded by parked vehicles, their growls drowning the rattle of camera shutters, they licked and tore at its crimson ribcage. Then a large female detached herself and sauntered towards us, casual with her power and glamorously compelling; as she moved nature seemed to make space around her.

Halting directly beneath my window, she glanced up. Her huge, unblinking golden eyes mirrored nothing—no warmth or intelligence—but the most dazzling certainty. Then she lay and began licking blood from her paws. Moses, our driver, whispered, "On no account put your hand outside." Was he *kidding*? The lioness lay just two feet below, replete and sleepy as fleas danced on her back. She looked homely as a dog, and to remind myself of what she could actually do I glanced across at the buffalo; it looked as if it had been hit by a truck. Then a crowd of Germans arrived who, puzzlingly, addressed her in English.

They called, "Hello!" and "How are you today?" and "You are the queen of the chunkle."

"Why are they talking like that?" I asked.

"Because they speak English to all natives of Tanzania," said Moses. "The French too—except to lions, then it's *Français*."

At dinner, sharing a table with two balding Australian travel agents, I mentioned the Germans. Jacko said, "Aw, the lions here only understand the local lingo. Mbut they're a mbit ndeaf, you ngot to shout. And never forget, those mbastards can mbite."

"You'll pick it up in no time," said Chas. He waved to a waiter. "Where's the ndunny, mate?"

Jacko asked, "How's the mbeef, tonight?"

The waiter, a bright young man from Dar, had evidently been listening in. He smiled faintly. "Toilet upstairs, sir. And the mbeef is, uh, ndelicious. Mbotswana's mbest."

*

Where, in the tropics, would you find kwanzas and iweis, takas and poishas, pulas and thebes, dalasis and bututs, cedis and pesewas, kips and ats, kwachas and tambalas, rufiyaas and laaris, ouguiyas and khoums, nairas and kobos, kinas and toeas, pa'angaas and seniti, talas and sene, kwachas and ngwees, riels and sen, dôngs and xus, kyats and pyas, gourdes, quetzals, birrs, balboas, ringgits, lempiras and meticals?*

Nothing evokes half-forgotten holidays like small caches of leftover currency. Pondering the shabby notes, you may recall getting your tongue around their names before—in a market, perhaps—actually starting to speak them. But money is not just a key to a language; engraved with pictures of dams and hydro-electric projects, flora and fauna, founding fathers, revolutionary heroes and defining moments, it also reveals what a country holds to be important about itself. I have a globetrotting BBC friend who refers to all tropical currencies as "grotties" and keeps a huge assortment in a biscuit tin. He threatens some day to change them, but having tried to change my own, I know he'll be received with the kind of invective not normally heard in a bank.

*

Just as the Omani government checked the suitability of any tourist applying for a visa, so a small Aboriginal tribe in the heart of Arnhem Land required an unequivocal endorsement from someone they trusted. One of those trusted most happened to be a clever London-

---

* Angola, Bangladesh, Botswana, the Gambia, Ghana, Laos, Malawi, Maldives, Mauritania, Nigeria, Papua New Guinea, Tonga, Western Samoa, Zambia, Cambodia, Vietnam, Burma, Haiti, Guatemala, Ethiopia, Panama, Malaysia, Honduras, Mozambique.

based Australian woman in the travel business. She arranged my entry, yet, mischievously imparting only a vague idea of what they had hidden away, left me wondering: Why all the fuss? Only there did I begin to understand its significance; Bronwyn's secretive tribe were, in fact, custodians of the Eighth Wonder of the World.

A bush-pilot dropped me at Umorrduk. At the strip I was met by Brian Rooke, a slim, bearded, distinguished-looking man, one-eighth Aboriginal, who reminded me that the region was strictly off-limits to whites. "You were lucky, the permits are harder to get than passports. It so happens Phyllis, my wife, is the lady who issues them."

Ochre dust billowed behind the ute as we set off through the ancestral lands of the Gummulkbun people. "There are only fifty-nine of us left. I'm actually from Flinders Island, down near Tazzy, but Phyllis is a traditional owner, and daughter of the clan chief. Our income used to come from buffalo, but when they got brucellosis and TB we had to think about tourists. Eventually the elders decided to take a few, as long as we restricted the numbers and kept them away from the sacred sites; at all times here you must be accompanied by one of our people."

We transited a series of landscapes so random and unrelated they seemed borrowed from other continents—rainforest, English wood-land, prairie (where wild Timor ponies grazed), veldt, formal European parks and a grassy summer steppe. The tented camp, set by a tree-lined waterhole, was run by Aboriginals whose numbers kept changing as, mysteriously, they came and went. (Yet all deferred to Brian; he was our Captain of the Bush, our *Capitão de Mato* or equatorial outpost commander.) Over a cold Foster's, white-bearded Tom told me about Sweetheart. A giant saltwater crocodile famous for attacking coastal shipping, it now hung, stuffed, in Darwin's museum. "Sweetheart sank more tonnage than the Japanese navy. First she rammed you, then she tore your bottom out, then she *ate your engine*. If you'd given the old girl a shake she'd have rattled like a money box."

At four in the morning, awakened by a terrific hullabaloo, I saw two wallabies slugging each other, standing toe-to-toe. At five a big mob of dingoes went through, at six I was woken again by light gilding the gums, tipping into dim hollows, making the birds sing.

And, with all this clamour and radiance, came the heady fragrance of eucalyptus—plus wood smoke from the breakfast fire.

"Got something a bit special lined up," said Brian, jumping into the ute. Moments later, halting by a low red sandstone shelf half-hidden by scrub, he jumped out again. Following him through a narrow defile, I saw an X-ray portrait of the yam god showing his spine, ribs and heart and, nearby, a rhino-sized animal painted in red ochre and charcoal. "A diprotodon. They became extinct fifteen thousand years ago, so the age of the picture is anyone's guess."

Next came a shadowy limestone ravine crowded with stunning murals, many done long before the birth of Christ. "They mixed the ochre with animal blood, bone marrow and fat. Crushed orchid stems were used as a fixative."

Scrambling up an ochre rock face we entered one of the most remarkable natural sites in the Southern Hemisphere—an imploded limestone cathedral open to the sky and arranged, almost playfully, as a series of aisles, apses, chapels and chancels. The colours of the rock—all derivatives of red, gold, brown, indigo and lavender—dazzled in the heat; high up the escarpment there were flying buttresses and crystalline formations mimicking stained glass. Over a period of twenty thousand years men utilizing those same colours had placed their paintings everywhere.

Glowing beneath overhangs and in dark, crypt-like caves, they went on and on; clamber out of one gallery and you entered another. In an amphitheatre on the brow of a hill I saw my first *mimi* picture— a tall, surreal stick figure representing a benevolent god who lived in the rock. "*Mimis* enter the rock by blowing on it," said Brian. "It just opens up and lets them in. A while back some white fellas, engineers from the Water Board, landed near here in a helicopter and went into a cave. Soon afterwards they were spotted coming out carrying a long object wrapped in canvas. Word got around they'd kidnapped a *mimi*. Later we got reports the *mimi* had been spotted in Sydney *driving a taxi*."

The final cave, entered at dusk on the way out, contained X-ray paintings of great age and sexual explicitness, some of the oldest pornography on earth. Tiny St Andrew's spiders had spun webs across the entrance, wild hibiscus grew nearby. I asked Brian if there were any other rock art sites in Arnhem Land. "Dozens," he said. "Go in any direction you like—it's full of them, many a lot bigger than this. The place has been painted from end to end."

We swam in the waterhole, ate steaks, had a few beers by the campfire. That night the mosquitoes bit so badly that at breakfast I asked if he had any remedy. He said, "Dead finish roots, boiled, should reduce the pain and swelling." He reached up to a shelf and produced a book of colour plates. "Meanwhile, you can check out some bush medicine paintings."

"You *paint* bush medicines?"

"In Arnhem Land, mate, you should worry about the things we don't paint."

He showed me a couple that might be prescribed for my condition. They were very fine—vivid, stylized ironwood leaves glowing in a fire before being crushed for application, blue and white gardenia leaves being prepared for the same purpose in runnels of bright flame.

*

The manager of a Balinese hotel told me of a middle-aged English couple who, annually, turned up for two weeks and never left the property. "They've been coming to this extraordinary island for ten years, and all they know is the airport road."

*

During the late nineteenth and early twentieth centuries, when the Eastern tropics held a profound fascination for Western literary men, certain hotels became key halts. One in particular offered the writers vice-regal accommodation, six-course breakfasts—washed down with Benedictine—and twelve-course dinners (of Bengal mutton, Chinese capons, Keddah fowls, Sangora ducks and so on). Their enthusiasm, publicly voiced, gave an obscure Bangkok hostelry near-legendary status. It, in turn, hasn't forgotten its debt to the writers. Indeed, a continuing regard for the art of story-telling helps make the Oriental a hotel regarded by many—certainly by me—as the world's finest.

In the lobby, late one thundery July afternoon, girls in silks brought iced champagne then, in a welcome that was almost choreographed, swept me off to reception. Beyond the Authors' Lounge (massed orchids, a discreet rattle of teatime china) lay the Noël Coward Suite with its golden four-posters, cavernous marble bathroom and elegant lobby; there I found bound copies of Coward's plays and expensive notepaper bearing my name. A stocky, middle-aged Thai in morning dress presented his card. "I am your butler," he said, then introduced his deputy, my under-butler. As the deputy unpacked my bag, his boss revealed the identities of some who had slept in those gilded beds: "Grace Kelly, Bob Hope, Prince Philip, the King of the Hellenes . . ."

"And what about Coward? Was he actually here?"

"Yes. He was here."

"Conrad too? Did he ever sleep in the Joseph Conrad Suite?"

It seemed that Conrad—his first command, the barque *Otago,* anchored just yards away on the Chao Phraya River—had baulked at the cost of the Oriental's rooms. "So maybe he stay aboard; some suites, you know, are called after the old sailing ships that visit Bangkok. But the authors—I think most of them have been in their suites: William Somerset Maugham, Graham Greene, Gore Vidal, James Michener, Barbara Cartland . . ."

"Barbara *Cartland*! Was she an old sailing ship?" (A stately square-rigger came to mind, with primrose sails and damask-shaded hull, manned by handsome, square-jawed Old Etonians.)

The deputy gave a sudden honking laugh, and offered to shave me; I said no and they left. The Oriental's atmosphere, already slightly carbonated, really began to fizz when, in the bar, a breezy, heavy-set American asked me why Maugham had been named for an English county. I said his parents probably supported its cricket team.

"So he could also have been, say, Middlesex Maugham."

I said that was an interesting idea. He nodded and, turning to the barman, asked for a Gore Vidal.

I said, "What is a Gore Vidal?"

"A cocktail of the house." He nodded towards a woman seated next to him. "She's having a John le Carré."

"My God," I marvelled. "It's like drinking in a library."

"Well, yeah—up to a point. Earlier a guy wanted a Tolstoy, and I tried Tom Wolfe. But I guess they're not on the reading list."

I asked for a P. G. Wodehouse.

The barman, making no comment, briskly mixed Gilbeys with Angostura. "There you go," he said, and slid the glass over. It was a large pink gin.

*

Breakfast always came at 8 a.m. sharp, delivered on silver trolleys by the butler, the under-butler and the under-butler's boy. On my last morning the butler said, "When you come back maybe you will be famous writer. Then we put your name on the door."

I thought this might be a tactic to earn him a bigger gratuity; but in fact it was to charm me out of the suite an hour early. He needed it for "a famous politician"—famous in Germany, it turned out, some Bundesrat high-flyer who had evidently been tipped as a future Chancellor. Waiting for a taxi, I idly wondered where he would take his holidays if he ever got the job. Which resorts could guarantee total seclusion for world leaders and global celebrities?

At the Hôtel Saint-Géran in Mauritius, favoured by football superstars, I'd once seen two multimillionaire strikers (one Dutch, one English) relaxing on the beach with their topless cover-girl wives while, in a palm grove behind, security men loitered. And Le Touessrok, nearby, kept an eye on minor royals like the Duke and Duchess of York—also, according to a deputy manager, Russians who turned up carrying briefcases crammed with hundred-dollar bills. "The only English they know is 'Best room'—though some can also say 'Royal suite.' They pay cash for everything. I have a couple now, he's in the Royal, she's in the De Luxe: $2,200 a night. And, on top of that, they're drinking us out of champagne."

(Earlier that day, in Port Louis, a fleshy young Muscovite smelling of Armani cologne and something unsettling, like gun oil, told me he was recruiting local women to turn peanuts into luxury "gogdail shnuks"—cocktail snacks—for the Moscow market. Each nut, he explained, had to be split, then hollowed out and filled with anchovy or curry paste before being tied back together with a strand of seaweed. A few rupees a day were being offered, cheap labour the key to this absurd tropical enterprise.)

The Mauritian economy revolved around sugar, molasses, rum, fertilizer, fishing and—certainly of interest to the vacationing Russians—diamond-cutting. Yet who could doubt that, in time, tourism would become its lodestar? Or that whole swathes of the equatorial zone might be transformed into beach resorts, game reserves, tented camps, forest lodges, golf courses and duty-free shopping precincts? The role of the indigenes then, quite simply, would be to keep rich folk from the temperate latitudes well fed and happy.

*

On Java there was a hotel with "dream conference facilities," a fully equipped fitness centre, a shopping arcade, an entertainment complex, numerous executive suites and a room where the Queen of Evil lived. Daily, to placate her, offerings of peanuts, flowers and clove-scented cigarettes were left outside the door.

On Tuesdays, at the folkloric evenings, barefoot girls jumped up and down on piles of dinner plates. Tiny and exquisite, they embodied a European dream of Asian womanly perfection yet, when European men saw each impassively demolishing several kilos of crockery, they blanched and avoided eye contact—just as the dancers, wrapping up the show, tried to establish eye contact with them. Chatting to the troupe afterwards, I learned all were available for "special room service."

Each night, at the Hilton in Antananarivo, dozens of beautiful Malagasy women came to pick up foreign men; those not invited to a guest's room headed for the lobby where, piled on sofas like sleeping seals, they dozed until dawn. One explained that since they were often given money by the foreign guests, it was dangerous for them to venture home in the dark.

*

As I write this a heat wave has settled over London. It's thirty-three degrees centigrade in the shade, and my friends complain of unbearable days and impossible nights. Yet some are planning winter breaks in countries where thirty-three degrees is a seasonal norm, and where even a leisurely evening stroll will leave them drenched in sweat.

Sweating, in fact, may be a function to which they have not given much thought; how many would know an apocrine from an eccrine? The latter are glands regulating temperature; evaporation of eccrine-secreted sweat cools the body and dissipates heat. Even in cold climates there is steady, if imperceptible, fluid release, while in torrid ones the output of moisture so dramatically exceeds the evaporation rate that in extreme conditions—say south India prior to the monsoon—a human may lose up to forty pints *per day.* Failure to replace it promptly can cause loss of consciousness, even death. (The apocrine, or scent glands, located around the armpits, navel, nipples and anogenital region, respond to stress or sexual stimulation; temperature has no bearing there.)

That's why well-meaning locals urge visitors to drink water; even if they're not thirsty, keep swallowing. And eat salt; salt depletion leads to heat prostration, with possible severe consequences. Water, though, remains the key and, Lord knows, there's rarely a shortage; in the tropics a million gallons can fall, in the space of minutes, on an area no larger than a tennis court. Yet the rainbows that follow tend to be ephemeral; diurnal winds soon whisk away the cloud, then it's back to the hot skies, sparkling seas and dazzling beaches that feature in all those glossy brochures.

The Hum Note

One day, while awaiting news of the bell's progress from Mr Brewis at the Whitechapel Foundry, I lunched near Broadcasting House with a producer who worked for BBC Radio 4. We had once made a programme in India about the monsoon and now, over a plate of Turkish road kill wrapped in vine leaves, she asked about my current plans. Naturally, I mentioned the bell. And when, pensively, she said, "You know, there might be an idea there," I groaned inwardly; turning up on Paama with an attractive younger woman to whom I wasn't married would, apart from causing all kinds of logistical problems, scandalize the population.

It was a place where close working relationships were permissible only with same-sex colleagues; any more flexible arrangement would automatically carry with it the presumption of adultery. (Maurice had seen to that.) Also, I was wary of talking into a microphone about so much private history. "It could be tricky, actually," I said, and she appeared to lose interest—then, a week later, called to say that her boss, unexpectedly keen, in fact wanted a two-part feature. I pretended delight (a dismayed silence at this point has crashed many a freelance career) and sought my wife's advice. She pointed out that though radio didn't pay much, the fee would help defray the cost of the bell. Every little helped. Privately I believed the programme would never get made.

*

Late in November 1999 I learned that Pentecost had been struck by an earthquake; there had been fatalities. The Zuikers, my Peace Corps friends now back in Cleveland, relayed two messages from a colleague, Chad Metzler, who had recently returned from Liro. "This will probably affect your bell project," they noted.

The first described how Pentecost's earthquake had struck Paama too, a 5.8 Richter aftershock—"the big ride," Metzler called it— coming shortly around midnight. At sunrise he began assessing the damage, and his descriptions eerily echoed what Maurice had witnessed almost a century earlier: whole sections of the coast tumbled into the sea, giant fissures splitting the ground, food gardens buried, gaping sink holes in villages. Yet nobody was hurt.

Earthquakes tear at the matrices of roots that wire gradients together. Hillsides—unsecured and destabilized, their soil loosened from the bedrock—require only a little lubricating rain to get launched; gravity does the rest.

The rain came on Boxing Day. Metzler's second dispatch, sent during the final hours of the millennium (when other South Sea islanders, in floral crowns and grass skirts, prepared to celebrate the new era for a worldwide television audience), reported catastrophic landslides. "Paama is in bad shape!" Still he reported no casualties— but added that Liro had been served with a mandatory government evacuation order.

"A fifty-metre-wide river of mud, stones (car-sized) and trees runs down to the sea," he told the Zuikers. "Your old house is knee-deep, the soccer ground is covered." He said the airfield, though bombarded with rocks, remained operational; more slides were feared. "The official word is that the government wants to move the villages which are in danger—but the stupid thing is no one will leave, they just say they'll make *kastom* and it will stop." Liro's people proved to be the most stubborn. Metzler, begging them to go, was being frustrated by an official named Holi Simon who insisted they remain where they were. "He's telling everyone they're OK, that they'll send food and it will be all right!"

I pictured the desolation. The "soccer ground" had been a paddock extending all the way from the guest house to the black beach. But what of the families living behind it, what of the clinic—and the church? Imagining it buried, flattened or swept out to sea, I asked my wife, "So what do we do with a two-thousand-quid bell nobody wants?" She said, "Hang it outside the front door."

I needed information and, knowing the *efil* was still open, faxed Norm Sanson. Practical as ever, he faxed back saying he would arrange to take the next Paama flight up himself—and if I wanted to contact anyone in Liro, should send him a "tick-the-box-type questionnaire." Yet a postscript contained more grim news. "Last night our first cyclone of the season passed close to Paama, no doubt exacerbating their problems."

Three natural disasters in a calendar month! How might Maurice have explained that? My scribbled communiqué to *Jif* Louis, after questions about himself and his family, concluded with:

Is the church still there? YES NO IT IS DAMAGED
If damaged, will you build it again? YES NO MAYBE
Do you still want the bell? YES NO SOME DAY

Norm, however, chose to show it to the VIP passenger riding in his second-pilot's seat. Holi Simon, who had enraged Metzler by urging everyone in Liro to stay put, turned out to be Vanuatu's Deputy Commissioner of Police, and a Liro man himself. He took out his pen and, there and then, produced a crisp ten-point summary—which Norm faxed back to me. Only the final point was positive: "The Maurice Frater Memorial Church is still standing. And they still need the bell you promised." This time Norm's postscript brought better news: Cyclone Iris, while damaging several islands nearby, had merely dumped rain on Paama.

Out of the blue, I received an e-mail from Holi Simon—a man I had never met.

"Happy New Year to you, Alex and family! Greetings from the people of Paama to you all!" After listing, village by village, the lost houses, he itemized the damage. It seemed anything left by the earthquake had been buried by the landslide. The tally of food gardens destroyed now came to 98 per cent, along with 90 per cent of "the water system" (a well supplying the Liro clinic had vanished beneath a torrent of mud, capped and sealed forever).

Now, though, they had acquired "chainsaws, a bulldozer, a truck, tarpaulins and vegetable seedlings." Supplies were promised by the French and New Zealand governments, Paama Disaster Committees had been set up in places as far away as New Caledonia. The first task was to ensure the school term started on schedule, the next to get community services functioning again. Everyone was working

very hard. He urged me to bring the bell and "visit old friends." He
concluded:

> Thank you for your precious time taken to read this note.
> Yours in His service
> Holi Simon (Man Paama)
> Deputy Commissioner of Police
> Port Vila
> Vanuatu.

*

Early in the first quarter of 2000, when delivery had been promised,
I learned from Mr Brewis that certain big jobs ("A fifty-eight-bell order
from *New York*!") kept pushing mine to the back of the queue. Holi,
echoing the expectations of the Liro folk, was impatient for news. As
time passed his messages grew fewer then—perhaps suspecting they
had been the victims of a practical joke—stopped altogether. I grew
fretful. My wife, exasperated, wanted me to cancel the bell and demand
my money back.

Sara, at the BBC, grew anxious. "They want to schedule the programmes. What should I tell them?"

"Not to hold their breath. Tell them the potential for things going
wrong is virtually unlimited."

I received a note from Alan Hughes, a Whitechapel director, asking
for the inscription. "Please remember that the bell is small and the
available space is therefore limited." My family, knowing no words we
had ever written would last as long as these, kept it simple: "Remem-
bering Maurice and Janie Frater · Liro 2000 AD." After I sent it in, he
typed it out and sent it back for final, *eternal* confirmation. I approved
of such attention to detail, while Mr Brewis regarded it as a positive
move. "We're getting close!"

From the Banks Line I obtained the sailing dates of their Port Vila
ships. E-mailing the news to Holi I told him, for the first time, about
the radio project. Sara I described in quasi-Reithian terms: a gifted,
resourceful, hard-working, widely respected producer wholly commit-
ted to the principles of public-service broadcasting. All true; her youth
and general sparkle they could discover for themselves. His response,
nervously awaited, was one of pleasure; everyone looked forward to

welcoming my "BBC delegation." Meals would be prepared by the Liro Community. "Transport by land will be provided by the Paama District Administrator, Mr. Redy Henry, and Sea Transport by Mr. Matias Andrew. All these will be free of charge. Elder White Yangen and Deacon Donald Nos have made seven announcements in the Church about your visit and are now awaiting confirmation on the dates. Best wishes, Your friend, Holi Simon."

I told Sara the way now seemed clear. She said, "Great. Let's get those dates sorted. People here are getting restless."

Airline seats were booked, along with rooms on Iririki. The BBC's insurance department asked her to list any hazards that might be encountered on the journey. She said, "I've told them about the diseases. But is there anything else?"

"Hurricanes and volcanic eruptions are possible. There's an outside chance of an earthquake, perhaps even a tidal wave."

"I see. And what kind of ship are we going to Paama on?"

"Some kind of copra steamer. Small."

"Will it have lifeboats?"

"Lifeboats!" The idea made me smile. "No."

"Should I put down sharks?"

"Yes, sharks would probably be a good idea."

She sighed. "This damn bell better be worth it."

*

Mr Brewis called one humid, overcast morning with thunder in the air. "You want the good news or the bad news?"

I took a deep breath. "Go ahead."

"It's ready! And, I must say, it sounds very sweet."

"But?"

"We forgot the inscription."

It took a second to sink in. *"Forgot?"*

"Must have slipped somebody's mind. But don't worry, we'll engrave it instead."

Wearily I said, "Mr Brewis, I want exactly what I ordered, a proper *inscribed* bell. You'll have to make me another one."

"It'll take at least a couple of weeks."

That meant it would miss the next boat.

"Air freight is the answer."

"Jesus! What's that going to cost?"

"Our transport specialists can tell you. But first they'll need the name and address of someone in Port Vila—a consignee who'll take delivery and deal with the paperwork."

I nominated my old friend Kal Kalsakau. His company, the magisterially named Cabinet d'Affaires du Pacifique, dealers in "Real Estate & Custom Lands," also acted as commercial agents.

Then a thought occurred. "What about instructions for getting it assembled and hung?"

"Full guidance notes will be packed with the bell."

"Guaranteed?"

"Absolutely. It's standard practice."

*

Many early bell-makers—who included St Dunstan and St Ethelwold—were itinerants who gathered their materials while travelling from job to job. In 1322 John of Gloucester, summoned to Ely to cast four large bourdon bells, got his copper in Northampton, and the reeds for his furnace—which he probably set up in the cathedral yard—around Thorney. During the Reformation, when all bells were forfeit to the Crown, their export was banned.

*

Kal phoned late on the evening of the day it was supposed to arrive in Port Vila. "There's no sign of it. We've ransacked the airport and, I promise, it wasn't on the plane."

My knees went shaky. "What do we do now?"

"I need the papers. The documentation you mentioned. From Whitechapel? They might tell us where to start looking."

"You should have had that ages ago."

"I've had nothing."

I rang Mr Brewis. "It hasn't arrived in Vila. And now Mr Kalsakau tells me he wasn't sent any documentation."

"Yes, he was. It's all packed in the box muzzle."

"Box muzzle?"

"It's with the bell."

"Mr Brewis, the bell is lost."

"Oh!" The distress evident in his voice—he plainly hoped he'd heard the last of me—was magnified furiously by Sara. "We're supposed to be flying out next week! They've already scheduled the programmes."

"Kal's on the case. It's got to be somewhere."

The days passed. As Sara's department heads badgered her, she badgered me; meanwhile the balance of the money, including freight, was being demanded by Mr Hughes; should we pay up? ("Should we *what*?" said my wife.)

Kal came through early one morning. "It's in Fiji."

"Fiji?" There was a nasty civil war going on in Fiji. "What the hell's it doing there?"

"Search me. Just by chance a friend happened to notice it in the Nandi cargo terminal, and saw it with my name on it. Air Vanuatu have cancelled all flights, but tomorrow they're laying on a special. To bring some stranded people home. He'll put it on that."

"Definitely?"

"It will be here by dinnertime."

I reminded him that, in a few days, I would be in a position to personally buy him a drink.

*

Port Vila, when we flew in on a sunny afternoon, had the shine of a town recently hosed by tropical rain. From Iririki I phoned and proposed a beer; he had meetings for the rest of the day, but suggested we come to his office next morning. Meanwhile the bell, safely in storage, would sail with us the following night. "You're due off at ten o'clock," he said. "From Star Wharf."

With an hour of daylight left I took Sara for a stroll through Vila and, proprietorially, as if showing off an ancestral estate, waited for her approval. Finally she said, "It's a bit *ramshackle*." Seeing it afresh through her eyes, I conceded that, yes, a lick of paint would not go amiss. "And the traffic!" The traffic, in truth, was terrible. "There are a lot more tourists than I'd expected." The tourists, merging with the vegetation to form a fuzzy, ill-defined background, had never really registered with me. On the Rue Higginson she took a digital recorder and a microphone from her bag. "Like to describe it?" I said I'd like to jot down a

few ideas first. She said, "It's probably better off the top of your head."
I described it, then, in her pale, strained smile, detected signs of real
alarm. But she spoke calmly. "Great! Want to try again?"

Meanwhile, where was Holi Simon? A man answering the phone at
Vila's police station said he had left the country, and Kal, ushering us
into his office next morning, thought this entirely possible. "Holi gets
about." He had, I noted, turned greyer and gained weight. "For you
there's been a change of plan. You're sailing in two hours. My assistant
is taking the bell down to Star Wharf right now."

"What's the rush?" asked Sara.

"The skippers are all chasing copra, they'd kill their first-born for a
consignment. Yours has probably just got some news."

I asked, "What's the ship?"

"Big one. The *Kimbe,* two hundred tons."

"The *Kimbe!* That used to be owned by Guy Benard. I once had
dinner with him. He brought her out from France, she's a gravel
carrier."

"Not any more." He handed me a letter. "The captain will ask for
this." Typed entirely in capitals, signed by Capt. Leith Nasak and Capt.
Gideon Kidley of the Western Pacific Marine, it was our boarding pass
to Paama.

Sara and I arrived at Star Wharf thirty minutes before departure
and, but for a twitching, wild-eyed man wolfing down a loaf of bread
under a tree, found the sun-blasted acre of concrete deserted. I asked
him what had happened to the *Kimbe.*

"Gone."

"Gone when?"

Cramming a crust in his mouth he gave me an oblique, oddly unfocused look; now I saw he had early cataracts. "Long time."

Sara, noting a giant light-diffracting spider's web in the tree under
which he sat, said, "Gosh, that's amazing. Want to tell me about it?"

Kal, perhaps the most easy-going person I'd ever known, displayed
signs of agitation when we reached his office. "I know! I heard! She was
just pulling out when my man arrived. They took the bell, but they
wouldn't wait for you."

"Can we talk to the skipper?"

"He's switched his radio off. The owners say he'll only switch it back on at sunset, we'll get him to pick you up at Lamen Bay, Epi. He should get there in about two days. You really need to go up tomorrow—but there's no plane till Monday."

This was Thursday. "The bell's being handed over on Sunday. Big service, special occasion."

Sara said, "And they'll need all of Saturday to get it assembled and hung."

"I understand that! I'm still thinking!" Now we were treated to the sight of this famously imperturbable man furiously rubbing his forehead. "We'll have to organize a diversion." He glanced anxiously at his watch. "But we can only do that at the airport."

There a cocky, heavily bearded young duty officer told us all northbound services were fully booked. Kal appeared not to hear. "My friends have to go to Lamen Bay tomorrow. They'll need seats on the early Santo plane, and the pilot will have to make a special stop." The Duty Officer gave a sardonic laugh. Kal took him by the elbow and led him away, returned moments later to say space had suddenly become available. Having added the diversion fee to the fares, he now came up with the grand total. "If you give me the money I'll see to it."

We gave him the money.

"There's also the question of getting back," I said.

"Scheduled flight from Paama on Tuesday. You're already booked."

I'd forgotten to mention that Tuesday happened to be the day we were due to head home to London. With our transmission dates horribly tight (programme details already faxed to the *Radio Times*) and more recording to be done in Vila, we wanted, if possible, to be off the island just hours after the bell's christening. "In on Saturday, out on Sunday. Sorry, mate." Calmly he said, "I'll do what I can," and walked off.

Sara blinked. "What an extraordinary man."

She already knew something about Kal. Born into a chiefly family, sent to my old Presbyterian boarding school in Melbourne (flogging being part of the core curriculum), he helped oversee Vanuatu's transition to independence and been appointed its first Finance Minister. Bored by politics, he returned to his home island, Ifira, and using island assets lying moribund in various half-forgotten bank accounts, built a nationwide trading company, with the profits created a welfare system for Ifira so enlightened it became a benchmark for communities throughout the Pacific. Now an elder statesman, a Melanesian patriarch and, naturally, a pillar of the Church, he commanded a lot of respect. "I suppose the Vanair Duty Officer finally realized who he was. And guessed the chiefs who own the airline would hate to upset him."

She said, "At least you'll finally get to see your bell."

"Maybe." I imagined it somewhere at sea, in the charge of a misanthropic, radiophobic master mariner obsessively sniffing the wind for coconut meat. Meanwhile, with an unexpected free afternoon, there was work to be done.

Reece Discombe, charmed by Sara, gave us orange pekoe tea, toasted buns and a ripping interview. A burly, charismatic old Aussie who first turned up in 1945 looking for salvage, he'd found such an abundance of sunken ships and other war-surplus materiel he never left. With his strong, growly voice and a vast portfolio of stories (recounted among the polished diving helmets, now displayed as decorative artefacts, in which he'd once walked the seabed), he was the first port of call for any media people arriving in Vila.

Though he claimed to have liked my father, his attitude to missionaries in general was hostile; evidently convinced that I, a chip off the old block, had become a closet proselytizer, he liked to mount the occasional sly attack. Today it came in anecdotal form. Noisily clearing his throat ("You'll enjoy this, Alex"), he said that, recently, while up in Santo recovering bodies from a World War Two bomber—in his eighties, he was working still—he'd come across a crowd of bush pygmies who stood "about a metre high." It was one of those moments anthropologists dream about, yet this lost Stone Age tribe all wore promotional T-shirts bearing the name—and web site details—of an ambitious, jungle-bashing American evangelist whose freelance activities were causing real alarm. I asked: Alarm to who? He smiled: Why, naturally, my friends and fellow-dissemblers, the mission establishment in Vila.

Sara, delighted, kept him talking for an hour—high-calibre stuff absolutely terrific for radio. Then he took me onto the terrace and pointed across to my birthplace. "Iririki was bought by a French speculator in 1850—but not for long. Your Presbyterians hung him up in chains till he'd pulled out of the deal . . ."

I laughed. "Oh, come on, Reece."

". . . literally left the poor bugger dangling from a tree. The French called it the British Isle, and that passage where all the yachts are was known as the English Channel. Down there, some years ago, I taught Sir David Attenborough to waterski."

At the airport, shortly after dawn, we found Kal chatting animatedly to an animated, amused-looking man wearing beautifully cut casual clothes; as they walked towards us I noted his easy air of authority. "Meet Holi Simon," Kal said. Delighted, I wrung Holi's hand. "Does this mean you're coming with us?"

"No, no," he laughed. "Later today I must go to New Guinea for a regional security conference; orders from the PM himself. But all is ready on Paama, you will be met by joyful crowds. And the *Kimbe* will collect you first thing tomorrow. Orders have been given. If the captain forgets we'll feed him to the fishes."

Holi's eyes shone with a humour and shrewdness not normally found among Melanesian police. The flight was called, people surged forward. Kal, brushing aside our thanks, said, "By the way, I've organized your trip back. You're coming with a friend of mine. On Sunday afternoon he's going to take his little seaplane up to Liro Bay and pick you up from the beach."

*

Lamen Bay was irradiated by sunlight and floored with fluorescent white sand; a dozen yachts lay moored precisely over their own shadows. I'd stayed at the Paradise Sunset Bungalows two years earlier and recalled that Tasso, the owner, knew many people on Paama—which lay only a dozen miles away. Now, as we strolled on the beach, I discovered he also knew a surprising amount about the bell. "From the same UK factory as Big Ben—we'll probably hear it over here! It's coming on the *Kimbe,* uh?"

"I hope so. When do you think she'll turn up?"

"Maybe tonight." Then he surprised me. "The new church at Liro is very nice. I was at the opening service—May 13. Truly a happy day. I went over in my launch." He pointed to a battered little metal boat upended, like storm wreckage, on the sand.

I gaped. "You went to Paama in *that?*"

"Sure. Also I took twenty people, a bullock and a pig." He had a richly amused laugh. "But it need two trips."

We came upon a burly man asleep in a hammock. Slack-mouthed and dribbling spit, hand cupped over his genitals, he lay in a narcoleptic stupor so profound he barely seemed to breathe.

"Is he all right?" I asked, concerned.

"Of course! Actually, he's a cop—on duty, too."

The police, he explained, while occasionally required to shoot a mad dog, or deal with aggressive drunks, mostly passed their days fishing or resting. "There is little crime here: what's the point? We have all we need, God provides." Anyone caught doing something bad, he added, would be packed off to Vila.

Once, in Vila, I heard a Radio Vanuatu announcer telling a suspected axe-murderer to get on a boat, come in and give himself up. Even men summoned from the most distant atolls always appeared eventually; it was *kastom* and practice. Aitutaki, in the Cook Islands, possessed no jail—only an unlocked room behind the post office where people checked themselves in and stayed until they felt comfortable about coming out. On Anguilla I learned about prisoners who broke out—to see friends, have a drink, visit the market—but then, without fail, broke back in again.

Tasso went for his siesta leaving me thinking about tropical criminality. A late afternoon sun gave Lamen Bay such dazzle the yachts now seemed weightless, chained down by their anchors. The word "transparent" came to mind—appropriate for a region where heat and humidity determined everything from housing to social interaction; people left their doors and windows open, wore loose clothes or no clothes at all, bathed together in seas and rivers, worked together in fields or gardens, lived their lives largely in the public domain. The privacy needed for the pursuit of crime was entirely alien to the transparency of the tropics—yet in certain areas, where God either hadn't provided wisely, or made the wrong kind of provision, crime was booming. So where had the Lord's plan gone wrong?

In Jamaica I was told by an airport cab driver that I should be wearing body armour; if this was a joke he certainly wasn't smiling. Here I found nervous tourists staying in impregnable, ring-fenced little city states which sought to evoke the lifestyles of the old plantocracies: no slaves, naturally, but plenty of smiling blacks who dispensed rum punches and called the women "mistress." (No Rastas either, no dreadlocks, no drug mules, no smack, no spliffs, no *nothin'* like that.)

Its edgy American vacationers depended on an excellent daily paper, the *Gleaner*, for information on events beyond the security guards and razor-wire. What were those crazy Jamaicans up to now?

The day I arrived they planned to welcome the Queen to Kingston. And, in case its readers mistook HMS *Lancaster*'s twenty-one-gun salute for yet another Yardie shoot-out, the paper urged them "not to be alarmed; only blank ceremonial rounds will be used." Normal life went on. Teachers and medical technologists planned a one-day strike. Police investigating a baby-stealing ring sought "a man who washes cars on Constant Spring Road." Health Minister Desmond Leakey—pictured rinsing his mouth as pensively as if tasting claret—attended the Jamaica launch of Listerine Cool Mint. A Kingston headmaster had received death-threats from the drug-pushers against whom he was waging a relentless campaign.

I stayed in the Good Hope Great House, a handsome Palladian structure overlooking the verdant Parish of Trelawney. Built by a white Jamaican-born sugar baron educated at Eton and Trinity College, Cambridge, it was now being run as a small, very exclusive hotel. Servant girls sang "The Holly and the Ivy" as they prepared dinner then, padding across a wild-orange-wood floor (which, having been polished for two hundred years by slaves, or the descendants of slaves, had the patina of an old violin), set the tables with crystal glasses, silver cutlery and white napery. A stout Dallas widow who visited regularly gave a contented little sigh. "This, my dear, is the real Jamaica."

Next morning, the *Gleaner*'s Letter of the Day said: "When I was in school I was proud to say: Tram, tram, tram, Jamaica marches on. On we go upon the road to glory. At the moment we are having an average of two murders a day. We shoot, rape and rob tourists . . . We have marched into a situation where the name Jamaica, when mentioned abroad, is enough to make others shiver . . . Let us shake off the shackles of death and destruction and get back on the road to prosperity where again we can say: Tram, tram, tram, Jamaica marches on."

Prince Philip, visiting a youth club, was serenaded with a rap version of "Don't Badda Wid De Coke, Jus Dash Away De Crack."

A local journalist told me, "America is now sending back all known criminals of Jamaican ancestry. These people may have lived in the States for two generations or more, and know nothing about Jamaica at all; they're just Yankee trash."

At his Port Antonio ranch Errol Flynn, noting the way bananas were shipped down the Rio Grande, conceived the idea of putting tourists on bamboo rafts. Now the owner of a roadside jerk joint, serving spicy grilled meat only yards from the wreckage of a drug-runner's crashed Cessna, said that recently gunmen had been taking pot-shots at the rafters. "So for the time being, my man, normal services are suspended."

*

As dusk fell on Lamen Bay two Australian couples in their early fifties landed from a blue-hulled schooner for a seafood dinner cooked by Tasso's wife. One of the men, tall and pot-bellied with a long, fleshy face, told me he worked for the Federal government but, teasingly, would say no more. So, over a chilled Tusker, finding out about Eric's role in his nation's affairs became a game of twenty questions. It emerged over the second beer.

Eric was a cop.

His friend said, "But Eric's only interested in the big picture. He goes to overseas security conferences—flies business class, thanks to us taxpayers—and makes policy recommendations to Canberra. Don't you, mate?"

Eric nodded. "In a nutshell."

"Ever come across a guy named Holi Simon?" I asked.

"Holi? Sure." He gave me an interested look. "He should be off to Moresby around now; I managed to slide out of that one. How come you know him?"

As soon as the bell was mentioned Eric's wife, owner of a North Sydney shoe shop, interrupted. With her spiky hair and intense manner, she wanted to know—if I didn't mind her asking—what it had cost. When I told her, she muttered, "Cripes, couldn't you beat them down a bit?" I found myself defending my purchase, a quality product built to last, even comparing it with the famously cheap, stupendously loud Victorian steel bells which, making a noise like colliding trains (each collision had a different tone and key), were judged to be an important technological breakthrough. Nobody, though, had given much thought to rust or corrosion, and in time they had to be abandoned—as did the 1947 instrument cast controversially from aluminium. (Looking chic and *very* twentieth century, its peal resembled the clanging of saucepans.)

Finishing my drink, I asked Eric which countries hosted the best security conferences. Malaysia, Kenya, Ecuador and Laos had his vote—all, it occurred to me, lying within the tropics. "So, obviously," I surmised, "there is such a thing as tropical crime."

"Are you *kidding*?" He began lecturing me: a cancer out of control, a spreading culture of lawlessness, political and military sponsorship at the highest levels—then, catching a warning glance from his wife (who saw me fumbling for my notebook), fell silent.

I said, "Well, could you define its nature?"

"OK, fair question. If we're going right back to basics, I'd say its causes were mostly agricultural."

Jerry, his friend, asked, "We're talking funny crops?"

"Not entirely. In many places it was—still is—to do with land. Take Lamen Bay here: strong community, families who've worked their gardens for generations, enough food to go round, everyone secure. But say, some day, all that changes. The kids drift off to the cities and find that opportunities for young, barely literate subsistence farmers are limited. Also, they'll want a commodity they never really *needed* before. Money. How do they get that? These country boys and girls may not be criminals, but they can start some interesting little crime waves."

Jerry said, "And remember what they had here before. God provides, but actually it was the tropics that did that, looked after their every need; from birth to death they were fed, housed and clothed, free of charge. Christ, they even provided free healthcare. If you were feeling crook the bush was your chemist, open twenty-four hours a day; you just popped down and helped yourself. And if anyone wanted specialist help, well, the fee for a witch doctor was a yam."

"Or a pig," I said.

"Or, for a big job, a wife."

Both wives smiled faintly.

He concluded, "So what was the point of money?"

Eric said, "Some adapted better than others. There's a story about a Chinese trader who opened a store in the Solomons. And one day he thought: These people are so ignorant I'll double my prices; they don't understand financial matters, they'll never even notice. But they did! And they collected all their money—every last farthing—and chucked it in the sea. The Chinaman was ruined."

Liking that tropical solution to an example of mean-spirited tropical exploitation, I asked what he made of Jamaica.

"Aw, look, Jamaica was always *about* money. An economy built on slavery? The forests that once supported the Caribs were cleared centuries ago for plantations (a few whites got very rich), so we can forget about God providing. Anyway, the population's now closing on three million and the labour market's swamped. So, if you can't get a job, what do you do?"

"Drugs are nature's bounty now," said Jerry.

"Yeah, and the trade puts food in an awful lot of mouths."

Jerry's earnest, plump Asian wife said, "It's still a nice spot. We've watched test matches there, I'd go back at the drop of a hat."

"But there are areas of Kingston," said Eric, "you should avoid after dark. Crime in the tropics? A lot of cities are reaching bursting point, crammed to the gunwales with desperate people. Kingston's just one. Anyone thinking of taking an evening stroll around, say, Bogotá, or Lagos, or Djakarta, or many other sinkholes I could mention, should carry a gun."

As they drifted off to eat I compiled my own list. Guyana's capital, Georgetown, had fine boulevards, a cathedral built entirely from tropical hardwoods, some arrestingly named districts—Ogle, Vigilance, Vryheid's Lust—and the world's lowest cricket ground. (Six feet below sea level, it produces freak atmospheric conditions that enable fast bowlers to perform with unparalleled viciousness; goat racing has a big following when no cricket is played.) Georgetown may be intimate and pretty yet, according to my guidebook, it was also the most dangerous city in South America.

One night, at a party, I asked an elegant woman wearing a black mantilla if this was true. She shrugged and told me that at home a

few months earlier, hearing screams, she had raced downstairs to
find her eighty-seven-year-old mother being pistol-whipped by two
male intruders; in the ensuing gun battle she shot them both dead.
"Ma refused to tell them where the safe was. They were country people. They always seem to operate in pairs. On the streets too." There,
using a technique called "choke and rob" (one goes for your wind-
pipe, the other your wallet), muggers had given Georgetown a siege
atmosphere.

In Antananarivo, Madagascar's acclivitous little capital, the Zoma
market bandits, circling like sharks, worked openly and in threes.
(Uncertain what to do when a trio began circling me, I doffed my hat
and made a theatrical bow; acknowledging this bravado with faintly
ironic nods, they slipped away.) Here, one night on the ill-lit Avenue
de l'Independence, listening to a sightless old man loudly declaiming
from a Braille Bible, I felt a sudden wetness on my hand and, reaching
a shop window, saw blood—a deep cut on the inside of my wrist. Yet
it had been done so fast, and with a blade so sharp, I hadn't felt a thing.
The nurse who dressed it said somebody, wanting my watch, had tried
to slash the strap.

Now, applying Eric's causal theory to the stabbing, I came up with
laterite rock; whoever did this had been driven to crime by its steel-
hard amalgamate of aluminium and iron hydroxide (valued by the
Khmer builders of Angkor Wat), unique to the tropics and containing
not a single element assimilable by plants. Gourou says that, due to this
"pedological leprosy," only thirty thousand square miles of Madagascar's two hundred and twenty-eight thousand are cultivable. Indeed,
part of the Malagas *tampoketsa* is so impermeable the peasants must
practise pot culture: chipping away with a spade they make a hole, fill
it with excrement and plant their seeds.

What kid would want a future like that? Add laterite to the woes
induced by deforestation, erosion, floods, droughts—and all the other
consequences of climate change—and the gravitational tug of the cities
becomes almost irresistible. Some tropical regions may, eventually,
contain rural settlements inhabited only by the sick, the idle, the old
and infirm.

*

At Lamen Bay a minimal surf broke with small crystalline sounds, hot embers of sunset smudged the horizon—but not a trace of ship's smoke. Where was my bell?

I found Sara in a dining room crowded with rowdy, hard-drinking yachties; a handwritten notice on the wall warned:

> *Jesus Christ*
> *Is the Head of this House*
> *The Unseen Guest at every meal*
> *The Silent Listener to every conversation.*

She sat with a cheery young Canadian couple who, during a week at Lamen Bay, had been woken twice by volcanic bombs on Lopevi, just across the water. They warned that the copra boats never lingered. "Keep your eyes skinned because they're not gonna come looking for you. If you're not on the beach, ready and waiting, they'll head right off."

"The captain's been told not to go without us."

"Told?" They exchanged knowing little smiles. "By who? Away from head office, those guys are a law unto themselves."

Tasso brought me a plate of grilled barracuda. I asked, "Any word on the *Kimbe*?"

"I think she arrive soon. But you must keep checking."

So, several times during the night, tireless Sara tapped at my door and led me, mutinous and groaning, to the lookout point. Since there was no sign of any vessel I had to provide narrative updates ("It's three in the morning and the sky is ablaze with stars"), along with descriptive stuff done by torchlight ("Here we have the tracks, I think, of a coconut crab").

The *Kimbe* anchored at five, a grey tender approached over a lumpy grey sea. "Hullo, Frater!" said the coxswain. As we hopped in he said, "Your bell is on the ship." I said, good-oh, but when would the ship get to Paama? He hesitated. "Today." I said, "What *time* today?" Sara said, "That's nice, keep chatting," but I was distracted by the ocean swells, and the lumpen, waterlogged way the *Kimbe* rolled about in them. Though small and squat, she was alarmingly high-sided. "So how do we get aboard?" He did not meet my eye. "There is a ladder."

We heard it before we saw it, a clanging piece of dangling scrap iron hung so high it was only accessible during the instant a wave peaked; then, using the wave's momentum, you leaped for the bottom rung and went up hand over hand. We drew alongside and I became aware of several simultaneous, but contradictory, forces at work: violent lateral ones caused by our swell-driven collisions with the hull, the hull's own rotational pitching and yawing and the vertical yo-yo motion of the surging tender.

Sara sprang like a lemur and, in a trice, had hauled herself to safety. "What a hoot!" she called. "Want to say something?" A wave came, the tender ascended and, even as the coxswain yelled "Now!" I glimpsed an elderly face, unshaven and bespectacled, glaring down from the bridge. This would be the same *kaptin* we had been pursuing for days, and a gust of rage sent me scrabbling up over his blooming rust and blistered paint. The instant my feet touched his filthy, junk-cluttered deck he began putting to sea.

In a tiny saloon several weary sailors, sprawled across Guy Benard's battered French upholstery, devoured huge breakfasts of rice and rancid boiled squid. *"Yu wantem sam kakae?"* enquired the cook. We said no, but he went to the galley and made us *kofe*. Then, for no apparent reason, the sailors all suddenly dropped their plates and shot out the door. Following, we found ourselves entering a small bay; on the beach a smoky fire burned, on deck a slight, smiling figure said, "Hullo, Frater, my name is Frank, I am the navigator, and Man Paama also." The fire, he added, signified there was copra waiting ashore.

As the tender charged in I saw smoke drifting from other bays, and knew we would reach Liro so late there would be little time for preparations. Frank read my mind. "You are worried about your bell. But we will cross at full speed. Tomorrow maybe the crew will come to church. I would like to be there. *My father was your grandaddy's boatman.*" He beamed while telling me that, and I was touched to hear it. (Sara, recording, gave a small nod of approval.) Now, back in Maurice's orbit, I felt a familiar sense of reality suspended, of stumbling about in a dead man's shoes—or big mission-issue boots—and worried again about what people would think when I showed up with a woman young enough to be my daughter.

But Frank, as I made the introductions, seemed very pleased to see her. "BBC, eh?" he murmured, and let out a soft whistle. Its World

Service, I was reminded, enjoyed such a reputation throughout the tropics that here and there the Corporation's pens—standard plastic rollerballs stamped with the triple-squared logo—were traded as currency. (In inflation-ridden Zambia a BBC pen had parity with chicken, in economically ruined Uganda—according to one reliable source—it could buy a woman.) Nation Speaking Unto Nation was what the BBC did, and on Paama, I realized, Sara would inspire respect; here, of all places, they were likely to appreciate the apostolic nature of her job—just as they would approve of our sleeping arrangements. They'd given me a billet somewhere in the village, and her the mission guest house; immensely entertained by my old-fogeyish anxiety, she had suggested we meet for Sunday breakfast in our pyjamas.

(Meanwhile, she'd arrived with several dozen BBC *pencils*. Radio being the poor relation—expected to make do with graphite while television hogged all the ink—they were all she could find when raiding the office stationery cupboard.)

Frank, untroubled by the microphone, described how whales often showed off their calves while passing Paama, tossing them in the air if you sang them a particular song. (Gravely he sang it for her.) When working, he said, he had little use for maps; six hundred thousand square miles of reef-strewn ocean containing three hundred islands, atolls, cays, rocks and sandbars were imprinted on his brain. Like the old Pacific canoemen with their stick charts, he knew where he was just by the sea's motion and temperament. The captain, meanwhile, skulked in his wheelhouse as on deck a dozen passengers dozed on mats and pillows embroidered with flowers and exhortatory messages: "Praise the Lord," "Dream of Jesus," "Love me tonight."

Finally the *Kimbe,* rolling around in waves high as houses, set off for Paama. Liro Bay, early in the afternoon, was flat as a fishpond, while Liro village, once quake-stricken and mud-ravaged, looked prosperous and prettier than ever. Yet, tucked away beneath its looming green mountain, it also looked empty. Where were Holi Simon's "joyous crowds"? As we watched our cargo—my first actual sighting of it—being winched into the tender, Frank muttered, "Saturday afternoon. Siesta time."

Ashore, the racket of its departing engine woke a boy asleep under a tree. Seeing an ageing, unshaven white man breathlessly wrestling a church bell up the beach, he jumped to his feet and ran away. The bell's silvery body, like a helmet set on a casket of ashes, was bolted to a pinewood box containing its constituent parts. As, squatting, I pondered it, Sara asked, "What do we do now?" I shrugged. At this point I had half-promised her some kind of welcome, perhaps even an appearance by the Paama Soul Singers; Liro's celebrated male-voice choir had, I suspected, formed a key part of her programme submission at Broadcasting House. She was standing by the sea recording the surf when the boy returned with a couple of friends. *"Gudaftenun,"* they said.

I said, *"Alo, fellers, nem blong mi Alex, nem blong woman ia Sara* from the BBC *mi wantem toktok long Jif Louis, plis."*

Louis, evidently, was resting. Well, could they help me lug this up to the church? And there, as it sat on the grass, people began turning up to inspect it. *"Smol, smol,"* murmured a beefy matriarch with shorn hair. I could see its size for myself and, irritated, invited her to test its weight. Even as she reached down—and I knew she would lift it like a bowl of fruit—an assertive young man arrived with a bag of tools. "This could be complicated work," he said to me. "You bring some literature?"

"It's in the box."

As he unbolted the bell he told me he was teacher at Liro's secondary school. Founded by Maurice, it had grown into a centre of excellence attracting bright kids from many neighbouring islands. Feeling a small surge of cognatic pride I helped him lift off the bell and crack open the box. Several dozen spectators had gathered as we extracted a coil of polypropylene rope with its red-white-and-blue sally, a pair of iron bookends, a spanner-like object, a fishing reel, packages of lock nuts, grub screws, washers and bolts. "We'll need diagrams for this," he said. Yes, indeedy! But when, finally, the box lay empty, it was clear we had nothing of the kind. "Christ!" I marvelled. *"They forgot the fucking instructions!"* People tut-tutted, but it was the profanity, rather than the obscenity, that distressed them; to these unworldly folk the latter might have been a pleasantry in, say, Swahili or Deep Wolof. Even while regretting both I wondered, furiously, how that Whitechapel mob had managed to keep trading for four hundred and thirty years.

Louis joined us. So did other white-bearded *jifs* and their frail consorts, the women in Mother Hubbards so stiffly starched they could have served as splints to keep them upright—Liro's aristocracy come to stare at a £2,000 piece of acoustic hardware that lay, mute and useless, in a quiet corner of their churchyard. Sara, who had flown twelve thousand miles to make *The Story of a Bell,* quietly asked if the bell could be rung. The clapper, I pointed, had been pre-attached; we'd get a sound all right, but would it ever peal and chime? She gave a tiny sigh of relief. "Just one clang will do."

The headstock, a length of sturdy machined metal, came fixed to the crown; lashed to the headstock was a twelve-inch iron bar with its ends bent in contrary directions. The bookends turned out to be bearings; they, along with the spanner-like lever, seemed to belong to the headstock. The reel, plainly, was the pulley that governed the rope— but where did we attach it, and how should the rope be anchored? The nuts, bolts and grub screws had purposes we could not fathom; the role of the bent iron bar remained a mystery. Sara made various suggestions, most (it emerged when "Notes of Guidance for the Installation of the Bell" finally reached me in London), on the right track. I was overcome, ultimately, by a strain of tropical bacteria which attacks the brain cells responsible for maintaining mental alertness—or, if you've been infected as badly as me, staying awake and trying to look interested.

*

Eighteenth-century headstocks, made and assembled by hand, featured stockhoops, straps, strap nuts, stays, soles, argent loops, dog plates, fillet holes, gudgeons, shroudboards and wheels of oak and ash. This one, by contrast, looked like a component machined for a missile. (Yet the foundryman who cast my bell, having first slagged the molten metal to remove impurities, then—like John of Gloucester in 1322— poled it with a willow branch: burning willow releases salicylic acid, a flux which aids fusion.)

*

As I slumped back others stepped forward. There was no attempt at debate, just advice and opinions offered by people all speaking at once. Much talk concerned the bent iron bar and, quite soon, a consensus developed: throw it away. Then I saw *Jif* Andrew Manoa, a bearded patriarch, beckon the boys who had met us on the beach. They slipped off to the bush and returned with two young rose-apple trees. Cut to equal lengths, trimmed and grooved, they were driven into the ground and a piece of metal piping laid between the two. "Bring the bell," commanded *Jif* Andrew. Using bits of frayed rope spliced to the head-stock, they got it hung.

"*Finis,*" he said.

It looked absurd. Everyone applauded.

"Will it work?" asked Sara.

"Only if you hold the clapper in your hand." I warned that a technique very similar to this had resulted in the destruction of the Liberty Bell. "It's called clocking; and if you get it wrong it'll crack like an egg."

"Can you ring it now?" enquired *Jif* Andrew.

"I suppose once wouldn't hurt. Shall we give it a try?"

"Hang on, I want to get this," said Sara.

An expectant hush fell. Fruit doves could be heard calling on the mountain as, taking a deep breath, I struck the clapper against the sound bow. It rang out strongly, a pure, sweet note that lingered in the air for a surprising time.

Everyone applauded.

It was decided that little more could be done for the present. A small leper woman, stump-fingered, adroitly draped the bell in a blue tablecloth bearing the words Jesus Loves Me. It would be removed, *Jif* Andrew said, only at the christening next morning.

"If it's going to be a christening," I pointed out, "perhaps you'll need a name."

He frowned. "For a bell?"

"Yes. It's not so unusual."

"Mike Tyson," said one of the boys who had helped hang it.

Jif Andrew grew thoughtful. "I think we will keep it simple, just have a service of dedication."

"Sure. That's fine by me."

Secretly, I rather liked Elvis.

*

A clapper's head, which attaches internally to the crown, may be flattened, forked, hooked, rounded, T-shaped or stirrup-topped. The ball, or the bit that actually strikes the bell (in medieval times it was a pear-shaped club on a flightless shank), is critical to good tone production, while the flight—the octagonal appendage at the shank's foot—provides momentum, propulsion and balance.

*

Jif Louis looked very frail. "Are you all right?" I asked.

He shrugged. "As you see. I am OK."

"Good." I had *samting* important to tell him, and hoped he would spread the word. "Look, Louis, I know how people gossip, so I don't want them getting the wrong idea. Sara is my colleague. We're here to work, and that's all. You understand me?"

His eyes widened. They took in a figure that had gone for decades without serious exercise, a face lit like a traffic light by years of whisky. "An old feller like *you?*" Even the wildest gossip needs roots that are credible and, laughing out loud, he patted my hand. "Alex! Alex!"

Oh, well, I thought, rather sourly, that's all right, then.

At 7 p.m. three women arrived at the mission guest house carrying fragrantly steaming dishes of fish, chicken, pork, rice, wild cabbage and *laplap.* When three men walked in with a gallon of kava in a plastic jerrycan, the women departed. To me they said, "We don't drink that stuff," to Sara their eyes said, Good luck, sister. The men, lounging on the floor with their musky smells and splayed bare feet, scoffed the food with their fingers and wiped their chins with the backs of their hands. "Eat! Eat!" they cried. *Toktok* would come later, over the kava out by the septic tank.

But, by the tank, I sensed unease. "Forget about the mike," I advised, "just chat." (My own first attempt at radio—a script pre-recorded years earlier at Broadcasting House—had caused the producer to burst through the door crying, "Christ Almighty, this isn't a Nuremberg Rally, you're talking to someone doing the ironing, or alone in a car.") Intimacy was the key and, relaxed by the kava, they did well, answered the questions, confirmed that the wizards who controlled Paama's rainfall and Lopevi's volcano were respectable citizens—unlike the weirdos who slid through walls to rape women and burgle their households.

As Sara changed a tape Ed mused, "We will be heard at the ends of the earth." He had a shaggy moustache and a nice bass voice. I said, "But who'd be listening?" He shrugged, not really interested. While everyone knew that the cool, temperate regions had snowy mountains, deciduous forests and big granite cities with gold-paved streets, I sensed that, for many here, such places always remained slightly out of focus; even the furthest reaches of the Torrid Zone—Africa, the Caribbean— were felt to be more homely, and the folks more sympathetic, and the way of life more familiar, than anything they'd find, say, just three hours' flying time away in New Zealand. (A Polynesian country now overrun by aloof European immigrants with their antisocial culture and cold-climate work ethic.)

At nine o'clock, full of low-grade narcotic, we broke up. I wished Sara sweet dreams and set off for a guest house in the village. Then my torch went out.

If the luminosity of stars can be measured in magnitudes, then so may degrees of darkness. And while this was a real sixth-magnitude night, it seemed as if something—perhaps atoms still carrying heat from the sun—was affecting the air in much the same way that, say, soap changed the nature of water; they made the darkness less dense. So, blundering along, I was able to reliably sense, rather than positively see, two posts with a small, swaddled shadow on top. I lit a cigarette and considered my position. First, if I had arrived at the bell I was going the wrong way. Second, if I removed the tablecloth and rang it, people would appear all right—nocturnal chimes warned of approaching cyclones or tsunami—but I would be left looking utterly foolish.

A small diurnal wind cleared some cloud. There was no moon to speak of, yet the village, under the Milky Way, took on a frosty sparkle. Maurice, a tropical sky specialist, always looked first to the Southern Cross—the Crux, he called it—with its long arm pointing almost directly at the south celestial pole, and its trademark stars, Acrux, Gacrux and the bluish-white Mimosa, among the twenty brightest in the firmament. I found it now, along with Sirius, Canopus and Columba—though not the elusive Small Magellanic Cloud. He once witnessed a big meteor storm here. It lit up the island like tracer shell and, he claimed, for several hours its radiant point kept exploding directly above his roof.

A man appeared, and halted. He seemed to be carrying an axe. *"Alo?"* he called. I told him I was looking for the guest house. He said, *"Yu wantem joj reshaos?"*—the church guest house? I said no, the other one. As, good-naturedly, he led me there, I learned he had been working late in his gardens. Though the land had been in his family for three generations it belonged to God; they were His caretakers. Later, in bed, I compared his environmental philosophy with that of the slovenly caboclos of Brazil. "For twelve hours," they admitted, "we do the land as much damage as possible, during the other twelve we sleep while God and the land put things right again." Their God was an indulgent agrotechnical genius who, nightly, organised the regenerational powers of the tropics. Here people utilised those powers just to keep God happy; He wasn't expected to lift a finger, merely admire the results. And where had that come from? On the verge of sleep I heard my grandfather's inspirational, actorish voice. "Everyone dig for Jesus!"

Liro's oxygen cylinder clanged its wake-up call at six thirty, half an hour later rang again, warning people to wash and get ready for church. By then Sara was boiling two small eggs that had been dropped off by the guest house's female janitor. Hunting for salt (liquefied in an old jam jar, it had the gluey, granular texture of old honey), I realized the eggs may have been an admirer's tribute. The women, showing Sara particular respect, seemed to like her quiet authority, and the focused way she went about her work. That an older man always deferred to her gave, I didn't doubt, a special talismanic power to their shiny BBC pencils. Yet, inevitably, a few elders worried she might be subverting their wives and daughters. When I told them that some of the BBC's top brass were women, they looked stunned. Plainly it was an organization out of control yet, from that moment on, they grinned obsequiously whenever she approached.

I had been asked to say "a few words" prior to the blessing. As the morning was balmy, with high altocumulus hazing the sun, I sat out on the septic tank to jot down notes: a reference, obviously, to my grandparents, how the bell came to be here, some data on Whitechapel and the way bells were made—though not the one thing they would all be aching to know: the price.

I wanted to say certain sentences in Bislama, and had been advised to consult the pastor, Reverend Jackson. A burly, quietly spoken man door-stepped on a busy Sunday morning, he patiently turned "My friends, some years ago you asked my family to bring a bell for this fine new church" into (scribbled down phonetically) *"All brata, more sista, some year we pass finis, yu fella ia askem me blong mi takem wan bell blong new fella joj ia."* After ten busy minutes he supplied the handover words *("Ia mi wan great honour mo respec blong mi givim bell ia")* and promised to translate the rest live, on the spot.

Back at the guest house Sara asked, "Want to rehearse a bit?" Reading it out aloud—counselled to take it slower—I realized her worry was not so much for a pastoral congregation in the South Seas, more for the half a million cosmopolitan Brits who tuned in to Radio 4 on Friday mornings. Aware of my unease about the project, she had behaved with immense sensitivity throughout; yet she had a programme to make (which would, in fact, win a national award) and was employing me to assist. However, as the oxygen cylinder summoned everyone to worship, I suddenly knew where my loyalties lay: I should have ignored the UK audience and made the whole damn speech in Pidgin.

Palm fronds had been stuck in the ground and sheaves of grass heaped on the bell; people in their Sunday best shook our hands. The pastor gave a welcoming address, and everyone clapped. I said my piece—how effortlessly he turned my halting English into sonorous Bislama—and said it to *them*. Everyone clapped. After he'd intoned, *"God papa, God pikinini . . . bless dem bell ia long name blong Jesus Kraes,"* I plucked the grass from the tablecloth, then the tablecloth from the bell, and banged the clapper smartly against the sound bow. *"Boinggggg,"* went the bell; and everyone clapped again.

It was done.

*

Tuners have their own vocabulary: barbing, skiving, skirting, flaking, naking, hewing and fluting are all tuning techniques, while the nominal, the quint, the tierce, the fundamental and the hum note are the elements of the five-tone principle they implant in a bell's memory. It is the tuner's job to isolate each octave span, then get them all vibrating harmoniously together.

*

We filed indoors for the service. "You sit with me," said *Jif* Louis. The leader of the all-male Paama Soul Singers hummed a long, warbling note, mouthed *"Wan, tu, tri!"* and off they went, delivering "Onward, Christian Soldiers" with an attack and cadence that made the hairs rise on the back of my neck. Then the pastor invited me to stand and speak about myself. Having no idea what to say, I spent two rambling, embarrassed minutes saying hardly anything at all. Louis, when I was seated again, said, "They want to hear about your life." Now I understood: How was my wife? What were my kids doing? Was I making plenty of money? How big was my house? "Also," he added, "the *English* situation." The *English* situation? "Drug addicts," he whispered, "the *Kwin* and Camilla. Can she marry Charles? Do you like Mr Blair? Will he look after us?" How, in other words, would New Labour deal with the old colonies? I was still mulling that over when the pastor announced that today's service would be taken by women. Louis winked—but suddenly the place was charged with energy and purpose. Wearing identical yellow dresses, they preached and prayed and chose the hymns. The place bustled. Everyone sat up straighter.

As the collection plate came our way, seeing me scrabbling in my pocket, he asked, "What is wrong with your hands?"

"It's something called Dupuytren's contracture."

Both, in truth, were starting to look like scuttling crabs. And, covertly extending them now, I noted the degrees of elevation had diminished even more.

"How did you get it?"

"I don't know. It could be ancestral."

Several dozen children lounged at the front. As the women retired for a short break, a tall, skinny man in a red shirt mounted the pulpit and spoke to them about the bananas of Puerto Rico. Unfurling a world map, he showed them where Puerto Rico was, described its plantations, the harvesting and packing of the fruit, the big refrigerated ships that carried them overseas and the place of the banana in Puerto Rico's tropical economy.

The women returned, refreshed, and the service moved on. Finally a handsome, youngish deaconess pronounced the blessing, and Louis and I, out in the sunshine, joined the throng strolling to the church hall. Thoughtfully he said, "Ancestral, uh? You know, I think Maurice had that."

I stared. "Maurice had *Dupuytren's?*"

"Or something similar. A problem. His fingers, I think. I remember the old people talking. So perhaps you get it from him."

"Well, I'll be blowed." I felt a new and powerful affinity with my grandfather; now we even had a deformity in common.

"What can they do for it?" asked Louis.

"Surgery. The operation's called a dermofasciectomy. It's the only treatment available."

"Good doctor?"

"Hope so."*

In the bamboo church hall a steaming pig, fresh from its earth oven, was being dismembered by perspiring women with bush knives. Behind them a raft of tables sagged beneath an epic feast: fish offered whole, filleted, grilled or simmered in coconut milk, chickens roasted, curried or casseroled, boiled crab served with a choice of chilli or mayonnaise, stir-fried prawns, beef barbecued or stewed and swimming in giblet gravy, mutton chops, veal goulash, fricasséed flying fox, a spicy seafood ragout, cold cuts, piles of rice, several kinds of *laplap*, salads and vegetables galore, giant bowls of custard, jelly and junket in fluorescent colours.

"This is simply amazing," I said, head reeling from a mix of emotion and sudden hunger. What had they *paid* for this?

"Oh, just a lunchtime snack."

Now came the part I hated: the women, work done, stood back diffidently as the men surged forward. Segregation was observed throughout the meal and speeches—only the men spoke—but not the presen-

---

* Though some months later, as I lay with an arm deadened by anaesthetic block, the doctor gave an exasperated sigh. "Your extensor tendon keeps sliding off the knuckle. See?" He dropped the screen to reveal a hand sliced almost in half, two bloody segments of tissue, muscle and bone neatly dissected and brilliantly spotlit. With a gloved fingertip he tugged at my slithery pink tendon as I mentally struggled to reunite it with its knuckle ("Come on! Get a grip!").

tation of gifts. The women, holding up two size-fifteen Mother Hubbard dresses, beckoned Sara forward, slipped both over her head and, cheering, transformed her into an ample island matron. The men, upstaged, gruffly handed me a giant conch—with a sonic range similar to the bell's—and a small replica of their church; made from astonishingly dense hardwood and fixed together with steel bolts, its weight made me stagger.

After a farewell hymn from the Soul Singers we all filed to the beach. Kal had estimated a three o'clock pick-up and, by four, as everyone continued to scan the sky, a curious unease was developing. They had sheltered and fed us, spent money on us, worked hard for us, overcome their stage *fraet* to be recorded by us, shown us kindness from the moment we stepped ashore. But now it was time to go. When, finally, we heard a distant engine, relief gave their shout extra resonance. But it was only an *aotbod*-powered boat, and the Elders, going into a huddle, sneaked anxious looks in our direction: what should they do now?

Late afternoon shadows were dimming Liro when, without warning, a tiny white seaplane burst from behind a hill, landed close inshore and parked with its floats on the sand. The pilot, a skinny, taciturn Australian named Matt, explained he'd had magneto trouble. "If we're going to make it back before dark we should go." Hastily we said our goodbyes. He called, "And I'll need a push." Sara and I, putting our shoulders to the struts, were joined by a dozen men. "Get in!" they yelled and, launching us like a canoe, shot the plane far out into the bay.

The engine wouldn't start. "*Still* not right," muttered Matt as, spinning lazily, we drifted off towards the shipping lanes. Several uneasy minutes passed before we lifted off and made a dipping pass across the village. Looking down on all those familiar houses and food gardens, at my grandparents' decayed tin-roofed manse and the new cruciform church with its shiny toy bell, I knew I would not be coming back.

Sara, busy taking pictures, cried, "I've never been in one of these, God, isn't it *small?*" The light was so heavy and thick we seemed suspended like a fly in amber; flames flickering across the windscreen signified a scatter of raindrops. I imagined hopping out ("See you guys later!") and porpoising along behind, buoyed up by this gravity-defying radiance all the way back to Vila. Sara yelled against the engine racket, "Today went pretty well, don't you think? I got some nice stuff. And the bell sounded great."

Actually, it had—perfectly tuned to the five-tone principle, as far as I could tell, and plainly displaying a balanced acoustic spread. Then, mulling over the past twenty-four hours, I suddenly saw Maurice in an entirely new way: as a tuner who once worked on me. Others were involved, no question, including my father and Frank Clarke (with, so to speak, their pitch pipes and trichordias), yet it was mainly the old man—busily naking, flaking and fluting away—who, without realizing what he was doing, implanted in my young mind the human variant of tropical sonance.

Bringing the bell to Paama had, finally, freed me from all that; if any of his five tones remained, it was likely to be the last—an echo, faintly recurring, that would soon fade into silence: the hum note.

The luminosity dissipated, leaving us tracking through a pinkish coralline sky. Epi lay below. The sun blazed furiously behind purple cloud which shortly, like a match touched to paper, it would consume; in two days, appearing blearily over Heathrow, it would have its work cut out just dispersing a light autumnal mist. Ahead, for me, lay the prospect of invigorating family walks, evenings drawing in, fires lit, a duvet on the bed, interesting new books and plays to look forward to, good television (and excellent radio), football under way again, the pleasures of a cool temperate country finally putting the summer behind it.

In the tropics there is no such moment: no equinox signals the resurgence of national energy; there summer's torpor is eternal.

That evening, taking a final stroll around Iririki, I bumped into a looming figure with a torch. Jacob, a six-foot Small Namba from Malekula island (Small Nambas wore penis gourds fashioned from a single leaf, Big Nambas hedgelike arrangements so dense that thicket warblers were said to nest in them), had once given me lunch at his village. Shaking hands, I recalled lounging on a palmleaf mat with twenty naked Presbyterians who, nibbling *laplap* dipped in chicken fat, declared that Malekula's last victim of cannibalism had been eaten on the same day Neil Armstrong walked on the moon.

Jacob, fully dressed now, murmured—perhaps a touch mischievously—"You walking with your spirits?"

Yet the night, fragrant and warm, contained only shadows. Taking a last look out over the harbour I saw the Southern Cross illuminating the seabed like swimming-pool lights. When a small copra boat went by the stars dissembled, then, dipping and sliding, came together again: the full set.

Acknowledgements

Hunting for anyone who had previously set out to describe the earth's hot, wet regions, I was fortunate enough to come upon two outstanding authorities—both French, and published half a century earlier. Claude Lévi-Strauss, writing about anthropology, remote places and the human condition in his magnificent *Tristes Tropiques,* gave me a measure of inspiration and some extraordinary stories, while Pierre Gourou's *The Tropical World (Les Pays Tropicaux),* while dated by the seismic changes that have since swept the area, still contains much that is relevant.

My primary source for the current state of tropical health was *The Wellcome Trust Illustrated History of Tropical Diseases,* a fascinating series of essays edited by Prof. Frank Cox—to whom I am indebted for a general introduction to the subject (over a very good lunch at the London School of Hygiene and Tropical Medicine) and a scrupulous reading of the relevant pages in the manuscript. I am grateful also to Derrick Beer, master geographer and ex-geography master, for sharing his knowledge of a world far removed from cool, temperate Wiltshire.

My account of the voyage of Ferdinand Quiros is based on the Hakluyt Society's *La Austrialia del Espíritu Santo* by Father Celsus Kelly OFM (a consummate work of scholarship done with wry affection for his subject). *Tropical Deforestation: The Human Dimension* is an accessible academic work on a subject of urgent topical interest. And *Bellfounding* by Trevor S. Jennings proved to be an invaluable little treasury of bell lore, history and casting techniques.

I, however, assembled and organized the material from all of the above. If any slip-ups occurred along the way, the fault is entirely my own.

My special thanks are due to the *Observer,* who sent me on numerous trips to the Torrid Zone; some material that first appeared in its pages has been incorporated here. One problem arising from writing about the region is not knowing when to stop: Picador's Charlotte Greig edited her way through a mass of tangled tropical undergrowth with immense patience, wisdom and skill; and further order was brought by Nicholas Blake's sharp and scholarly eye. My agent, David Godwin, was, as always, a strong, steadying presence. And, finally, without my family's eternally good-humoured and enduring support, the tropics would have remained just a big, warm, wet idea bubbling away at the back of my mind.

Bibliography

"Asterisk" (Robert James Fletcher), edited by Bohun Lynch: *Isles of Illusion: Letters from the South Seas* (London: Century Hutchinson, 1986)

Burns, Sir Alan: *Fiji* (London: Her Majesty's Stationery Office, 1963)

Coates, Austin: *Western Pacific Islands* (London: Her Majesty's Stationery Office, 1970)

Cox, Prof. F. E. G. (ed.): *The Wellcome Trust Illustrated History of Tropical Diseases* (London: The Wellcome Trust, 1996)

Denoon, Donald (ed.): *The Cambridge History of the Pacific Islanders* (Cambridge: Cambridge University Press, 1997)

Desowitz, Robert: *Tropical Diseases: From 50,000 BC to 2500 AD* (London: Flamingo, 1997)

Edwards, Philip (ed.): *The Journals of Captain Cook* (London: Penguin Books, 1999)

Frater, Maurice: *Midst Volcanic Fires* (London: James Clarke & Co. Ltd, 1922)

Gourou, Pierre (trans. E. D. Laborde): *The Tropical World* (London: Longmans, Green & Co. Ltd, 1958)

Grenfell Price, A. (ed.): *The Explorations of Captain James Cook in the Pacific* (New York: Dover Publications, Inc., 1971)

Harcombe, David, and Denis O'Byrne: *Vanuatu* (Hawthorne, Victoria: Lonely Planet Publications, 1995)

Harrisson, Tom: *Savage Civilisation* (London: Victor Gollancz Ltd, 1937)

Hislop, Ian (ed.): *Private Eye* (London: Pressdram Ltd, 1992)

Jacomb, Edward: *France and England in the New Hebrides* (Melbourne: George Robertson & Company, 1914)

Jennings, Trevor S.: *Bellfounding* (Princes Risborough: Shire Publications Ltd, 1999)

Kelly, Celsus OFM: *La Austrialia del Espíritu Santo: The Journal of Fray Martín de Munilla O.F.M,* 2 vols. (Cambridge: The Hakluyt Society at the University Press, 1966)

Lawson, Will: *Pacific Steamers* (Glasgow: Brown, Son & Ferguson, Ltd, 1927)

Lévi-Strauss, Claude (trans. John and Doreen Weightman): *Tristes Tropiques* (London: Jonathan Cape, 1973)

Lindsrom, Lamont: *Sophia Elau, Ungka the Gibbon, and the Pearly Nautilus* (findarticles.com: *Journal of Pacific History,* 1998)

Martin, John MD: *An Account of the Natives of the Tonga Islands by Mr William Mariner* (Edinburgh: Constable & Co., 1827)

Paton, M. Whitecross: *Letters and Sketches from the New Hebrides* (London: Hodder and Stoughton, 1905)

Quammen, David: *The Song of the Dodo* (London: Hutchinson, 1996)

Scarr, Deryck: *Fragments of Empire: A History of the Western Pacific High Commission 1877–1914* (Canberra: Australian National University Press, 1967)

Sponsel, Leslie E., Thomas N. Headland, and Robert C. Bailey (eds): *Tropical Deforestation: The Human Dimension* (New York: Columbia University Press, 1996)

Theroux, Paul: *The Happy Isles of Oceania: Paddling the Pacific* (New York: G. P. Putnam's Sons, 1992)

Tryon, Darrell: *Evri samting yu wantem save long Bislama be yu fraet tumas blong askem: A Traveller's Guide to Vanuatu Pidgin English* (South Pacific: Media Masters Pidgin Post Publications)

Wheatley, J. I.: *A Guide to the Common Trees of Vanuatu* (Port Vila: Department of Forestry, 1992)

A NOTE ABOUT THE AUTHOR

Alexander Frater has contributed to various publications and has been a contracted *New Yorker* writer. As chief travel correspondent of the London *Observer* he won an unprecedented number of British Press Travel Awards. His books *Beyond the Blue Horizon* and *Chasing the Monsoon* have been made into major BBC television films. He lives in London, though whenever time and money allow he is likely to be found skulking deep in the hot, wet tropics.

This book was set in Adobe Garamond. Designed for the Adobe Corporation by Robert Slimbach, the fonts are based on types first cut by Claude Garamond (c. 1480–1561). Garamond was a pupil of Geoffroy Tory and is believed to have followed the Venetian models, although he introduced a number of important differences, and it is to him that we owe the letter we now know as "old style." He gave to his letters a certain elegance and feeling of movement that won their creator an immediate reputation and the patronage of Francis I of France.